The Afterlives of Extraction: Alternatives and Sustainable Futures

International Development Policy

Editor-in-Chief

Ugo Panizza

Guest Editors

Filipe Calvão
Matthew Archer
Asanda Benya

VOLUME 16

The titles published in this series are listed at *brill.com/idp*

Visit *International Development Policy* online
http://www.devpol.org and *http://debate.devpol.org*

International Development Policy—**Previous Titles**

1 *Africa: 50 Years of Independence*, No. 1, Geneva: Graduate Institute Publications, 2010, ISSN print 1663-9383 | ISSN online 1663-9405 | ISBN: 9782940415274.
2 *Energy and Development*, No. 2, Basingstoke/Geneva: Palgrave Macmillan/ Graduate Institute Publications, 2011, ISBN: 9780230282483.
3 *Aid, Emerging Economies and Global Policies*, No. 3, Basingstoke/Geneva: Palgrave Macmillan/Graduate Institute Publications, 2012, ISBN: 9781137003409.
4 *Religion and Development*, No. 4, Basingstoke/Geneva: Palgrave Macmillan/ Graduate Institute Publications, 2013, ISBN: 9781137329370.
5 *Education, Learning, Training: Critical Issues for Development*, No. 5, Leiden|Boston/ Geneva: Brill Nijhoff/Graduate Institute Publications, 2014, ISBN: 9789004281141.
6 *Large-Scale Land Acquisitions: Focus on South-East Asia*, No. 6, Leiden|Boston/ Geneva: Brill Nijhoff/Graduate Institute Publications, 2015, ISBN: 9789004304741.
7 *Combining Economic and Political Development: The Experience of MENA*, No. 7, Leiden|Boston/Geneva: Brill Nijhoff/Graduate Institute Publications, 2017, ISBN: 9789004336452.
8 *Development as a Battlefield*, No. 8, Leiden|Boston/Geneva: Brill Nijhoff/ Graduate Institute Publications, 2017, ISBN: 9789004349520.
9 *Alternative Pathways to Sustainable Development: Lessons from Latin America*, No. 9, Leiden|Boston/Geneva: Brill Nijhoff/Graduate Institute Publications, 2017, ISBN: 9789004351660.
10 *African Cities and the Development Conundrum*, No. 10, Leiden|Boston/Geneva: Brill Nijhoff/Graduate Institute Publications, 2018, ISBN: 9789004387928.
11 *The ILO @ 100: Addressing the Past and Future of Work and Social Protection*, No. 11, Leiden|Boston/Geneva: Brill Nijhoff/Graduate Institute Publications, 2019, ISBN: 9789004399006.
12 *Drug Policies and Development: Conflict and Coexistence*, No. 12, Leiden|Boston/ Geneva: Brill Nijhoff/Graduate Institute Publications, 2020, ISBN: 9789004440487.
13 *Gender in Peacebuilding: Local Practices in Indonesia and Nigeria*, No. 13, Leiden|Boston/ Geneva: Brill Nijhoff/Graduate Institute Publications, 2021, ISBN: 9789004498464.
14 *Governing Migration for Development from the Global South*, No. 14, Leiden|Boston/ Geneva: Brill Nijhoff/Graduate Institute Publications, 2022, ISBN: 9789004522763.
15 *The Lives of Extraction. Identities, Communities and the Politics of Place*, No. 15, Leiden |Boston/Geneva: Brill Nijhoff/Graduate Institute Publications, 2023, ISBN: 9789004538849.

Geneva Graduate Institute
Graduate Institute of International and Development Studies
Institut de hautes études internationales et du développement
Research Office
P.O. Box 1672
1211 Geneva 1
Switzerland
devpol@graduateinstitute.ch
http://www.devpol.org
http://debate.devpol.org
http://graduateinstitute.ch

The Afterlives of Extraction: Alternatives and Sustainable Futures

Edited by

Filipe Calvão, Matthew Archer and Asanda Benya

BRILL | NIJHOFF

LEIDEN | BOSTON

Library of Congress Cataloging-in-Publication Data

Names: Calvão, Filipe, editor. | Archer, Matthew, editor. | Benya, Asanda, editor.
Title: The afterlives of extraction : alternatives and sustainable futures / edited by Filipe Calvão, Matthew Archer and Asanda Benya.
Description: Leiden ; Boston : Brill, [2024] | Series: International development policy, 1663-9383 ; volume 16 | Includes bibliographical references and index.
Identifiers: LCCN 2023040570 (print) | LCCN 2023040571 (ebook) | ISBN 9789004538856 (paperback ; alk. paper) | ISBN 9789004686182 (ebook)
Subjects: LCSH: Mineral industries–Environmental aspects. | Mines and mineral resources–Environmental aspects. | Sustainable development. | Economic development–Social aspects.
Classification: LCC HD9506.A2 A365 2024 (print) | LCC HD9506.A2 (ebook) | DDC 333.8/51–dc23/eng/20230927
LC record available at https://lccn.loc.gov/2023040570
LC ebook record available at https://lccn.loc.gov/2023040571

Typeface for the Latin, Greek, and Cyrillic scripts: "Brill". See and download: brill.com/brill-typeface.

ISSN 1663-9383
ISBN 978-90-04-53885-6 (paperback)
ISBN 978-90-04-68618-2 (e-book)
DOI 10.1163/9789004686182

This book is printed on acid-free paper and produced in a sustainable manner.

Contents

Preface

International Development Policy is a critical source of analysis of development policy and international cooperation trends, aimed at an audience of scholars, policymakers and development professionals. It offers a diverse range of academic views from both industrialised countries and emerging economies.

International Development Policy is edited by the Graduate Institute of International and Development Studies, an institution of research and higher education dedicated to advancing world affairs. Located in Geneva, at the heart of an international centre of multilateral governance, the Graduate Institute benefits from a rich legacy linked to the founding of the international system and the League of Nations in the 1920s, and the emergence of the developing world in the 1960s.

http://www.devpol.org

http://graduateinstitute.ch/research

We extend our thanks to the Swiss Agency for Development and Cooperation (SDC) and the Republic and State of Geneva—Service for International Solidarity (SSI) for their financial support.

Schweizerische Eidgenossenschaft
Confédération suisse
Confederazione Svizzera
Confederaziun svizra

Swiss Confederation

REPUBLIC
AND STATE
OF GENEVA

POST TENEBRAS LUX

Figures and Tables

Figures

Tables

Abbreviations

ABOP	Party for General Liberation and Development, Suriname
Alcoa	Aluminium Company of America
ANC	African National Congress
ASM	artisanal small-scale mining
BAPEX	Bangladesh Petroleum Exploration and Production Company Limited
B-BBEE	broad-based black economic empowerment
BC	British Columbia
BCE	before the Common Era
BEE	black economic empowerment
BELA	Bangladesh Environmental Lawyers' Association
BIA	Bureau of Indian Affairs, United States
BITS	Bilateral Investment Treaties
CHEMP	Communities, Heritage and Environmental Management Plan, Australia
CICODEV	Pan-African Institute for Citizenship, Consumers, and Development
CNCR	National Council for Consultation and Cooperation of the Rural Population, Senegal (Conseil National de Concertation et de coopération des Ruraux)
CNY	Chinese yuan renminbi
COMEST	UNESCO World Commission on the Ethics of Scientific Knowledge and Technology
CORFO	Production Promotion Corporation, Chile
CRAFS	Reflection and Action Network on Land in Senegal (Réflexion et d'Action sur le Foncier au Sénégal)
DES	Department of Environment and Science, Queensland, Australia
DFO	Department of Fisheries and Oceans, Canada
DGA	General Water Directorate, Chile
DMIRS	Department of Mines, Industry Regulation and Safety
DONG	Danish Oil and Natural Gas
DR	Department of Resources, Queensland, Australia
DRC	Democratic Republic of Congo
EAS	environmental assessments, Canada
EBA	European Battery Alliance
EBG	Evangelische Broedergemeente
EDCS	ecological distribution conflicts
EGD	European Green Deal
EIA	Environmental Impact Assessment, Australia
EITI	Extractive Industry's Transparency Initiative

EJ	environmental justice
ENDA Pronat	Association for the Environment and Development Action for the Natural Protection of Lands (Association pour l'Environnement et Developpement Action pour une Protection Naturelle des Terroirs), Senegal
EP Act (WA)	Environmental Protection Act 1986, Western Australia
EP Act Qld	Environmental Protection Act 1994, Queensland, Australia
EPBC Act	Environment Protection and Biodiversity Conservation Act 1999, Australia
ESIAS	Environmental and Social Impact Assessments, Australia
EU	European Union
EV	electric vehicle
FAO	Food and Agriculture Organization, UN
GF1	GAIA Fund 1
GFM	GAIA Fund Managers
GMOS	genetically modified organisms
ICMM	International Council on Mining and Metals
ICSID	International Centre for the Settlement of Investment Disputes, World Bank Group
IISD	International Institute for Sustainable Development
IML	imperial mode of living
IPBES	Intergovernmental Science-Policy Platform on Biodiversity and Ecosystem Services
IPCC	Intergovernmental Panel on Climate Change
IPP	independent power producer
IRP	Integrated Resource Plan for Electricity, South Africa
ISDS	investor-state dispute settlement
ITIE Senegal	Initiative pour la transparence dans les Industries Extractives du Sénégal
JICA	Japan International Cooperation Agency
KEOH	Association Kédougou Encadrement Orientation et Développement Humain
KTV	karaoke box
kWh	kilowatt-hour
LME	London Metal Exchange
MAC	Mining Association of Canada
MCF	thousand cubic feet (unit of measure)
MCP	Mine Closure Plan, Australia
MDB	multilateral development bank
MDRCS	Mine Development Review Committees, Canada

MMPO	Major Mine Permitting Office, British Columbia, Canada
MoA	mode of appropriation
MoE	mode of extraction
MoP	mode of production
MoU	Memorandum of Understanding
MR&C	mine rehabilitation and closure
Mt	megatonne, or 1 billion kilogrammes (unit of measure)
NABU	Nature and Biodiversity Conservation Union, Germany
NCBD	National Committee to Protect Resources of Bangladesh
NGO	non-governmental organisation
NIEO	New International Economic Order
NOAMI	National Orphaned/Abandoned Mines Initiative, Canada
NRDC	Natural Resources Defense Council
NTA	Native Title Act 1993, Australia
OPSAL	Plurinational Observatory of Andean Salt Flats
OWD	Our World in Data
PPP	public–private partnership
PRCP	Progressive Rehabilitation and Closure Plan, Australia
PSCs	Production Sharing Contracts
PSNR	Permanent Sovereignty over Natural Resources
PWYP	Publish What You Pay
RADDHO	African Assembly for the Defence of Human Rights (Rencontre Africaine pour la Défense des Droits de l'Homme), Senegal
RDP	Reconstruction and Development Programme, South Africa
REI4P	Renewable Energy Independent Power Producer Procurement Programme, South Africa
RtR	right to repair
SADEV	Solidarité Action Développement
SANCO	South African National Civic Organisation
SATCU	South African Congress of Trade Unions
SBM	the Surinaamsche Bauxiet Maatschappij
SDGs	Sustainable Development Goals, UN
SMA	Superintendency of Environment, Chile
SPV	special purpose vehicle
SQM	Sociedad Química y Minera de Chile
SSRC Act	Strong and Sustainable Resource Communities Act 2017, Australia
STS	science and technology studies
Suralco	the Suriname Aluminum Company
TCWF	Tsitsikamma Community Wind Farm, South Africa
TDT	Tsitsikamma Development Trust, South Africa

TIC	The Invisible Committee
TØI	Institute of Transport Economics, Norway
TSM	Towards Sustainable Mining (initiative and framework, Canada)
TWAIL	the Third World Approach to International Law
TWh	terawatt-hour (unit of measure)
UN	United Nations
UNCITRAL	United Nations Commission on International Trade Law
UNDP	United Nations Development Programme
UNDRIP	United Nations Declaration on the Rights of Indigenous Peoples
UNDROP	United Nations Declaration on the Rights of Peasants
UNGA	United Nations General Assembly
USD	United States dollar
USGS	United States Geological Survey
WSC	Wall Street consensus
ZAR	South African rand

Notes on Contributors

Matthew Archer

Matthew Archer studies corporate sustainability, sustainable finance and sustainable development through the lens of political ecology and environmental anthropology. He is currently a lecturer in sustainability in the Department of Environment and Geography at the University of York.

Ramón M. Balcázar

is a PhD candidate in Rural Development at the Autonomous Metropolitan University of Mexico—UAM and Coordinator at OPSAL (the Plurinational Observatory of Andean Salt Flats). Taking a participatory approach, his militant research is situated at the intersection of multilateral climate policies and the subsequent expansion of green extractivism throughout Indigenous/rural territories in the Andean puna. His expertise lies in rural development, agroecology, neo-extractivism, climate justice, socio-environmental movements, just transition and post-development.

Javiera Barandiarán

is associate professor in Global Studies at the University of California, Santa Barbara. Her work explores the intersection of science, environment, and development in Latin America. Her research on lithium has been awarded support from the Mellon Foundation and the National Science Foundation, and has been published in *World Development*. In 2022, she received the Berlin Prize from the American Academy in Berlin for her lithium work.

Asanda Benya

Asanda Benya is a labour sociologist based at the University of Cape Town. She works at the intersection of gender, class and race. She researches the extractives industries, gendered workplace subjectivities, labour and feminist movements.

James J. A. Blair

is assistant professor of Geography and Anthropology at California State Polytechnic University, Pomona. Blair holds a PhD in Anthropology from The Graduate Center, City University of New York. His work centers on energy, water and environmental justice in the Americas. In addition to his research, Blair has professional experience in environmental policy as an international advocate for the Natural Resources Defense Council (NRDC).

Emille Boulot

is a Lionel Murphy Foundation Scholar and a Leadership for the Ecozoic fellow and is pursuing a PhD at McGill University. She is also a lecturer in the Faculty of Law of the University of Tasmania.

Filipe Calvão

Filipe Calvão is an economic and environmental anthropologist broadly interested in the intersection of nature, culture and capital in postcolonial Africa. He is an associate professor at the Graduate Institute of International and Development Studies (IHEID) and a trained gemmologist and diamond grader. His research examines the politics, ecologies and economies of mineral extraction, with a current focus on the nexus between digitalization, work and extractivism.

Ben Collins

is a postdoctoral research fellow at the School of Public Policy and Global Affairs at the University of British Columbia. He is also an Economics for the Anthropocene (E4A) graduate, and a PhD graduate at McGill University.

Alexander Dunlap

is a visiting research fellow at the University of Helsinki. His work has critically examined police–military transformations, market-based conservation, wind energy development, and extractive projects more generally in Latin America and Europe. He is the author of *Renewing Destruction: Wind Energy Development, Conflict and Resistance in a Latin American Context* (Rowman & Littlefield, 2019), the co-author of *The Violent Technologies of Extraction: Political Ecology, Critical Agrarian Studies and the Capitalist Worldeater* (Palgrave, 2020), and the co-editor of *Enforcing Ecocide: Power, Policing and Planetary Militarization* (Palgrave, 2022).

Paul Robert Gilbert

is a senior lecturer in International Development at the University of Sussex. His research has focused on extractive industry expertise, finance, and violence, predominantly in Bangladesh. With Clea Bourne, Max Haiven and Johnna Montgomerie, he is editor of *Entangled Legacies of Empire: Race, Finance & Inequality* (Manchester University Press, 2022).

Håvard Haarstad

is professor of Human Geography and director of the Centre for Climate and Energy Transformation at the University of Bergen (Norway).

Dorothea Hamilton
is a human geographer who graduated from the Philipps University of Marburg in Geography and Peace and Conflict Studies. She later taught at the Justus Liebig University of Giessen, where she also wrote her PhD, on resource conflicts in Latin America. Her research interest lies in understanding when nature becomes a means of conflict or of peace.

Simon Lobach
is working towards a PhD in International History and Politics at the Geneva Graduate Institute, with a focus on environmental history. He already holds degrees in History and in Latin American Studies, and has worked as a consultant on environment-related projects for several years, mainly within the United Nations. His current research focuses on histories of bauxite and aluminium across Amazonia, including Brazil, Suriname, Guyana and Venezuela.

Amanda Maxwell
is managing director of the International Program at NRDC. Maxwell's work focuses on promoting clean energy, cleaning up dirty fuels, improving air quality, and protecting wildlife and wildlands throughout Latin America. She received her Bachelor's degree in History and Spanish from Middlebury College and her Master's in International Politics and Economics from Charles University in Prague. She has also studied at the Universidad de Buenos Aires.

Ryan Parsons
is an assistant professor of Sociology and Southern Studies at the University of Mississippi. His research explores linkages between geographic and social mobility, ethnic stratification, rural development, and inequality in a range of national and subnational contexts. He holds a PhD in Sociology and Social Policy from Princeton University.

Erik Post
is a PhD candidate in geography at the University of British Columbia. His research explores the articulation of violence, geopolitics, and extractivism. He obtained his Master's degree in International Affairs at the Geneva Graduate Institute. Prior to his PhD research, he worked for the European Commission, the Dutch Ministry of Foreign Affairs, International Crisis Group, and the Belgian Network for Sustainable Development.

Louisa Prause
is a postdoctoral researcher at the Humboldt Universität zu Berlin, where she is part of the Agricultural and Food Policy Group and the Biomaterialities Research Group. Her research and teaching focuses on socioecological transformations, the bio-economy, the digitalisation of agriculture, land and mining conflicts, and social movements, with a regional focus on Africa and Europe.

Michelle Pressend
is academic coordinator of the African regional hub of TRAJECTS, the Transnational Centre for Just Transitions in Energy, Climate and Sustainability, and a lecturer in Political Ecology at the University of Cape Town. She is also a PhD candidate in Anthropology in association with Environmental Humanities South at the same university.

Devyn Remme
is a PhD candidate at the University of Bergen (Norway). She holds an interdisciplinary BSc in The Environment and Resources and an MPhil in Geographies of Sustainable Development.

Kjetil Rommetveit
is associate professor at the Centre for the Study of the Sciences and the Humanities at the University of Bergen (Norway).

Siddharth Sareen
is associate professor of Energy and Environment at the Department of Media and Social Sciences at the University of Stavanger and associate professor II at the Centre for Climate and Energy Transformation at the University of Bergen, both in Norway.

Sina Trölenberg
works at a German non-governmental organisation in the areas of climate justice and project management with organisations from Central America and Europe. She holds an MSc in Human Geography from the University of Giessen, where she focused on human–environment interactions, political ecology and environmental peacebuilding, with a regional emphasis on Colombia and Germany. Her BA in Geography and Spanish Studies was awarded by the University of Münster.

CHAPTER 1

Introduction: Global Afterlives of Extraction

Filipe Calvão, Asanda Benya and Matthew Archer

Abstract

This volume of *International Development Policy* brings together post-extractivist imaginaries, diverse and ever-evolving forms of resistance and contestation, and a growing recognition of the paradox of 'green' extractivism. Despite the pervasive narrative that more rather than less mining is necessary to achieve decarbonisation, there is now growing recognition that the current model of economic development based on fossil fuels and resource extraction is not sustainable in the long term. The introduction to this volume acknowledges the complex and ongoing legacies of extraction and the urgent need to move beyond extractive models of development and towards alternative pathways that prioritise social justice, environmental sustainability, democratic governance, and the well-being of both human and non-human beings.

1 Introduction

Debates around resource extraction, capitalism and development are situated within broader discussions about the relationship between economic growth and socio-environmental sustainability. On the one hand, proponents of the familiar developmentalist approach argue that extraction is a necessary precondition for socio-economic development and poverty reduction, and could be carried out in a socially and environmentally responsible manner. Recently, the mining industry adopted this narrative to position itself, which it has done successfully, at the centre of discussions around green transitions and sustainable futures, arguing persuasively that *more* rather than *less* mining is necessary to achieve decarbonisation goals while maintaining economic growth. Critics of extractivism, on the other hand, argue that environmental degradation, social inequality and human rights abuses are an inevitable consequence of resource extraction and perpetuate a system of accumulation that prioritises profits over people and the planet. Attempts to improve the purported 'sustainability' of mining operations, it is argued, are little more than 'greenwashing'.

 | DOI:10.1163/9789004686182_002

These debates have taken on added urgency in recent years, as concerns about climate change and the limits of natural resources have come to the fore. There is now growing recognition that the current model of economic development based on fossil fuels and resource extraction is not sustainable in the long term and that alternative models of development are needed. These alternative models of development prioritise social equity, environmental sustainability, and the well-being of people and communities over the interests of multinational corporations and global capital. More radical proposals, however, critique these 'alternative models *of* development' and argue instead for 'alternatives *to* development'. Gudynas, for example, argues that alternative models are locked into and operate within the dominant development logic. These models call for minor adjustments here and there, be it reducing harm, improving societal contributions, or the inclusion of those previously excluded. 'Alternatives *to* development', meanwhile, critique the development logic and its institutions altogether, advocating instead for 'radically different strategies, based on other ideological foundations' (Gudynas, 2013,169).

As we engage with these critical debates, several questions emerge that speak to the complex and contested nature of extraction and its afterlives: Is the move towards responsible extraction accompanied by a new politics of resistance? Can the predatory logic of extractivism be reformed to maintain only those activities necessary for the reproduction of life and not the extraction of natural resources for profit, or would such concessions require the fundamental alteration of processes of resource extraction? Are different modes of extraction possible within current structures of production and accumulation? Can extraction be decolonised? And what could post-extractivist futures look like?

Social scientists have contributed to these debates by offering critical analyses of the social, cultural and political dimensions of resource extraction and by documenting the impacts of extraction on local communities, cultures and environments. Through a study of the power relations and political processes that shape resource extraction and its impacts, these scholars have also highlighted the agency and resistance of communities and social movements that seek to challenge the dominant model of resource extraction and to advocate for alternative models of development that prioritise social and environmental justice. In the current moment, when technical solutions for decarbonisation, mining electrification, and the digitalisation of mineral supply chains are being developed, a sociocultural perspective on these challenges and opportunities is more important than ever.

This volume of *International Development Policy* on the lives and afterlives of extraction focuses on landscapes, economies and practices of post-extractivism. Our use of 'afterlives' and 'post-extraction' in this, the second volume does not imply a complete departure from the themes explored in the first volume, such as community, identity, and social reproduction. Nor does it necessarily imply a neat teleological temporal conception of 'phases' of extraction. Instead, we view these phases and themes as entangled with and integral to the larger debates on the lives and afterlives of extraction, and seek to build on the critical insights offered in the first volume by exploring alternative pathways for development and sustainable futures. Where the first volume asked how people are involved in, impacted by, and responsive to extractive processes, the second volume asks how the logic of extractivism persists—and is resisted—as the contested futures of extraction continue to unfold. Taken together, the two volumes show how the pasts, presents and futures of mining, the spaces and places of extraction, and the logics of extractivism and anti-extractivism are invariably mediated by politics that transect spatial and temporal scales. In what follows, we briefly situate the vigorous debate around extractive capitalism and extractivism, and industry approaches to sustainability and responsibility, before presenting conclusions on alternative pathways for life beyond extractivism.

2 Extractive Capitalism

The neo-liberal reforms that followed structural adjustment programmes in Africa in the 1970s and 1980s and the Latin American debt crisis in the 1990s opened economic sectors across the global South to increased private and foreign participation. In Latin America in particular, the fast-paced growth of the Chinese economy created a commodities super-cycle that hampered industrialisation. In response, national governments expanded and deepened industrialisation efforts based on resource extraction, causing a 're-primarisation' of Latin American economies in what has been described as a shift from the 'Washington Consensus' to the 'Commodities Consensus' (Svampa, 2015). The development model implemented by various Latin American 'post–neo-liberal' governments in the early twenty-first century, known as 'neo-extractivism', increased dependency on international commodity markets, foreign currency and transnational corporations, whereas the state would be assigned the role of a mere regulator of extractive activities, with responsibilities for capturing resource rents (Acosta, 2013; Burchardt and Dietz, 2014). The economic development policies that buttressed resource nationalism across the continent in turn provoked fierce contestation from anti-extractive and Indigenous movements (Riofrancos, 2020).

Against this backdrop, extractive activities have intensified and expanded across the world. Extraction has been described as 'any form of economic activity that relies on or benefits from resources or relations that are external to it' (Mezzadra and Neilson, 2019, 134), commonly denoting the appropriation of natural and human resources for profit, often with little to no regard for the social and environmental impacts of these practices, at a high volume and intensity with little or no processing and mainly geared towards exports (Gudynas, 2018; Pereira and Tsikata, 2021; Ye et al., 2020). It conventionally operates by appropriating lands and resources and women's social reproductive forces, and disproportionately impacts Indigenous peoples, Black communities, and people of colour, who are all subject to displacement, dispossession, and environmental degradation. This highlights the need for intersectional approaches to both extractivism and resistance to it (Hernández Reyes, 2019).

The long-standing interdisciplinary literature on resource extraction has sought to broaden its conceptual purview and empirical horizon by questioning resource extraction's underlying patterns, logics and systematicity. In so doing, scholars have examined how the inherent violence, injustice and inequality of capitalism as an extractive regime structurally sustains its operations and permeates its exploitative logics. This system of value extraction is historically indebted to colonial and plantation economies and to contemporary imperialist projects, or the ways in which capitalism has been and continues to be shaped by racial hierarchies and inequalities (Appel, 2019). 'Racial extractivism' (Preston, 2017) perpetuates forms of violent white settler colonialism, imperialism and logics of modernity that attempt to erase Indigenous jurisdiction, government and life itself. The systemic and structural nature of the problems associated with both extractive capitalism and racial capitalism are most apparent at the sites where they intersect.

Likewise, new propositions around the concept of extractivism (oftentimes pluralised to denote the diverse forms it can take and the diverse processes and impacts involved) define it as a widespread modality of capital accumulation, characterised by dispossession, heightened value extraction and planetary spatial reach (Arboleda, 2020; Nygren et al., 2022; see Post, this volume, for a more comprehensive overview of these debates and the co-extensive duality of capitalism and extractivism). Chagnon et al. (2022, 762) define extractivism as an 'organizing concept' that 'arranges and synthesizes a body of knowledge to serve as the basis for progressive interventions', reflecting the emergence of global extractivism as a way of organising life. For Mezzadra and Neilson (2019), extractive logics appear to be spreading to other realms of capitalist activity, leading some to argue that capitalism has entered a new stage of extractivism and giving rise to a plethora of plural 'extractivisms': financial, intellectual, digital, or green, to name only a few. Indeed, as several contributions to this volume demonstrate, both the logic of extractivism and efforts to resist it have spread far beyond the confines of more conventional extractive zones to enter what Watts (2021) calls an age of 'hyper-extractivism'.

In order to facilitate the superseding of extractivism, this volume strives to clarify some of the analytical muddiness associated with the concept. As important as these conceptual debates are, however, the remainder of this introduction focuses on specific pathways being carved out by the extractive industry to shield itself from criticism, and on the delineation of an alternative programme for a post-extractivist world.

3 Extractivism and Sustainability

As humans become a new geological force to be reckoned with in the Anthropocene (Chakrabarty, 2021), the need for sustainable alternatives to extractivism is more urgent than ever. Sustainability and extractivism are often at odds with each other, and with good reason: the social and environmental impact of extractive industries has been amply documented (see Chapter 1 in Calvão, Archer and Benya, 2023). For its detractors, sustainable mining is a strategic ploy that inadvertently generates new conflicts, human vulnerabilities and environmental degradation, even as it seeks to mitigate the effects of extractivism or develop new sustainable alternatives. In diverse contexts, anthropologists and political ecologists have shown how corporate social responsibility and corporate sustainability initiatives often contribute to the entrenchment of corporate rule, particularly vis-à-vis dispersed, less organised workers such as artisanal miners, and the communities they inhabit (Welker, 2014; Calvão, Mcdonald and Bolay, 2021). For some, the very idea of environmentally and socially responsible extractive industries is an oxymoron (Benson and Kirsch, 2010). Notwithstanding, the field of sustainable and responsible initiatives has gained prominence in the extractive landscape to preclude potential criticism, warranting its closer scrutiny.

Critical work on transparency and traceability initiatives in particular has shown how purported efforts to enhance the visibility of minerals and other globally traded commodities as they move from sites of extraction through sites of processing and exchange often generate new spaces of opacity and reinforce the value-extracting potential of multinational corporations (Calvão and Archer, 2021; Thylstrup et al., 2022). Under the guise of ethics or responsibility, accountability or transparency, approaches to sustainability and sustainable development in the extractive sector have spurred important conversations in both policy and academic circles. Is it possible to leverage mining for sustainable development, or to conceive of truly sustainable and socially responsible action within the horizon of the contemporary economic model of production? Can we have impactful action without significant structural transformations at the political and economic levels?

As we understand it, sustainable development must always acknowledge the historically imbricated structural and systemic inequality of the current political–economic model. We also seek to identify the blind spots and potential structural gaps associated with programmes, initiatives and discourses of sustainability—namely in the following three areas: ethical commodities, certification initiatives, and corporate governance.

The emergence of a global 'register of responsibility' in the field of ethical consumption (Barnett et al., 2011, 2) is best illustrated by what James Carrier (2010) calls 'ethical commodities', or material objects infused with value-producing moral attributes rendered legible as 'ethical'. Consumers become arbiters capable of distinguishing between objects with seemingly identical properties, where one has verifiable standards ensuring respect for certain ethical qualities, of which 'conflict-free' diamonds is perhaps the most widely and arguably successful case (Bell, 2023; Calvão, 2020). Notwithstanding, the ethical label offers limited avenues for actual social change, and fails to address the structural dimensions of human insecurity or environmental destruction.

This consumer legibility is often achieved through certification practices, whereby an independently accredited entity validates the ethical qualities it seeks to make transparent. Over the last two decades, certification regimes have become an industry in their own right, mobilising trade organisations, certification management organisations, and, increasingly, due diligence and traceability mechanisms. And yet traceability and certification regimes presuppose an unbroken chain from producer to consumer where a product can retain its 'ethicality' within a system of economic and social relations that actively reproduces existing power relations. New, digital-based solutions for certification and traceability, including the implementation of blockchain-based traceability and tracking initiatives, are presented as an alternative to paper-based forms of certification. These are aimed at disintermediating the certification process by creating alternative modalities for data input and management, although informational asymmetries emerge among participants in the supply chain, often reinforcing already existing exclusionary practices (Calvão and Archer, 2021) to the detriment of an 'ethics of invisibility' aspired to by some as an alternative to colonial forms of predation, as in the case of Congolese 'digital miners' (Smith, 2021, 27).

Corporations have been commonly associated with the implementation of sustainability programmes, from corporate social responsibility (CSR) initiatives to the more recent environmental, social and corporate governance (ESG) framework. With the support of proponents of so-called philanthrocapitalism and benefit sharing arrangements, the business case for corporate responsibility has gathered support by extending economic value to social welfare and sustainability. By the same token, its critics argue that the power of corporations should be curtailed rather than extended into new arenas of economic and social life often at the expense of the state's responsibilities. We see CSR as integral to an emergent 'ethical' capitalism, but not as dissociated from other corporate social technologies of coercion, co-option and control (Kirsch, 2014; Welker, 2014; Verweijen and Dunlap, 2021; Frederiksen and Himley, 2019). Rather than seeing CSR as the silver bullet for underdevelopment, we follow research that seeks to understand how corporate power is exercised through CSR programmes and what is the corporate vision of progress, sustainability and development underpinning such initiatives.

Finally, the ESG framework—environmental, social and (corporate) governance—has emerged as a financial response with which to remedy some of the woes in the extractive industries. For fund managers and investment companies, a financial product packaged around the idea of 'doing good' now offers a plausible alternative to the costs—financial or other—of doing 'bad' or non-sustainable business. Yet, these ESG products still comprise only a tiny fraction of the total capital invested in private equity, and it is far from consensual that the problems in the sector can be addressed within the horizon of these financial mechanisms, let alone that the responsibility for sustainable investment should be assigned to Wall Street executives. Proponents of the power of ESG (and of finance more broadly) as a force for good in the context of global sustainability claim that various indices and ratings of companies' ESG performance allow investors to account for reputational, regulatory and other risks, especially in 'dirty' businesses like mining. In effect, however, a focus on ESG allows investors to justify their continued support for extractive, carbon-and pollution-intensive industries while enhancing their own power over the invested firms, shifting the terms of the conversation around sustainability from social and environmental risks to a concern with the extent to which these risks 'translate' to financial risks for investors themselves (Archer, 2022). In our understanding, the growing focus on ESG in the context of extractive industries reveals the naked truth of the oxymoronic relationship between (moral) purpose and profit, and may offer only a limited solution to a problem that requires a far more muscular intervention.

4 Whose Responsibility, for What?

In addition to these sustainability initiatives, mineral supply chains have been differently codified in terms of standards, legal frameworks and guidelines, in a precipitous rush for 'responsible' schemes. The dual effect of the increased complexity of this regulatory landscape and the fragmented nature of the field of voluntary initiatives raises important questions regarding the inevitable overlap between standards, the lack of clarity on their purpose and scope, and the extent to which these corporate-led 'technical fixes' (Le Billon and Spiegel, 2022) may serve to render opaque problems of unequal wealth distribution and of labour or environmental exploitation.

These initiatives coalesce around due diligence mechanisms and responsible sourcing programmes. With the Voluntary Principles on Security and Human Rights, established in 2000, extractive companies sought to institutionalise human rights due diligence mechanisms. Through modes of interpellation, disclosure and mitigation—mostly focused on human rights violations—due diligence was eventually extended to the entirety of mineral supply chains with the rise of conflict minerals. The Organisation for Economic Co-operation and Development (OECD) Due Diligence Guidance for Responsible Supply Chains of Minerals from Conflict-Affected and High-Risk Areas, first launched in 2010 with subsequent later editions in 2013 and 2016, operationalised a due diligence framework, in what was to become a foundational moment for responsible sourcing within licit production networks. Though fundamental, the OECD guidance offers only an open and voluntary framework, but it has been complemented with other initiatives with regulatory force, from the US Dodd–Frank Act (2010) to the European Union's Conflict Minerals Regulation (2021), each correspondingly drawing from international law agreements, from the International Labour Organization's Tripartite Declaration of Principles concerning Multinational Enterprises and Social Policy (1977) to the UN Guiding Principles on Business and Human Rights (2011).

For some, these regulations are toothless in the face of the overwhelming task at hand. These due diligence mandates and guidelines are mostly operationalised through voluntary adherence to their principles—when not developed by corporate standards—and remain contingent upon their specific target commodity, region or segment of the supply chain. If subject to compliance, accreditation and external verification procedures, these responsibility initiatives and standards still represent a form of self-legitimacy in the eyes of consumers, while overlooking environmental dimensions not addressed in most existing dimensions. More broadly, if increased transparency is assumed to enhance accountability, the exclusionary effects of (digital) data production become more prominent in the critical discussion over the distribution of benefits and costs along the extractive process.

Aside from abiding by—and at times embracing—a growing body of standards and regulations, the mining industry has pre-emptively sought to 'offset' its most direct environmental harms, often reinforcing the influence of major multinational corporations in the process. Biodiversity offsetting schemes in an 'extraction–conservation nexus' (Le Billon, 2021) attempt to compensate for biodiversity loss in one place by protecting biodiversity somewhere else, essentially granting mining companies a license to destroy vulnerable habitats as long as they channel a negligible amount of money towards these purported offsets (Seagle, 2012; Brock, 2020). Apart from the mind-boggling 'logic' of such schemes, recent work has highlighted the way these offsetting mechanisms add yet another layer of dispossession and land grabbing (Kill et al., 2016; Bidaud et al., 2018).

5 Greening Extractivism for the 'Clean' Energy Transition: Mining the Future

Extractivism is marked by a range of temporalities, expectations and futures. These include predictions and orientations towards past and future resource booms and busts, as well as the ways in which different actors anticipate future resource needs and scarcities. One of the key ways in which extraction is situated in dominant visions of a sustainable future—paradoxically, according to many critics—is as a necessity rather than a hindrance. Organisations such as the International Energy Agency and the European Commission anticipate significant increases in the amount of rare earth elements and other metals and minerals required to meet the rising 'clean' energy demand seen as necessary for the green transition.

This apparent contradiction, referred to as 'green extractivism' by a growing number of scholars (Bruna, 2023; Voskoboynik and Andreucci, 2021), has emerged as a defining feature of contemporary discussions around sustainability and sustainable development. The notion of green extractivism highlights the persistence of both extractivism as an ideology and extraction as a resource-intensive practice of removing non-renewable resources from the earth, highlighting how technological and spatial fixes to global sustainability threaten to reproduce and even extend the long colonial shadows of extraction into the future (Jerez and Garces, 2021). Green extractivism perpetuates and expands so-called extractive zones and land grabbing across Indigenous lands in particular (Dunlap, 2019).

One important stepping stone towards the energy transition has been the adoption of new technologies capable of holding true to the promise of that transition while fostering the expansion of new extractive frontiers, from the depths of deep-sea mining to so-called rare earth elements (Klinger, 2017). Electrification, automation and digitalisation have become integral to mining operations, with various case studies highlighting the use of these technologies, from fully automated electric truck fleets and drilling operations to data analytics, remote operations, digital sensors, asset tracking, blockchain technology and drone mapping (Bellamy and Pravica, 2011; Ellem, 2015; Dadhich, Bodin and Andersson, 2016; Calvão and Gronwald, 2019; Kiziroglou et al., 2017). Sensors and sensing technology are playing a significant role in mining operations by analysing and modeling different variables in real time, helping detect potential spillages and breakdowns in shafts, or other hazards (Ralston et al., 2014). These real-time monitoring sensors are meant to protect workers and prevent accidents, despite troublesome surveillance and privacy concerns. Algorithms have also become integral to sourcing minerals, in part given declining ore grades and a decrease in mineral deposit discovery rates (Kaplan and Topal, 2020). From machine learning techniques to 3D models to optimise ore control, digital software solutions are now part and parcel of exploration and geologic settings. In yet another pivotal development, some critical minerals such as graphite or, more commonly, gemstones such as diamonds can be fully produced in specialised laboratories, away from nature (Ali, 2017; Calvão and Bell, 2021). These developments are, as it were, also a key component of the mining industry's claim that it is becoming more responsible—a claim often employed in the face of criticisms that more mining is specious in the context of sustainable development—since they improve the lives of workers by making extractive processes safer and more efficient.

The rise of these digital technologies introduces a range of new challenges and opportunities. On the one hand, they can enable greater precision in mining operations, reducing waste and minimising the environmental impact of extractive activities. They can also provide new opportunities for data collection and analysis, potentially leading to more informed and sustainable decision-making (Cosbey et al., 2016). However, digital mining also raises questions about the ownership and control of data, the potential for increased surveillance and control over workers, and the potential for the continued exploitation of natural resources. With these technologies, there is an accentuated expansion of new resource frontiers, as new mineral deposits become reachable by robotised and remote-controlled machines, reproducing old patterns of accumulation and dispossession, oftentimes in the name of the 'green transition'.

In these different instances, automation and digitalisation are presented as twin pathways to increased efficiency, safety and productivity in mining operations, despite diminishing job availability and, importantly from the industry standpoint, the risk of labour strife. More broadly, these innovations would seem to anticipate a future that seeks to partially replace human labour with intelligent machines, and, in the case of digital solutions, with intermediaries with unmediated accountability. The consequences of these transformations, and the ulterior motive of the reduction in what is after all the most 'tangible benefit' for communities in the vicinity of extractive operations—waged labour—warrant reflection, and a novel conceptualisation of the emergent relationship entangling humans and machines, material and digital processes, and synthetic and natural resources (Calvão, Bolay and Bell, 2021). In other words, these transformations question the very role of nature in largely synthetic and artificial processes, and the various political, epistemological, ecological and social conditions underpinning a future that looks like it will be increasingly defined by the emergence of synthetic products, digital technologies and autonomous machines.

6 Alternatives: Decoloniality, Degrowth, Resistance

The first step towards an alternative post-extractivist world entails undoing a pattern of exploitation resting on inequality, violence, and dispossession, or what Anibal Quijano (2000) calls the 'colonial matrix of power'. Developing his critique of the 'European paradigm of rationality/modernity', Quijano calls for this epistemic delinking by pointing out the need 'to extricate oneself from the linkages between rationality/modernity and coloniality, first of all, and definitely from all power which is not constituted by free decisions made by free people' (2007, 171). The framework of decoloniality, drawing from the original impulses of Caribbean intellectuals and later expanded by Latin American scholars (Mignolo and Escobar, 2013; Mignolo and Walsh, 2018), has gained widespread traction in the critique of extractive capitalism (Murrey and Jackson, 2019; Yusoff, 2018; Gómez-Barris, 2017).

Race, like gender, is one central vector by which this colonial matrix of power operates. It is widely recognised that capitalism is shaped and maintained by specific articulations of race and gender. As such, race and gender are integral to the extraction of value from people and the environment (Robinson, 1983; Tilley and Shilliam, 2021). Despite formal decolonisation in the mid-twentieth century, the hierarchies of power that structured colonial forms of domination have not subsided. For Nelson Maldonado-Torres (2007, 243), coloniality 'refers to long-standing patterns of power that emerged as a result of colonialism, but that define culture, labour, intersubjective relations, and knowledge production well beyond the strict limits of colonial administrations', impacting at once logics of economic extraction and knowledge structures. The crisis of the neo-liberal model, in Artur Escobar's (2007) 'modernity/coloniality research program', has fundamentally paved the way for imagining a new post-moment, be it of development, capital, or extraction.

This decolonial turn calls, first, for a moment of 'epistemic disobedience' (Mignolo, 2011) that breaks with the historical amnesia and silences (Trouillot, 1995) imposed by Euro-modernity and its structures of power. This includes practices of 'localwashing'—akin to 'greenwashing'—by corporate extractive actors as they seek to accrue legitimacy in the process of erasing, racialising, and making invisible the violence of appropriation, displacement and extraction (Murrey and Jackson, 2019). Second, this project involves developing a decolonisation programme that fosters alternatives conceived as the 'radical deconstruction of the cultural base of development' (Gudynas, 2011, 442).

For the extractive industries, as shown in many of the chapters in both of the present volumes (Calvão, Archer and Benya, 2023 and this volume), this would involve recognising and respecting Indigenous sovereignty and self-determination, significant structural and systemic changes, and addressing the historical and ongoing harms caused by extractive activities. The return of land and resources to local communities, the recognition of local and Indigenous knowledge and governance systems, or the establishment of alternative economic models that prioritise the well-being of local communities and environmental sustainability would be possible pathways in the decolonial programme. In that regard, a decolonial critique has been productively deployed to question existing power relations and reaffirm a sense of place by setting a new framework for environmental and energy justice (Tornel, 2022; for a critique of environmental justice, see Dunlap, this volume).

A post-extractivist degrowth approach holds the potential of challenging the dominant paradigm of neo-liberal capitalism and its reliance on extractivism for economic growth by offering alternative pathways towards more sustainable and equitable modes of production and consumption. Degrowth advocates a deliberate contraction of economies, particularly in the global North, to reduce resource use and prioritise social and ecological well-being over economic growth (see Gezon and Paulson (2017) for a review). This means adopting a post-extractivist focus beyond extractivism as the primary driver of development and promoting alternative forms of production and governance that prioritise social and environmental sustainability (Escobar, 2015). Degrowth strategies, however, come with their own limitations—namely the exacerbation of existing global inequalities (Huber, 2022). As Jason Hickel recently pointed out in his call for an 'anti-colonial politics of degrowth' (2021), what lies ahead—and is no small task—entails reconciling eco-socialism with anti-imperialism, degrowth with class politics.

However, the feasibility and potential impact of these alternative approaches remain contested, particularly within the context of the current global economic system, and the present volume contributes to the reconsidering of resistance from a decolonial, post-extractivist perspective. Certainly, protest and resistance movements opposed to extractivism have gained visibility and prominence throughout the world. In some instances, particularly in Latin America, notions of *buen vivir* (*Sumak kawsay* in the original Quechua formulation, or *Suma Qamaña* in Aymara, often reduced to its simpler denotation of living well or good living) have informed state and social policies and directly contributed to the vitality of social movements. In 2008 and 2009, respectively, the constitutions of Ecuador and Bolivia adopted the principles of *buen vivir* (Gudynas, 2011), with the former recognising the rights of nature. And yet the effects of this adoption—and the risks of the 'metaphorization of decolonization' (Tuck and Yang, 2012)—are not without shortcomings that call for reflection by researchers and activists alike.

First, the constitutional inscription of these ethical and social principles, and the support of grassroots anti-extraction movements and Indigenous communities for progressive governments in Latin America, did not signify the end of state-led resource nationalism policies. In fact, as Thea Riofrancos suggests for Ecuador (2017, 11), the 'transition from neoliberalism to a new, post-neoliberal version of resource nationalism was not a total rupture with prevailing power structures'. Instead, this strategic adoption of radically critical and plural epistemic traditions laid bare the firm establishment of extractivist principles and the difficulty of superseding them in the existing socio-economic order. In some cases, again in Ecuador, these principles of *buen vivir* are deployed to justify development initiatives in direct opposition to the well-being of Indigenous communities. For the Amazonian Waorani nation, according to Bravo Díaz (2021), development infrastructures associated with oil extraction recast *Sumak kawsay* as 'harmful'. As extractive actors reposition themselves at the forefront of a sustainable transition to a low-carbon economy, it bears remembering that similar strategies may be deployed to oppose anti-extractive movements and justify expanded extractive activities.

Second, there is oftentimes an underlying expectation that all Indigenous peoples ought to resist extractivism, at the risk of not being 'properly' Indigenous or defenders of nature and sustainable ecological livelihoods if they do not. For myriad reasons—including jobs and tangible material benefits—consent, rather than resistance, can at times be the chosen pathway for Indigenous communities, and is not always at odds with the commoditisation of value (see Babidge (2016) for a discussion of the 'indigenous ethics of resources' in light of the contested value of water in the Atacama desert). Researchers and activists risk instrumentalising and essentialising Indigenous world views in the name of an idealised view of what their legitimate concerns should be. In the process, anti-extractivist positions may be blind to more subtle renditions of the divide between support for and opposition to extractivism. In Michael Cepek's (2016 633) 'cautionary tale for advocates of indigenous struggles', there are limits to the imposition of a cosmological view for the purpose of political action, regardless of how righteous said positions may be. In fact, he argues, turning 'Cofán [Amazonian people] anti-oil activism into a cosmopolitical war for the coancoans' well-being would carry significant risks[1]'—namely, limiting and delegitimising the possibility of pursuing a politically engaged alliance between communities and activists. These are important lessons to retain as social movements across the world seek to mobilise new energy to craft expanded alliances against extractivism (see Hamilton and Trölenberg, Prause, and Gilbert, this volume).

7 Chapter Overview

The volume is organised into three sections, each unfolding different aspects of the afterlives of extraction and exploring various alternatives and possibilities for the future. The first section, 'Post-extractivism: Debates and Practices', critically engages with the concept of post-extractivism and the various political, economic and social practices that emerge in the aftermath of extraction. The underlying question is tied to the (im)possibility, within existing structures of production and accumulation, of alternative models of extractivism that prioritise social and environmental sustainability. While resource efficiency, circular economies and alternative ownership models could offer plausible—and potentially palliative—measures, the existing structures of production

1 Coancoans, in the A'ingae language spoken by the Cofán people, are mythical subterranean beings; the association of oil with their blood remains a disputed point.

and accumulation are deeply entrenched in profit and growth interests that trump sustainability and equity, which will inevitably condition the feasibility of these alternative models.

Erik Post opens the volume with a wide-ranging analysis of the plural and often contested notion of 'extractivisms', tracing its genealogy from the specific context of the exploitation of Latin American natural resources to the more recent—but very clearly related—debates around 'clean' and 'renewable' energy. In doing so, Post theorises extractivisms as 'modes of extraction' facilitating the exploitation of mineral and energy resources that are fundamental to the reinforcement of an 'imperial mode of living' wherein the structures of everyday life are reliant on an exploitative relationship with both labour and the natural world. His analysis yields a complex understanding of extractivisms as deeply entangled with capitalism, even if the two are not, to use Post's phrasing, 'coterminous'.

In a critical examination of green growth and its chameleonic ability to camouflage itself within apparently different discourses, Alexander Dunlap questions the extent to which 'justice' remains a useful analytic with which to critically theorise and contest the ever-expanding logic of extractivism. He observes that the ambiguity of the notion of 'environmental justice' has enabled its co-option by actors perpetuating modernist visions of development that remain deeply committed to growth. Like Post, Dunlap pushes us to consider the substantial overlaps between industrialism, capitalism and extractivism, calling for renewed attention to be paid to the structural factors undermining both the notion and the pursuit of environmental justice. Dunlap argues that large-scale mining and infrastructure projects, including—and perhaps especially—those labelled necessary for the so-called green transition, perpetuate violence against Indigenous people and other groups that are often marginalised, often to an extent that is essentially indistinguishable from the more blatant instances of violence that mining companies and other multinational corporations inflict.

Shifting away from these expansive theoretical concerns, Ryan Parsons offers a detailed ethnographic analysis of what happens after the mining industry leaves a particular area, focusing on a town surrounded by increasingly defunct iron ore mines. His account resonates with the concerns raised by Post and Dunlap, showing how post-extraction does not necessarily mean post-extractivism and signalling an important distinction present in both volumes of this double volume—that between extraction as a set of practices and extractivism as a political–ideological approach to the exploitation of resources, natural or otherwise. In this village in Yunnan, which has now come to rely on tourism to support its population, Parsons shows how local cultural practices quickly took the place of iron ore as an exploitable resource, reproducing the logic of extractivism in the assumption that 'peripheral' cultures are there to be commodified and consumed by relatively well-off people living in the 'core'.

Emille Boulot and Ben Collins find a similar tension between post-extraction and post-extractivism. In their comparative analysis of mine closures on Indigenous lands in Australia and Canada, they argue that even extensive legal frameworks for the closure and rehabilitation of mining sites are insufficient without the active participation and ownership of Indigenous peoples. Importantly, they suggest, legislation often pertains only to environmental indicators, with little regard for the social, cultural and economic afterlives of polluted mine sites, or the Indigenous people inhabiting them.

The second section, 'Resilience, Contestation and Resistance', explores the strategies that communities, social movements and organisations use to resist extractivism and create alternative pathways for development, demonstrating the value of a comparative approach in particular. This section speaks to the tension between the growing calls for responsible extraction and the resistance movements that have emerged in response to the harms caused by extractive industries. While some argue that responsible extraction can be achieved through technological and regulatory means, others contend that true responsibility can only be achieved through a fundamental shift in the politics and power dynamics underlying extractive industries. This includes giving voice and agency to affected communities, respecting Indigenous land rights, and promoting alternative economic models that prioritise environmental and social sustainability.

Simon Lobach's chapter offers an important cautionary tale of resource extraction failing to deliver on its promise of modernity and development, and of the limits to formal decolonisation when one disregards human, social, and environmental contexts. The chapter meticulously examines the complex history of Suriname's bauxite and aluminium sector, and the country's industrialisation efforts with regard to bauxite mining and hydroelectricity generation. Suriname was the world's main exporter of bauxite in the 1940s, but the chapter sheds light on the confluence of technical, economic, political and social factors leading to the withdrawal of foreign investors and the demise of the country's project of bringing the entirety of the bauxite–alumina–aluminium value chain to Suriname. This post-extractive 'aluminium landscape', Lobach suggests, requires that attention be paid to the consequences of industrialisation efforts that disregarded the livelihoods and well-being of local Maroon communities, be it through displacement, environmental damage, or political violence, all of which persisted beyond the original bauxite boom.

Dorothea Hamilton and Sina Trölenberg examine protests against the felling of 85 hectares of forest in central Germany, which they interpret through the lens of 'contested extractivism'. Alongside rich empirical evidence of the protesters' complex and diverse relationships with the forest they were trying to protect, Hamilton and Trölenberg contribute to our understanding of anti-extractivism by probing the limits of the notion of extractivism's applicability outside the specific Latin American mining context from which it emerged. They argue that the felling of trees to build an *autobahn* between industrial centres in Western Europe is also an example of extractivism and that through engaging with theories of the 'good life' that are fundamental to anti-extractivism in Latin America, commonalities between geographically dispersed anti-extractivist activities and post-extractivist imaginaries start to cohere.

Where Hamilton and Trölenberg compare anti-extractivist protests in German forests to anti-extractivist movements around mining sites in Latin America, Luisa Prause examines a case where the distinct modes of extractivism associated with mining and with industrial agriculture overlap. In Senegal, those seeking better working conditions in either the agricultural or the mining sector often have similar goals to one another and even employ similar strategies. They also face comparable threats from extractivist development projects. There are differences, however—namely, the distinct temporalities of the impact of mining and of industrial agriculture on land, as well as the different laws regulating these industries. Prause finds that these differences make coalition building between the two sectors difficult, and calls for critical attention to be paid to the differences between modes of extractivism—even as the idea that 'everything is extractivism' grows in popularity—in order to understand the diverse ways people might resist their logics.

Through his analysis of resistance to coal mining and both offshore and onshore gas exploration in Bangladesh, Paul Gilbert shows how different priorities can lead to similar forms of resistance. While some oppose the extraction of hydrocarbons because of concerns around climate change and land tenure, others (namely resource nationalists) are less concerned about the social and environmental impacts of extraction than what they perceive as the exploitation of Bangladesh's resources by foreign corporations. Gilbert's account highlights a key facet of extractivism, the extraction of a resource in one place for the benefit of people living in a different place, marking an important distinction between extractivism as a logic (which, from the perspective of some global or local 'centre' views the 'periphery' as a source of raw materials) and extraction as a practice.

Finally, the third section, '"Green" Extractivism and Its Discontents', interrogates the growing trend of 'green' extractivism and the contradictions and tensions inherent in the promotion of natural resource extraction as a means to transition to a low-carbon economy. Taken together, these authors offer critical insights into the complex and paradoxical relationship between extractive industries and the future of sustainability and climate change mitigation driven by the imperatives of more 'green' extraction.

James Blair, Ramón Balcázar, Javiera Barandiarán and Amanda Maxwell examine the mineral most commonly associated with the green transition: lithium. Deploying and developing the notion of 'alterlives', they show how brine evaporation in the Puna de Atacama affects the lives of Indigenous people in particular, but also plant and animal life, not only at the sites of extraction but both upstream and downstream in the lithium supply chain, where chemicals are manufactured and where they pollute surrounding environments for generations. Having expounded what they refer to as the 'alterlives of green extractivism', Blair and co-authors helpfully indicate several directions in which policies to address these inequities might move, from integrating Indigenous knowledge and science into the environmental monitoring framework to a precautionary moratorium on brine evaporation.

Michelle Pressend similarly problematises the ostensible benefits of the 'green' energy transition. Through extensive fieldwork, she shows how a community in South Africa's Eastern Cape, despite its early and largely enthusiastic embracing of wind energy, has failed to profit from the material benefits of the green transition and the promises of the renewable energy technological 'fix'. This is due, in part, to the fact that so-called clean energy developments do little to address the underlying structures of exclusion and dispossession that are fundamental to neo-liberal development. Despite their land being expropriated for the installation of windmills, members of the community Pressend studies are unable to access the energy those windmills produce, which remains prohibitively expensive.

Finally, through a case study of the global supply chains of the raw materials necessary for Norway's celebrated embrace of electric vehicles (EVs), Devyn Remme, Siddharth Sareen, Håvard Haarstad and Kjetil Rommetveitand probe the tension between 'sustainability' efforts in the global North and the extractivist logic that such efforts reproduce and rely on in their orientation with regard to the global South. It might come as no surprise that a petro state like Norway externalises the social and environmental impacts of its relatively sparse population's welfare. However, in advocating a global value chains approach to this complex relationship, Remme and co-authors offer a way of organising critical analyses of green extractivism around both the nodes that constitute global value chains and the way these nodes relate to one another.

By contrasting post-extractivist imaginaries, diverse and ever-evolving forms of resistance and contestation, and a growing recognition of the paradox of 'green' extractivism, this volume acknowledges the complex and ongoing legacies of extraction and the urgent need to move beyond extractive models of development and towards alternative pathways that prioritise social justice, environmental sustainability, democratic governance, and the well-being of both human and non-human beings. Through different conceptual approaches and in different empirical contexts, the contributions to this volume demonstrate the alarming obduracy of the logic of extractivism, even—and perhaps especially—in the growing support for the so-called green transition. These interventions caution us against the assumption that anti-extraction is anti-extractivist, that post-extraction is post-extractivism, and they critically attune us to the systemic nature of extractivism in a way that both connects and transcends any specific site or scale.

Acknowledgements

The guest editors wish to thank all the contributors to this special thematic issue. We are deeply indebted to the anonymous reviewers and to the discussants that offered their time and generous feedback during the authors' workshop: Philippe Le Billon, Jerry Jacka, Marc Hufty, Kuntala Lahiri-Dutt and Muriel Côte. Our gratitude is extended particularly to the editorial board of International Development Policy, to Dave Brooks, and for the indefatigable work of Marie Thorndahl.

References

Acosta, A. (2013) 'Extractivism and Neoextractism: Two Sides of the Same Curse', in M. Lang and D. Mokrani (eds) *Beyond Development: Alternative Visions from Latin America* (Amsterdam: Transnational Institute).

Ali, Saleem (2017) 'The ecology of diamond sourcing: from mined to synthetic gems as a sustainable transition', *Journal of Bioeconomics*, DOI: 19. 10.1007/s10818-016-9241-8.

Appel, H. (2019) *The Licit Life of Capitalism. US Oil in Equatorial Guinea* (Durham: Duke University Press).

Arboleda, M. (2020) *Planetary mine: Territories of extraction under late capitalism* (London: Verso).

Archer, M. (2022) 'The ethics of ESG: Sustainable finance and the emergence of the market as an ethical subject', *Focaal*, 2022(93), pp. 18–31.

Babidge, S. (2016) 'Contested value and an ethics of resources: Water, mining and indigenous people in the Atacama Desert, Chile', *The Australian Journal of Anthropology*, 27, pp. 84–103.

Barnett, C., P. Cloke, N. Clarke, and A. Malpass (2011) *Globalizing Responsibility: the Political Rationalities of Ethical Consumption*, RGS-IBG Book Series (Oxford: Wiley-Blackwell).

Bellamy, D. and L. Pravica (2011) 'Assessing the impact of driverless haul trucks in Australian surface mining', *Resources Policy*, 36, pp. 149–158, DOI: 10.1016/j.resourpol.2010.09.002.

Bell, L. (2023) *Under Pressure: Diamond Mining and Everyday Life in Northern Canada* (Toronto: Toronto University Press).

Benson, P., and S. Kirsch (2010) 'Corporate oxymorons', *Dialect Anthropol.*, 34, pp. 45–48, DOI: 10.1007/s10624-009-9112-y.

Bidaud, C., K. Schreckenberg and J.P. Jones (2018). The local costs of biodiversity offsets: Comparing standards, policy and practice. *Land Use Policy*, 77, pp. 43–50.

Bravo Díaz, A. (2021) '"Sumak Kawsay Is Harmful for All of Us": Oil Roads and Well-being among the Waorani in Ecuadorian Amazonia', *Latin American Perspectives*, 48(3), pp. 51–68, DOI: 10.1177/0094582X211004909.

Brock, A. (2020) 'Securing accumulation by restoration—Exploring spectacular corporate conservation, coal mining and biodiversity compensation in the German Rhineland', *Environment and Planning E: Nature and Space*, DOI: 10.1177/2514848620924597.

Bruna, N. (2023) 'The Rise of Green Extractivism. Extractivism, Rural Livelihoods and Accumulation in a Climate-Smart World' (Abingdon: Routledge).

Burchardt, H. J., and K. Dietz (2014) '(Neo-) extractivism–a new challenge for development theory from Latin America' *Third World Quarterly*, 35(3), pp. 468–486.

Calvão, F., M. Archer and A. Benya (eds.) (2023) *The Lives of Extraction. Identities, Communities and the Politics of Place,* International Development Policy | Revue internationale de politique de développement, 15 (Geneva, Boston: Graduate Institute Publications, Brill-Nijhoff), DOI: 10.4000/poldev.5226.

Calvão, F. (2020) 'Transparent Minerals and Opaque Diamond Sources' in Ferry, E., A. Vallard, A. Walsh (eds.), *The Anthropology of Precious Minerals* (Toronto: University of Toronto Press), pp. 147–63.

Calvão, F. and M. Archer (2021) 'Digital extraction: Blockchain traceability in mineral supply chains', *Political Geography*, 87, 102381, DOI: 10.1016/j.polgeo.2021.102381.

Calvão, F., M. Bolay and L. Bell (2021) 'Dis/connection Matters: Natural, Synthetic, and Digital: Introduction', *Tsantsa*, 26, pp. 7–17, DOI: 10.36950/tsantsa.2021.26.7680.

Calvão, F., C. Mcdonald, and M. Bolay (2021) 'Cobalt mining and the corporate outsourcing of responsibility in the Democratic Republic of Congo', *The Extractive Industries and Society*, 8, DOI: 10.1016/j.exis.2021.02.004.

Calvão, F. and V. Gronwald (2019) *Blockchain in the Mining Industry: Implications for Sustainable Development in Africa*, Policy Insights, 74 (Johannesburg: South African Institute of International Affairs).

Carrier, J. (2010) 'Protecting the Environment the Natural Way: Ethical Consumption and Commodity Fetishism' *Antipode*, 42(3), pp. 672–689.

Cepek, M. (2016) 'There might be blood: Oil, humility, and the cosmopolitics of a Cofán petro-being: There might be blood', *American Ethnologist*, 43, pp. 623–635, DOI: 10.1111/amet.12379.

Chagnon, C. W., F. Durante, B. K. Gills, S. E. Hagolani-Albov, S. Hokkanen, S. M. J. Kangasluoma, H. Konttinen, M. Kröger, W. LaFleur, O. Ollinaho and M. P. S. Vuola (2022) 'From Extractivism to Global Extractivism: the Evolution of an Organizing Concept', *The Journal of Peasant Studies*, pp. 1–33, DOI: 10.1080/03066150.2022.2069015.

Chakrabarty, D. (2021) *The Climate of History in a Planetary Age* (Chicago: The University of Chicago Press).

Cosbey A., Mann H., N. Maennling, P. Toledano, J. Geipel and M. D. Brauch (2016) *Mining a Mirage? Reassessing the shared-value paradigm in light of the technological advances in the mining sector* (Winnipeg: International Institute for Sustainable Development), https://www.iisd.org/publications/report/mining-mirage-reassessing-shared-value-paradigm-light-technological-advances (accessed on 12 May 2023).

Dadhich, S., U. Bodin and U. Andersson (2016) 'Key challenges in automation of earth-moving machines', *Automation in construction*, 68, pp. 212–222, DOI: 10.1016/j.autcon.2016.05.009.

Dunlap, A. (2019) *Renewing destruction: Wind energy development, conflict and resistance in a Latin American context* (London: Rowman & Littlefield).

Ellem, B. (2015) 'Geographies of the labour process: automation and the spatiality of mining. Work', *Employment & Society*, 30, DOI: 10.1177/0950017015604108.

Escobar, A. (2015) 'Degrowth, postdevelopment, and transitions: a preliminary conversation', *Sustainability Science*, 10(3), pp. 451–462, DOI: 10.1007/s11625-015-0297-5.

Escobar, A. (2007) 'Worlds and Knowledges Otherwise. The Latin American modernity/ coloniality research program', *Cultural Studies*, 21(2 and 3), pp. 179–210, DOI: 10.1080/09502380601162506.

Frederiksen, T. and M. Himley (2019) 'Tactics of dispossession: Access, power, and subjectivity at the extractive frontier', *Transactions of the Institute of British Geographers*, 45, DOI: 10.1111/tran.12329.

Gezon, L. and S. Paulson (eds) (2017) 'Degrowth, culture and power', *Journal of Political Ecology*, 24, pp. 425–666.

Gómez-Barris, M. (2017) *The Extractive Zone. Social Ecologies and Decolonial Perspectives* (Durham, NC: Duke University Press).

Gudynas, E. (2018) 'Extractivisms. Tendencies and consequences', in R. Munck and R. Wise (eds.) *Reframing Latin American Development* (Abingdon: Routledge).

Gudynas, E. (2013) *Transitions to post-extractivism: directions, options, areas of action. Beyond Development: Alternative Visions from Latin America* (Amsterdam: Transnational Institute), pp. 165–188.

Gudynas, E. (2011) 'Buen Vivir: Today's tomorrow', *Development*, 54, pp. 441–447, DOI: 10.1057/dev.2011.86.

Hernández Reyes, C. E. (2019) 'Black women's struggles against extractivism, land dispossession, and marginalization in Colombia', *Latin American Perspectives*, 46(2), pp. 217–234.

Hickel, J. (2021) 'The anti-colonial politics of degrowth', *Political Geography*, 88, 102404. DOI: 10.1016/j.polgeo.2021.102404.

Huber, M. (2022) *Climate Change as Class War: Building Socialism on a Warming Planet* (London: Verso).

Jerez, B. and I. Garces (2021) 'Lithium extractivism and water injustices in the Salar de Atacama, Chile: the colonial shadow of green electromobility', *Political Geography*, 87, 102382, DOI: 10.1016/j.polgeo.2021.102382.

Kaplan, U.E. and E. Topal (2020) 'A New Ore Grade Estimation Using Combine Machine Learning Algorithms', *Minerals*, 10(847), DOI: 10.3390/min10100847.

Kill, J., G. Franchi, and R. Hall (2016) *Rio Tinto's biodiversity offset in Madagascar: Double landgrab in the name of biodiversity* (Montevideo: World Rainforest Movement and Re: Common).

Kirsch, S. (2014) *Mining Capitalism: the Relationship between Corporations and Their Critics* (Oakland: University of California Press).

Kiziroglou, M. E., D. E. Boyle, E. M. Yeatman and J. J. Cilliers (2017) 'Opportunities for Sensing Systems in Mining', in IEEE Transactions on Industrial Informatics, 13(1), pp. 278–286, 10.1109/TII.2016.2636131.

Klinger, J.M. (2017) *Rare Earth Frontiers: from Terrestrial Subsoils to Lunar Landscapes*, (Ithaca: Cornell University Press).

Le Billon, P. (2021) 'Crisis conservation and green extraction: biodiversity offsets as spaces of double exception', *Journal of Political Ecology*, 28, DOI: 10.2458/jpe.2991.

Le Billon, P. and S. Spiegel (2022) 'Cleaning mineral supply chains? Political economies of exploitation and hidden costs of technical fixes', *Review of International Political Economy*, 29(3), 768–791, DOI: 10.1080/09692290.2021.1899959.

Maldonado-Torres, N. (2007) 'On the Coloniality of Being', *Cultural Studies*, 21(2–3), pp. 240–270, DOI: 10.1080/09502380601162548.

Mezzadra, S. and B. Neilson (2019) *The Politics of Operations: Excavating Contemporary Capitalism* (Durham: Duke University Press).

Mignolo, W. (2011) 'Epistemic Disobedience and the Decolonial Option: a Manifesto', *TRANSMODERNITY: Journal of Peripheral Cultural Production of the Luso-Hispanic World*, 1(2), DOI: 10.5070/T412011807.

Mignolo, W. and C. Walsh (2018) *On Decoloniality: Concept, Analytics, Praxis* (Durham: Duke University Press).

Mignolo, W. and A. Escobar (eds) (2013) *Globalization and the Decolonial Option* (Abingdon: Routledge).

Murrey, A. and N. Jackson (2019) 'A Decolonial Critique of the Racialized "Localwashing" of Extraction in Central Africa', *Annals of the American Association of Geographers*, 110, pp. 1–24, DOI: 10.1080/24694452.2019.1638752.

Nygren, A., M. Kröger, and B. Gills (2022) 'Global Extractivisms and Transformative Alternatives', *The Journal of Peasant Studies*, pp. 1–26, DOI: 10.1080/03066150.2022.2069495.

Pereira, C. and D. Tsikata (2021) 'Contextualising extractivism in Africa', *Feminist Africa*, 2(1), pp. 14–47.

Preston, J. (2017) 'Racial Extractivism and White Settler Colonialism: an Examination of the Canadian Tar Sands Mega-Projects', *Cultural Studies*, 31(2–3), pp. 353–375, DOI: 10.1080/09502386.2017.1303432.

Quijano, A. (2007) 'Coloniality and modernity / rationality', *Cultural Studies*, 21: 2, pp. 168–178, DOI: 10.1080/09502380601164353.

Quijano, A. (2000) 'Coloniality of Power, Eurocentrism and Latin America', *Nepantla*, 1(3), pp. 533–580.

Ralston, J., D. Reid, C. Hargrave and D. Hainsworth (2014) 'Sensing for advancing mining automation capability: a review of underground automation technology development', *International Journal of Mining Science and Technology*, 24, DOI: 10.1016/j.ijmst.2014.03.003.

Riofrancos, T. (2020) *Resource Radicals: from Petro-Nationalism to Post-Extractivism in Ecuador* (Durham: Duke University Press).

Robinson, C. (1983) *Black Marxism: the making of the Black radical tradition* (The University of North Carolina Press).

Seagle, C. (2012) Inverting the impacts: Mining, conservation and sustainability claims near the Rio Tinto/QMM ilmenite mine in Southeast Madagascar. *Journal of Peasant Studies*, 39, pp. 447–477, DOI: 10.1080/03066150.2012.671769.

Smith, J. H. (2021) *The Eyes of the World. Mining the Digital Age in the Eastern DR Congo* (Chicago: The University of Chicago Press).

Svampa, M. (2015) 'Commodities consensus: Neoextractivism and enclosure of the commons in Latin America', *South Atlantic Quarterly*, 114(1), pp. 65–82.

Tilley, L. and R. Shilliam (eds.) (2021) *Raced Markets* (Abingdon: Routledge).

Thylstrup, N. B., M. Archer and L. Ravn (2022) 'Traceability', *Internet Policy Review*, 11(1), pp. 1–12.

Tornel, C. (2022) 'Decolonizing energy justice from the ground up: Political ecology, ontology, and energy landscapes' *Progress in Human Geography*, 47(1), pp. 43–65. DOI: 10.1177/03091325221132561.

Trouillot, M.-R. (1995) *Silencing the Past: Power and the Production of History* (Boston: Beacon Press).

Tuck, E. and K. Yang (2012) 'Decolonization Is Not a Metaphor. Decolonization. Indigeneity', *Education & Society* 1(1), pp. 1–40, DOI: 10.25058/20112742.n38.04.

Verweijen, J., and A. Dunlap (2021) 'The evolving techniques of the social engineering of extraction: Introducing political (re) actions "from above" in large-scale mining and energy projects', *Political Geography*, 88, 102342.

Voskoboynik, D. M., and D. Andreucci (2021) Greening extractivism: Environmental discourses and resource governance in the 'Lithium Triangle'. *Environment and Planning E: Nature and Space*, 5(2), 787–809, DOI: 10.1177/25148486211006345.

Watts, M. (2021) 'Hyper-Extractivism and the Global Oil Assemblage', in J. Shapiro and J.-A. McNeish (eds.) *Our Extractive Age: Expressions of Violence and Resistance* (Abingdon: Routledge), pp. 207–248.

Welker, M. (2014) Enacting the Corporation. An American Mining Firm in Post-Authoritarian Indonesia (Los Angeles: University of California Press).

Ye, J., J. D. van der Ploeg, S. Schneider and T. Shanin (2020) 'The Incursions of Extractivism: Moving from Dispersed Places to Global Capitalism', *The Journal of Peasant Studies*, 47(1), pp. 155–183.

Yusoff, K. (2018) *A Billion Black Anthropocenes or None* (Minneapolis: University of Minnesota Press).

PART 1

Post-extractivism: Debates and Practices

CHAPTER 2

Expanding Extractivisms: Extractivisms as Modes of Extraction Sustaining Imperial Modes of Living

Erik Post

Abstract

The rapacious planetary extraction of energy and materials and associated socioecological violence have culminated in overlapping ecological, social, and political crises. With the advent of global initiatives that seek to address these crises and signs of post-pandemic recovery programmes deepening extraction, 'extractivisms' are at a critical juncture. Discussions over extractivisms, their relation to capitalism, and implications for creating alternative post-extractivist futures have proliferated in recent years. As a result, definitions have multiplied and expanded, which has led to ambiguity and prompted calls to better define and conceptualise extractivisms. This chapter contributes to this exercise in three ways: First, it details a genealogy of extractivisms that originates in Latin American scholarship, expands to 'global extractivisms', and culminates in conceptual expansions that progressively divorce the concept from the extraction of energy and materials. Second, it addresses how Marxian thought has theorised the relationship between capitalism and the biophysical world and analyses four recent interventions to clarify why extractivisms are pivotal to but cannot be equated with capitalism. Third, the chapter synthesises insights from these discussions to argue that extractivisms are best conceived of as particular 'modes of extraction' that provide the energetic and material basis for 'imperial modes of living'. It concludes with reflections on how more sustainable and peaceful futures must be premised on transitions to 'post-extractivisms' and 'post-imperial solidarity modes of living'.

1 Introduction[1]

The harnessing of energy and materials for human purposes from the web of life (Moore, 2015)—extraction—increased markedly in the latter half of the twentieth century. The United Nations (UN) International Resource Panel's

1 Conflict of interest and funding. No potential conflict of interest was reported by the author.

 | DOI:10.1163/9789004686182_003

most recent *Global Resources Outlook* (International Resource Panel, 2019, 39) documents that from '1970 to 2017, annual global extraction of materials grew from 27.1 billion tons to 92.1 billion tons [...] [while] material demand per capita grew from 7.4 tons in 1970 to 12.2 tons per capita in 2017'. Post-pandemic recovery programmes and high commodity prices in part also due to the Russian invasion of Ukraine are likely to further spur extraction (Benites and Bebbington, 2020; Le Billon et al., 2021; World Bank Group, 2022). Most of this extraction is achieved through modes of renewable and non-renewable resource extraction that Gudynas (2009, 188) coined as forms of 'extractivism', referring to 'activities that remove great quantities of natural resources that are not then processed (or are but only in a limited fashion) and that leave a country as exports'.[2] Extractivisms have been able to expand and deepen to such an extent that they 'have become the main driving force of ecological change on a continental scale' (Gudynas, 2021, 20). Extractivisms are also associated with multidimensional forms of violence (Glaab and Stuvøy, 2021; Navas, Mingorria and Aguilar-González, 2018; Post, 2022), which unevenly drive and exacerbate overlapping planetary social and political crises. UN Special Rapporteur Achiume (Achiume, 2019, 3), for example, penned a report on how 'global extractivism' causes 'poverty and underdevelopment' as well as 'dependency and inequality'. This inequality is vividly illustrated by the fact that inhabitants of 'the wealthiest countries consume, on average, ten times as many materials as [those of] the poorest countries' (Schandl et al., 2018, 836; see Figure 2.1).

Recognition of extractivisms' profound socioecological implications has given rise to a critical conjuncture in the context of which the concept, its relation to global capitalism, and pathways to alternative futures are hotly debated. In tandem, definitions and conceptual frameworks of extractivisms have multiplied, leading to an analytical muddiness that makes it 'essential to clarify the concept of extractivism' (Gudynas, 2021, 4; also see, Nygren, Kröger and Gills, 2022; Shapiro and McNeish, 2021; Szeman and Wenzel, 2021). This involves theorising the relationship between extractivisms and capitalism since 'extractive logics [...] seem to be spreading to other realms of capitalist activity, prompting claims that capitalism has entered a new stage of extractivism' (Mezzadra and Neilson, 2019, 38). As a result, 'understanding the wide variety of dynamics that are connected to extraction seems to be more pertinent than ever before' (D'Angelo and Pijpers, 2022, 3).

2 All English translations of matter quoted from non-English sources are the author's.

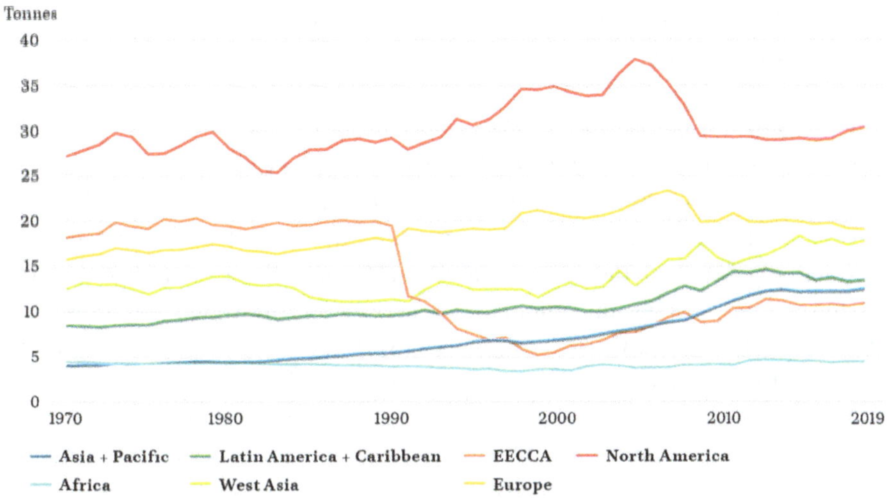

FIGURE 2.1 Per capita material footprint of consumption by seven world regions 1970–2019 in tonnes
SOURCES: AUTHORS, BASED ON DATA FROM THE UNEP AND IRP GLOBAL MATERIAL FLOWS, DATABASE: HTTPS://WWW.RESOURCEPANEL.ORG/GLOBAL-MATERIAL-FLOWS-DATABASE/ (ACCESSED ON 20 DECEMBER 2022)

In this chapter, I propose that extractivisms are 'modes of extraction'—the historical strategic relations facilitating the extraction of energy and materials (Bunker, 1985)—that provide the material basis for what Brand and Wissen (2021, 39) term the 'imperial mode of living' (IML): the practices built into political, economic, and cultural structures of everyday life that rely on 'unlimited access to labour power, natural resources and sinks'. In mobilising this concept, I follow Hanaček and co-authors' (2020, 9) suggestion to develop 'more integrated, regional and global understandings of economic interdependencies and relations'. To do so, I first survey a genealogy of the concept of extractivisms. Second, I discuss how Marxian thought has theorised the relationship between capitalism and the biophysical world and analyse four recent interventions that elucidate why extractivisms are pivotal to, but not coterminous with, capitalism. Third, I discuss the concept of modes of extraction and argue that those coupled with imperial modes of living constitute extractivisms. I conclude with reflections on the ramifications for post-extractive transitions to more sustainable and peaceful futures premised on post-imperial solidarity modes of living, and highlight future research avenues.

2 From Latin American to Global Extractivisms and Conceptual Expansions

2.1 *Latin America and the Commodities Consensus*

Although the term 'extractivism' has a longer genealogy (see, for example, Moran, 1982, 25), discussions of '*extractivismo*' proliferated during the early twenty-first century in Latin American academia and political life as the consequences of the expansion of energetic and material extractive frontiers initiated in the 1990s became apparent (Acosta et al., 2011; Delgado Ramos, 2013; Schuldt et al., 2009). Gudynas's (2009, 188) definition provided in the introduction to this chapter is the most well known definition proposed in these discussions. It entails that the extractive activities must meet three conditions: (i) a high volume and intensity of extraction, (ii) little to no processing, and (iii) exportation of a majority of the resources. Extractivisms can operate through non-renewable and renewable resources—the former, for example, including when pearls, timber, guano, rubber, seafood or agricultural products are extracted at volumes that exceed regeneration capacities. Gudynas pluralises extractivisms to indicate this variability and notes that particular forms create distinct impacts that include population displacement, ecological degradation, and the commodification of social life and the environment. In the aggregate, extractivisms' socioecological transformations are highly destructive, in their most extreme forms wholly preventing socioecological systems from sustaining life (Gudynas, 2021).

This literature builds on the insight of dependency theory that former colonies remained 'trapped' in continued resource extraction and exportation after being forced into it under colonial unequal exchange relations (Cardoso and Faletto, 1998). Svampa (2019, 7), for example, writes that 'since the time of the conquest (1492), Latin American territories have been subject to [...] a mode of accumulation [...] characterised by the export of raw materials and by a scheme of subordinate insertion in the world economy'. Since the legitimacy of 'modern' Latin American independent states was and continues to be premised on achieving economic growth to promote progress, modernisation and development, extractivisms became 'development models' rearticulated under successive imperial and neo-colonial regimes (Alimonda, 2011; 2015; Brand, Dietz and Lang, 2016). Following a waning of resource exports' centrality to Latin American economies after the 1960s (Ocampo, 2017), extractivisms returned with a vengeance in the 1990s. Neo-liberal reforms following the Latin American debt crisis opened Latin American extractive sectors to increased private and foreign participation, while Chinese industrialisation created a commodities super-cycle and hampered Latin American industrialisation (Acquatella, Bello and Berríos, 2019; Stallings, 2020). In response, Latin American governments expanded and deepened extractivisms, causing a 're-primarization' of Latin American economies that Svampa (2013, 30; emphasis in the original) refers to as a 'shift from the *Washington Consensus* [...] to the *Commodities Consensus*'.

While emphasising the continuity between historical and contemporary forms of extractivisms, these accounts highlight the particularities of so-called neo-extractivism: the development model implemented by various Latin American left-wing and 'post–neo-liberal' 'pink tide' governments in the early twenty-first century. Neo-extractivism's defining feature is the reassertion of the state in regulating extractive activities and capturing resource rents to transform dependent economies and fund social programmes. Rather than transforming economies, however, neo-extractivism deepened dependence on international commodity markets, foreign finance and transnational corporations (Bebbington and Bebbington, 2013; Burchardt and Dietz, 2014; Petras and Veltmeyer, 2014). With due respect to Ferguson (2015), 'post–neo-liberal' social programmes created 'compensatory' states that deploy conditional cash transfers for political legitimacy and to avert more radical proposals for economic redistribution and multidimensional well-being (Andreucci and Radhuber, 2017; Gudynas, 2012; Tilzey, 2019). These programmes also imply 'the incorporation of other worlds into the world defined by development' (Bebbington et al., 2018, 15), buttressing teleological narratives of progress, modernity and development (Lang and Mokrani, 2013; Marston and Perreault, 2017).

Regardless of the particularities of neo-extractivisms, Carbonnier, Campodónico and Tezanos Vázquez (2017, 14) conclude that they 'do not seem to have translated into radically different outcomes' when compared with 'conventional' extractivisms. Arsel, Hogenboom and Pellegrini (2016, 881) explain that both types of Latin American regime operate under an 'extractive imperative', according to which extractivisms 'enjoy teleological primacy [...] [and have] taken over the logic of other state activities'. In teasing out the similarities and differences between (neo-)extractivisms, this literature focuses almost exclusively on Latin America. Yet some scholars writing in the Latin American tradition note that extractivisms 'began to be structured with the conquest and colonisation of the Americas, Africa and Asia' and became 'a constant in the economic, social and political life of many countries in the global South' (Acosta, 2013, 6263).

2.2 *Global Extractivisms*

Following the popularisation of the concept in Latin America, 'extractivism' increasingly featured in analyses of similar phenomena in Africa and central and Southeast Asia (Ayelazuno, 2014; Dietz and Engels, 2017; Lahiri-Dutt, 2018).

Beyond the so-called global South, North American scholarship explored how 'racial extractivism' perpetuates 'forms of violent white settler colonialism [...] to continue exploiting the natural environment while attempting to erase Indigenous forms of legal jurisdiction, government and ultimately life' (Preston, 2017, 356–370). While Preston develops racial extractivism through an analysis of the Canadian tar sands (also, see Westman, Joly and Gross, 2020), similar dynamics in Canada are observed concerning land banks (Scobie, Finau and Hallenbeck, 2021), the Mackenzie Valley pipeline (Coulthard, 2010), and iron ore extraction (Nachet, Beckett and MacNeil, 2021), and the transborder Keystone XL pipeline (Coulthard, 2014; Curley and Lister, 2020), as well as concerning (slave) plantations (Bauerly, 2017; Benson, 2012; Haraway, 2016), Louisiana's Cancer Alley (Davies, 2022) and hydrocarbon, coal and uranium mining in Navajo territories in the United States (Curley, 2019).

These resonances across regions and temporalities lead UN rapporteur Achiume (2019, 6–7) to use the term 'global extractivism', noting that it 'cannot properly be understood without reference to its colonial origins [...] first in the Americas and then in Asia and Africa'. Global extractivism is the most spatially and temporally expansive conception of this 'development model', covering the *longue durée* on the planetary scale. The capaciousness of global and racial extractivisms can be contrasted with scholars who maintain the planetary spatial scope but apply narrower temporal and conceptual terms. For example, Adaman, Arsel and Akbulut (2019, 518–519; emphasis mine) define extractivism as a '*new* regime of accumulation' and the 'dominant economic model' undergirding the 'neoliberal developmentalism' of populist leaders.

2.3 *Conceptual Expansions*

Recent literature has also sought to expand extractivisms conceptually. Chagnon, Hagolani-Albov and Hokkanen (2021, 176–180; also, see Calvão, 2019; Calvão and Archer, 2021) examine how 'digital and data extractivism [...] intersect with natural resource and financial extractivisms in their underlying logic and processes', noting that 'digital infrastructures depend on natural resource extraction, while at the same time natural resource extraction is increasingly driven by the digital'. Le Billon (2021, 220; also, see Hope, 2020) identifies an extraction–conservation nexus to indicate how 'logics of conservation and extraction [...] are in many ways coming together'. Del Bene, Scheidel and Temper (2018) coin 'renewables extractivism' to capture how renewable energy infrastructures are entangled with (neo-)extractivisms. Voskoboynik and Andreucci (2021, 16; emphasis in the original) describe the discursive strategy through which 'extraction and valorisation of mineral resources is rendered not only compatible with "sustainable development," but *necessary* to it' as 'green extractivism' (also, see Blair et al., Chapter 10 in this volume). Dunlap and Arce (2021, 180) deploy 'green extractivism' to refer to how renewable energy infrastructures appropriate and distribute value similarly to conventional extractivisms while causing comparable socioecological destruction (also, see Pressend, Chapter 11 in this volume). Conservation, renewables, and green extractivisms can be subsumed under the category 'eco-extractivism' deployed by Núñez, Benwell and Aliste (2020, 3) to describe 'the accumulation of land justified in terms of environmental protection or environmentally friendly projects [...] undertaken by large investors whose other investments are in extractive industries'. Bruna (2022, 142) drops the connotation of extractive industries by defining 'green extractivism' generally as 'a vehicle for the appropriation of nature through the implementation of land-based projects funded through climate change policies'.

Further divorcing extractivisms from the physical extraction of energy and materials, several approaches point to how 'extractive logics' appropriate value from social worlds. Grosfoguel (2016, 132) develops 'cognitive and epistemic extractivism' to describe 'a mentality that [...] seeks to extract ideas like it extracts raw materials in order to colonise them by subsuming them within the parameters of Western culture and epistemology'. This is underpinned by an 'ontological extractivism', denoting 'a way of being and being in the world that appropriates from others without consent and without thinking or worrying' (Grosfoguel, 2016, 138). Other examples concern so-called urban extractivism (Duplat, 2017) and financial extractivism (Gago and Mezzadra, 2017). The 'emergence of global extractivism as a way of organizing life' and the proliferation of critical research lead Chagnon and co-authors (2022) to define it as an 'organizing concept' that arranges and synthesizes a body of knowledge.

This mushrooming of definitions of extractivisms risks diminishing the terms' analytical purchase and obscures both the important qualitative differences between modes of appropriation and their unifying element: being interrelated with capitalism. The next section addresses how Marxian thought has theorised this interrelationship and whether the seeming ubiquity of extractivisms and extractivist logics entails a novel world historical system of extractivism.

3 Extractivisms, Capitalism, and Civilisation

According to Marx (1990, 198), capitalist production operates akin to a 'social metabolism' (*Stoffwechsel*), transforming energy and materials through a 'metabolic interaction' (Foster, 1999). Labour acts as 'the point of contact [...] where biophysical resources pass into the circuits of social metabolism' (Malm, 2016, 19). Under capitalist social relations only human labour is considered as generating economic value. A labour theory of value therefore 'defines value as socially necessary labour-time' alienated from the socioecological conditions required for its existence and reproduction (Huber, 2018, 149). Under capitalist production, huge swaths of the web of life are thus not valued while other ways of valuing, such as aesthetic, social, cultural, or ecological, are marginalised (Martinez-Alier, 2002; Martinez-Alier et al., 2010; Moore, 2017; 2018). Capital thus 'produces' specific natures (Smith, 2008), which is why so-called natural resources can 'only be defined in relationship to the mode of production which seeks to make use of them' (Harvey, 1974, 265).

Wolf (2010, 75) refers to modes of production (MoPs) as historical 'set[s] of social relations through which labour is deployed to wrest energy from nature by means of tools, skills, organisation, and knowledge'. These combine relations and forces of production, the latter including the 'resources' that form 'the means and objects of labour' (Jessop, 1990, 289–290). Graeber (2006, 61–63) notes that conceptualisation of MoPs is 'theoretically quite undeveloped' and that 'the "forces of production" are rarely much invoked'. Yet the forces of production co-determine the historical forms that MoPs take. In thermodynamic terms, no growth can feed upon itself, which is why expanded production, characteristic of the capitalist MoP, requires continued extraction of energy and material (Leff, 2021). Luxemburg (2003, 379) theorises that capitalist crisis tendencies manifest when 'the development of the productive forces is arrested'. These tendencies must be counteracted by expansion into an 'outside', or elsewhere, of non-capitalist social formations and biophysical environments. This explains why Arrighi and Silver's (1999, 28) four world-historical 'cycles of accumulation' occasioned a progressive 'increase in the collective power over third parties or nature by the entire system's dominant group'.

Building on these precepts, Harvey (2003, 145) argues that the ascent of the US to global hegemon initiated a neo-liberal world system plagued by crises of over-accumulation that cause capital to increasingly engage in 'accumulation by dispossession' and the continuous appropriation of 'assets' at low or zero cost, including 'colonial, neo-colonial, and imperial processes of appropriation of assets (including natural resources)'. From this perspective, extractivisms are instantiations of accumulation by dispossession. Harvey's (2003, 153) assertion that accumulation by dispossession had 'become the dominant form of accumulation' portends recent arguments that extractivisms define contemporary capitalism. A brief discussion of four interventions that agree upon the increasing centrality of extractivisms to capitalism but disagree on whether extractivisms and capitalism have become coextensive will elucidate the utility of the concept of modes of extraction (MoEs) as distinct from MoPs and modes of appropriation (MoAs).

3.1 *Extractivisms as Pivotal to, But Not Coterminous with, Capitalism*

In a recent discussion paper, Ye et al. (2020, 158–169) hypothesise that extractivism as a 'development model […] characterised by accumulation by dispossession' has become the 'new, and increasingly favoured, *modus operandi* of capital' in 'an organised, and internally coherent, system for ongoing value extraction'. This new economic system has ten defining features: (1) it creates monopolies over the resources that are (to be) extracted, (2) relying on 'infrastructural elements' that (3) are linked in 'chains' and controlled by 'operational centres' with monopoly control over vital links; (4) through this control, operational centres appropriate value and accumulate wealth shared between actors in the centres, which (5) are characterised by a close intertwinement between state and private groups; (6) this creates and deepens inequalities that are themselves co-constitutive of extractivism, (7) even if the resulting wealth occasionally funds development or distributive policies; (8) in terms of production in *sensu stricto*, extractivism represents production without the reproduction of the required material resources; (9) this generates 'windfall profits' and 'boom–bust cycles' that (10) ultimately result in barrenness. The centralising effect of these dynamics gives rise to emergent centres, even if these defy meta-geographical categories of core–periphery and global North/South. Whereas this, the first of our four interventions is highly generative, its conclusion that capitalism has entered a new stage of extractivism is refuted by the other three interventions.

Arboleda concurs, in *The Planetary Mine* (2020, 25), that the planetary geography of Chilean copper extraction exemplifies 'a more advanced stage of the same system of capitalist domination', yet rejects equating this with extractivisms. Defining an entire economic system based on a singular (extractivist) logic 'can obfuscate the equally relevant function of labour exploitation, impersonal compulsions, fetishisation, and all those economic processes' not tied to extractivisms that remain crucial to capital accumulation on a global scale (Arboleda, 2020, 245–248). Arboleda posits that the determining logic of extractivisms is the '*production of relative surplus value at the world scale*' (Arboleda, 2020, 6; emphasis in the original). Concrete extractivisms are expressions of the universal content of capital in its historically and geographically specific forms that

> yields a new territoriality of extraction whose immanent content cannot be fully elucidated by the *loci classici* of state-centric concepts of political

> economy […] [but is] also objectified in those unspectacular, nearly imperceptible practices and habits that constantly weave together the fabric of everyday life in the twenty-first-century city: sending an email, driving to work, ordering groceries through the internet.
>
> ARBOLEDA, 2020, 13

Connecting the scales of planetary relations and everyday life is a fertile approach to theorising the relationship between capitalism and the operations that appropriate value from capital's outsides.

This is Mezzadra and Neilson's central concern in *The Politics of Operations* (2019, 164), in which they interrogate how 'aggregate capital' extracts value from its 'multiple outsides', '[w]hether this outside takes the form of mineral deposits, land, biological materials, or social cooperation'. Operations in extraction, logistics and finance have become entangled 'and thus emerge as distinctive criteria of capitalism in its present global formation' while overall 'the composition and logics of aggregate capital are increasingly marked by the prevalence and pivotal status of *extractive* operations' (Mezzadra and Neilson, 2019, 163; emphasis in the original). Extractive operations in finance appropriate wealth to be produced in the future through social cooperation, including the gendered and racialized forms of sociality 'produced' by the self-, un-, and underemployed and those engaged in social reproductive labour. Operations in logistics extract value by coordinating the connection and valorisation of the 'relative spatial positioning' of production processes, leveraging 'a kind of drawing power over diverse labour regimes and meshes of social cooperation' (Mezzadra and Neilson, 2019, 164). Nevertheless, Mezzadra and Neilson are 'hesitant to argue that extractivism constitutes a new paradigm of capitalism' (2019, 38–39). Like Arboleda, they propose that capitalism emerges from 'the articulation of extractive operations with other operations of capital, which involve heterogeneous forms of labour and exploitation' (Mezzadra and Neilson, 2017, 197). The heterogeneity and planetary scope of these articulations render 'the geography of contemporary capitalism far more complex than suggested by such binaries as global North and global South or centre and periphery', indicating a need to attend to how capital 'hits the ground' (Mezzadra and Neilson, 2017, 7). Besides affirming the importance of the 'aggregate' world capitalist market scale, the interpenetration of extraction, finance and logistics in extracting value from capital's multiple outsides demonstrates the need to trace the concrete socioecological relations through which capital 'hits the ground'.

Lastly, Dunlap and Jakobsen propose a different reason why capitalism and extractivisms ought not to be equated, even if the latter are 'taking on planetary significance'. In *The Violent Technologies of Extraction* (2020, Chapter 1, 1–12), they develop the notion of 'total extractivism' to describe 'the imperative driving the global capitalist economy, centred on the deployment of violent technologies aiming at integrating and reconfiguring the earth and absorbing its inhabitants, meanwhile normalising its logics, apparatuses and subjectivities, as it violently colonises and pacifies various natures'. They diverge from Ye et al.'s analysis on three grounds. First, rather than concentration and centralisation, they point to the decentralised nature of infrastructural, logistical and financial systems in facilitating contemporary value extraction, concurring with Arboleda and Mezzadra and Neilson. Second, echoing research on extractive 'leftover' and 'residue' economies (Jaramillo, 2020; Pijpers et al., 2021) and eco-extractivisms, they argue that barren landscapes represent not extractivisms' endpoints, but opportunities for novel extractivisms to emerge. Third, and most significantly, Dunlap and Jakobsen (2020, Chapter 2, 13–41) trace total extractivism's imperative beyond the capitalist historical horizon to roots in the creation of complex social formations through power, which is 'much older than capitalism or colonialism, but civilisation itself'. While driven by strategies for capital accumulation, total extractivism is ultimately about reproducing the hierarchical social formations of 'civilisation'. Because non-capitalist civilisational social formations can still be premised on hierarchies that integrate, reconfigure and absorb human and non-human worlds into civilisational metabolisms, Dunlap and Jakobsen caution against conflating post-capitalisms with post-extractivisms. Thus, they advocate for 'abolishing the myth of human supremacy' and other hierarchical relations underpinning civilisational reproduction (2020, Chapter 6, 119–131).

In the next section, I argue that extractivisms are 'modes of extraction' that sustain the 'imperial mode of living'. This provides a way out of the cacophonous proliferation of definitions and approaches, increasing analytical rigour and specifying extractivisms' relationship with capitalism while incorporating issues highlighted by these four interventions and raised in attempts to conceptually expand extractivisms.

4 Extractivisms as Modes of Extraction Sustaining Imperial Modes of Living

4.1 *Modes of Extraction*

In *Underdeveloping the Amazon: Extraction, Unequal Exchange, and the Failure of the Modern State* (1985), Bunker argued that the rapacious extraction of energy and materials from the Brazilian Amazon organised through a series of 'modes of extractions' (MoEs) caused the region's 'development of underdevelopment'. MoEs describe the 'systemic connections' between the extraction of energy and materials and 'class structures, the organisation of labour, systems of exchange and property, the activities of the state, the distribution of populations, the development of physical infrastructures, and the kinds of informations, beliefs, and ideologies which shape social organisation and behaviour' (Bunker, 1985, 23). MoEs are not categorical units that sort specific systemic connections into one bucket or another, they render visible the strategic relationships that shape the terms under which energy and materials are extracted. MoEs thus fill the blind spot in analyses of MoPs identified by Graeber, by describing a set of relationships that 'produce' a component of the 'forces of production', ensuring the 'metabolic interaction' underpinning the 'development of the forces of production'. In line with Arboleda and Mezzadra's and Neilson's reservations, MoEs are not paradigmatic for world-historical systems *tout court* since they dialectically couple with MoPs, forming mutually dependent relations.

Gudynas (2016, 96, translation by author) has proposed a similar move, deploying 'modes of appropriation' (MoAs) to refer to 'the distinct types of organisation and dynamics that characterise the extraction of natural resources'. However, Marxian scholarship conventionally describes MoAs as the entire ensemble of relations that are the 'extra-economic preconditions' for a specific MoP (Jessop, 1990, 290). Covering all 'extra-economic preconditions', MoAs is thus an expansive notion, including among other things the institution of private property and a host of modalities of 'accumulation by extra-economic means' (Glassman, 2006). The latter include the ways in which capital appropriates value from social cooperation, such as the gendered and racialised labour of social reproduction (Federici, 2014; Mies, 2014), as well as from affective interactions and cultural artefacts (Hardt and Negri, 2000; Post and Calvão, 2020). They also comprise the commodification of ecological processes into so-called ecosystem services beyond the strict extraction of energy and materials, such as ecotourism or biodiversity capitalisation and offsetting schemes (Fletcher et al., 2019). This expansiveness obfuscates important differences between these modalities.

By excluding the appropriations not implicated in the extraction of energy and materials, the notion of MoEs enables greater analytical precision while being expansive enough to incorporate elements of other MoAs when relevant. In its broad spatio-temporal applicability, MoEs enables comparative research on the heterogeneous historical and contemporary sets of relations organising energy and material extraction. As stressed by Arboleda and Mezzadra and Neilson, these relations are not geographically restricted to the location where extraction occurs. In describing articulations of planetary interconnections rather than clearly delineated local phenomena, MoEs escapes the regional particularism of most Latin American accounts of (neo-)extractivisms without losing sight of the spatio-temporal specificity of such relations. Moreover, MoEs are not exclusively limited to coupling with capitalist MoPs, dovetailing with Dunlap and Jakobsen's concerns.

In Meso-American polities conquered by the Aztec Triple Alliance, for example, the imperial elite appointed 'a supervisor called a *calpixqui*' who 'collected wealth goods in the form of tribute', often retooling existing MoEs to supply the 'state treasuries' in the imperial centre with 'cacao, cotton, natural rubber, paper; specific minerals [...] and products that come from specific habitats' (Hirth, 2016, 49–50). Auguring the agricultural MoEs deployed in Latin America by the Spanish empire, the 'feudal conquest by the Aragon Crown in 1229' of Mallorca created manorial *cavalleries* for extraction of 'payment of tithes and feudal rents in kind' (Tello et al., 2018, 486–489). The extraction of agricultural goods cultivated by Indigenous slavery in the early Portuguese colonial regime in Brazil was likewise organised through a non-capitalist system of *seigneury* imported from Portugal (De Carvalho, 2015). Banaji (1977, 18) writes that even in the seventeenth century 'capitalist slave plantations' in the Caribbean were ultimately linked to the MoP of 'feudal estates in Poland through a complicated network of basically mercantile and financial interests'. More recently, MoEs have been coupled with the Soviet MoP, such as the early and appalling 'forcible extraction of grain from the countryside' (Kagarlitsky, 2008, 257), cotton cultivation through forced labour around the Aral Sea (Spoor, 1998) and mining in Soviet republics such as Kyrgyzstan (Ocaklı et al., 2021).

Beyond historical diversity, MoEs can also coexist and interpenetrate. As suggested by one of the reviewers of this chapter, the various modes of artisanal and small-scale mining exemplify this heterogeneity, including through 'different configurations that form around' the 'interface' of small-and large-scale mining (Kemp and Owen, 2019, 1094; also, see Mujere, 2023; Verbrugge and Geenen, 2019). A sketch of the multiple MoEs organising metals mining in the contemporary Amazon further illustrates this. These range from localised traditional forms of mining that are mostly executed by individuals or family groups and rely predominantly on intensive human labour and low capital costs, to small-scale mining operations run by licit and illicit entrepreneurs with access to more capital and employing labour through debt peonage and other forms of forced labour as well as waged or product payment, to cooperative and semi-cooperative organisations that can have access to significant capital and exhibit internal wage subordination while often operating in cooperation with state-owned enterprises, to the state-owned mining enterprises that operate in a manner akin to that of the large-scale private mining multinationals also present in the region. People can also variously engage in distinct MoEs at different moments. Amazonian smallholder communities, for example, maintain 'different combinations of agriculturalist and extractivist activities', shifting between both to ensure sustenance and sufficient cash (J. A. Fraser et al., 2018, 1383).

Importantly, not all MoEs are synonymous with extractivisms. Instead, I propose to use the term extractivisms to describe MoEs that are coupled with imperial modes of living.

4.2 *Sustaining Imperial Modes of Living*

Similar to later arguments about 'ecologically unequal exchange' and 'ecological debt' (Dorninger et al., 2021; Martinez-Alier, 2002), Bunker (1985, 22) insists that 'modern' social formations 'can only emerge in regions where industrial modes of production derive large amounts of energy and matter from subordinate modes of extraction [...] [that] create unequal exchange'. In thermodynamic terms, the extraction of energy and materials from regions creates entropic peripheries if no equivalent amount of energy and/or materials is returned (Leff, 2021). As detailed in section 2 of this chapter, such subordination is associated with political, economic and social inequalities. Following Arboleda, Mezzadra and Neilson, and Dunlap and Jakobsen, these dynamics cannot be captured in meta-geographical categories of interstate, centre/periphery and global North/South dynamics. Instead, these asymmetric socioecological relations cut across nations, incorporating and excluding population strata according to class, gender and race inequalities. This generates emergent and relational supra-and subnational centre–periphery dynamics that sustain the social metabolism of 'the imperial mode of living'.

Brand and Wissen (2021, 39–40, emphasis in the original) conceive of 'the imperial mode of living' (in the singular) to describe how 'everyday life in the capitalist centres is essentially made possible by shaping social relations and society–nature relations *elsewhere*, i.e. by means of (in principle) unlimited access to labour power, natural resources and sinks'. The adjective 'imperial' denotes that the IML is 'based on exclusivity' and can be sustained 'only as long as an "outside"'—which can be geographically near or far—exists to extract from and externalise socioecological destruction towards (Brand and Wissen, 2021, 7). The IML thus 'presupposes an imperialist world order [...] [and] creates asymmetric interdependencies between various places and territories [...] in a way in which the mechanisms of reproduction in one part pose severe restrictions for the practices of a majority of people in other parts' (Brand and Wissen, 2022, 76). Whereas the concepts of 'global labour arbitrage', 'labour aristocracy' and 'super-exploitation' describe the IML's organising effect on labour processes (Cope, 2019; Marini, 1991; Smith, 2016), I propose that extractivisms denote the IML's organising effect on the socioecological relations that ensure access to energy and materials.

In line with Arboleda's, Mezzadra and Neilson's, and Dunlap and Jakobsen's joint attention to the scales of planetary relationships and everyday life, the IML 'points towards the norms of production, distribution, and consumption built into the political, economic, and cultural structures of everyday life for the populations of the global North [...] [and] increasingly in the countries with "emerging" economies of the global South' (Brand and Wissen, 2021, 41). In contrast to Dunlap and Jakobsen, Brand and Wissen (2021, 42) propose that the IML represents 'an essential moment in the reproduction of [a] capitalist society' whose norms have their origins in Eurocentric conceptions of progress, modernity and development that emerged with the colonial encounter and capitalist world market. While 'initially limited to furnishing the upper classes with luxury goods' (Brand and Wissen, 2021, 83), the IML progressively incorporated larger bourgeois strata of the global population, becoming entrenched in the nineteenth century through discourses of progress, modernity and development. Historically, populations that resisted being enrolled in the MoEs, MoAs and MoPs undergirding the IML were ruthlessly oppressed and violently dominated. Successful socio-economic struggles have often culminated in the (re)integration of peoples into an extended and consolidated IML. In this way, ever-larger sections of the global population have been persuasively enticed with imperial privileges. This progressive incorporation of populations into the IML constitutes a 'kind of compromise between the interests of those in power and the demands and desires of their subalterns' (Brand and Wissen, 2021, 70).

Building on Gramsci's approach to hegemony, Foucault's understanding of critique and subjectivation, and Bourdieu's notions of habitus and lifestyle, Brand and Wissen highlight the intimate link between everyday practices and subjectivity. The IML's lived everyday practices co-produce subjects who internalise its norms, developing psycho-emotional attachments that make them desire enrolling or remaining in it. In addition, the IML provides 'conditions for income-generating production, just as the acquisition of products (home appliances, industrialized food, cars, smartphones) makes everyday life easier' by lowering the cost of social reproduction. These conditions also 'broaden the spectrum of leisure activities and possible travel goals' while creating a sense of security in crisis situations (Brand and Wissen, 2021, 53). For many, the IML thus entails 'the opportunity to have a subjectively fulfilled [...] [and] materially more comfortable life' (Brand and Wissen, 2021, 117). The IML is not universally experienced in the same manner. Its hegemony is 'secured through complex spatial strategies that reproduce highly uneven social structures' stratified along class, gender, race and other dimensions (Brand and Wissen, 2022, 77).

The IML only became hegemonic in the global North under Fordism through the 'generalisation' and 'universalisation' of 'modern' or 'Western' consumption norms. During this period, many middle classes in 'non-Western' societies came to adopt similar modes of living as those in the capitalist centres, constituting 'a peripheral IML' that equally relied on 'access to cheap labour power and nature elsewhere for the production of commodities for the world market, as well as for internal use' (Brand and Wissen, 2022, 80). From the 1970s onward, 'neoliberal globalisation' deepened the IML in the global North and expanded it to the planetary scale 'due to the rise of emerging economies [...] [where] it is becoming the dominant model of prosperity, even for those who have not yet been integrated into the imperial mode of living' (Brand and Wissen, 2021, 114). Brand and Wissen point to OECD, UNDP and ILO statistics to indicate that around 1.9 billion people could be designated as living a middle-class life in 2010, often implying the IML. However, rather than classifying some absolute category of individuals as falling within or outside the IML, it is a relational concept describing emergent supra-and subnational centre–periphery dynamics that link victims and beneficiaries, contenders and collaborators. These 'relations of dominance and subordination' give rise to an 'articulated hierarchy' that cannot be abstractly deduced but that is historically specific and constructed as part of the analysis (Hall, 2018, 196–202).

With due respect to Dunlap and Jakobsen, who trace extractivisms to 'civilisation itself', I prefer Brand and Wissen's more restrictive temporal range from the colonial moment onwards for two reasons. First, while hierarchies and domination certainly existed before and will last beyond the capitalist horizon, the historical co-constitution of colonialism and the capitalist world market marks significant differences in the prevalent modes of living and MoEs. According to Fraser (2014), this inaugurated a novel 'institutionalised social order' that structurally differentiated a) production from social reproduction, b) humanity from 'nature', c) the political from the economic, d) public from private power, and e) the 'domestic' from the 'inter-national' in a Westphalian system of states. Concomitantly, an 'epochal shift' occurred 'in what was *valued* [...], from land productivity under conditions of seigneurial power to labour productivity under the hegemony of the modern world market' (Moore, 2017,

610; emphasis in the original). Together, these changes occasioned a cascading series of technological inventions and a set of technics that unleashed spatio-temporal dynamics through which 'everything moved faster—*a lot faster*', including the extraction of materials and energy. I therefore concur with Durante Kröger and LaFluer (2021, 20–24), who locate the ontological roots of extractivisms in ancient Greek natural law and Roman property law, yet argue that 'what differentiates the ancient deforestations and other extractions from the past 500 years of extractivism[s] is the scale, and the greater domination of certain mindsets, by the advancement of modern technology alongside political and military power'.

Second, this more restricted temporal application does not normalise extractivisms as inherent to civilisation, which makes it difficult to conceive of alternative post-extractivist modes of living suited to large-scale social formations. While critical scholarship and praxis should strive toward the dissolution of all kinds of hierarchies between human and non-human beings, lumping together all historical forms of domination and inequality mythologises the past, obscuring more than it reveals (Graeber and Wengrow, 2021). I nevertheless acknowledge that imperial modes of living (in the plural) could be repurposed to analyse continuities and differences in the strategic relationships shaping everyday life and the extraction of materials and energy along Dunlap and Jakobsen's civilisational time frame, which would be an interesting but separate research agenda. The coupling of an undisputedly imperial mode of living in the Aztec Triple Alliance with certain MoEs described above points in this direction. Future modes of living could also be structurally organised in non-capitalist ways without becoming less imperial.

Regardless of the IML and extractivisms' precise historical origins, maintaining and deepening the IML and extractivisms has become a contemporary 'imperative' for governments as this functions as the societal pact stabilising the contradictions inherent in relying on in principle unlimited labour, resources, and sinks. The powerful psycho-emotional attachment of dominators and dominated alike to the IML in part explains this persistence in the face of overwhelming socioecological destruction. Nevertheless, the IML is not a total system of domination and is always challenged by alternative modes of living and counter-hegemonic subjectivities. In fact, the socioecological destruction of extractivisms provokes counter-hegemonic proposals and 'insubordinate' subjects that point to the possibility of transitioning to post-imperial solidarity modes of living. Let me conclude with brief reflections on such transitions and highlight relevant avenues for research.

5 Transitioning to Post-imperial Solidarity Modes of Living

Further universalising the imperial mode of living and the extractivisms on which it depends deepens the genocidal–ecocidal trajectory of overlapping planetary crises (Dunlap, chapter 3 in this volume). As the United Nations Secretary-General (2021) stated at the twenty-sixth Conference of the Parties, '[e]ither we stop it—or it stops us [...] Enough of brutalising biodiversity. Enough of killing ourselves with carbon. Enough of treating nature like a toilet. Enough of burning and drilling and mining our way deeper. We are digging our own graves'. Despite this rhetoric, the UN's flagship 'plan of action' *Transforming our World: the 2030 Agenda for Sustainable Development* (UNGA, 2015) insufficiently challenges the imperial mode of living. As illustrated by the renewables, green, and eco-extractivisms discussed in section 2 of this chapter, capitalist approaches to sustainable development perpetuate and deepen extractivisms (Remme et al., Chapter 12 in this volume). Given their increasing prominence at the current juncture, analysis of the entanglements between discourses of sustainability and so-called net-zero and nature-based solutions with extractivisms and their role in stabilising the imperial mode of living is a critical task. Further historical comparative research on extractivisms, imperial modes of living, and associated socioecological violence is also necessary if we are to further understand and challenge their intractability and perceived normality.

Equally—if not more—urgent is research on transitions to post-imperial solidarity modes of living that are part of 'a great transformation *beyond the capitalist mode of production* [...] [with] very different forms of the societal appropriation of nature' (Brand, Görg and Wissen, 2020, 166–170, emphasis in the original). The Global Tapestry of Alternatives, serving as 'the global confluence of alternatives', congregates many examples of modes of living that are striving towards 'fundamental, systemic, radical transformation' (Kothari, 2020, 247). The *Post-Development Dictionary* is a related survey of concrete and conceptual alternatives that propose 'profound shifts in the spheres of [the] economy, politics, society, culture, and lived sexuality' towards a 'pluriversal world' in which many worlds can be embraced and coexist in dignity and peace (Kothari et al., 2019, xxxv).

One strain of these proposals concerns degrowth, defined as a 'radical political and economic reorganization leading to drastically reduced resource and energy throughput' (Kallis et al., 2018, 291; also, see Fitzpatrick, Parrique and Cosme (2022) and Mastini, Kallis and Hickel (2021), and Hamilton and Trölenberg, Chapter 8 in this volume). This reduction is not universal and must be accompanied by an increase in the material and energetic basis of other peoples' modes of living to guarantee a dignified life for all (Hickel, 2021). The fact that some modes of extraction can provide the energetic and material bases for post-imperial solidarity modes of living is highly relevant in this respect. The so-called eco-territorial turn in Latin America highlights that many struggles by Indigenous communities for sovereignty and territorial well-being are *not only against extractivisms but for alternative futures* developed through Life projects that articulate with broader social and environmental struggles to create new counter-hegemonic subjectivities (Andreucci et al., 2017; Blaser, Feit and McRae, 2004; Escobar, 2008; Post, 2022; Svampa, 2019; also, see Prause, Chapter 7 in this volume). Activists and scholars who are part of this eco-territorial turn have developed proposals for post-extractivist modes of living beyond Indigenous communities and territories (Acosta, 2014; 2017; Gudynas, 2011; 2017; 2021; Hollender, 2015; Lang and Mokrani, 2013). According to Riofrancos (2020, 168), these 'represent the most important contributions of contemporary Latin American critical thought to leftist politics around the world' since they inform and synergise with decolonial and transition efforts around the world (Brand, Boos and Brad, 2017; Escobar, 2015; Nourani Rinaldi, 2022). Analysing which modes of extraction can support post-imperial solidarity modes of living thus presents a vital research avenue. To avoid reproducing colonial patterns of knowledge production (Cusicanqui, 2010; Mignolo and Walsh, 2018), this research should be conducted in collaboration with communities realising post-imperial futures.

Because of already-existing destruction and the prospect of post-pandemic recovery programmes deepening and expanding extractivisms, transition efforts cannot solely focus on post-imperial futures but must be accompanied by state-led efforts to address the cascading planetary crises. Analysis of extractivisms' relationship with the state and the interstate geopolitical system is crucial for identifying promising levers for change. Activists, researchers and policymakers should adopt what Luxemburg (1903) termed 'revolutionary Realpolitik', setting and pursuing achievable goals through the most effective means while simultaneously striving to overcome the existing order. To reclaim a powerful rallying cry popularised by Luxemburg, the future is one of post-extractivisms or barbarism.

Acknowledgements

The chapter benefited from Philippe Le Billon's generous and constructive comments as well as from the incisive questions and suggestions raised by colleagues who participated in the January 2022 Workshop on the Lives and

Afterlives of Extraction hosted by the Geneva Graduate Institute. I also wish to thank the two anonymous reviewers for their engagement with my ideas and their excellent suggestions. Thanks to Matthew Archer, Asanda Benya and Ndongo Sylla, as well as the editorial teams at the Geneva Graduate Institute and Brill for their support. Lastly, I wish to express my gratitude to Filipe Calvão for his encouragement.

References

Achiume, T. (2019) *Global Extractivism and Racial Equality: Report of the Special Rapporteur on Contemporary Forms of Racism, Racial Discrimination, Xenophobia and Related Intolerance*, No. A/HRC/41/54 (Geneva: UN Human Rights Council).

Acosta, A. (2017) 'Post-Extractivism: from Discourse to Practice—Reflections for Action', in G. Carbonnier, H. Campodónico and S. Tezanos Vázquez (eds.) *Alternative Pathways to Sustainable Development: Lessons from Latin America, International Development Policy*, 9 (Leiden and Boston: Brill/Nijhoff), DOI: /10.4000/poldev.2356.

Acosta, A. (2014) 'Post-Crecimiento y Post-Extractivismo: Dos Caras de La Misma Transformación Cultural', in G. Endara and C. Larrea M. (eds.) *Post-Crecimiento y Buen Vivir: Propuestas Globales Para La Construcción de Sociedades Equitativas y Sustentables* (Quito, Ecuador: Friedrich-Ebert-Stiftung).

Acosta, A. (2013) 'Extractivism and Neoextractism: Two Sides of the Same Curse', in M. Lang and D. Mokrani (eds.) *Beyond Development: Alternative Visions from Latin America* (Amsterdam: Transnational Institute).

Acosta, A., E. Gudynas, F. Houtart, H. Ramírez Soler, J. Martínez Alier and L. Macas (eds.) (2011) *Colonialismos Del Siglo XXI: Negocios Extractivos y Defensa Del Territorio En América Latina*, Antrazyt (Barcelona: Icaria Editorial).

Acquatella, J., O. Bello and F. Berríos (2019) 'Evidencia Estadística de Superciclos en las Series de Precios de los Metales y el Petróleo, 1900–2015', in *La Bonanza de los Recursos Naturales para el Desarrollo: Dilemas de Gobernanza*, LC/PUB.2019/13-P (Santiago de Chile: CEPAL), pp. 231–255.

Adaman, F., M. Arsel and B. Akbulut (2019) 'Neoliberal Developmentalism Authoritarian Populism and Extractivism in the Countryside: the Soma Mining Disaster in Turkey', *The Journal of Peasant Studies*, 46(3), pp. 514–536, DOI: 10.1080/03066150.2018.1515737.

Alimonda, H. (2015) 'Mining in Latin America: Coloniality and Degradation', in R.L. Bryant (ed.) *International Handbook of Political Ecology* (London: Edward Elgar Publishing), pp. 149–161.

Alimonda, H. (ed.) (2011) *La Naturaleza Colonizada: Ecología Política y Minería En América Latina, Colección Grupos de Trabajo* (Buenos Aires: Consejo Latinoamericano de Ciencias Sociales).

Andreucci, D., M.J. Beltrán, I. Velicu and C. Zografos (2017) 'Capital Accumulation, Hegemony and Socio-Ecological Struggles: Insights from the ENTITLE Project', *Capitalism Nature Socialism*, 28(3), pp. 18–27, DOI: 10.1080/10455752.2017.1355930.

Andreucci, D. and I.M. Radhuber (2017) 'Limits to "Counter-Neoliberal" Reform: Mining Expansion and the Marginalisation of Post-Extractivist Forces in Evo Morales's Bolivia', *Geoforum*, 84, pp. 280–291, DOI: 10.1016/j.geoforum.2015.09.002.

Arboleda, M. (2020) *Planetary Mine: Territories of Extraction Under Late Capitalism* (London and New York: Verso).

Arrighi, G. and B.J. Silver (1999) *Chaos and Governance in the Modern World System*, Contradictions of Modernity 10 (Minneapolis: University of Minnesota Press).

Arsel, M., B. Hogenboom and L. Pellegrini (2016) 'The Extractive Imperative and the Boom in Environmental Conflicts at the End of the Progressive Cycle in Latin America', *The Extractive Industries and Society*, 3(4), pp. 877–879, DOI: 10.1016/j.exis.2016.10.013.

Ayelazuno, J.A. (2014) 'The 'New Extractivism' in Ghana: a Critical Review of Its Development Prospects', *The Extractive Industries and Society*, 1(2), pp. 292–302, DOI: 10.1016/j.exis.2014.04.008.

Banaji, J. (1977) 'Modes of Production in a Materialist Conception of History', *Capital & Class*, 1(3), pp. 1–44, DOI: 10.1177/030981687700300102.

Bauerly, B. (2017) *The Agrarian Seeds of Empire: the Political Economy of Agriculture in US State Building*, Studies in Critical Social Sciences 100 (Boston: Brill).

Bebbington, A., A.-G. Abdulai, D.H. Bebbington, M. Hinfelaar and C.A. Sanborn (2018) *Governing Extractive Industries: Politics, Histories, Ideas* (Oxford: Oxford University Press).

Bebbington, A. and D.H. Bebbington (2013) 'Post-What? Extractive Industries, Narratives of Development and Socio-Environmental Disputes Across the (Ostensibly Changing) Andean Region', in H. Haarstad (ed.) *New Political Spaces in Latin American Natural Resource Governance* (New York: Palgrave Macmillan).

Benites, G.V. and A. Bebbington (2020) 'Political Settlements and the Governance of Covid-19: Mining, Risk, and Territorial Control in Peru', *Journal of Latin American Geography*, 19(3), pp. 215–223, DOI: 10.1353/lag.2020.0081.

Benson, P. (2012) *Tobacco Capitalism: Growers, Migrant Workers, and the Changing Face of a Global Industry* (Princeton: Princeton University Press).

Blaser, M., H.A. Feit and G. McRae (eds.) (2004) *In the Way of Development: Indigenous Peoples, Life Projects, and Globalization* (London and New York : Zed Books).

Brand, U., T. Boos and A. Brad (2017) 'Degrowth and Post-Extractivism: Two Debates with Suggestions for the Inclusive Development Framework', *Current Opinion in Environmental Sustainability*, 24, pp. 36–41, DOI: 10.1016/j.cosust.2017.01.007.

Brand, U., K. Dietz and M. Lang (2016) 'Neo-Extractivism in Latin America—One Side of a New Phase of Global Capitalist Dynamics', *Ciencia Política*, 11(21), pp. 125–159, DOI: 10.15446/cp.v11n21.57551.

Brand, U., C. Görg and M. Wissen (2020) 'Overcoming Neoliberal Globalization: Social-Ecological Transformation From a Polanyian Perspective and Beyond', *Globalizations*, 17(1), pp. 161–176, DOI: 10.1080/14747731.2019.1644708.

Brand, U. and M. Wissen (2022) 'Spatialising the Imperial Mode of Living—Rethinking a Concept', *DIE ERDE—Journal of the Geographical Society of Berlin*, pp. 75–83, DOI: 10.12854/erde-2022-613.

Brand, U. and M. Wissen (2021) *The Imperial Mode of Living: Everyday Life and the Ecological Crisis of Capitalism* (London and New York: Verso).

Bruna, N. (2022) 'Green Extractivism and Financialisation in Mozambique: the Case of Gilé National Reserve', *Review of African Political Economy*, 49(171), pp. 138–160, DOI: 10.1080/03056244.2022.2049129.

Bunker, S.G. (1985) Underdeveloping the Amazon: Extraction, Unequal Exchange, and the Failure of the Modern State (Chicago: University of Chicago Press).

Burchardt, H.-J. and K. Dietz (2014) '(Neo-)Extractivism—a New Challenge for Development Theory from Latin America', *Third World Quarterly*, 35(3), pp. 468–486, DOI: 10.1080/01436597.2014.893488.

Calvão, F. (2019) 'Crypto-Miners: Digital Labor and the Power of Blockchain Technology', *Economic Anthropology*, 6(1), pp. 123–134, DOI: 10.1002/sea2.12136.

Calvão, F. and M. Archer (2021) 'Digital Extraction: Blockchain Traceability in Mineral Supply Chains', *Political Geography*, 87, 102381, DOI: 10.1016/j.polgeo.2021.102381.

Carbonnier, G., H. Campodónico and S. Tezanos Vázquez (2017) 'Alternative Development Narratives, Policies and Outcomes in the Andean Region', in G. Carbonnier, H. Campodónico and S. Tezanos Vázquez (eds.) *Alternative Pathways to Sustainable Development: Lessons from Latin America*, International Development Policy, 9 (Leiden and Boston: Brill/Nijhoff), DOI: 10.4000/poldev.2346.

Cardoso, F.H. and E. Faletto (1998) 'Dependencia y Desarrollo en América Latina: Selección', in *Cincuenta Años del Pensamiento de la CEPAL: Textos Seleccionados* (Santiago: Fondo de Cultura Económica/CEPAL), pp. 475–499.

Chagnon, C.W., F. Durante, B.K. Gills, S.E. Hagolani-Albov, S. Hokkanen, S.M.J. Kangasluoma, H. Konttinen, M. Kröger, W. LaFleur, O. Ollinaho and M.P.S. Vuola (2022) 'From Extractivism to Global Extractivism: the Evolution of an Organizing Concept', *The Journal of Peasant Studies*, 49(4), pp. 1–33, DOI: 10.1080/03066150.2022.2069015.

Chagnon, C.W., S.E. Hagolani-Albov and S. Hokkanen (2021) 'Extractivism at Your Fingertips', in J. Shapiro and J.-A. McNeish (eds.) *Our Extractive Age: Expressions of Violence and Resistance* (London: Routledge), pp. 176–188.

Cope, Z. (2019) *The Wealth of (Some) Nations: Imperialism and the Mechanics of Value Transfer* (London: Pluto Press).

Coulthard, G.S. (2014) *Red Skin, White Masks: Rejecting the Colonial Politics of Recognition, Indigenous Americas* (Minneapolis: University of Minnesota Press).

Coulthard, G.S. (2010) 'Place Against Empire: Understanding Indigenous Anti-Colonialism', *Affinities: a Journal of Radical Theory, Culture, and Action*, 4(2), pp. 79–83.

Curley, A. (2019) 'T'áá Hwó Ají t'éego and the Moral Economy of Navajo Coal Workers', *Annals of the American Association of Geographers*, 109(1), pp. 71–86, DOI: 10.1080/24694452.2018.1488576.

Curley, A. and M. Lister (2020) 'Already Existing Dystopias: Tribal Sovereignty, Extraction, and Decolonizing the Anthropocene', in *Handbook on the Changing Geographies of the State* (Cheltenham: Edward Elgar Publishing).

Cusicanqui, S.R. (2010) *Ch'ixinakax Utxiwa Una Reflexión Sobre Prácticas y Discursos Descolonizadores* (Buenos Aires: Retazos : Tinta Limón Ediciones).

D'Angelo, L. and R.J. Pijpers (eds.) (2022) *The Anthropology of Resource Extraction* (London: Routledge).

Davies, T. (2022) 'Slow Violence and Toxic Geographies: 'Out of Sight' to Whom?', *Environment and Planning C: Politics and Space*, 40(2), pp. 409–427, DOI: 10.1177/2399654419841063.

De Carvalho, B. (2015) 'The Modern Roots of Feudal Empires: the Donatary Captaincies and the Legacies of the Portuguese Empire in Brazil', in R. Palan and S. Halperin (eds.) *Legacies of Empire: Imperial Roots of the Contemporary Global Order* (Cambridge: Cambridge University Press), pp. 128–148, DOI: 10.1017/CBO9781316271674.006.

Del Bene, D., A. Scheidel and L. Temper (2018) 'More Dams, More Violence? A Global Analysis on Resistances and Repression Around Conflictive Dams Through Co-Produced Knowledge', *Sustainability Science*, 13, pp. 617–633, DOI: 10.1007/s11625-018-0558-1.

Delgado Ramos, G.C. (ed.) (2013) *Ecología Política Del Extractivismo En América Latina: Casos de Resistencia y Justicia Socioambiental, Colección Grupos de Trabajo* (Buenos Aires: Consejo Latinoamericano de Ciencias Sociales).

Dietz, K. and B. Engels (2017) *Contested Extractivism, Society and the State* (London: Palgrave Macmillan UK).

Dorninger, C., A. Hornborg, D.J. Abson, H. von Wehrden, A. Schaffartzik, S. Giljum, J.-O. Engler, R.L. Feller, K. Hubacek and H. Wieland (2021) 'Global Patterns of Ecologically

Unequal Exchange: Implications for Sustainability in the 21st Century', *Ecological Economics*, 179, 106824, DOI: 10.1016/j.ecolecon.2020.106824.

Dunlap, A. and M.C. Arce (2021) 'Pacifying Autonomous Land Defenders in Oaxaca, Mexico: Human Rights Groups as Social Warfare Mechanisms', in M. Menton and P. Le Billon (eds.) *Environmental Defenders* (London: Routledge), pp. 180–198.

Dunlap, A. and J. Jakobsen (2020) *The Violent Technologies of Extraction: Political Ecology, Critical Agrarian Studies and the Capitalist Worldeater* (Cham: Palgrave Pivot), DOI: 10.1007/978-3-030-26852-7.

Duplat, A.M.V. (ed.) (2017) *Extractivismo Urbano: Debates Para Una Construcción Colectiva de Las Ciudades* (Buenos Aires: Fundación Rosa Luxemburgo ; Ceapi ; El Colectivo).

Durante, F., M. Kröger and W. LaFluer (2021) 'Extraction and Extractivisms: Definitions and Concepts', in J. Shapiro and J.-A. McNeish (eds.) *Our Extractive Age: Expressions of Violence and Resistance* (London: Routledge), pp. 19–30.

Escobar, A. (2015) 'Degrowth, Postdevelopment, and Transitions: a Preliminary Conversation', *Sustainability Science*, 10(3), pp. 451–462, DOI: 10.1007/s11625-015-0297-5.

Escobar, A. (2008) *Territories of Difference: Place, Movements, Life, Redes* (Durham: Duke University Press).

Federici, S.B. (2014) *Caliban and the Witch* (New York: Autonomedia).

Ferguson, J. (2015) *Give a Man a Fish: Reflections on the New Politics of Distribution* (Durham and London: Duke University Press).

Fitzpatrick, N., T. Parrique and I. Cosme (2022) 'Exploring Degrowth Policy Proposals: a Systematic Mapping with Thematic Synthesis', *Journal of Cleaner Production*, 365, 132764, DOI: 10.1016/j.jclepro.2022.132764.

Fletcher, R., W.H. Dressler, Z.R. Anderson and B. Büscher (2019) 'Natural Capital Must Be Defended: Green Growth as Neoliberal Biopolitics', *The Journal of Peasant Studies*, 46(5), pp. 1068–1095, DOI: 10.1080/03066150.2018.1428953.

Foster, J.B. (1999) 'Marx's Theory of Metabolic Rift: Classical Foundations for Environmental Sociology', *American Journal of Sociology* (The University of Chicago Press), 105(2), pp. 366–405, DOI: 10.1086/210315.

Fraser, J.A., T. Cardoso, A. Steward and L. Parry (2018) 'Amazonian Peasant Livelihood Differentiation as Mutuality-Market Dialectics', *The Journal of Peasant Studies*, 45(7), pp. 1382–1409, DOI: 10.1080/03066150.2017.1296833.

Fraser, N. (2014) 'Behind Marx's Hidden Abode: for an Expanded Conception of Capitalism', *New Left Review*, April, https://newleftreview.org/issues/ii86/articles/nancy-fraser-behind-marx-s-hidden-abode (accessed on 31 August 2022).

Gago, V. and S. Mezzadra (2017) 'A Critique of the Extractive Operations of Capital: toward an Expanded Concept of Extractivism', *Rethinking Marxism*, 29(4), pp. 574–591, DOI: 10.1080/08935696.2017.1417087.

Glaab, K. and K. Stuvøy (2021) 'The Politics of Violence in Extractivism: Space, Time, and Normativity', in J. Shapiro and J.-A. McNeish (eds.) *Our Extractive Age: Expressions of Violence and Resistance* (London: Routledge), pp. 31–47.

Glassman, J. (2006) 'Primitive Accumulation, Accumulation by Dispossession, Accumulation by 'Extra-Economic' Means', *Progress in Human Geography*, 30(5), pp. 608–625, DOI: 10.1177/0309132506070172.

Graeber, D. (2006) 'Turning Modes of Production Inside Out: Or, Why Capitalism Is a Transformation of Slavery', *Critique of Anthropology*, 26(1), pp. 61–85, DOI: 10.1177/0308275X06061484.

Graeber, D. and D. Wengrow (2021) *The Dawn of Everything: a New History of Humanity* (New York and London: Penguin).

Grosfoguel, R. (2016) 'Del «Extractivismo Económico» al «Extractivismo Epistémico» y «Extractivismo Ontológico»: Una Forma Destructiva de Conocer, Ser y Estar en el Mundo', *Tabula Rasa*, 24, pp. 123–143.

Gudynas, E. (2021) Extractivisms: Politics, Economy and Ecology, *Critical Development Studies*, 5 (Halifax and Winnipeg: Fernwood Publishing: Practical Action Publishing).

Gudynas, E. (2017) 'Value, Growth, Development: South American Lessons for a New Ecopolitics', *Capitalism Nature Socialism*, 30(2), pp. 234–243, DOI: 10.1080/10455752.2017.1372502.

Gudynas, E. (2016) 'Modos de Producción y Modos de Apropiación, Una Distinción a Propósito de Los Extractivismos', *Actuel Marx/Intervenciones*, 20, pp. 95–121.

Gudynas, E. (2012) 'Estado Compensador y Nuevos Extractivismos: Las Ambivalencias Del Progresismo Sudamericano', *Nueva Sociedad*, 237, pp. 138–146.

Gudynas, E. (2011) 'Desarrollo, Postextractivismo y "Buen Vivir"', *Pueblos*, 69, pp. 19–21.

Gudynas, E. (2009) 'Diez Tesis Urgentes Sobre El Nuevo Extractivismo. Contextos y Demandas Bajo El Progresismo Sudamericano Actual', in J. Schuldt, A. Acosta, A. Barandiarán, A. Bebbington, M. Folchi and A. Alayza (eds.) *Bolivia, Extractivismo, Política y Sociedad* (Quito: Centro Andino de Acción Popular & Centro Latinoamericano de Ecología Social), pp. 187–225.

Hall, S. (2018) 'Race, Articulation, and Societies Structured in Dominance [1980]', in D. Morley (ed.) *Essential Essays, Stuart Hall, Selected Writings* (Durham: Duke University Press).

Hanaček, K., B. Roy, S. Avila and G. Kallis (2020) 'Ecological Economics and Degrowth: Proposing a Future Research Agenda From the Margins', *Ecological Economics*, 169, 106495, DOI: 10.1016/j.ecolecon.2019.106495.

Haraway, D.J. (2016) *Staying with the Trouble: Making Kin in the Chthulucene, Experimental Futures: Technological Lives, Scientific Arts, Anthropological Voices* (Durham: Duke University Press).

Hardt, M. and A. Negri (2000) *Empire* (Cambridge: Harvard University Press).

Harvey, D. (2003) *The New Imperialism* (Oxford and New York: Oxford University Press).

Harvey, D. (1974) 'Population, Resources, and the Ideology of Science', *Economic Geography*, 50(3), pp. 256–277, DOI: 10.2307/142863.

Hickel, J. (2021) 'What Does Degrowth Mean? A Few Points of Clarification', *Globalizations*, 18(7), pp. 1105–1111, DOI: 10.1080/14747731.2020.1812222.

Hirth, K.G. (2016) *The Aztec Economic World: Merchants and Markets in Ancient Mesoamerica* (Cambridge: Cambridge University Press).

Hollender, R. (2015) 'Post-Growth in the Global South: the Emergence of Alternatives to Development in Latin America', *Socialism and Democracy*, 29(1), pp. 73–101, DOI: 10.1080/08854300.2014.998472.

Hope, J. (2020) 'The Anti-Politics of Sustainable Development: Environmental Critique from Assemblage Thinking in Bolivia', *Transactions of the Institute of British Geographers*, 46(1), pp. 208–222, DOI: 10.1111/tran.12409.

Huber, M. (2018) 'Resource Geographies I: Valuing Nature (Or Not)', *Progress in Human Geography*, 42(1), pp. 148–159, DOI: 10.1177/0309132516670773.

International Resource Panel (2019) *Global Resources Outlook 2019: Natural Resources for the Future We Want* (Nairobi: United Nations Environment Programme).

Jaramillo, P. (2020) 'Mining Leftovers: Making Futures on the Margins of Capitalism', *Cultural Anthropology*, 35(1), pp. 48–73, DOI: 10.14506/ca35.1.07.

Jessop, R. (1990) 'Mode of Production', in J. Eatwell, M. Milgate and P. Newman (eds.) *The New Palgrave Marxian Economics* (London: Macmillan), pp. 289–296.

Kagarlitsky, B. (2008) *Empire of the Periphery: Russia and the World System* (London: Pluto Press).

Kallis, G., V. Kostakis, S. Lange, B. Muraca, S. Paulson and M. Schmelzer (2018) 'Research On Degrowth', *Annual Review of Environment and Resources*, 43(1), pp. 291–316, DOI: 10.1146/annurev-environ-102017-025941.

Kemp, D. and J.R. Owen (2019) 'Characterising the Interface Between Large and Small-Scale Mining', *The Extractive Industries and Society*, 6(4), pp. 1091–1100, DOI: 10.1016/j.exis.2019.07.002.

Kothari, A. (2020) 'Earth Vikalp Sangam: Proposal for a Global Tapestry of Alternatives', *Globalizations*, 17(2), pp. 245–249, DOI: 10.1080/14747731.2019.1670955.

Kothari, A., A. Salleh, A. Escobar, F. Demaria and A. Acosta (eds.) (2019) *Pluriverse: a Post-Development Dictionary* (New Delhi: Tulika Books and Authorsupfront).

Lahiri-Dutt, K. (2018) 'Peasant Mineral Resource Extractivism and the Idea of Scarcity', in M.C. Dawson, C. Rosin and N. Wald (eds.) *Global Resource Scarcity: Catalyst for Conflict or Cooperation?, Earthscan Studies in Natural Resource Management* (London and New York: Routledge Taylor & Francis Group).

Lang, M. and D. Mokrani (eds.) (2013) *Beyond Development: Alternative Visions from Latin America* (Amsterdam: Transnational Institute).

Le Billon, P. (2021) 'Defending Territory from the Extraction and Conservation Nexus', in M. Menton and P. Le Billon (eds.) *Environmental Defenders* (London: Routledge).

Le Billon, P., P. Lujala, D. Singh, V. Culbert and B. Kristoffersen (2021) 'Fossil Fuels, Climate Change, and the COVID-19 Crisis: Pathways for a Just and Green Post-Pandemic Recovery', *Climate Policy*, 21(10), pp. 1347–1356, DOI: 10.1080/14693062.2021.1965524.

Leff, E. (2021) *Political Ecology: Deconstructing Capital and Territorializing Life* (Cham: Palgrave Macmillan), DOI: 10.1007/978-3-030-63325-7.

Luxemburg, R. (2003) *The Accumulation of Capital* (London: Routledge).

Luxemburg, R. (1903) 'Marxist Theory and the Proletariat', *Vorwärts*, 14 March.

Malm, A. (2016) *Fossil Capital: the Rise of Steam Power and the Roots of Global Warming* (London and New York: Verso).

Marini, R.M. (1991) *Dialéctica de la Dependencia* (Mexico City: Era).

Marston, A. and T. Perreault (2017) 'Consent, Coercion and Cooperativismo: Mining Cooperatives and Resource Regimes in Bolivia', *Environment and Planning A: Economy and Space*, 49(2), pp. 252–272, DOI: 10.1177/0308518X16674008.

Martinez-Alier, J. (2002) *The Environmentalism of the Poor: a Study of Ecological Conflicts and Valuation* (Northhampton: Edward Elgar Publishing).

Martinez-Alier, J., G. Kallis, S. Veuthey, M. Walter and L. Temper (2010) 'Social Metabolism, Ecological Distribution Conflicts, and Valuation Languages', *Ecological Economics*, 70(2), pp. 153–158, DOI: 10.1016/j.ecolecon.2010.09.024.

Marx, K. (1990) *Capital: a Critique of Political Economy*, Volume 1 (London and New York: Penguin Books in association with New Left Review).

Mastini, R., G. Kallis and J. Hickel (2021) 'A Green New Deal Without Growth?', *Ecological Economics*, 179,. 106832, DOI: 10.1016/j.ecolecon.2020.106832.

Mezzadra, S. and B. Neilson (2019) *The Politics of Operations: Excavating Contemporary Capitalism* (Durham: Duke University Press).

Mezzadra, S. and B. Neilson (2017) 'On the Multiple Frontiers of Extraction: Excavating Contemporary Capitalism', *Cultural Studies*, 31(2–3), pp. 185–204, DOI: 10.1080/09502386.2017.1303425.

Mies, M. (2014) *Patriarchy and Accumulation on a World Scale: Women in the International Division of Labour* (London: Zed books).

Mignolo, W. and C.E. Walsh (2018) *On Decoloniality: Concepts, Analytics, Praxis, On Decoloniality* (Durham: Duke University Press).

Moore, J.W. (2018) 'The Capitalocene Part II: Accumulation by Appropriation and the Centrality of Unpaid Work/Energy', *The Journal of Peasant Studies*, 45(2), pp. 237–279, DOI: 10.1080/03066150.2016.1272587.

Moore, J.W. (2017) 'The Capitalocene, Part I: on the Nature and Origins of Our Ecological Crisis', *The Journal of Peasant Studies*, 44(3), pp. 594–630, DOI: 10.1080/03066150.2016.1235036.

Moore, J.W. (2015) *Capitalism in the Web of Life: Ecology and the Accumulation of Capital* (London and New York: Verso).

Moran, E.F. (1982) 'Ecological, Anthropological, and Agronomic Research in the Amazon Basin', *Latin American Research Review*, 17(1), pp. 3–41.

Mujere, J. (2023) 'Chromite Mining Cooperatives, Tribute Mining Contracts, and Rural Livelihoods in Zimbabwe, 1985–2021' in F. Calvão, M. Archer and A. Benya (eds.) *The Lives of Extraction. Identities, Communities and the Politics of Place*, International Development Policy | Revue internationale de politique de développement, 15 (Geneva, Boston: Graduate Institute Publications, Brill-Nijhoff), DOI: 10.4000/poldev.5226.

Nachet, L., C. Beckett and K.S. MacNeil (2021) 'Framing Extractive Violence as Environmental (In)Justice: a Cross-Perspective from Indigenous Lands in Canada and Sweden', *The Extractive Industries and Society*, 100949, DOI: 10.1016/j.exis.2021.100949.

Navas, G., S. Mingorria and B. Aguilar-González (2018) 'Violence in Environmental Conflicts: the Need for a Multidimensional Approach', *Sustainability Science*, 13(3), pp. 649–660, DOI: 10.1007/s11625-018-0551-8.

Nourani Rinaldi, P. (2022) 'The Age of Transition: Postdevelopment and North-South Synergies', *Latin American Perspectives*, 49(1), pp. 237–256, DOI: 10.1177/0094582X211060381.

Núñez, A., M.C. Benwell and E. Aliste (2020) 'Interrogating Green Discourses in Patagonia-Aysén (Chile): Green Grabbing and Eco-Extractivism as a New Strategy of Capitalism?', *Geographical Review*, 112(5), pp. 1–19, DOI: 10.1080/00167428.2020.1798764.

Nygren, A., M. Kröger and B. Gills (2022) 'Global Extractivisms and Transformative Alternatives', *The Journal of Peasant Studies*, 49(4), pp. 1–26, DOI: 10.1080/03066150.2022.2069495.

Ocaklı, B., T. Krueger, M.A. Janssen and U. Kasymov (2021) 'Taking the Discourse Seriously: Rational Self-Interest and Resistance to Mining in Kyrgyzstan', *Ecological Economics*, 189, 107177, DOI: 10.1016/j.ecolecon.2021.107177.

Ocampo, J.A. (2017) 'Commodity-Led Development in Latin America', in G. Carbonnier, H. Campodónico and S. Tezanos Vázquez (eds.) *Alternative Pathways to Sustainable Development: Lessons from Latin America*, International Development Policy, 9 (Leiden and Boston: Brill/Nijhoff), DOI: 10.4000/poldev.2354.

Petras, J.F. and H. Veltmeyer (2014) *Extractive Imperialism in the Americas: Capitalism's New Frontier*, Studies in Critical Social Sciences volume 70 (Leiden and Boston: Brill).

Pijpers, R.J., E. van de Camp, E. Fisher, L. Massaro, J. Calvimontes, L. D'Angelo and C. Lanzano (2021) 'Mining 'Waste': Repurposing Residues in Artisanal and Small-Scale Gold Mining', *Etnofoor*, 33(2), pp. 13–40.

Post, E. (2022) 'Proyectos de Muerte and Proyectos de Vida: Indigenous Counter-Hegemonic Praxis to Sustainable Development in the Sierra Norte de Puebla, Mexico', *The Journal of Peasant Studies*, pp. 1–30, DOI: 10.1080/03066150.2022.2082286.

Post, E. and F. Calvão (2020) 'Mythical Islands of Value: Free Ports, Offshore Capitalism, and Art Capital', Arts, 9(4), 100, DOI: 10.3390/arts9040100.

Preston, J. (2017) 'Racial Extractivism and White Settler Colonialism: an Examination of the Canadian Tar Sands Mega-Projects', *Cultural Studies*, 31(2–3), pp. 353–375, DOI: 10.1080/09502386.2017.1303432.

Riofrancos, T. (2020) *Resource Radicals: from Petro-nationalism to Post-extractivism in Ecuador, Radical Américas* (Durham: Duke University Press).

Schandl, H., M. Fischer-Kowalski, J. West, S. Giljum, M. Dittrich, N. Eisenmenger, A. Geschke, M. Lieber, H. Wieland, A. Schaffartzik, F. Krausmann, S. Gierlinger, K. Hosking, M. Lenzen, H. Tanikawa, A. Miatto and T. Fishman (2018) 'Global Material Flows and Resource Productivity: Forty Years of Evidence', *Journal of Industrial Ecology*, 22(4), pp. 827–838, DOI: https://doi.org/10.1111/jiec.12626.

Schuldt, J., A. Acosta, A. Barandiarán, A. Bebbington, M. Folchi, A. Alayza and E. Gudynas (2009) *Extractivismo, Política y Sociedad* (Quito: Centro Andino de Acción Popular & Centro Latinoamericano de Ecología Social).

Scobie, M., G. Finau and J. Hallenbeck (2021) 'Land, Land Banks and Land Back: Accounting, Social Reproduction and Indigenous Resurgence', *Environment and Planning A: Economy and Space*, 0308518X211060842, DOI: 10.1177/0308518X211060842.

Shapiro, J. and J.-A. McNeish (2021) *Our Extractive Age: Expressions of Violence and Resistance* (London: Routledge), DOI: 10.4324/9781003127611.

Smith, J. (2016) *Imperialism in the Twenty-First Century: Globalization, Super-Exploitation, and Capitalism's Final Crisis* (New York: Monthly Review Press).

Smith, N. (2008) *Uneven Development: Nature, Capital, and the Production of Space* (Athens: University of Georgia Press).

Spoor, M. (1998) 'The Aral Sea Basin Crisis: Transition and Environment in Former Soviet Central Asia', *Development and Change*, 29(3), pp. 409–435, DOI: 10.1111/1467-7660.00084.

Stallings, B. (2020) *Dependency in the Twenty-First Century? The Political Economy of China-Latin America Relations, Cambridge Elements in Politics and Society in Latin America* (Cambridge: Cambridge University Press).

Svampa, M. (2019) *Neo-Extractivism in Latin America: Socio-Environmental Conflicts, the Territorial Turn, and New Political Narratives, Elements in Politics and Society in Latin America* (Cambridge: Cambridge University Press).

Svampa, M. (2013) ''Consenso de Los Commodities' y Lenguajes de Valoración En América Latina', *Nueva Sociedad*, 244, pp. 30–46.

Szeman, I. and J. Wenzel (2021) 'What Do We Talk About When We Talk About Extractivism?', *Textual Practice*, 35(3), pp. 505–523, DOI: 10.1080/0950236X.2021.1889829.

Tello, E., G. Jover, I. Murray, O. Fullana and R. Soto (2018) 'From Feudal Colonization to Agrarian Capitalism in Mallorca: Peasant Endurance Under the Rise and Fall of Large Estates (1229–1900)', *Journal of Agrarian Change*, 18(3), pp. 483–516, DOI: 10.1111/joac.12253.

Tilzey, M. (2019) 'Authoritarian Populism and Neo-Extractivism in Bolivia and Ecuador: the Unresolved Agrarian Question and the Prospects for Food Sovereignty as Counter-Hegemony', *The Journal of Peasant Studies*, 46(3), pp. 626–652, DOI: 10.1080/03066150.2019.1584191.

UNGA (United Nations General Assembly) (2015) *Transforming Our World: the 2030 Agenda for Sustainable Development*, No. A/70/L.1.

United Nations Secretary-General (2021) *UN Secretary-General: COP26 Must Keep 1.5 Degrees Celsius Goal Alive*, United Nations Framework Convention on Climate Change, https://unfccc.int/news/un-secretary-general-cop26-must-keep-15-degrees-celsius-goal-alive (accessed on 31 August 2022).

Verbrugge, B. and S. Geenen (2019) 'The Gold Commodity Frontier: a Fresh Perspective on Change and Diversity in the Global Gold Mining Economy', *The Extractive Industries and Society*, 6(2), pp. 413–423, DOI: 10.1016/j.exis.2018.10.014.

Voskoboynik, D.M. and D. Andreucci (2021) 'Greening Extractivism: Environmental Discourses and Resource Governance in the 'Lithium Triangle'', *Environment and Planning E: Nature and Space*, 5(2), pp. 787–809, DOI: 10.1177/25148486211006345.

Westman, C.N., T.L. Joly and L. Gross (eds.) (2020) *Extracting Home in the Oil Sands: Settler Colonialism and Environmental Change in Subarctic Canada, Arctic Worlds* (London and New York: Routledge Taylor & Francis Group).

Wolf, E.R. (2010) *Europe and the People Without History* (Berkeley: University of California Press).

World Bank Group (2022) *Commodity Markets Outlook: the Impact of the War in Ukraine on Commodity Markets* (Washington D.C.: World Bank Group).

Ye, J., J.D. van der Ploeg, S. Schneider and T. Shanin (2020) 'The Incursions of Extractivism: Moving From Dispersed Places to Global Capitalism', *The Journal of Peasant Studies*, 47(1), pp. 155–183, DOI: 10.1080/03066150.2018.1559834.

CHAPTER 3

The Structures of Conquest: Debating Extractivism(s), Infrastructures and Environmental Justice for Advancing Post-development Pathways

Alexander Dunlap

Abstract

The green economy and 'green growth' are not solutions to ecological and climate catastrophe. The dominate trajectory of techno-industrial development has to be reconsidered and placed within ecological limits. The 'social', related to environmental and climate justice, tends towards subordinating the ecological in the maintenance of modernist infrastructures, and thus towards breaking efforts to achieve socio-ecological harmony. The following examines the realities of resource extractivism, but also tensions within academic debates on these matters. This entails locating an important 'grey area' within these debates, which has significant implications for imagining pathways to address ecological and climate catastrophe. This grey area—questioning the difference between extractivism and industrialism—also persists within archetypal positions on land acquisition and shades of reform in environmental justice studies, and, to a lesser degree, in the (academic) decolonial literature. This chapter contends that environmental justice reinforces modernist development, necessitating and expanding extractivism and ecologically destructive infrastructures. By highlighting ambiguities in critical literatures, it seeks to provide political clarity, reinforcing personal and collective self-determination and, secondarily, to encourage public policy to begin taking climate catastrophe seriously.

1 Introduction

Extractivism and infrastructure are the two sides of the socio-ecological coin. The extraction of human and non-human life to 'develop' states, grow economies and modernise infrastructures, while responsible for creating living possibilities and enchantments (Alexander, 2008; Harvey and Knox, 2012), is undeniably the modality of development that is responsible for socio-ecological and climate catastrophe (Kallianos, Dunlap and Dalakoglou, 2022). 'The invention of the boat', as Paul Virilio ((2008 [1983]), 46) reminds us, 'was the

© GENEVA GRADUATE INSTITUTE, 2024 | DOI:10.1163/9789004686182_004

invention of shipwrecks. The invention of the steam engine and the locomotive was the invention of derailments. The invention of the highway was the invention of three hundred cars colliding in five minutes'. Ward Churchill (2003) and Winona LaDuke and Sean Aaron Cruz (2012), taking this further, remind us that colonial genocide–ecocide process on Turtle Island are foundational to nuclear weapon production. Colonial conquest and the 'Indian Wars' established the means to exterminate Hiroshima and Nagasaki via atomic bombs dropped on Japan.[1] With the wider public recognition of climate change, we can now say that the invention of capitalist industrialisation (as we know it) has consolidated the pathways towards ecological and climate catastrophe.

Technological progress, its speed, convenience and possibilities, offered existential purpose and enamoured people (Harvey and Knox, 2012; Anand, Gupta and Appel, 2018), meanwhile masking, ignoring and externalising the underside and 'costs' of this wonder—'[t]he negative side of technology and speed was censored', as Virilio ((2008 [1983]), 46) contends. This underside is not only accidents and disasters as Virilio indicates, but an entire self-reinforcing and administering institutional network of extractivism and infrastructure powered by capitalism(s). This, of course, refers specifically to material-intensive, or 'hard', infrastructures, such as roads, pipes, power lines, data centres, power stations and more (Anand, Gupta and Appel, 2018; Tarvainen, 2022), which function as the skeleton of capitalism, the shape of modernity, the driving force of extractivism. Patrick Wolfe's (2006, 388) contention that colonial 'invasion is a structure not an event', indicates—past and present—how the modernist process seeks to literally 'steamroller' and absorb Indigenous peoples and ecologies, revealing how political economy maintains this socio-ecological apparatus of conquest. Wolfe's 'structure' refers to settler colonialism and colonial societies, their political economy and forms of political organisation—the state (Dunlap, 2018; 2020). Viewing statist[2] infrastructures as conquest reminds us of the extent to which intense socio-ecological destruction is tolerated and normalised within the current institutions and economies. This is to say that colonial/statist[3] invasion is also infrastructural

1 This, of course, was in the name of defeating an enemy, even if 'conventional bombing had already achieved such a high level of destruction that atomic bombs could not inflict dramatically more damage' (Pape, 1993, 155).

2 Statist also implies corporate. The state is a framework; albeit imperfect/contested, it facilitates political economy and everything that entails.

3 Colonial and/or statist forms is a matter of temporality, making the state the current and evolving form of the colony model. State-making, necessitates 'internal' colonialism to organize people and ecologies in the service of centralized power, which organizes the possibilities

(Dunlap and Arce, 2022, 461; Tornel, 2020), which implies the necessity of rethinking and changing 'resource' extraction practices and modern infrastructural construction (Kallianos, Dunlap and Dalakoglou, 2022), which extends to bureaucratic, judicial and mental infrastructures. Mental infrastructures are formed by systematically bombarding people with efforts at subjectivity persuasion (e.g. 'brain washing') by private industries and governments in order to cultivate particular forms of public conduct and consumer practices (Bernays, [1928]2005; Herman and Chomsky, [1989]2010; Verweijen and Dunlap, 2021). If people want to mitigate ecological crisis, they must become responsive and challenge the persistence of ecologically destructive infrastructures and begin (re)transforming their habitation practices to support their environments. This chapter seeks to address an anthropocentric extractive and infrastructural bias that predominates within extractive and environmental justice (EJ) literatures. This bias relates to how people chart (multi-scalar) extractive supply webs, the state and 'justice' phraseology. Critical approaches, the chapter argues, still suffer from 'infrastructural coloniality' (Dunlap, 2021a, 6), which underestimates the accumulation and interdependence of extractivism(s) and enables them through processual and egalitarian concerns that maintain the supremacy of modernist infrastructures over ecosystems. Infrastructural coloniality frequently results in 'selling out' ecosystems/habitats, thereby subordinating nonhuman life (e.g. animals, rivers, mountains, trees and habitats) to the desires of various human populations under the influence of colonial mentalities and, later, industrial-'technocapitalist' desires. Civilisation, Empire, Monarchy and Colonialism, guided by various statist forms and economic logics, have progressed alongside technological developments, which reinforce each other to continue industrial capitalist trajectories into cybernetic and computational capitalism(s) that remain normal features of (statist) market societies.

This chapter proceeds by examining the realities of extractivism and infrastructure, but also the political perspectives and ideologies that enable them. The 'social', related to environmental and climate justice, tends towards subordinating the ecological to the maintenance of modernist infrastructures. By attempting to reconcile capitalism with ecology, there is risk of stultifying efforts at achieving socio-ecological harmony. Harmony, in opposition to extractivism, refers to creating reciprocal and relational health within habitats/ecosystems; so, for example, to not degrade or over-exploit any humans or nonhumans. The following examines the realities of resource extractivism, but also

of becoming a 'colonial power'. Once states emerge, a campaign of 'external' colonization in the service of capitalist accumulation and modernist developmental can then take hold.

tensions within academic debates on these matters. This entails locating an important 'grey area' within the debate, which has significant implications for imagining pathways to confront ecological and climate catastrophe. This grey area—questioning the difference between extractivism and industrialism[4]—which also persists within the different seven archetypal positions within land acquisition, discussed below, and corresponds to reformism with environmental justice studies and, to a lesser degree, 'academic decolonial scholarship' (Dunlap, 2022, 3). This chapter contends that environmental justice systematically promotes inclusion into the project of modernist development, necessitating and expanding extractivism and modernist infrastructures. By highlighting ambiguities in critical literatures, this chapter seeks to provide clarity, reinforcing personal and collective self-determination and, secondarily, to encourage public policy to begin taking climate catastrophe seriously. In its conclusion, the chapter advocates (decolonial) degrowth reforms and post-development pathways aimed at mitigating socio-ecological catastrophe.

2 Extractivism: Recognising the Depth of Socio-ecological Destruction

Energy demand is rising. According to Our World in Data (OWD), the amount of mined material has only grown exponentially. In 1880, approximately 43.2 million metric tons of minerals were consumed. By 2013 this figure had increased to 2.64 billion metric tons of iron ore, tungsten, bauxite, copper, and so on (OWD, 2021a), a figure projected to grow as the rapid roll-out of low-carbon infrastructures for the 'green energy transition' (Hickel, 2020; EC, 2020, 4) and economic growth continues. Low-carbon infrastructures, the World Bank recognises (Hund et al., 2020, XI), 'are in fact significantly more material intensive in their composition than current traditional fossil-fuel-based energy supply systems'. This includes expansive spatial demands, consuming large swaths of land and hillsides (Mulvaney, 2019). 'The global population doubled between 1970 and 2017, yet the extraction of materials (including

4 This chapter avoids the concept of 'infrastructuralism' as it has many diverse meanings and raises various questions. Yet, Rubenstein and colleagues (2015, 579) ask an important question: 'When are we justified in decrying the intrusions of infrastructure and when ought we to defend the progress it does, sometimes, represent?' This question underlines this chapter, but also maintains a democratic illusion that 'we'—people— have a choice over planning, developmental decisions and how computational technologies are integrated into institutions and markets.

fossil fuels for energy) tripled, from 27.1 billion tonnes to 92.1 billion tonnes per year', explains Meadhbh Bolger and colleagues (2021, 6). The increase of material consumption coincides with a rising energy consumption, totalling 171,240 terawatts in 2019, with oil accounting for 53,181, coal 44,109, and gas 38,517 terawatt-hours (TWh). (OWD, 2021b). Meanwhile, '75% of the terrestrial environment and 40% of the marine environment are already severely altered, combined with an alarming and rapid loss of biodiversity, with close to one million species facing extinction' (Bolgher et al., 2021). Despite all the enchantments of capitalism and modernity (Alexander, 2008; Harvey and Knox, 2012), current modes of extractivism, infrastructural development and urbanisation are far from being ecologically sustainable. This places greater importance on the debates and existing gaps within the literature on extractivism.

Given increasing rates of material and energy consumption across all sectors, claims of an energy transition are unjustified (Bell, Daggett and Labuski, 2020). While there is a socio-technical energy transition currently in action that is restructuring infrastructural organisation, development and capital accumulation, there is only one long-term energy transition, or continuity—it points in the direction of industrialisation and mass consumption (Dunlap, 2021a). This trajectory should raise concerns for all the inhabitants of the planet. The green capitalist solutions—such as market-based conservation, carbon capture and storage, offsetting, and low-carbon infrastructures—promoted by governments at the 26th Conference of the Parties to the United Nations Framework Convention on Climate Change are inadequate (Böhm and Sullivan, 2021; Stoddard et al., 2021). The responsibility for socio-ecological catastrophe rests with governments, corporations and international bodies. Meanwhile, governments and companies systematically work to repress environmental, Indigenous and anti-capitalist movements attempting to mitigate socio-ecological crises and defend ecosystems. While Indigenous groups and other land defenders continue to protect their territories from mines, pipelines and wind turbines, the responses from (mainstream) environmentalists celebrating low-carbon infrastructures and, implicitly, so-called 'green mining' appears painfully inadequate. On the 14 November 2021 Wet'suwet'en issued an eviction order against the Coastal GasLink pipeline, demonstrating an example of enforcing treaty rights and protecting ecosystems (IGD, 2021). This, however, has resulted in the intensification of police, security and paramilitary occupation of Wet'suwet'en land (Temper, 2019), policing Indigenous and other bodies challenging extractive and infrastructure projects (Simpson and Le Billon, 2021). While committed resistance to socio-ecological destruction continues, there remains a general lack of confrontation and commitment from policy makers and established movements alike.

This lack of commitment from policy makers, however, is rather unsurprising. Governments are intended to facilitate (and expand) territorial control, infrastructural development and economic growth (e.g. profiteering) no matter the consequences, as it appears. The European Green Deal (EGD) remains an exemplar in the energy sector (Dunlap and Laratte, 2022, 2), where the extractive realities related to the 'rapid rollout of renewable energy deployment' remain either ignored or only acknowledged in the matter related to supply-chain bottlenecks and critical raw material insecurity (in terms of foreign dependence). The rapid roll-out of low-carbon infrastructures is leading to land grabbing via expulsion orders (including Declarations of Public Utility or Projects of Common Interest), which reinforce the neo-liberalisation of the European energy market through the EGD. The EGD, moreover, seeks to expand energy markets, high-voltage power line (HVPL) infrastructures, (extractive-intensive) digitalisation and 'smart' censor schemes, and the rapid expansion of wind, solar and other low-carbon infrastructures (Dunlap and Laratte, 2022). The EGD, we must remember, was heavily influenced by the Sustainable Development Goals (SDGs)—specifically in the energy sector—and will replicate similar problems of socio-ecological dispossession (Larsen, Haller and Kothari, 2022). Policy reactions to climate change have resulted in efforts to 'decarbonise' hydrocarbon and mineral extraction companies by employing carbon capture schemes and natural gas and powering resource extraction via low-carbon infrastructures (E&M, 2022; Equinor, 2022), which ignores the hydrocarbon-dependent and mineral-intensive realities of low-carbon infrastructures themselves (Dunlap and Marin, 2022). While policy frontiers remain limited, or disappointing, political and environmental movements—especially the younger ones (e.g. Extinction Rebellion)—could benefit from learning from longstanding struggles and committed land defenders. With the struggle in Lützerath fighting the open-pit Garzweiler lignite coal mine (Brock, 2023), it appears the climate justice movement is learning through the harsh lessons of green political party betrayal, police repression and, inversely, the importance of embracing a diversity of tactics in their struggles.

The concern here is how movements are defanged and divided, often from within. The recent debates on extractivism are telling, crossing over into academia. This general concern with extractivism and infrastructure, presented in this chapter, questions the totality of state and capital (Dunlap and Jakobsen, 2020; Kass, 2022), viewing the entire structure of political economy as a machine of socio-ecological conquest.[5] The debates over the definition of

5 This does not deny that conquest and modernist development can have, thinking of Foucault, 'positive' or enchanting features to facilitate political control (Verweijen and Dunlap, 2021; Rubenstein, Robbins and Beal, 2015).

extractivism actually illuminate key political tensions and fault lines that create discursive, but also practical, divisions. Extractivism, according to Eduardo Gudynas (2009), involves acquiring large volumes of raw material for export, profiting national or international business classes (or governments, in the case of neo-extractivism), while breaking down existing sectors and social and ecological relationships. Extractivism entails a high intensity of environmental degradation and, finally, corresponding deleterious labour opportunities and conditions (Gudynas, 2009; see also Lang and Mokrani (2013) Nygren, Kröger, and Gills (2022)). The volume of material extracted (e.g. timber, minerals, hydrocarbons, produce, or biodiversity), the intensity of that extraction, and the destination and concentration of ownership by foreign or national industries are, it can be said, the main attributes of extractivism. While boundary making is useful for conceptual development, extractivism—contrary to the view of Eduardo Gudynas (2021)—in practice has few if any boundaries. And worse, the perverseness of the phenomenon is normalised and thereby underestimated.

This raises the issue of calling 'everything extractivism' (see EXALT (2020); Gudynas (2021); Chagnon et al., 2022). The primary concern of calling everything extractivism, as Gudynas (2021, 4) warns, is that 'almost any activity could be considered extractivism' and 'rigour and precision [will be] lost'. A lack of rigor and precision generates 'ambiguity', which—Gudynas (2021, 4) explains—allows advocates of mineral and oil companies 'to insist that any use or abuse of Nature was ultimately extractivism, and therefore it should be tolerated and protected as a fundamental condition for humanity [sic] survival'. An example of this, as illustrated by Ben Mckay (2020, 106), is Evo Morales' ex-Vice President García Linera, who justifies extractive operations this way. On the contrary, the misuse and manipulation of information by mining companies and politicians *should never temper our criticisms or assessments*. Otherwise, like the concerns with environmental justice discussed below, the ecological is sacrificed in the name of the 'social', the 'industrial' or the 'good' of the nation, perpetuating socio-ecological imbalance and crisis.

Gudynas's points, then, raise a central question at the core of calling 'everything' extractivism: How can industrial capitalist operations not be extractivism? (Dunlap, 2021b, 4). What is not extractivism within an industrial capitalist system? Important criteria for judging whether something is extractivist, Dunlap and Jakobsen (2020, 14–15) contend, is assessing what development initiatives or operations produce or leave in their wake and how they structure the future. This implies assessing development based on the product and end result of socio-ecological conditions. This resonates with Markus Kröger's (2022) 'political economy of existences', which examines the process of landscape change, or, more accurately, exterminations and reconfigurations that transform rainforests into soy monocrop plantations or wetlands into strip malls. Is the soil, water, food, non-human, climate and relational qualities being improved or degraded by development operations? Maybe the outcome is variegated, yet this asks whether particular activities—developments, constructions, forms of organisation and relationships—are socio-ecologically sustainable or renewable.

Establishing renewability is challenging, but it remains a remedy to extractivism and ecological catastrophe. Various Indigenous traditions and practices that, before the onset of industrialisation (Deloria, 1999; Hatfield et al., 2018; Ulloa, 2020), cohabited and continue to this day to cohabit with the planet are certainly examples of (real) socio-ecological sustainability and renewability or, at least, are closer to it. (Neo)colonialism, modernity and capitalism, and their products, are spreading everywhere—creating ruptures with renewable socio-ecological relationships. Winona LaDuke and Deborah Cowen (2020, 253) remind us that human activity should be 'rooted in a practice of relationality that understands human and more-than-human life as kin, as familial relations' (see also Simpson, 2014). Acknowledging, respecting and living with non-human life (e.g. animals, trees, rivers, mountains), and challenging anthropocentrism and materialism (in the mechanical philosophy sense), offers important pathways to challenge extractivism—as countless Indigenous land defenders do across the world (Blaser, 2013; Escobar, 2020; Springer et al., 2021)—and to begin conceptualising real socioecological renewability. This means remembering, as Leanne B. Simpson (2014, 9–10) explains, that humans are 'dependent upon intimate relationships of reciprocity, humility, honesty and respect with all elements of creation, including plants and animals' (see also Escobar, 2020). Extractivism denies this reality, instead viewing everything as a 'resource' and a commodity to be taken, marketed, and sold (Grosfoguel, 2016; Simpson, 2019). This also relates to the 'predator prey bargain', popularised by Derrick Jensen (2006, 179),[6] which conceptualises, based on Indigenous practices, our responsibility with regard to consumption and, by extension, 'resource use'.

> If you live on a piece of land-if you own a piece of land-if you consume the flesh that is on that land, you are now responsible for the continuation of that land and its health. You are now responsible for the health of

6 While *Endgame* is an appreciated classic, citing Jensen's work here is in no way an endorsement of his later statements, political positions and media collaborations.

> all the various communities who share that land with you. And because members of this community will consume your flesh, too, they will be just as responsible for the continuation and health of your community. At that point you will own the land, and it will own you.
>
> JENSEN, 2006, 197

This conceptualises how to organise systems based on care and renewability, as opposed to plunder and extractivism. Moreover, it is a reminder that we share our habitats with other peoples, which also stresses that if people damage or destroy their habitats, they are destroying themselves. The anarchist slogan, 'destroy what destroys you', obtains greater significance from this perspective. The carelessness of and the destruction wrought by modernist development have gone on so long that they are resulting in climate change and weather extremes (Hickel, 2020). This understanding, then, adds to our conceptualisation of renewability as well as of extractivism. Extractivism is thus defined as cutting, fracturing, taking, usurping and disregarding humans and non-humans without intention or plan to fully and adequately redress the resulting violence and harm.

Definitions of renewability and extractivism are established above, but the question persists: How can industrial capitalist operations not be extractivism? Based on institutional structure and development priority, academics—and people generally—have become accustomed to and enamoured by the products of extractivism. This normalised—everyday—infrastructural reality of roads, individualized automobility, utilitarian architecture, pipes and power lines, to name a few, have consumed people wilfully, begrudgingly or somewhere in between and beyond. Remembering how Walter Rostow weaponized capitalist consumerism to win the Cold War (Cullather, 2013, 161), we might understand convenience and entertainment as capitalist 'weapons of mass destruction' against the planet. Modernist infrastructural regimes allow us to ignore, or even to forget, how we accommodate capitalism, industrialisation and our (forced or voluntary) servitude to the development of computational technologies. As the Mining Association of Canada (MAC, 2021) exclaims: 'Before it's yours, its mined'.[7] Thus, this bounded definition of extractivism, put forward by Gudynas (2021) and many others (Mckay, 2020; Ye et al., 2020), is accused of ignoring the complex financial and material supply webs of monocultures, research labs, schools, hospitals, police, prisons and all the rest that depends on plundering habitats for either materials or energy

7 Thanks to Philippe Le Billon for pointing this out to me.

production (Dunlap, 2021b). In order for agro-extractivism to be possible in the first place, there needs to be an entire political-economic regime—the structure of conquest—in place to create the means, scale and intensity that allows agro-extractivism: chemical factories—extracting, dividing and synthesising nature—to produce pesticides and/or fertilisers; the scientific expertise and laboratories to research, develop and create genetically modified organisms (GMOs); and, now, the existing supply webs behind the application of digital technologies in agriculture, which 'appropriate decision-making based on the flow of data from individual farms and farmers' (Stone, 2022, 3). While Glenn Stone (2022) refers to this as 'surveillance agriculture', indicating how agriculture is becoming digitalized, automated and eroding control from farmers, the purpose here is to emphasises how extractive processes, or extractivism(s), are connected at various intensities through production supply webs, violent histories, economic and financial actors, and/or institutions. Agro-extractivism requires mining, and more of it as it digitalises and intensifies. The 'innovation economy', Antti Tarvainen (2022, 2) reminds us, depends on, emerges from, and systematically affirms settler colonialism, meanwhile refining 'the violence of technocapitalism' and 'data colonialism'. The relevance of 'global extractivism' as an organising concept (Nygren, Kröger and Gills, 2022; Chagnon et al., 2022), affirms its relevance, as extractivism, infrastructural colonisation, and economic forces proliferate, transcend borders, intersect, and depend on multiple extractive companies and trajectories.

Coming to terms with the reality that 'everything is extractivism' within the dominant development paradigm is important to any effort to resituate the present planetary situation—and the action that should follow. This extractive reality should also allow people to resituate how they conceive of politics, conflict, political organisation and, consequently, 'justice' the last of which is discussed in the next section. Academically, if not practically, the imperative exists to take the socio-ecological damage and harm created by industrial, bureaucratic and capitalist systems seriously. Non-humans, the Indigenous, the marginalised, peoples that consume little materials and energy, moreover, are the least responsible for this socio-ecological catastrophe (Bolger et al., 2021), which is not to forget the psychosocial decay and discontent emanating from modernist affluence of high-income countries and neighborhoods (Lane, 2000; Alexander, 2008). Properly recognising the scope of this problem is the first step. Technologies and infrastructures, however, can be appropriated. This appropriation indicates the importance of taking the 'best' innovations from this global development process. If socio-ecological transformation is to take place, it will require serious and committed efforts to redress the violence done by techno-capitalism and to build new types of (post)developmental infrastructures.

Finding a way between industrialism and extractivism, Markus Kröger (2022, 47–49) views extractivism through different intensities across a seven-point scale from-1 to 5. This is instructive to, first, create greater specificity within the extractivisms' debate and, second, to resituate our understanding of industrial activities so that we may re-conceptualise our productive relationships with our ecosystems and the planet.

5 = hyperextractivist
4 = very extractivist
3 = notably extractivist
2 = partially extractivist
1 = limitedly extractivist
0 = non extractivist
−1 = anti-extractivist

Anti-extractivism includes recognising non-human life and practicing food procurement, housing and daily life in a way that supports habitats and begins restoring ecosystems subjected to extractivist relationships and habitats. 'Green' buildings, 'convivial' technologies,[8] agro-ecology, permaculture, and degrowth systems designed with and connected to habitats and people remain an important direction in which to develop (see Jacke and Toensmeier (2005); Lockyer and Veteto (2013); Rosset and Altieri (2017); and Hickel (2020)). Developing post-development, degrowth, non-and anti-extractivist pathways remains a global challenge for humanity, which is something that Peter Gelderloos (2022) imagines and outlines in the last chapter of *The Solutions Are Already Here*. Current practices of resistance to megaprojects (Menton et al., 2020; Dunlap, 2022), convivial living and ecological restoration spanning Latin America—including the Viva Campinas Network (Rosset and Altieri, 2017), Proceso de Liberación de la Madre Tierra in Colombia (Reyes and Santamaría, 2020), the Teia dos Povos network, and the Cultive Resistência collective in Brazil—are excellent, self-organised initiatives (Gelderloos, 2022). This entails, as Julia Schöneberg and colleagues show (2022, 2), that despite geographical diversity, cultural specificities and, even, a lack of formal

8 'Convivial technologies' refer to tools designed within the socio-ecological fabrics of a given bioregion. This might include activity limited the production and types of tools used for their impact on people, nonhumans and ecosystems. Socially and ecologically conducive technologies allow autonomous and creative engagements among its users and the environment. Convivial technologies are scaled, social and environmentally responsible technologies, connected to broader social ecologies.

organised movements, 'strategies of reciprocity, solidarity, and commoning' are 'means for survival and/or provide alternative pathways for societal and economic transformation'. These movements and political struggles are, however, violently repressed by governments, companies and subverted by the myths of 'green growth'(see Hickel, 2020)—green capitalism as a viable solution to socio-ecological and climate catastrophe. Extractivism remains a weapon against life, meanwhile producing infrastructures to control, capture and enchant—facilitating dependency, false hopes and addiction (Harvey and Knox, 2012; Anand, Gupta and Appel, 2018; Kallianos, Dunlap and Dalakoglou, 2022). The challenge from our environments, the planet and ceaseless technocapitalsit 'fixes'—delivering technological enchantment, convenience, and mobility—has culminated in is generalised socio-ecological catastrophe. There is no shortage of opposition and resistance to the present path of extractivist development. Like extractivism debates, however, there is an avoidance of confronting the realities of industrialisation and capitalism, which extends to Marxian scholars conceptualizing anti-capitalism as state capitalism, modernist development and 'socialist accumulation'. This translates into inadequate reform that tends towards ignoring the destructive trajectory of colonial powers have created for this planet.

3 The Dilemmas of Extractivism and Infrastructure: Environmental Justice?

Avoidance of considering industrialisation as inherently extractivist has similarities within the environmental justice and, to a degree, decolonial studies (see Dunlap, 2022). Environmental conflicts—whether they are struggles against mines, infrastructure, or plantations—differ from one another, but there are archetypal political positions that also surface (see Hall et al., (2015); Geenen and Verweijen (2017); Dunlap (2019b; 2021d); Prause and Le Billon (2021)). First (see Table 3.1) there are the people who are in favour of large-scale development projects, viewing them as opportunities, pathways towards material well-being and modernity. The land deal, then, is received positively by all parties involved. Second is the position in which people are in favour of the development project, but are adversely incorporated into the project and subjected to various and unequal forms of exploitation and deteriorating labour conditions in the service of national or transnational capital accumulation. The third position is representative of people who are indifferent to and/or opportunistic with regard to the project, 'flip-flopping' between whatever position will serve their personal material and social interest. Fourth, people are against—and even resent—the project but actively collaborate with the companies and/or political representatives involved in order to gain access to work and various political, economic, and material benefits. This position recognises the large socio-ecological problems that lead to resistance but whether due to poverty, obligation or ambition people (often begrudgingly) choose to collaborate with extractivist projects and their representatives. Fifth, is a general acceptance of the conceptual idea (e.g. mines, wind turbines, plantations), but profound concerns regarding the terms of project incorporation and benefits, revenue sharing, social development funds and who bares the socio-ecological impacts of the project (Jakobsen, 2022). The next position blurs into position six, where people who are against the project but want differentiated forms of social development. For example, they may not want a field of corporate wind turbines, but would like a community-scale wind factory or micro-scale projects to provide them with the energy they need (Dunlap, 2018). There is a spectrum of alternative or post-development positions related to self-organised grassroots, or 'do-it-yourself' initiatives, which are either completely autonomous or supported by non-governmental organisations (NGOs), municipalities or state funds. State, and to a lesser degree NGO, funding can create intense internal political debate, controversy and divisions within political movements and networks (see Dunlap and Correa-Arce, 2022). Finally, overlapping with the previous point, the seventh archetypal position is the total rejection of the imposed project. This position is typically cultivated by previous experiences with political parties or development projects or through existing commitments to livelihood or cultural–spiritual practices (Blaser, 2013; Conde and Le Billon, 2017; Dunlap, 2019b; Escobar, 2020). This general, seven-point spectrum of positions within environmental conflicts blurs and mutates between armed and criminal organisations, yet what is significant here is that the more recalcitrant positions of total rejection tend to be erased, minimised, or blurred with more liberal positions within the academic literature.

These positions are, however, largely movable and changeable in every direction. Mining and infrastructure companies work diligently, usually after effective opposition, to gain the 'social acceptance' from locals necessary to commence and operate extractivist projects. The 'social engineering of extraction' documents how companies, whether building wind turbines (Dunlap, 2018), mining gold (Geenen and Verweijen, 2017) or operating coal mines (Brock and Dunlap, 2018), work by any means to persuade people to accept resource extraction projects (see also Le Billon and Sommverville, 2017). This entails constructing local interests as the same as company objectives, meanwhile sending the message that resistance to project development is

TABLE 3.1 Land control archetypes

Land contracting	Mutually agreed upon transfer of land with little to no controversy within the community. An ideal business transaction with full information on market values and socio-ecological costs, and, more importantly, general agreement from all involved and surrounding parties.
Deceptive land deal	Land transfers or contractual deals based on manipulation, deception, and lies. This generates (minor) community discord and resentment when the terms agreed to are more unfavourable than expected and the levels of incorporation and benefit sharing are more unequal than originally imagined. Benefits are limited and/or concentrated around selected actors (often reinforcing power and gender disparities). Political mobilisations can begin, or fail to get off the ground.
Land deal opportunism	The land deal and/or project remains exploitative and unequal with regard to benefit sharing and ecological impact, yet people use the arrival of land deals, and resistance to them, as opportunities for negotiation and (adverse) inclusion into the projects.
Land deal panic	The land deal is more akin to a land grab with noticeable economic exploitation, ecological impacts, unequal benefit sharing and a local concentration of wealth, but people choose to submit—'give up'—at some point in the process and collaborate with the companies and/or their representatives or local intermediaries. Land deal panic represents the successful dividing and pacification of resistance.

TABLE 3.1 Land control archetypes (*cont.*)

Land deal injustice	Acceptance of the development project, but local representatives, towns, or communities take an active stance in order to secure greater inclusion in project planning and (re) negotiation of the terms of the project. Desires for project inclusion and greater benefit sharing can manifest in larger contestations and conflicts. Manifestations and uprisings are used by actors to (re)negotiate terms and conditions.
Land grabbing contestation	The land deal is land grabbing (i.e. deception, coercion, and dispossession), generates mass mobilisations and concerted resistance, and attracts the attention of NGOs. Despite ardent opposition, the desire for development and inclusion results in protesting for environmental justice to balance local socio-ecological and developmental concerns.
Land grabbing rejection	This is the ardent rejection of land grabbing, reflecting a political maturity, or cynicism, that does not believe that projects from state, national or transnational actors will ever respect the land, culture or bring development. In fact, this position believes that particular development projects will bring (greater) exploitation. The total rejection of the project remains the trajectory for residents and land defenders. This position overlaps with aspirations of political autonomy, resulting in combative direct-action strategies, legal strategies, and political mobilisation. This position overlaps, and at times clashes, with the 'Land grabbing contestation' position.

SOURCE: AUTHOR

futile, using legal regimes, police, the military and private security companies (Dunlap, 2020; Verweijen and Dunlap, 2021). The social engineering of extraction has been discussed in the context of deep-sea mining in the Pacific (Childs, 2019) copper mining in Peru (Dunlap, 2019a) and Ecuador (Leifsen, 2020), coal mining in Mozambique (Wiegink, 2020) and Colombia (Jakobsen, 2020), hydraulic fracturing in the UK (Brock, 2020), ilmenite mining and conservation enclosures in Madagascar (Huff and Orengo, 2020) and nuclear development in India (Kaur, 2021). Social engineering and counter-insurgency, Alleen Brown and colleagues show (2017), are also instrumental to the development of hydrocarbon pipelines on multiple sites (Brown, 2021). The efforts of extraction companies to shape the perceptions, interests and, even, the subjectivities of inhabitants (Frederiksen and Himley, 2020) are nothing new, but the persistence of these activities and the lack of institutional opposition should raise serious concerns. Company-led manipulation and coercion to enforce infrastructure and extractivist projects are institutionally normalised, if always contested and negotiated (Rajak, 2011; Dunlap, 2019b; Ulloa, 2020; Kröger, 2021; 2022), and deserve greater consideration within environmental justice studies.

Environmental justice, as a term, emerges from struggles against environmental racism and waste incinerators in the United States in the 1980s (Pulido and De Lara, 2018). 'Mainstream' environmental justice, as it has been called (Menton et al., 2020, 3), adheres to roughly five dimensions. *Distributional justice* focuses on the distribution of environmental 'costs' and 'benefits' from a particular development project, such as revenue sharing, material benefits, land-use changes and so on. *Recognition justice* seeks to establish social equity and dignity by respecting socio-cultural difference and collectivities. *Procedural justice* examines the procedural aspects of development projects, seeking to advance popular participation in project design, siting, and implementation. *Capabilities* seeks to establish and ensure people have the capacity to engage and participate in development projects. While environmental justice has experienced conceptual expansion (Pellow, 2016; Ulloa, 2017; Pulido, 2017; Temper, 2019; Rodriguez, 2020), it has emerged as an umbrella term, encompassing various political tendencies and struggles that relate to the environment. Environmental justice is synonymous with all ecological and territorial struggles (see Akbulut et al., 2019; Scheidel et al., 2020; Temper et al., 2020). This has led to adapting the concept to more expansive understandings, for example making it applicable to Indigenous groups. '[E]nvironmental self-determination', Astrid Ulloa (2017, 176) explains, 'refers to Indigenous notions of environmental justice that come from a sense of responsibility and interrelations between human and nonhumans' and is 'based on other valuations and rights relating to territory, culture, and the nonhumans'. Recognising the shortcomings of mainstream environmental justice (EJ), Leah Temper (2019) proposes a decolonial environmental justice to better represent Indigenous self-governance, socio-ecological relationships and epistemologies (see also Menton et al., 2020; Rodriguez, 2020). The term justice, while rightly interrogated by decolonial EJ scholars, mostly for its limited Western or singular connotations, is preserved or augmented to suite Indigenous struggles.

Branding all socio-ecological and territorial struggles as 'environmental justice struggles' necessitates further consideration. Discussing the issue of 'popular justice' with French Maoists, Michel Foucault ([1972]1980) reminds us that justice tends to conjure up specific spatial infrastructures (e.g. the court and tables) and ideologies (e.g. liberalism). Justice is a loaded term with different histories and meanings, yet simultaneously enacts claims of 'neutrality' in relation to each litigant, no prejudgment before a trial, dominant epistemological conceptions of justice, and the necessity of authority to enforce decisions. People 'do not rely on an abstract universal idea of justice' explains Foucault 1980, 8) referring to acts of popular justice. Instead, people rely only on their own experience, that of the injuries they have suffered, that of the way in which they have been wronged, in which they have been oppressed; and finally, their decision is not an authoritative one, that is, they are not backed up by a state apparatus which has the power to enforce their decisions, they purely and simply carry them out.

Foucault raises structural concerns regarding the concept of justice, specifically around processes of deliberation, institutional arrangements and enforcement, which have consequences for the meaning but also how environmental justice brands or directs struggles. What political frameworks govern or represent struggles and what actors does this framework empower? And, like Laura Pulido (2017, 524) contends in the United States, it is questionable over the last 35 years of environmental justice struggles 'if the environments of vulnerable communities have actually improved'.

Similar to extractivism debates, mainstream environmental justice tends to favour industrial capitalism and its corresponding statist infrastructures. Justice presupposes situations that necessitate a mediator or an authority to dispense justice—whether it be environmental, energy, climate, or other varieties of justice (Jenkins et al. 2016). Highlighting this issue, Lina Álvarez and Brendan Coolsaet (2020, 55) explain how solutions to environmental injustice are conceived within the realm of the state, which delimits political autonomy, implies epistemic valuations (and devaluations), and imposes a rights-based framework wedded to bureaucratic administration that affirms statist control (Dunlap, 2021c). The managing of Indigenous territories in North America through the Bureau of Indian Affairs (BIA) in the United States and Department of Indian Affairs and Northern Development in Canada remain notable examples of (neo)colonial control mechanisms (Churchill, 2003; Coulthard, 2014).

All political issues intersect within state governance frameworks (Dunlap, 2021c). Recognising this issue, Temper (2019, 104) explains that 'justice must include self-governing authority; that rather than distribution (of nature), environmental justice calls for breaking down the dualism between humans and nature, and beyond recognition, what is needed is epistemic justice and self-affirmation'. While this expansive version of EJ is highly welcomed, it also refashions the concept of EJ to signify anything related to ecological struggle and environmental liberation. Self-government speaks to autonomous and anarchistic struggle. With the exception of efforts to decolonise (Ulloa, 2017; Pulido, 2017; Temper, 2019; Álvarez and Coolsaet, 2020), environmental justice studies depend on and celebrate the state as a framework of justice or, at the least, EJ is theoretically assuming or systematically ambiguous on the matter of statism.

Distinctions are made between environmental justice movements, environmental conflicts, and NIMBY ('not in my backyard') struggles (Akbulut et al., 2019), yet all environmental conflicts or contestations are labelled as environmental justice struggles in the Environmental Justice Atlas (Scheidel, et al., 2018, 2020; Temper et al., 2020).[9] This risks erasing militant autonomous and anti-colonial actions by absorbing them into justice frameworks, which also tend towards extending normative Western conceptions of 'social movements' that assume a particular form of (bureaucratic) organising and underwriting the prevalence of 'property damage' and 'sabotage' in non-violent political struggles (cf Scheidel et al., 2020).[10] These tactics are legitimate, if dubbed illegal by a system mandating and regulating accelerating extractivism and urbanization (Sovacool and Dunlap, 2022). Individuals and action groups and various militant actions tend to be erased under normative conceptions of social movements (e.g. Gandhian civil disobedience),[11] which ignores or sidelines the multiplicity of self-organisation and/or militancy related to uprisings in general or relegates it to groups in the 'global South' (e.g. Zapatistas or

9 The Invisible Committee (TIC, 2015), while more militant, did a similar thing by relating all riots and uprisings from the period 2009–15 as part of the 'imaginary party' ushering in a new historical epoch.

10 As a contributor to, reader and fan of the EJAtlas, I note that there has been a (strict) non-violence bias built into the questioner, which leaves out the arguably important grey area of vandalism/property destruction instrumental to protest and social change. This issue appears to have been rectified approximately two years ago with the inclusion of 'property destruction/arson' and 'sabotage'. Yet 'property destruction' does not always have to be related to 'arson'. It could be artistic expression and disgruntled public communication.

11 There has been a lack of critical reflection on Gandhi's role (as a colonial collaborator), tactics and general shortcomings by academics and activists (see Gelderloos, 2007).

Indigenous collectives). Raúl Zibechi (2012, 268) counters 'social movement' labelling by describing the multiplicities of struggles and tensions as 'societies in movement', which speaks to the diversity and multiplicity of actors, forms of organisation and methods of fighting. Are all ecological struggles—rooted in autonomous self-determination, militant struggle and insurrectionary action—environmental justice struggles? The line between offering support to those engaged in ecological conflicts and integrating these conflicts into an academic framework and assumed social movement etiquette can reinforce statist/counter-insurgent categories of 'good/bad'[12] protests or actions. This raises questions regarding political strategies (e.g. reinforcing or breaking with parliamentary or colonial governance systems) and the objectives of numerous actors (politicians, NGOs, farmers, anarchists, and the undecided). While many academic and NGOs situate themselves within the environmental justice framework, what are the ideologies, feelings and language propelling these struggles?

The close association of environmental justice with ecological distribution conflicts (EDCs) further enunciates this concern. EDCs are defined by Arnim Scheidel and colleagues (2018, 587) as 'social conflicts arising over the unequal distribution of environmental benefits, such as access to natural resources, fertile land, or ecosystem services, as well as over unequal and unsustainable allocations of environmental burdens, such as pollution or waste'. Ignoring the anthropocentric and utilitarian language of 'ecosystem services' employed, the emphasis on distribution and unequal benefits makes environmental justice susceptible to liberal reformism necessitating statist legal frameworks. The 'state', Ulloa reminds us (2017, 176–7), 'is a principal actor in constructing ideas of territory and nature, and in generating territorial confrontations'. Advocates of environmental justice, critical or otherwise, often find themselves lobbying and demanding that the state pay attention and administer recognition and/or justice. This relates to the monopoly, or partial monopoly, of violence that the state maintains—consequently raising issues of political agency, capabilities to enact self-determination and sustaining politico-ecological autonomy. Reliance on the state, while logical in many ways, potentially forecloses opportunities for political struggle, but—moreover—risks transposing Western conceptions of justice onto long-established customary law and territorial struggles facing counter-insurgency warfare by state and corporate actors. The state organises dependency, imposing its relevance and existence by

12 See Gelderloos (2013; 2022) and Dunlap (2019a) on protest and action standards crafted as 'good/bad'.

enchanting populations, meanwhile dispensing coercion and deception (Kass, 2022). Temper (2019) cogently confronts this tendency within environmental justice studies, yet the justice framework continues to instill real or imagined vulnerabilities within ecological conflicts. 'Epistemic justice', for example, still suffers from the liberal sensibility of 'making visible and politically relevant ways of knowing that have been marginalized as a result of the imposition of a dominant knowledge system over others' (Temper, 2019, 98). Establishing visibility to gain media attention for environmental struggles and preserve (sacred) spiritual, ecological or medicinal knowledge to integrate into state archives or knowledge apparatuses still relies on the myth of liberalism, which forms a scaffolding for colonial/statist society. Foucault ([1978]1998), James Scott (1998; 2009), anarchists (Bonanno, [1977]1998; Green Anarchy Collective, 2012; Loadenthal, 2017), and autonomists (Holloway, 2010; TIC, 2009; Culp, Lana and Rosales, 2015) demonstrate how creating statist 'legibility', or visibility in general, can have a double-edged effect by advancing discursive or material knowledge of people, places and non-humans (branded as 'resources') to statist and corporate powers seeking to enact conquest, control and production strategies. Legibility, cultural visibility, and geographical mapping, it could be argued, are the 'first steps' towards colonial/statist control—the original purpose of (colonial) anthropology and geography![13] As valuable as epistemic justice might be, maybe *epistemic affirmation or evasion* might represent another set of pathways for the long-term survival or resurgence of traditional knowledges, practices and peoples. Authorities cannot conquer or make illegal what they do not know exists. This can be double-edged as well, yet remains another avenue for consideration.

The state, decolonial or otherwise (Anthias, 2018; Vela-Almeida, 2018; Dunlap, 2022), is an extractivist system dependent on particular infrastructural and political forms that, to varying degrees, exemplify resource and energy intensive statist bureaucracies. This presents two substantial barriers to environmental justice. First, the past and present extractivist foundations and evolution of the state, which daily celebrates ecologically unfriendly infrastructures, logistics, and energy use. Second, the problem of 'reason of state' (*raison d'état*), where the state as an entity prioritises its own existence and survival above anything else (Agamben, 2005; Dunlap, 2014). The state, and its reason, is currently threatening the biosphere and climate through its existence and its maintenance and protection of economic actors (Hickel, 2020;

13 See Churchill (2012), Bryan and Wood (2015) and Weston and Djohari (2020) for more on this topic.

Whyte, 2020; Dunlap and Brock, 2022). The problem with environmental justice is the implicit belief that the state is neutral and capable of administering justice, when in reality it is just the opposite (or remains complicit, in areas of 'weak states'), spreading extractivism and material and energy-intensive infrastructures—the imperative of industrial market economies. This is manifest by governments selectively (or under political pressure) administering social justice. Recognising the problem of 'coloniality', Temper (2019, 98)—along with so many others—asserts with (normative) postcolonial logics that 'physical control of territories has ended, the cultural logic of colonialism still operates, and silences other ways of doing, being and knowing'. This standard phrase from decolonial theory, while true, underestimates how modernist infrastructures continue coloniality through the physical control of territories, landscapes, habitats and ecosystems (Dunlap, 2021a, 6)—alluding to 'infrastructural coloniality' and statist hang-ups, reproduced through 'academic decolonial theory', that accept statist and infrastructural domination as acceptable if they are 'non-Western' or 'pluri-national' (Dunlap, 2022, 3, 10–11). This raises issues regarding how people self-identify (Dunlap, 2020). Do people identify with colonial/statist institutions or their infrastructures—'*our* nation', 'democratic' decisions (via voting) and infrastructure—or are they understood as structures of conquest, domestication and ecocidal processes inherited and imposed on one's life? How people relate to, understand and view bureaucracies, modern infrastructures and economies will have significant political consequences.

Scholars have criticised how the principles of environmental justice inadequately address the realities of resource control, racism, patriarchy and militarisation (Pulido and De Lara, 2018; Velicu and Barca, 2020; Brock and Stephens-Griffin, 2021). Transposing ideas of 'environmental equity' that are 'intrinsically linked to an idea of environmental exploitation' to other contexts, Álvarez and Coolsaet (2020, 55) remind us. There is a risks of subordinating or silencing sensitive ecological concerns that reject this exploitation, including those of the more militant and self-determined actors mentioned above (see also Dunlap, (2021d)). The message conveyed, at least by mainstream environmental justice, is 'that this exploitation does not necessarily need questioning as long as its most harmful effects are being distributed equitably within society' (Álvarez and Coolsaet, 2020, 55; Temper, 2019). The central mechanism is compensation, which scholars demonstrate 'commodifies justice in the language of cheap licenses for development projects to operate' (Velicu and Barca, 2020, 265). The fact remains, companies cannot compensate for climate change or watching your friends and family—human and non-human—being wounded (in the broader sense of the word) or killed. Compensation and making equivalences[14] to justify extractive development and conservation enclosures is a notable mechanism for ensuring climate and ecological catastrophe. Compensation, then, emerges as a self-reinforcing socio-technical infrastructure designed to facilitate continued land control and extractivism. Environmental justice, as criticised by Ulloa (2017), Pulido (2017), Temper (2019), Álvarez and Coolsaet (2020), Menton and colleagues (2020), Rodriguez (2020) and Dunlap (2021c), is statist and anthropocentric and, ironically, reinforces modernist development. The result has been an attempt at decolonising environmental justice studies (Ulloa, 2017; Temper, 2019; Álvarez and Coolsaet, 2020; Rodriguez, 2020), in order to respect and afford agency to non-human life, celebrate self-determined autonomy, and allow a total rejection of socio-ecologically destructive development projects. This means drawing on the non-academic works arising from movements and combative communiques (Rodriquez, 2021; Mullenite, 2021; Loadenthal, (2017)). In sum, emphasis on the distribution of socio-ecological harms and benefits as well as inclusive participation within extractive project preserves the modernist project. Moreover, distributive and inclusive EJ approaches can marginalise sensitive ecological concerns, thwart combative energies and finally further mystifies alternative post-developmental pathways. Post-development, again, seeks locally produced, small-scale and non-capitalist solutions to habitation, energy production, medicine and food procurement. Emphasis on distributing the 'costs' and 'benefits' and permitting greater participation within modernist development shields people from the difficult questions of how to stop ecological catastrophe and organise forms of habitation and development complementary to humans, but more so to non-humans (Ulloa, 2020), such as rivers, mountains, trees and the numerous communities of flora and fauna. This is not about what 'people want'—we know that desires are shaped and engineered—but about *how* people can create socio-ecological harmony with our habitats and planet and avoid extractivist approaches that require the exploitation and killing of humans and non-humans.

Environmental justice is about inclusion into the project of modernist development (Temper, 2019), necessitating and expanding extractivism and modernist infrastructures. These distributional and inclusive reforms are obviously welcomed and fought-for social additions, but at the same time they do not adequately challenge the structure of industrial capitalism or the 'Worldeater' (Dunlap and Jakobsen, 2020). Technocapitalism is the elephant in the climate catastrophe room. As Irina Velicu and Stefania Barca (2020, 267) explain, the

14 See Sullivan (2017) for epistemic problems of compensation and offsetting.

emphasis EJ places on compensation, distribution, and procedure, 'tend[s] to lock the working class within a political horizon limited to maintaining the same system, accepting its exploitation and structural inequalities'. Justice theory 'reproduces a paternalistic and inequalitarian logic of emancipation', Velicu and Barca (2020, 268) contend following Jacques Rancière, 'verifying, confirming, and thus, reifying inequalities while setting the ideal of equality in a future that never seems to arrive'. Justice theories tend towards reformism (Brock and Stephens-Griffin, 2021), meanwhile luring people into believing that courts will legislate against extractivism and 'leave it in the ground' so that habitats remain undisturbed and waters uncontaminated. The more common result, however, is that infrastructures of inequality and extractive development are frequently affirmed by courts. The piecemeal and retributive reforms—often fought for militantly—and that keeping mines closed or preventing them from ever (re)opening remains a long-term and continuous struggle, a truth to which the Tía Maria project in Peru (Dunlap, 2019a) and the numerous cases referenced above or documented in the Environmental Justice Atlas can attest (Scheidel et al., 2020). Reforms, when placed next to the coercive violence of riot police, paramilitaries and long prison sentences (Gelderloos, 2022), appear better than the alternatives—and understandably so. This, however, does not change the harsh reality that political violence maintains the present socio-ecological situation (Dunlap and Brock, 2022). Political pacification is constantly hiding behind a veil, changing its clothes, and feeding on our productive energies to perpetuate political economy and its extractive activities.

This issue, as with the debates on extractivism, represents a failure to adequately question the roots of the capitalist machine that is responsible for systematic ecological destruction and inequality. Environmental justice reforms and social development, combined with the political violence of the military, police, and extrajudicial forces, have a way of enticing people to 'sell out' or stop fighting for their habitats and culture, leaving larger technocapitalist structures intact. This acknowledges the psychosocial trap—a sort of 'Stockholm syndrome'—that infrastructures and politics create (Dunlap and Correa-Arce, 2022). The psychosocial trap avoids challenging modernist progress itself and stifles the difficult academic debates around the civilisational, societal or post-developmental transformations necessary to sustain the planet. Infrastructural development, or colonisation (Dunlap, 2020; Dunlap and Correa-Arce, 2022), is an apparatus of social warfare designed to reinforce extractivism, exploitation and planetary ecological conquest.

Critical or decolonial environmental justice seeks to address this destructive gap, but even decolonial theory exclaiming the need for self-determination and statist powers giving 'land back' based on original treaty agreements tends to avoid the issue of capitalist industrialisation by relegating it to Indigenous leadership (see Liboiron (2021)) or non-Western governments (Dunlap, 2022).[15] Indigenous self-determination and returning land is mandatory, but the history of colonial Indigenous administration, (postcolonial) governance, and internalising colonial structures still presents a challenge to those confronting extractivism and modernist development. Cogently provoking the roots upholding the politico-economic structures of conquest, Fredy Perlman (1984, 58) once asked: 'What concentration camp manager, national executioner or torturer is not a descendant of oppressed people?' Decolonial environmental justice, while challenging the environmental justice imperative to include people 'within existing governance structures' and recognising how it 'is a less appropriate fit for the settler-colonial context' as 'Indigenous peoples have to address their claims within a sovereignty they do not recognize' (Temper, 2019, 105), ends up wrongly assuming that statist frameworks, law and institutions are then appropriate for non-Indigenous people. While anti-colonial struggles differ from other anti-capitalist contestations, this categorisation remains divisive. Environmental justice frameworks only being 'a less appropriate fit for the settler-colonial context' ignores autonomous and (eco) anarchist struggles that reject state/corporate governance frameworks and laws, but also the common ground—or complicity—between people that recognise the state and capital as obstructions to socio-ecological well-being. This division, moreover, reveals that it is difficult for people to remember, see or feel how non-indigenous peoples or 'settlers' do not identify with statist institutions, laws and the modernist/extractivist way of life. Let militant autonomist and anarchist struggles across the globe (Holloway, 2010; Loadenthal, 2017; Dunlap, 2022) that reject government itself be a reminder that the issues of state, ecocide and political subjugation are not strictly limited to Indigenous people.[16] While environmental justice studies recognise the need for self-governance within Indigenous territory, the problem of power-hungry politicians, bureaucratic controls, and political pacification techniques still persists, in addition to wider national colonial-political occupation.

Environmental conflicts have movable positions, as already mentioned—subjectivities are influenced, people persuaded and regions shaped to accept extractivist projects (see Verweijen and Dunlap, 2021). Environmental justice, for all its popularity, frequently avoids the difficult questions of challenging

15 For an extended discussion of 'academic decolonial theory' see Dunlap (2022).

16 '[D]ecolonising participatory parity' (Temper, 2019, 105) has arguably been an issue since the rise of democracy as a social control mechanism.

the state and its corresponding infrastructural regimes outside individual projects or the global problem and extractive reality of modernity itself. The by-product of this political preference is omitting autonomist and anarchistic land defenders, either Indigenous or non-Indigenous from the political or academic conversation (Dunlap, 2021d; 2022; Gelderloos, 2022). This presumably is because they reject the existing regime of modernist development, which is conferred an inherently elevated status by industrialised societies and is familiar to the habitus of researchers. Even when environmental justice scholars rightfully reject the state, for example: "[W]e should help expose the fraudulent nature of the state, how it has sought to co-opt EJ communities, its support of racial capitalism and its willingness to forsake poisoned communities" (Pulido, 2017: 530). Anarchists—Indigenous (Dunlap, 2022), black (see Ervin, 2021 [1979]; Anderson, 2021) or otherwise—who have been at war with the state for centuries are omitted, which extends to enduring anarchist anti-colonial action and solidarity (Ó Donghaile, 2010; Ferretti, 2018; Dunlap, 2022). Autonomist and anarchist positions are legitimate, yet frequently mined selectively or buried within environmental justice research.

The task remains—to acknowledge the legitimacy of recalcitrant autonomist positions in permanent conflict, meanwhile theorising and practicing post-development practices that exercise degrowth and convivial infrastructures. Why cling to 'environmental justice' when we are talking about anti-colonial, autonomous, socio-ecological struggles or, even, uncompromising citizen initiatives? While reform positions remain a dominant tendency within environmental conflicts—making environmental justice suitable for a wide audience, even ecocidal governments—why impose a concept of justice, with its colonial, liberal and academic baggage, that necessitates constant reformulations (e.g. critical, decolonial, abolitionist)? Why not call the struggles what they are, foregrounding the uncompromising elements concerned with habitats being consumed by extractivism, infrastructure and technocapitalist projects? Addressing ecological and climate catastrophe means struggling where we live and unravelling the difference between industrialisation and extractivism, and the shortcomings or multiplicities of justice(s), in order to create clear visions of how to create real renewability in our habitats in the best ways possible.

4 Conclusion: New Ways of Conceiving Infrastructure

The socio-ecological impacts of industrialism, capitalism and technological progress are extensive, and the proposed mitigation pathways and discussions—even those proposed by the concept of environmental justice—are either limited or inadequate. This chapter, following Virilio, is a call for greater attention to the daily harms being perpetrated by industrialism and extractive capitalism. Critical approaches, the chapter demonstrates, still suffer from infrastructural coloniality, which underestimates the accumulation and inter-dependence of extractivism(s). This relates to the statism and coloniality of environmental justice frameworks, which tend to enable extractivism and infrastructural domination despite processual and egalitarian concerns. This, moreover, results in subordinating non-human life (including animals, rivers, mountains, trees and habitats) to the desires of various human populations operating under the influence of technocapitalism. Recognising the spaces between extractivism and capitalism remain fundamental for expanding post-development alternatives, while acknowledging the strengths of environmental justice in resisting the expansion of extractivism, but also its discursive and material weak points.

Environmental justice offers important reformist pathways, yet this reformism appears inadequate and anthropocentric. The 'justice' in environmental justice, or in energy justice for that matter (Jenkins et al., 2016),[17] ignores holistic ecological concerns, extensive material requirements for infrastructure and offers an inadequate pathway to the resolution of socio-ecological catastrophe. Decolonial environmental justice scholars acknowledge these issues (cf. Pellow (2016); Ulloa (2017); Pulido (2017), Temper (2019); Álvarez and Coolsaet (2020); Menton et al. (2020) and Rodriguez (2020)), yet further reflection is still warranted. Participatory inclusion, visibility of knowledges, identifying infrastructural coloniality, and designating self-governance and/or the militant rejection of the state solely for Indigenous peoples indicate a need for further reflection on our relationship and integration within technocapitalist systems. At worst, environmental justice studies, thinking of Gelderloos's (2022, 86) critique of NGOs, risk normalising development and state institutions, creating divisions between the Indigenous and non-Indigenous even when these share a common cause, and falling into legal traps of 'good/bad' militant tactics that isolate dedicated land defenders. The act of viewing habitats as commodities or 'ecosystem services' to be controlled and exploited, instead of as *living with* and *a part of us*, remains a pressing issue. The perspective of ecological economics, relying on reductive data sets, high levels of conceptual abstraction, macro/mega level approaches and short-term fieldwork, contributes to these

---

17 For detailed criticism of energy justice please see Tornel (2022) and Partridge (2022). This chapter was written before the publication of these works.

weak points within environmental justice studies. There remains, overall, a discursive and practical risk that reformist approaches are slowly transforming people into accomplices that assist in subjugating ecosystems and people to the trajectory of modernist progress. We have to become more critical of our immediate environments (e.g. Universities) and the materials and energy they use, and transform them in socio-ecologically enriching directions, as challenging as that task may be.

The alternative is to affirm post-development pathways that reject development or create culturally/locally appropriate and convivial developmental solutions that ensure shelter and access to water and high-quality foods, prevent the spread of toxic waste, and affirm ecologically co-creative modes of production and alternative technologies (Kothari et al., 2019; Gelderloos, 2022). This could also be complemented by (decolonial) degrowth approaches (Nirmal and Rocheleau, 2019), which actively seek to re-conceptualise growth and to degrow capitalism, and consequently extractivism (Hickel, 2020; Mastini, Kallis and Hickel, 2021; Trainer, 2019). If public policy has any purpose, thinking of Hickel (2020), it will be to cut back on destructive chemical and extractive industries, eliminate planned obsolescence or 'desired obsolescence' (e.g. product upgrade purchases), revamp repair and recycling processes, recentre development on use value, rather than exchange value, cut the advertising budgets that manufacture mass consumption, and expand public goods and direct democracy. In short, to organise policy that promotes collective emotional and social well-being, with the impacts on ecosystems and the climate as a central priority, because—after all—we are our habitats. We must radically change the material, energy and socio-ecological relationships of existing infrastructures. There are numerous ways to cultivate subjective well-being, yet—as has been known for some time—market democracies tend to generate social discontent, dependency and addiction (Lane, 2000; Alexander, 2008). Ecological crisis, social uprisings, depression, anxiety and ill health are opportunities to create socio-technical and ecological change, to use critical knowledge to make genuine social change to remediate harms, restore ecosystems, and create socio-ecological systems and forms of habitation that are genuinely renewable. If these changes are not made—where rebellion, suicide, and cries for help are met with political violence—if we pretend that structural issues do not exist, and if, overall, we intensify matters through the European Green Deal and UN Sustainable Development Goals, then the road to immiseration will be affirmed, and only dystopia awaits.

Acknowledgements

I am grateful for the comments, patience and support offered by the editors, Matthew Archer and Filipe Calvão. This chapter benefited greatly from the edits and comments of, and discussions with, Philippe Le Billon and Sage. The time, energy and suggestions of the two reviewers contributed to the text of this chapter, especially their in-text comments, which proved constructive and productively stimulating—a luxurious benefit to have during a review process, thank you. Lastly, I am grateful for Sabo's companionship and care that makes its way into this chapter.

References

Agamben, G. (2005) *State of Exception* (Chicago: University of Chicago Press).

Akbulut, B., F. Demaria, J.-F. Gerber and J. Martínez-Alier (2019) 'Who Promotes Sustainability? Five Theses on the Relationships Between the Degrowth and the Environmental Justice Movements', *Ecological Economics*, 165(1), pp. 1–12, DOI: 10.1016/j.ecolecon.2019.106418.

Alexander, B.K. (2008) *The Globalization of Addiction: a Study in Poverty of the Spirit* (New York: Oxford University Press).

Álvarez, L. and B. Coolsaet (2020) 'Decolonizing environmental justice studies: a Latin American perspective', *Capitalism Nature Socialism*, 31, pp. 50–69.

Anand, N., A. Gupta and H. Appel (2018) *The Promise of Infrastructure* (Durham: Duke University Press).

Anderson, W.C. (2021) *The nation on no map: Black anarchism and abolition* (Chico: AK Press).

Anthias, P. (2018) *Limits to Decolonization: Indigeneity, Territory, and Hydrocarbon Politics in the Bolivian Chaco* (Ithaca, New York: Cornell University Press).

Bell, S.E., C. Daggett and C. Labuski (2020) 'Toward Feminist Energy Systems: Why Adding Women and Solar Panels is Not Enough', *Energy Research & Social Science*, 68, pp. 1–13.

Bernays, E. (2005 [1928]) *Propaganda* (New York: Ig Publishing).

Blaser, M. (2013) 'Notes Toward a Political Ontology of 'Environmental' Conflicts', in L. Green (ed.) *Contested Ecologies: Dialogues in the South on Nature and Knowledge* (Cape Town: HSRC Press), pp. 13–27.

Böhm, S. and S. Sullivan (2021) *Negotiating Climate Change in Crisis* (London: Open Book Publishers).

Bolger, M., D. Marin, A. Tofighi-Niaki and L. Seelmann (2021) *'Green mining' is a myth: the case for cutting EU resource consumption*, European Environmental Bureau

& Friends of the Earth Europe, https://eeb.org/wp-content/uploads/2021/10/Green-mining-report_EEB-FoEE-2021.pdf (accessed on 20 October 2021).

Bonanno, A.M. (1998 [1977]) *Armed Joy* (London: Elephant Editions).

Brock A. (2023) *Life at Lützerath*, The Ecologist, https://theecologist.org/2023/jan/19/life-lutzerath (accessed on 28 February 2023).

Brock, A. (2020) "Frack off": towards an Anarchist Political Ecology Critique of Corporate and State Responses to Anti-fracking Resistance in the UK', *Political Geography*, 82, pp. 1–20, DOI: 10.1016/j.polgeo.2020.102246.

Brock, A. and A. Dunlap (2018) 'Normalising Corporate Counterinsurgency: Engineering Consent, Managing Resistance and Greening Destruction around the Hambach Coal Mine and beyond', *Political Geography*, 62(1), pp. 33–47, DOI: 10.1016/j.polgeo.2017.09.018.

Brock, A. and N. Stephens-Griffin (2021) *Policing Environmental Injustice*, IDS Bulletin, pp. 1–20, DOI: 10.19088/1968-2021.130.

Brown, A. (2021) *Corporate Counterinsurgency: Indigenous Water Protectors Face Off With an Oil Company and Police Over a Minnesota Pipeline*, The Intercept, 7 July, https://theintercept.com/2021/07/07/line-3-pipeline-minnesota-counterinsurgency/ (accessed on 10 October 2022).

Brown, A., W. Parrish and A. Speri (2017) *Leaked Documents Reveal Counterterrorism Tactics Used at Standing Rock to 'Defeat Pipeline Insurgencies'*, The Intercept, 27 May, https://theintercept.com/2017/05/27/leaked-documents-reveal-security-firms-counterterrorism-tactics-at-standing-rock-to-defeat-pipeline-insurgencies/ (accessed on 10 October 2022).

Bryan, J. and D. Wood (2015) *Weaponizing Maps: Indigenous peoples and Counterinsurgency in the Americas* (New York: The Guilford Press).

Chagnon, C.W., F. Durante, B.K. Gills, S.E. Hagolani-Albov, S. Hokkanen, S.M.J. Kangasluoma, H. Konttinen, M. Kröger, W. LaFleur, O. Ollinaho and M.P.S. Vuola (2022) 'From Extractivism to Global Extractivism: the Evolution of an Organizing Concept', *The Journal of Peasant Studies*, 49(4), pp. 1–34, DOI: 10.1080/03066150.2022.2069015.

Childs, J. (2019) 'Greening the Blue? Corporate Strategies for Legitimising Deep Sea Mining', *Political Geography*, 74, pp. 1–11, DOI: 10.1016/j.polgeo.2019.102060.

Conde, M. and P. Le Billon (2017) 'Why Do Some Communities Resist Mining Projects While Others Do Not?' *The Extractive Industries and Society*, 4(3), pp. 681–697, DOI: 10.1016/j.exis.2017.04.009.

Coulthard, G.S. (2014) *Red Skin, White Masks: Rejecting the Colonial Politics of Recognition* (Minneapolis: Minnesota University Press).

Churchill, W. (2003) *Acts of Rebellion: the Ward Churchill Reader* (New York: Routledge).

Churchill, W. (2012) 'Confronting Western Colonialism, American Racism, and White Supremacy: Ward Churchill and Pierre Orelus in Dialogue', in P.W. Orelus (ed.) *A Decolonizing Encounter: Ward Churchill and Antonia Darder in Dialogue* (New York: Peter Lang), pp. 56–112.

Cullather, N. (2013) *The Hungry World: America's Cold War Battle Against Poverty in Asia* (Cambridge: Harvard University Press).

Culp, A., E.D. Lana and J. Rosales (2015) *Hostis 2: Beyond Recognition* (Berkeley: Ardent Press).

Deloria, V. (1999) *Spirit & Reason: the Vine Deloria, Jr., Reader* (Golden: Fulcrum Publishing).

Dunlap, A. (2022) "I don't want your progress! It tries to kill … me!' Decolonial Encounters and the Anarchist Critique of Civilization', *Globalizations*, pp. 1–27, DOI: 10.1080/14747731.2022.2073657.

Dunlap, A. (2021a) 'Spreading 'Green' Infrastructural Harm: Mapping Conflicts and Socio-ecological Disruptions within the European Union's Transnational Energy Grid', *Globalizations*, pp. 1–25, DOI: 10.1080/14747731.14742021.11996518.

Dunlap, A. (2021b) 'Book Review: the political economy of agrarian extractivism: Lessons from Bolivia, by Ben McKay', *Journal of Agrarian Change*, pp. 1–6.

Dunlap, A. (2021c) 'Toward an Anarchist Decolonization: a Few Notes', *Capitalism Nature Socialism*, 32(4), pp. 62–72, DOI: 10.1080/10455752.2021.1879186.

Dunlap, A. (2021d) 'More Wind Energy Colonialism(s) in Oaxaca? Reasonable Findings, Unacceptable Development', *Energy Research & Social Science*, 82, 102304, DOI: 10.1016/j.erss.2021.102304.

Dunlap, A. (2020) 'The Politics of Ecocide, Genocide and Megaprojects: Interrogating Natural Resource Extraction, Identity and the Normalization of Erasure', *Journal of Genocide Research*, 23(2), pp. 212–235, DOI: 10.1080/14623528.2020.1754051.

Dunlap, A. (2019a) "Agro sí, mina NO!' The Tía Maria Copper Mine, State Terrorism and Social War by Every Means in the Tambo Valley, Peru', *Political Geography*, 71, pp. 10–25, DOI: 10.1016/j.polgeo.2019.02.001.

Dunlap, A. (2019b) *Renewing Destruction: Wind Energy Development, Conflict and Resistance in a Latin American Context* (London: Rowman & Littlefield).

Dunlap, A. (2018) 'Insurrection for Land, Sea and Dignity: Resistance and Autonomy against Wind Energy in Álvaro Obregón, Mexico', *Journal of Political Ecology*, 25(1), pp. 120–143, DOI: 10.2458/v25i1.22863.

Dunlap, A. (2014) 'Permanent War: Grids, Boomerangs, and Counterinsurgency', *Anarchist Studies*, 22(2), pp. 55–79.

Dunlap, A. and A. Brock (2022) *Enforcing Ecocide: Power, Police and Planetary Militarization* (Cham: Palgrave).

Dunlap, A. and D. Marin (2022) 'Comparing Coal and 'Transition Materials'? Overlooking Complexity, Flattening Reality and Ignoring Capitalism', *Energy Research & Social Science*, 89, pp. 1–9, DOI: 10.1016/j.erss.2022.102531.

Dunlap, A. and J. Jakobsen (2020) *The Violent Technologies of Extraction: Political Ecology, Critical Agrarian Studies and The Capitalist Worldeater* (London: Palgrave).

Dunlap, A. and L. Laratte (2022) 'European Green Deal necropolitics: Exploring 'Green' Energy Transition, Degrowth & Infrastructural Colonization', *Political Geography*, 97(1), pp. 1–17.

Dunlap, A. and M. Correa-Arce (2022) "Murderous Energy' in Oaxaca, Mexico: Wind Factories, Territorial Struggle and Social Warfare', *Journal of Peasant Studies*, 49(2), pp. 455–480, DOI: 10.1080/03066150.2020.1862090.

EC (European Commission) (2020) *Critical Raw Materials for Strategic Technologies and Sectors in the EU—A Foresight Study* (Brussels: European Comission), https://ec.europa.eu/docsroom/documents/42881 (accessed on 15 September 2021).

E&M (*Energy and Mines Magazine*) (2022) '19 Recently announced renewables in mining projects and commitments by Australian mines', *Energy and Mines Magazine*, 41–19, https://energyandmines.com/2022/05/energy-and-mines-magazine-issue-41/ (accessed on 10 October 2022).

Equinor (2022) *Energy Transition Plan*, 22 March, (Stavanger, Norway: Equinor), https://www.equinor.com/content/dam/statoil/documents/sustainability/energy-transition-plan-2022-equinor.pdf (accessed on 10 October 2022).

Ervin, L.K. (2021 [1979]) *Anarchism and the Black revolution* (London: Pluto).

Escobar, A. (2020) *Pluriversal Politics* (Durham: Duke University Press).

EXALT (2020) *Video EXALT Symposium 2020: Opening Plenary: Roundtable Discussion* (Helsinki: University of Helsinki), https://www.youtube.com/watch?v=7XMMyyv_bSQ (accessed on 10 October 2022).

Ferretti, F. (2018) 'Revolutions and their places: the anarchist geographers and the problem of nationalities in the Age of Empire (1875–1914)', in: F. Ferretti, G. Barrera, A. Ince and F. Toro (eds.) *Historical geographies of anarchism—Early critical geographers and present-day scientific challenges* (Abingdon: Routledge), pp. 113–128.

Foucault, M. (1998 [1978]) *The Will To Knowledge: the History of Sexuality: 1* (London: Penguin Books).

Foucault, M. (1980 [1972]) 'On Popular Justice: a Discussion with Maoists', in C. Gordon (ed.) *Power/Knowledge: Selected Interviews & Other Writings, 1972–1977* (New York: Pantheon Books), pp. 1–36.

Frederiksen, T. and M. Himley (2020) 'Tactics of Dispossession: Access, Power, and Subjectivity at the Extractive Frontier', *Transactions of the Institute of British Geographers*, 45(1), pp. 50–64, DOI: 10.1111/tran.12329.

Geenen, S. and J. Verweijen (2017) 'Explaining Fragmented and Fluid Mobilization in Gold Mining Concessions in Eastern Democratic Republic of the Congo' *The Extractive Industries and Society*, 4(4), pp. 758–765, DOI: 10.1016/j.exis.2017.07.006.

Gelderloos, P. (2022) *The Solutions Are Already Here: Strategies of Ecological Revolution from Below* (London: Pluto).

Gelderloos, P. (2013) *The Failure of Nonviolence. From the Arab Spring to Occupy* (St. Louis: Left Bank Books).

Gelderloos, P. (2007) *How Nonviolence Protects the State* (Zinelibrary.info).

Green Anarchy Collective (2012) *Uncivilized: the Best of Green Anarchy* (Berkeley: Ardent Press).

Grosfoguel, R. (2016) 'Del extractivismo económico al extractivismo epistémico y ontológico', *Revista Internacional de Comunicación y Desarrollo* (*RICD*), 1, pp. 123–143.

Gudynas, E. (2021) *Extractivism: Politics Economy and Ecology* (Black Point: Fernwood Publishing).

Gudynas, E. (2009) 'Diez tesis urgentes sobre el nuevo extractivismo', in J. Schuldt, A. Acosta and A. Barandiarán (eds.) *Extractivismo, política y sociedad* (Quito: Centro Andino de Acción Popular (CAAP) and Centro Latinoamericano de Ecología Social (CLAES)).

Hall, R., M. Edelman, S.M. Borras, I. Scoones, B. White and W. Wolford (2015) 'Resistance, Acquiescence or Incorporation? An Introduction to Land Grabbing and Political Reactions 'from Below'', *Journal of Peasant Studies*, 42, pp. 467–488, DOI: 10.1080/03066150.2015.1036746.

Harvey, P. and H. Knox (2012) 'The Enchantments of Infrastructure', *Mobilities*, 7(4), pp. 521–536, DOI: 10.1080/17450101.2012.718935.

Hatfield, S.C., E. Marino, K. P. Whyte, K.D. Dello and P.W. Mote (2018) 'Indian Time: Time, Seasonality, and Culture in Traditional Ecological Knowledge of Climate Change', *Ecological Processes*, 7, pp. 1–11, DOI: 10.1186/s13717-018-0136-6.

Herman, E.S. and N. Chomsky (2010 [1989]) *Manufacturing Consent: the Political Economy of the Mass Media* (New York: Random House).

Hickel, J. (2020) *Less is More: How Degrowth Will Save the World* (London: Random House).

Holloway, J. (2010) *Crack Capitalism* (London: Pluto).

Huff, A. and Y. Orengo (2020) 'Resource Warfare, Pacification and the Spectacle of 'Green' Development: Logics of Violence in Engineering Extraction in Southern Madagascar', *Political Geography*, 81, 102195, DOI: 10.1016/j.polgeo.2020.102195.

Hund, K., D. La Porta, T.P. Fabregas, T. Laing and J. Drexhage (2020) Minerals for Climate Action: the Mineral Intensity of the Clean Energy Transition (Washington D.C.: The World Bank Group), http://pubdocs.worldbank.org/en/961711588875536384/Minerals-for-Climate-Action-The-Mineral-Intensity-of-the-Clean-Energy-Transition.pdf (accessed on 16 November 2020).

IGD (2021) 'Canadian Tire Fire #20: Floods in Southern BC, Raids on Wet'suwet'en Territory, #AllOutForWedzinKwa Solidarity Actions Spread', *IGD*, 22 November, https://itsgoingdown.org/canadian-tire-fire-20/ (accessed on 10 October 2022).

Jacke, D. and E. Toensmeier (2005) *Edible Forest Gardens, Volume II: Ecological Design and Practice for Temperate-Climate Permaculture* (Burlington: Chelsea Green Publishing).

Jakobsen L.J. (2022) 'Extractive subjectivity in a corporate coal mining site in Colombia', *Geoforum*, pp. 1–10, DOI: 10.1016/j.geoforum.2022.07.007.

Jakobsen, L.J. (2020) 'Corporate Security Technologies: Managing Life and Death along a Colombian Coal Railway', *Political Geography*, 83, pp. 1–10, DOI: 10.1016/j.polgeo.2020.102273.

Jenkins, K., D. McCauley, R. Heffron, H. Stephan and R. Rehner (2016) 'Energy Justice: a Conceptual Review', *Energy Research & Social Science*, 11, pp. 174–182, DOI: 10.1016/j.erss.2015.10.004.

Jensen, D. (2006) *Endgame, Vol. 1: the Problem of Civilisation* (New York: Seveb Stories Press).

Kallianos, Y., A. Dunlap and D. Dalakoglou (2022) 'Introducing Infrastructural Harm: Rethinking Moral Entanglements, Spatio-Temporal Modalities, and Resistance(s)', *Globalizations*, pp. 1–24, DOI: 10.1080/14747731.2022.2153493.

Kass, H. (2022) 'Food anarchy and the State Monopoly on Hunger', *The Journal of Peasant Studies*, pp. 1–20, DOI: 10.1080/03066150.2022.2101099.

Kaur, R. (2021) 'Nuclear Necropower: the Engineering of Death Conditions around a Nuclear Power Plant in South India', *Political Geography*, 85(1), pp. 1–12, DOI: 10.1016/j.polgeo.2020.102315.

Kothari, A., A. Salleh, A. Escobar, F. Demaria and A. Acosta (2019) *Pluriverse: a Post-Development Dictionary* (Delhi: University of Colombia Press).

Kröger, M. (2022) *Extractivisms, Existences and Extinctions: Monoculture Plantations and Amazon Deforestation* (London: Routledge).

Kröger, M. (2021) *Iron Will: Global Extractivism and Mining Resistance in Brazil and India* (Ann Arbor: University of Michigan Press).

LaDuke, W. and D. Cowen (2020) 'Beyond Wiindigo.Infrastructure', *South Atlantic Quarterly*, 119(2), pp. 243–268, DOI: 10.1215/00382876-8177747.

LaDuke, W. and S.A. Cruz (2012) *The Militarization of Indian Country* (East Lansing: Michigan State University Press).

Lane, R.E. (2000) *The Loss of Happiness in Market Democracies* (New Haven: Yale University Press).

Lang, M. and D. Mokrani (2013) *Beyond Development: Alternative Visions from Latin America* (Amsterdam: Transnational Institute).

Larsen, P.B., T. Haller and A. Kothari (2022) 'Sanctioning Disciplined Grabs (SDG s): from SDGs as Green Anti-Politics Machine to Radical Alternatives?', *Geoforum*, 131, pp. 20–26, DOI: 10.1016/j.geoforum.2022.02.007.

Le Billon, P. and M. Sommerville (2017) 'Landing Capital and Assembling 'Investable Land' in the Extractive and Agricultural Sectors', *Geoforum*, 82, pp. 212–224, DOI: 10.1016/j.geoforum.2016.08.011.

Leifsen, E. (2020) 'The Socionature That Neo-Extractivism Can See: Practicing Redistribution and Compensation Around Large-Scale Mining in the Southern Ecuadorian Amazon', *Political Geography*, 82(1), pp. 1–12, DOI: 10.1016/j.polgeo.2020.102249.

Liboiron, M. (2021) *Pollution Is Colonialism* (Durham: Duke University Press).

Loadenthal, M. (2017) *The Politics of the Attack: Communiqués and Insurrectionary Violence* (Manchester: Manchester University Press).

Lockyer, J. and J.R. Veteto (2013) *Environmental Anthropology Engaging Ecotopia: Bioregionalism, Permaculture, and Ecovillages* (Berghahn: Berghahn Books).

MAC (Mining Association of Canada) (2021) *Before it's yours, it's mined*, 30 September, https://mining.ca/resources/posters/before-its-yours-its-mined/ (accessed on 10 October 2022).

Mastini, R., G. Kallis and J. Hickel (2021) 'A Green New Deal without growth?', *Ecological Economics*, 179, pp. 1–9, DOI: 10.1016/j.ecolecon.2020.106832.

McKay, B.M. (2020) *The Political Economy of Agrarian Extractivism: Lessons from Bolivia* (Rugby: Practical Action Publishing Limited).

Menton, M., C. Larrea, S. Latorre, J. Martinez-Alier, M. Peck, L. Temper and M. Walter (2020) 'Environmental Justice and the SDGs: from Synergies to Gaps and Contradictions', *Sustainability Science*, 15, pp. 1621–1636, DOI: 10.1007/s11625-020-00789-8.

Menton M. and P. Le Billon (2021) *Environmental Defenders: Deadly Struggles for Life and Territory* (London: Routledge).

Mullenite, J. (2021) 'Toward Broader Anarchist Geographies', *ACME: an International Journal for Critical Geographies*, 20(2), pp. 206–213.

Mulvaney, D. (2019) *Solar Power: Innovation, Sustainability, and Environmental Justice* (Berkeley: University of California Press).

Nirmal, P. and D. Rocheleau (2019) 'Decolonizing Degrowth in the Post-Development Convergence: Questions, Experiences, and Proposals from Two Indigenous Territories', *Environment and Planning E: Nature and Space*, 2(3), pp. 465–492, DOI: 10.1177/2514848618819478.

Nygren, A., M. Kröger and B. Gills (2022) 'Global Extractivisms and Transformative Alternatives', *The Journal of Peasant Studies*, 49(4), pp. 734–759, DOI: 10.1080/03066150.2022.2069495.

Ó Donghaile, D. (2010) 'Anarchism, anti-imperialism and "The Doctrine of Dynamite"', *Journal of Postcolonial Writing*, 46(3–4), pp. 291–302, DOI: 10.1080/17449855.2010.482380.

OWD (Our World in Data) (2021a) *Metal Production over the Long Term, World, 1880 to 2013* (Oxford: University of Oxford), https://ourworldindata.org/grapher/metal-production-long-term (accessed on 10 October 2022).

OWD (Our World in Data) (2021b) *Global Energy Consumption: How Much Energy Does the World Consume?* (Oxford: University of Oxford), https://ourworldindata.org/energy-production-consumption (accessed on 10 October 2022).

Pape, R.A. (1993) 'Why Japan Surrendered', *International Security*, 18(2), pp. 154–201, DOI: 10.2307/2539100.

Partridge, T. (2022) *Energy and Environmental Justice Movements, Solidarities, and Critical Connections* (Cham: Palgrave McMillan).

Pellow, D.N. (2016) 'Toward a Critical Environmental Justice Studies: Black Lives Matter as an Environmental Justice Challenge', *Du Bois Review: Social Science Research on Race*, 13(2), pp. 221–236, DOI: 10.1017/S1742058X1600014X.

Perlman, F. (1984) *The Continuing Appeal of Nationalism* (Ferndale: Fifth Estate).

Prause, L. and P. Le Billon (2021) 'Struggles for Land: Comparing Resistance Movements Against Agro-Industrial and Mining Investment Projects', *The Journal of Peasant Studies*, 48(5), pp. 1100–1123, DOI: 10.1080/03066150.2020.1762181.

Pulido, L. (2017) 'Geographies of race and ethnicity II: Environmental racism, racial capitalism and state-sanctioned violence', *Progress in Human Geography*, 41(4), pp. 524–533, DOI: 10.1177/0309132516646495.

Pulido, L. and J. De Lara (2018) 'Reimagining 'Justice' in Environmental Justice: Radical Ecologies, Decolonial Thought, and the Black Radical Tradition', *Environment and Planning E: Nature and Space*, 1(1–2), pp. 76–98, DOI: 10.1177/2514848618770363.

Rajak, D. (2011) *In Good Company: an Anatomy of Corporate Social Responsibility* (Palo Alto: Stanford University Press).

Reyes, B.V. and R.A. Santamaría (2020) 'Liberación de la Madre Tierra: Resistencia del pueblo nasa en el Norte del Cauca', *Revista Estudios Socio-Jurídicos*, 22(1), pp. 203–231, DOI: 10.12804/revistas.urosario.edu.co/sociojuridicos/a.7641.

Rodriguez, I. (2020) 'Latin American Decolonial Environmental Justice', in B. Coolsaet (ed.) *Environmental Justice* (London: Routledge), pp. 78–93.

Rosset, P.M. and M.A. Altieri (2017) *Agroecology: Science and Politics* (Rugby: Practical Action Publishing).

Rubenstein, M., B. Robbins and S. Beal (2015) 'Infrastructuralism: An Introduction', *Modern Fiction Studies*, 61(4), pp. 575–586. https://www.jstor.org/stable/26421821.

Scheidel, A., D. Del Bene, J. Liu, G. Navas, S. Mingorría, F. Demaria, S. Avila, B. Roy, I. Ertör, L. Temper and J. Martínez-Alier (2020) 'Environmental Conflicts and Defenders: a Global Overview', *Global Environmental Change*, 63, pp. 1–12, DOI: 10.1016/j.gloenvcha.2020.102104.

Scheidel, A., L. Temper, F. Demaria and J. Martinez-Alier (2018) 'Ecological Distribution Conflicts as Forces for Sustainability: an Overview and Conceptual Framework', *Sustainability Science*, 13(3), pp. 585–598, DOI: 10.1007/s11625-017-0519-0.

Schöneberg, J., D. Haudenschild, H. Darvishi, S. Momeni and A. Ziai (2022) 'The Many Faces of Post-Development: Alternatives to Development in Tanzania, Iran and Haiti', *Sustainability Science*, pp. 1223–1234, DOI: 10.1007/s11625-022-01164-5.

Scott, J.C. (2009) *The Art of Not Being Governed: an Anarchist History of Upland Southeast Asia* (New Haven: Yale University Press).

Scott, J.C. (1998) *Seeing Like a State: How Certain Schemes to Improve the Human Condition Have Failed* (New Haven: Yale University Press).

Simpson, M. (2019) 'Resource Desiring Machines: the Production of Settler Colonial Space, Violence, and the Making of a Resource in the Athabasca Tar Sands', *Political Geography*, 74, pp. 1–12, DOI: 10.1016/j.polgeo.2019.102044.

Simpson, L.B. (2014) 'Land as Pedagogy: Nishnaabeg Intelligence and Rebellious Transformation', *Decolonization: Indigeneity, Education & Society*, 3(3), https://jps.library.utoronto.ca/index.php/des/article/view/22170 (accessed on 10 October 2022).

Simpson, M. and P. Le Billon (2021) 'Reconciling Violence: Policing the Politics of Recognition', *Geoforum*, 119, pp. 111–121, DOI: 10.1016/j.geoforum.2020.12.023.

Springer, S., J. Mateer, M. Locret-Collet and M. Acker (2021) *Undoing Human Supremacy: Anarchist Political Ecology in the Face of Anthroparchy* (London: Rowman & Littlefield).

Sovacool, B.K. and A. Dunlap (2022) 'Anarchy, war, or revolt? Radical perspectives for climate protection, insurgency and civil disobedience in a low-carbon era', *Energy Research & Social Science*, 86, pp. 1–17, DOI: 10.1016/j.erss.2021.102416.

Stoddard, I., K. Anderson, S. Capstick, et al. (2021) 'Three Decades of Climate Mitigation: Why Haven't We Bent the Global Emissions Curve?', *Annual Review of Environment and Resources*, 46, pp. 653–689, DOI: 10.1146/annurev-environ-012220-011104.

Stone, G.D. (2022) 'Surveillance Agriculture and Peasant Autonomy', *Journal of Agrarian Change*, 22(3), pp. 1–24, DOI: 10.1111/joac.12470.

Sullivan, S. (2017) 'What's Ontology Got to Do With It? On Nature and Knowledge in a Political Ecology of the 'Green Economy'', *Journal of Political Ecology*, 24(1), pp. 217–242, DOI: 10.2458/v24i1.20802.

Tarvainen, A. (2022) 'The Modern/Colonial Hell of Innovation Economy: Future as a Return to Colonial Mythologies', *Globalizations*, pp. 1–23, DOI: 10.1080/14747731.2022.2048460.

Temper, L. (2019) 'Blocking Pipelines, Unsettling Environmental Justice: from Rights of Nature to Responsibility to Territory', *Local Environment*, 24(2), pp. 94–112, DOI: 10.1080/13549839.2018.1536698.

Temper, L., S. Avila, D. Del Bene, et al. (2020) 'Movements Shaping Climate Futures: a Systematic Mapping of Protests Against Fossil Fuel and Low-Carbon Energy Projects', *Environmental Research Letters*, 15(12), pp. 1–23, DOI: 10.1088/1748-9326/abc197.

TIC (The Invisible Committee) (2015) *To Our Friends* (Los Angeles: Semiotext(e)).

TIC (The Invisible Committee) (2009) *The coming insurrection* (Los Angeles: Semiotext(e)).

Tornel, C. (2020) 'Petro-populism and infrastructural energy landscapes: the case of Mexico's Dos Bocas Refinery', *Nordia Geographical Publications*, 49(5), pp. 6–31, DOI: 10.30671/nordia.98353.

Tornel, C. (2022) 'Decolonizing energy justice from the ground up: Political ecology, ontology, and energy landscapes', *Progress in Human Geography*, 47(1), pp. 43–65, DOI: 10.1177/03091325221132561.

Trainer, T. (2019) 'Remaking Settlements for Sustainability: the Simpler Way', *Journal of Political Ecology*, 26(1), pp. 202–223, DOI: 10.2458/v26i1.22972.

Ulloa, A. (2020) 'The Rights of the Wayúu People and Water in the Context of Mining in La Guajira, Colombia: Demands of Relational Water Justice', *Human Geography*, 13(1), pp. 6–15, DOI: 10.1177/1942778620910894.

Ulloa, A. (2017) 'Perspectives of Environmental Justice from Indigenous Peoples of Latin America: a Relational Indigenous Environmental Justice', *Environmental Justice*, 10(6), pp. 175–180, DOI: 10.1089/env.2017.0017.

Vela-Almeida, D. (2018) 'Territorial Partitions, the Production of Mining Territory and the Building of a Post-Neoliberal and Plurinational State in Ecuador', *Political Geography*, 62, pp. 126–136, DOI: 10.1016/j.polgeo.2017.10.011.

Velicu, I. and S. Barca (2020) 'The Just Transition and Its Work of Inequality', *Sustainability: Science, Practice and Policy*, 16(1), pp. 263–273, DOI: 10.1080/15487733.2020.1814585.

Verweijen, J. and A. Dunlap (2021) 'The Evolving Techniques of the Social Engineering of Extraction: Introducing Political (Re)actions 'from Above' in Large-Scale Mining and Energy Projects', *Political Geography*, 88, pp. 1–9, DOI: 10.1016/j.polgeo.2021.102342.

Virilio, P. (2008 [1983]) *Pure War* (Los Angeles: Semiotext(e)).

Whyte, D. (2020) *Ecocide: Kill the Corporation Before It Kills Us* (Manchester: Manchester University Press).

Weston, G. and N. Djohari (2020) *Anthropological Controversies: the "Crimes" and Misdemeanors that Shaped a Discipline* (London: Routledge).

Wiegink, N. (2020) 'Learning Lessons and Curbing Criticism: Legitimizing Involuntary Resettlement and Extractive Projects in Mozambique', *Political Geography*, 81, 102192, DOI: 10.1016/j.polgeo.2020.102192.

Wolfe, P. (2006) 'Settler Colonialism and the Elimination of the Native', *Journal of Genocide Research*, 8(4), pp. 387–409, DOI: 10.1080/14623520601056240.

Ye, J., J.D. van der Ploeg, S. Schneider and T. Shanin (2020) 'The Incursions of Extractivism: Moving from Dispersed Places to Global Capitalism', *The Journal of Peasant Studies*, 47(1), pp. 155–183, DOI: 10.1080/03066150.2018.1559834.

Zibechi, R. (2012) *Territories in Resistance: a Cartography of Latin American Social Movements* (Oakland: AK Press).

CHAPTER 4

Logics of Extraction and of the Valorisation of Culture: the Role of Post-extraction Investment in the Creation of Inequality in China

Ryan Parsons

Abstract

What sort of social and economic arrangements are enabled by an extractive economy and its successors? How are patterns of social stratification influenced by these processes? Drawing on ethnographic evidence collected in a tourist destination town in Yunnan that is surrounded by iron mines, I argue that the underlying logics of extractivism persist into the development of a service sector economy (in this case, tourism). The specific case documents economic and social change in a community being reshaped by an emergent cultural tourism industry. New logics of extractivism are motivated by an assumption that peripheral capital is raw and unchanging and exists to be processed, monetised, and consumed by core elites. Even as the makeup of economic sectors change, the national periphery continues to be a site of raw resources to be extracted and valorised by elites and other stakeholders from urban cores. The effect of this extractive tourism industry is to flatten, ossify, and 'legibilise' culture in ways that prioritise performance and experience over the agency of local people. The resulting reformation of cultural practice creates new forms of inequality, here marked by gender and ethnicity.

1 Introduction

What sort of social and economic arrangements are enabled by an extractive economy and its successors? How are patterns of social stratification influenced by these processes? Drawing on ethnographic evidence collected in a tourist destination town in Yunnan, China, that is surrounded by iron mines, I document how the evolution of state-controlled mining industries enables state capacity expansions that are marked by increasing inequality between core and periphery, increasingly centralised control over local cultural life, and the entanglement of these process within larger national transformations. I approach the role of extractivism in this context starting from the

© GENEVA GRADUATE INSTITUTE, 2024 | DOI:10.1163/9789004686182_005

internal colonialism framework as initiated by Clark (1989) and Hechter (1999). Building on past analysis of how subnational development follows an exploitative, colonial trajectory, I ask how the transition out of a primary industry extractivism (in this case, mining) towards a service economy (here marked by ethnic and cultural tourism) carries forward the same logics of extraction. The central thesis of this analysis is that development out of extractivism risks ossifying an orientation towards peripheral economies in which all life in the periphery can be processed and consumed by urban elites. In such a case, rural development becomes halted, delayed, or redirected as development patterns adhere to the interest of urban elites, absentee capitalists, and state power. The extraction that follows can be described as a form of *cultural extraction*: cultural forms are reduced to easily managed, predictable units for consumption by urban-based tourists who use these brief experiences as a vehicle for making meaning out of their own lives. In order for this venture to succeed, cultural and social development must be arrested and governed to ensure a reliable experience for urban consumers. This 'arresting' functions to represent a local culture as pre-modern, authentic, or otherwise uninfluenced by the modernisation and development associated with urban cores. The chapter proceeds as follows. First, I synthesise the relevant literature on internal colonialism and extractivism in order to provide a theoretical foundation for the chapter's argument. Then I introduce the case and analytic strategies used. Finally, I explore how this argument unfolds in cultural industries in a complex ethnic hierarchy, before concluding with implications for development policy. In particular, I suggest that development policy meant to promote transitions to more equitable economic structures runs the risk of reproducing and entrenching underlying dynamics of inequality.

2 State Formation and Cultural Extractivism

Extractivism and its entanglement with development processes have been a common concern for social scientists, particularly with regard to cases drawn from Latin America. The present literature review surveys relevant arguments related to extractivism and its critiques, then highlights elements of the internal colonialism literature as a means to extend critique of extractivism to the present case. The literature review suggests two intertwined questions: As local and regional economies transition out of an extractive (primary) economy, how does the underlying ideological orientation that structures extractivism persist? Secondly, how does the conceptual schematic of state formation described in the internal colonialism literature help explain development that facilitates a transition out of extractivism?

A broad overview of extractivism and its successor ideologies can be found in the introduction to this volume and in Calvão, Archer and Benya (2023). Other writings on extractivism have offered new visions of the relations underpinning extractivism while pushing beyond case studies of tangible, 'natural' resources such as ores and rare earth metals. Calvão and Archer (2021), for example, describe how blockchain technologies embedded in mining supply chains create their own forms of social and political value by reinforcing narratives of sustainability. Gago and Mezzadra (2017) use the example of the extractive logic inherent in patents for soya bean seeds—local knowledge is taken and codified in corporate intellectual property, which shifts value away from its source. These authors' analysis yields an important foundation for an expanded analysis of extractivist structures; the use of the extractivism concept ought to yield insights beyond cases of raw materials and instead should explore the 'fundament features of the logic of contemporary capitalism's functioning' (Gago and Mezzadra, 2017, 577).

2.1 *State Formation and the Periphery*

Analysis of the existing literature further builds on the nature of core and periphery development at the subnational level. This configuration of framing and data analyses extends the theoretical literature on internal colonialism as described by Hechter (1999) who envisions the process of internal colonialism as the result of an 'uneven wave of modernisation over state territory' that

> creates relatively advanced and less advanced groups. As a consequence of this initial fortuitous advantage, *there is crystallization of the unequal distribution of resources and power between the two groups.* The superordinate group, or core, seeks to stabilize and monopolize its advantages through policies aiming at the institutionalization of the existing stratification system. It attempts to regulate the allocation of social roles such that those roles commonly defined as having high prestige are reserved for its members ... [resulting in] a cultural division of labor.
>
> HECHTER (1999, 9); emphasis added

Though Hechter's thesis was often discussed during the 1980s and 1990s (and has been less prominent in the literature since), it was rarely thoroughly applied to China. An exception is work by Gladney (1994; 2004), who uses internal colonialism to frame his analyses of media representation of China's ethnic minorities, particularly Uyghurs. Gladney (2004) argues that representations of minority groups in China are fashioned to assert the homogeneity and superiority of China's Han ethnic majority group, which makes up more than 90 per cent of China's population. The present chapter extends this theoretical tradition by more explicitly considering the state's role in managing symbolic life, and the function of private sector investors in this work. By doing so in connection to an analysis of cultural extraction, the chapter demonstrates how unequal core–periphery relationships persist through economic transformations.

A theoretical step towards this extension comes from Bourdieu, Wacquant, and Farage's (1994) analysis of the state's actions to legitimate itself. Their argument builds on the Weberian notion of the state as the monopolist of legitimate violence by incorporating the state's control over symbolic violence (and symbolic life more generally):

> The state is the *culmination of a process of concentration of different species of capital*: capital of physical force or instruments of coercion (army, police), economic capital, cultural or (better) informational capital, and symbolic capital. It is this concentration as such which constitutes the state as the holder of a sort of meta-capital granting power over other species of capital and over their holders.
>
> BOURDIEU, WACQUANT, AND FARAGE'S (1994, 4); emphasis in the original

This last point about 'meta-capital' is key to the internal colonialism process and its role in transposing one model of extraction from that of raw resources to that of intangible culture. Cultural forms found in the margins of the state precede formal state presence (e.g., the indigenous traditions of the Huayao Dai discussed below long predate the foundation of the contemporary Chinese regime). Successful entrenchment of the centralised state in the supposed periphery requires the ability to define symbolic life as cultural capital that can be exchanged for economic capital, which can then be used elsewhere in the national economy. According to Bourdieu, Wacquant, and Farage (1994), the modern state's role as a monopolist over the relations between these different capitals has a natural corollary: interpretations of capital's relative values among the governed—laypersons' notions of why certain cultural or social practices have a certain value—are subordinated to new official 'exchange rates'. Thus, as states and regions contend with the relative value of a primary resource (such as iron ore) and an intangible resource (such as the value embedded in cultural tourism), it is the role of the state to decide, informally or explicitly, what the relative value of these things is and how to allocate and redistribute that value.

Limitations in both of these literatures provide motivation for the present study. The extractivism literature has primarily focused on neo-liberal and capitalist interventions and attempts to counter or reform those interventions. Moreover, prior work has frequently engaged with Latin American case studies in countries that are frequently embroiled in the liberalisation agenda of 'Washington Consensus' institutions. Similarly, the internal colonisation framework has overlooked countries outside of the neo-liberal or laissez-faire capitalist sphere of influence. By engaging with a case from contemporary China, this chapter extends analysis in both these traditions to a case in which the state exercises a strong influence over development in an integrated way; the same cadres who determine provincial economic development strategies are also engaged in questions of ideological concern, social development, and international politics (Donaldson, 2011). While corporate and private sector interests are certainly present in contemporary China, they often work in tandem with (or are subordinated to) state interests.

3 Date, Case, and Methods

This chapter draws on fieldwork conducted in southwest China over the summers of 2016, 2017 and 2018. The primary site is a town I refer to as 'Red River'—a growing town with close to 10,000 residents. The town is surrounded by smaller villages with populations ranging from a few dozen to several hundred. The region has historically been home to several ethnic groups, chiefly the Huayao branch of the Dai minority. In recent years the town has become a Han majority town, but the surrounding villages are primarily Dai.

3.1 *The Huayao Dai of Southwest China*

The Huayao Dai (花腰傣; they also refer to themselves as the Daiya, 傣雅) are a branch of the Dai minority group found in Southeast Asia. The Dai overall number more than 7 million, with the majority (6.3 million) to be found in Myanmar, more than 100,000 in Thailand and Laos, and the remaining 1.1 million in southwest China (Tao, 2003). Though the majority of the Dai people practice Theravada Buddhism, the Huayao Dai are one of the few groups in China that still practice an indigenous religion. Their faith is a blend of animist and pantheistic traditions that are often melded with elements from Buddhists sects and other Chinese folk traditions.

The religious practices of the Huayao Dai are centred around two roles: the *beima* and the *longtou*. The *beima*, typically an older woman, occupies a position similar to a priest or shaman. Her job is to ensure that the spirits associated with the village are content and settled in their appropriate realm. Typical duties include funerary rights to ensure a smooth transition to the next life; annual exorcisms of each home in the village, which encourage departed family members to return to the appropriate spiritual dwelling; divinations and blessings for villagers' ad hoc needs; and sacrifices and other rites for the village's primary gods or spirits. The most important spirits to the Huayao Dai are associated with trees, in particular the banyan tree.

The *longtou* occupies a position similar to a deacon in Christian traditions. They are bi-vocational, and husband and wife pairs often serve jointly. The *longtou*'s primary job is to assist the *beima* in obligatory rituals such as funerals and exorcisms. *Longtou*s also serve as elders in the village, overseeing the secular affairs of the community (this aspect of their social role has waned in recent years as state governments take hold). There is no prescribed number of *beima*s and *longtou*s that a village must have; people select into these positions on the basis of personal experiences and divination rituals. For example, most of the *beima*s discussed in this essay acquired their ability to speak in tongues and enter the spiritual realm after surviving a serious illness or injury during early adulthood. Most of the villages in the Red River area had at least two *beimas*; the number of *longtou*s varies from one to more than a dozen.

The town is situated between a range of low, jagged mountains and the Red River, also called the Gasa River, which gives the town its name. While the town is densely populated and packed with multistorey residential and commercial buildings, it is surrounded by a dozen smaller villages that have historically relied on agriculture. Beginning in the mid-2000s, the local government was able to substantially increase its revenues via levies on the profits of mining taking place in the surrounding mountain ranges. Much of this extra tax revenue has been invested in tourist enterprises, particularly *nongjiale*s (rural guest houses that allow tourists to participate in rural life) and performance venues. One of the major attractions each year is the Water Splashing Festival, a holiday that occurs each April in Buddhist Dai communities. The traditional function of the festival is to highlight the commencement of a new year with a ritualistic cleaning of Buddha statues and Buddhist temples, and the festival culminates in a playful, village-wide water fight—modern celebrations often feature water guns and water balloons. Even though the Huayao Dai in Red River are not Buddhist, the local government began promoting the Water Splashing Festival as a means of attracting large numbers of tourists.

3.2 *Ethnographic and Analytic Approach*

This chapter draws on fieldwork conducted in Yunnan during 2016, 2017 and 2018. During 2016 I travelled to Red River with a small group of anthropologists based at Yunnan University and stayed in a village that I will refer to as Orchid Valley. I returned in 2017 and 2018. Work in Red River consisted primarily of interviews and participant observation. I observed and occasionally participated in religious rituals in Orchid Valley and nearby villages. I also frequently attended or participated in events designed for tourists: guided tours of nearby mountains, song and dance performances of Huayao Dai mythology, and traditional meals set in tourist restaurants. The ethnographic approach adopted in this research is particularly well suited to a study of the emergent traits of development strategies within national peripheries. This particular case, because of its unique confluence of state, market, and local cultural forces, highlights what Katz (1997, 412) calls the 'rarely occurring but generally relevant interactional situations' that offer insight into more general social processes. By extending analysis over a multi-year period and leveraging participant observation in a range of social contexts, the data described here are able to identify key tensions in development processes by tracking how social change aligns with official state narratives.

Data were also collected through formal, semi-structured interviews with around 40 residents of Red River and surrounding villages. Interviewees were aged 18–85, collectively represented four ethnic groups, and were spread around Red River and a half dozen adjacent villages. While several themes were present in each interview, I followed Small's (2009) sequential approach to interview design: emergent themes and provoked questions were allowed to influence each future interview inductively. Thus, interview data capture a comprehensive range of salient public issues in the region. Candidates for formal interviews were recruited until the number of new emergent themes diminished significantly. Formal interview data are supplemented by casual conversations with people such as taxi drivers, restaurant staff, and neighbours of my village guesthouse. Data are presented below as excerpts from contemporary field notes or as contextual notes to explore connections to the existing literature.

Red River's residents are ensconced in steep mountain ranges and patches of flat land along the banks of the eponymous river, but the wider world is rapidly establishing a foothold in previously remote villages and neighbourhoods. My approach to developing the theoretical argument for this chapter follows the extended case method discussed by Burawoy (1998) and Burawoy et al. (2000). My fieldwork sought to explore Red River across both time and space. In addition to literal explorations of the regions connections to larger cities and the expansion of my fieldwork over three years, conversations also touched on perceptions of the region's evolution, imagined futures for the region and its families. My 'hook' into a larger global process (see Burawoy,

1998) is the penetration of supply chains into Red River and the spectre of outside investors. These nascent supply chains constitute primary industries (mining, bananas, dragon fruit), secondary industries (home construction, paper manufacture), and tertiary industries (the tourism sector).

The Huayao Dai are one of several sub-branches of the Dai ethnic group, but in this chapter I use the terms Dai and Huayao interchangeably; all Dai who live in Red River are members of the Huayao Dai branch. In the empirical sections below, I present data from field notes and from conversations with participants alongside my own analysis.

4 Transitioning from Extractive Mining to Extractive Tourism

Bai Taitai is a Huayao Dai woman in her early 30s and an entrepreneur in Orchid Valley—she and her husband, Zhou Laoban, have expanded their home to create space for guests, mostly residents of urban China looking to experience rural life in a *nongjiale*, or guesthouse (Park, 2014). Their home is large and new, with concrete walls painted a bright off white. The house has six bedrooms: one shared by her, her husband, and her two young children, one for her parents, and four reserved for guests, who pay around USD 7.50 (50 Chinese yuan renminbi (CNY)) per night. A balcony on the second floor overlooks the home's courtyard and poultry coops, and the roof is flat with ample room to lay out grain to dry in the sun and to sleep under the stars during cool summer nights.

Bai has a serious demeanour that belies her sharp and dry wit. She oversees a household with four generations of Huayao Dai women—her mother and father live in the bedroom next to hers, her grandmother divides her time between Bai's home and a neighbouring cousin's home, and a baby daughter follows her in a plastic walker. Bai's wardrobe highlights the cultural changes between her mother's generation and her own—she typically wears a cotton t-shirt, capris, and a sun hat while working in the home's courtyard alongside her mother, who wears a plain white blouse, a black skirt embroidered with Huayao Dai patterns, and cone-shaped rice hat.

Her husband, Zhou Laoban, is a muscular Han man from a mountainside village about an hour away. He worked in construction for most of his teens and early twenties, and met Bai Taitai while building houses in Orchid Valley. Now he works intermittently as a demolitions expert in the iron mines that encircle Red River and its satellite villages. The work pays well and he typically only has to work a few hours a day when the mine boss needs something blasted. I ask Bai if she worries about her husband's safety—'What good does it do to worry?'

she replies while feeding the baby strips of dried apricot. Bai and I often talked about her life in Orchid Valley and the town of Red River while I lived with her and her family. Mining and the subsidies it enables have transformed the cultural and economic lives of families around Red River. The mines themselves still operate, but are far enough away from villages like Orchid Valley to not upset the idyllic image cultivated by tourism entrepreneurs.

Scholars of tourism in developing spaces have noted the possibility of functional similarities between extractivism and tourism. In an analysis of the rise of ecotourism in Honduras, Loperena (2017, 621) notes that both 'entail mostly outward-oriented production, market valorisation of natural and cultural resources, and processes of dispossession in areas with high economic potential'. Each of these dimensions is present in the emerging tourist economy of Red River. Consumption of cultural and ecotourism is marketed heavily to ethnic Han Chinese tourists from urban China and international tourists from Thailand, and the cultural experiences for sale are largely flattened to cohere with the demands of a market economy. Tourism is also fundamentally reshaping the political economy of Red River as villages are marked for either tourist or industrial development and residents face the risk of violent dispossession (Devine and Ojeda, 2017). While some models of post-extractivism tourism (coupled with logics of degrowth and local sovereignty) have successfully evaded these parallels with primary resource extractivism (e.g., Chassagne and Everingham, 2019), the transition to tourism in Red River has been marked by widening inequality at the expense of local indigenous populations.

I arrived in Orchid Valley for the first time in 2016, the night before a major funeral; the husband of a local *beima* had just died. The occasion brought in family and friends from nearby counties and townships, many of whom were able to contextualise Red River's development:

> We asked Yang, a distant cousin of the deceased from a neighbouring township, about the outlook for his village and the communities around him. The government of Yunnan had somewhat arbitrarily decided that Red River and its constituent villages would be a centre for Dai-related tourism in the region, while his own village continued to rely on agriculture. The villages connected to Red River township enjoyed generous subsidies from the government. Peasant households rented out their land to banana and rice plantations, guaranteeing a passive income of several thousand [CNY] [several hundred USD] per year. Households who opened bed and breakfasts were also entitled to a [CNY] 10,000 [USD 1,500] [...] annual subsidy.

> Prospects for men and women my age were still somewhat grim. Yang told us that many young people sought out part time jobs in the [county's administrative capital], the women as office or clerical workers, and the men at nearby iron mines. The mines are particularly treacherous; Yang tells us that someone dies at a mine every day. Despite the dangers, work at the mines pays well, netting the young Dai men several hundred [CNY] [several dozen USD] per day. The easy cash brings its own challenges; Yang tells us that many young men spend their pay on KTV [karaoke] parlours (which implicitly function as brothels as well) before the next day's work begin[s]. After they marry, we ask, do Dai men still seek out this type of part time work? Yes, Yang replies; after working there long enough they learn [...] to watch for the falling rocks.
>
> Author's field note, July 2018

Yang's comments about the high death rates in the mines underscore the high toll that extractivism extracts from local populations, as do his comments about the capriciousness of the tourism development plan. The seemingly random distribution of mining risk and tourist fortune reflects the state's role in facilitating development: the conversion of mining subsides into narrow tourism ventures has been directed by local cultural management cadres. The arbitrary selection of 'winners' and 'losers' could be seen within the Red River area. The town of Red River is surrounded by a dozen smaller villages ranging in size from 100 to 700 households. Each is within walking distance of Red River's downtown strip, which contains department stores, hotels, and the long-distance bus station. Some, like Orchid Valley, have seen rapid growth in rural accommodation, restaurants, entertainment venues, and other instantiations of the tourism industry. Other villages, however, have been excluded from this growth. A few weeks after my initial visit to Orchid Valley, I visited a peasant farmer named Dao Li on the other side of town in a village called Pingzhai:

> Dao Li's home in the village of Pingzhai, about two kilometres south-southwest of Orchid Valley, has stood for nearly a century. The structure was home to her grandparents, parents, and now to her, her second husband, and her children. Dao Li, a 38-year-old Huayao Dai woman, is now preparing for the home's demolition. The home shows its age: the walls are exposed brick, the walls dirt, the second floor held up by wooden beams. Parts of the roof over the outer rooms of the house have collapsed, revealing the sunny sky overhead. The village around her home is equally humble; even the chickens are a little rougher around the edges than those in Orchid Valley. Dao is one of the poorest people I have spoken to

> in China, and perhaps anywhere. She tells us the income she generates from subsistence farming and other source[s] totals around 4,000 [CNY] (just shy of USD 600) per year.
>
> Author's field note, July 2018

Many of the homes in Pingzhai were in a similar condition. While Pingzhai was roughly as far away from downtown Red River as was Orchid Valley, almost none of its households had been able to collect subsidies for rural accommodation offerings or other small businesses. Pingzhai is relatively close to a paper mill—Red River's only industrial employer—and the odour is pervasive when the winds blow southwest. Pingzhai also lies at the intersection of the roads that lead up to the natural tourism destinations of the mountains—a waterfall, a mountain pass, and several scenic vistas. Ironically, this proximity to these other tourist destinations undercuts Pingzhai's tourist potential by increasing traffic and undermining its 'rural' character. Contrasting families like Bai Taitai's (from Orchid Valley) and Dao Li's (in Pingzhai) highlights the inequalities created by the transition to culturally extractive tourism. Bai and her family live in a large, new home and enjoy a consistent passive income from their allotment of farmland and their guesthouse. Dao, by contrast, lost out on these very same opportunities: her farmland allotment was on poor soil and the local government expressed little interest in developing tourism for Pingzhai.

By and large, the expansion of the tourism industry in Red River funded by iron mining revenues has led to the evolution (rather than the replacement) of the extractivist form of governance. Central to this analysis is recognition that while the type of resources being moved has shifted from iron to culture, the underlying patterns of exploitation inherent in extractivism (Mezzadra and Neilson, 2017) are still present.

5 Ossifying and Flattening Culture

Bai Dage is an affable restauranter in his mid-30s. He is a heavy drinker, often entertaining guests and luminaries at his village restaurant well into the evening with bottles of *baijiu* shared in front of a KTV machine. The restaurant consists of a rectangular dining pavilion with waist-high cinderblock walls and a corrugated metal roof; adjacent to the dining room is an open-air kitchen that overlooks a poultry pen containing chickens, geese, ducks, and an occasional turkey. The restaurant sits beside a four-lane road at the top of a gentle terraced hill leading down to Orchid Valley, the village he administers on behalf of the Party. Between the road and dining pavilion Bai has dug a quarter-acre fish pond that provides the staple protein for his restaurant. The fields are dotted with slim papaya trees; in the cool of the morning neighbours let out a water buffalo, which lazily chews through the weeds of a yet-to-be-planted rice paddy.

I often—on my walks out of the village and into town before the heat of the late morning sun rolled in—found Bai sitting on a stool in the dining area. My route involved a shortcut over a cinderblock retaining wall that divides the fish pond from a stand of dragon fruit vines; at the end of the wall pedestrian guests duck under a young papaya tree and step into the dining room. On a typical late June morning, the shirtless, wiry Bai grimaced and laughed his way through the day's hangover, looking out through his aviator sunglasses over the dragon fruit vines and rice paddy that took up most of the hill between him and the village. I start my research for the day sitting across from Bai and chat with him about the vegetables he needs to buy at the market today. Over the previous few days I had accompanied Bai on the quick motorcycle taxi ride into Red River, the nearby town, and followed him as he scouted out the best deal for 'collard greens', mangos, mint, pork, and whatever else he planned to serve that day. 'Why don't I go into town today with your list? I want to practice my Dai', I offer. Bai laughs gently—I'm not ready yet.

Bai has done well for himself. He occupies a formal position as leader of his village—a secular, political role that puts him in constant contact with the powers that be in town and, occasionally, in the county government. But he is also heir to the village's religious authority—his father had previously served as a spiritual leader, but abdicated upon his son's appointment to avoid any appearance of dynastic aspirations. Bai talked often about faith in the village and what it meant to him, his family, his son—the most concise answer he ever gave on matters of belief was, 'You don't believe in it, until you have to'. Parents die and need to be cared for on their journey to the next place, children get sick and the doctor's medicine does not work fast enough. Bai's candid acknowledgement of the instrumentality of his faith reflects the need to adopt the 'modern' outlook necessary for his secular role while still maintaining a core sense of ethnic identity.

Bai's dual sources of authority were not without their tensions, especially when it came time to believe in the local religion. A tragic murder in town was one such time; he told us a story about the magic and politics required to set this right. The following field note retells the story:

> After a local *beima*'s grandson murdered her son-in-law, the people of the village began to experience problems with his ghost bothering them.

> There's an additional type of spiritual leader called the *yamou*, men who provide services similar to Taoist priests (exorcisms, spells, etc.). In his role as village chief, Dage asked a *yamou* from outside the village—one that is more powerful than the local *yamou*—to help. The village collectively spent [CNY] 20,000 [...] [around USD 2,800] for a ward/spell to settle all of the village's spiritual affairs at once.
>
> Dage plays an active role in this story [both] because he is [...] the formal, elected leader of the village and because he is a bit sceptical about the power that the traditional spiritual leaders have here. He was given the ward in the form of a printed written formula of some sort. The spell would be cast/carried about by one of the village *longtous*, but the *longtou* is illiterate so Dage had to practice reading the spell to convey it to him. He recounts the following experience:
>
> He was practicing the spell but did not read it completely. After casually reading parts of it he heard a voice and saw a large spirit—he describes it as some mixture of a large tree and a giant—which told him to turn around. As soon as he did he found himself in the middle of his fishpond. A friend, who had been in the bathroom at the time, came out and found him treading water.
>
> Author's field note, July 2018

This story captures the liminal position Bai finds himself in often—the Communist party leader and son of a priest, anxious about the village's spiritual health but also about ceding too much control to a magician, finds himself punished by forces he does not understand because he is trying to straddle two worlds. This tension is emblematic of the challenges of participating in culture forms caught up in changing conditions of modernity (van Gennep, 2004), and Bai finds himself navigating collisions of modernisation and culture throughout his community.

As a concept, culture is, of course, immensely complex both conceptually and practically. Tourists, as consumers of culture, often have narrower expectations in mind. Urry and Larsen (2011, 1119) describe the performance of service in the tourism industry as a 'bodily performance that needs to please, seduce or entertain, especially visually'. The subsidised cultural industry in Red River ossifies certain cultural practices in time for the enjoyment of tourists from China's urban cores. The elements of spiritual life that were so integral to the lived experiences of Huayao Dai residents, particularly middle-aged and older residents, were difficult to commodify. Tourists instead prefer to see easily accessible, and unchanging, forms of culture that adhere to prior notions of what minority life looks like on society's margins (Cohen, 1988; De Haes and Archer, 2017).

Instead, performances and elements of material culture that are easier to sell take precedence. One impact of this shift is the reification of gender inequalities, particularly in terms of occupational sorting. The streets of downtown Red River's are punctuated with statues of lithe and colourful young women in traditional Dai garb. The pedestal of each statue bears a short paragraph describing some aspect of Huayao Dai material and performance culture: traditional sewing methods, dances, musical traditions. The village of Orchid Valley has benefited from the construction of a large amphitheatre and outdoor restaurant. Groups of tourists sit at large banquet tables and watch as young Dai women dance to a soundtrack of songs (in Mandarin) that narrate Dai creation myths. The role of gender in stratifying opportunities in the emergent culture industry was made apparent in a conversation with a local cadre in the cultural management bureau. Dao Xiaomei, a native of Red River and a Huayao Dai woman in her early thirties, spoke about the specific opportunities available to young adults in the area:

> The conversation continues to focus on the outlook for [...] young Dai men and women. Their faith is split between acknowledging the importance of their elder's faith (which they view as superstition) and a more modern trust in science and contemporary medical practices.
>
> At this point, Dao Xiaomei becomes a more central part of the conversation. She recounts several anecdotal experiences she has had moving between traditional and modern practices when raising her child, and opens the conversation to a broader discussion about discrimination and pride in ethnic identity. It wasn't long ago, she says, that ethnic minority groups were subject to heavy discrimination. 'Why aren't you Han?' she recalls being asked. Pride in her Dai identity is easier and stronger now, and Dao views a goal of her job to [be to] encourage and protect that pride. She relates how she used to be too embarrassed to wear traditional Dai clothing even outside of her own home; she now wears them to trips to Beijing and Shanghai. The Dai have gained the ability to take pride in traditional embroidery and fashions.
>
> I ask about what men take pride in—and the answer is less clear. The men are more heavily engaged in agriculture, mining, and other heavy labour, and much of their free time (she reminds us) is taken [up] by alcohol. Sexism is apparently a serious issue in the area. This is apparent from what we have inferred about education in Gasa. Though Dao Xiaomei's Mandarin is articulate and intelligently spoken, very few adult

> women have been able to speak well enough to communicate with us. It is mostly the men that have received extensive education in Mandarin.
>
> It seems that the economy is the source of this gender stratification and [the] corresponding difference in cultural engagement. Men are enticed by the high incomes offered by mining, construction, and other manual labour sectors; women are more likely to engage in [the] commercialisation of culture, such as dance performance and embroidery work. 'Culture' has become synonymous with 'cultural products'.
>
> Author's field note, Jun 2017

The gendered nature of cultural development was stratified by age; while material and performance culture provided employment opportunities for young women, the shift away from spirituality was impacting a key source of employment and status for older women. The *beima*s and other traditional religious figures were increasingly marginalised, as tourists exercised an outsize influence on the ways in which culture was performed. Dances and songs could be scripted for an audience; religious rituals could not. Tensions in the gendered nature of cultural development in Red River featured prominently even in official marketing for the region, as evidence by the county government's English language web page about Red River:

> 'Judge a man by the land he farms on, and the girl by the embroidery she makes', a local saying circulates among the Huayao Dai ethnic people in Xinping County, where most girls at the age of six or seven begin to learn how to stitch.
>
> For Huayao Dai ladies, embroidering has become a way to pursue beauty, a way to perfect themselves and also a way to express what they most likely think romantic.
>
> Dai ethnic communities of [Red River] are such places where you can see young girls getting together here and there, devoting themselves to the years-old hereditary craft.
>
> Yunnan Provincial Tourism Administration, 2018

The patterns that Dao Xiaomei noted in reflecting on her own experiences are made explicit by the government's tourism office: Red River was a place where outsiders could come watch women sew and dance, and leave with fond memories and embroidered souvenirs. The goal of such tourism, beyond economic enrichment and development, was the development and cultivation of urban citizens. Extracting 'authentic' experiences from people serves as a means of inspiring new forms of modernity among contemporary urban Chinese residents (Cohen, 1988; Walsh and Swain, 2004).

6 The Creation of Hierarchy

A final consequence of the transition from natural resource extraction to culture extraction is the impact of externally funded, core-centric development on local hierarchies. Prior sections of this chapter have described examples of the spatial inequalities inherent in this process: certain villages and townships are chosen as tourist centres, leaving others to persist in mining and farming. They have also noted the impact that reshaping and flattening culture has on gender inequality, as women are encouraged to seek employment in hospitality and young men are pressured to move out for work. While earlier analyses of tourism in China suggested that the valorisation of ethnic culture might lessen tensions in contemporary China (e.g. Sofield and Li, 1998), in practice tourism has seen the creation of new types of inequality embedded in the absolute growth of the region.

This model of development creates new forms of inequality and stratification within and across these spaces as well. Most notable in the case of Red River has been the rise of increasingly crisp and rigid ethnic hierarchies. While Red River has become the national centre of cultural tourism for the Huayao Dai, the Huayao Dai make up only 40 per cent of the area's population. A significant portion of the population belong to China's Han ethnic majority. The economic life of downtown Red River is dominated by Han-owned business:

> Later a friend and I attempt to do a survey of a 'typical' block off the main street by cataloguing the types of business and facts about their proprietors, but our results are pretty mundane. Our site, a block of New Street, contains on one side (from south to north): an Asus dealer[ship] run by Dai, a pig feed store, a water store, a Dai rice store, a closed insurance business, something under construction, an alley of apartments, a fishing store with a group of drunk Huayao Dai men eating outside (they invite me to drink with them; I decline), a convenience store, a closed salon, a small playground, an old house, another old house set to be demolished—拆 [chai, "demolish"] painted on the wall—and a row of closed warehouse type buildings. The other side of the street is less interesting, mostly newer houses and a couple of convenience stores. In short, the flurry of tourist activity in Red River seems concentrated along a few

> blocks of the main road; once you go back a few blocks (especially away from the river and towards the mountain) there's much less activity.
>
> Author's field note, August 2018

Similar, albeit subtle, inequities between Dai and Han families are visible at the downtown market that is held every five days. The market occupies a large pavilion covered with a patchwork of corrugated tin roofing. The pavilion is surrounded by small, permanent shopfronts and restaurants. The interior of the pavilion is filled with rows of tables where vendors set up stalls selling meat, vegetables, tofu, and home goods. The perimeter pavement between the rectangle of tables and the shopfronts is littered with mats on which vendors, mostly elderly women, sell mangos and other fruits. An informal survey of the market during late summer suggests that Han migrants occupy favourable positions and sell the most lucrative products:

> A quick census of the interior stalls (that is, the permanent tables) suggests that 10 per cent of the vendors are obviously Dai women (i.e., wearing the hats or have tattoos or stained teeth). We don't have a good way to identify Dai men, so a generous estimate would suggest that a [quarter] of these vendors are Dai. On the other hand, all of the women selling vegetables and herbs on mats on the surrounding [pavement] are Dai. I buy some bajiao bananas [CNY 2 RMB/*jin*],[1] mangos [CNY 4/*jin*] and a bunch of mint [CNY 2.5] to take back to Bai Dage's restaurant. The outermost ring of stores are the permanent storefronts that gird the market; these appear to be owned primarily by outsiders. For instance, we walk past stores selling Guizhou and Zhejiang wares; their respective owners say they are migrants. The handful of bricks-and-mortar stores with Dai employees are modest noodle joints.
>
> Author's field note, July 2018

In addition to the Huayao Dai and Han, the Red River area has communities of Hui, Hani, and Yi people. Each of these groups constitutes a minority population in China, which is 95 per cent Han. One consequence of the rapid emergence of a tourist sector devoted explicitly to the Huayao Dai culture is that other ethnic groups have become marginal to the service economy in town. Conversations with members of these groups revealed a certain ambivalence about this feature of local development; they noted that their own

1 One *jin* is approximately 500 grams.

attachments to Red River felt contingent or less valid, but they also recognised that opportunities to capitalise on this growth were distinctly limited. Yang Chaode, an Yi man in his 50s, owns a hotel halfway up the mountain between Red River and the mountain range's natural tourism sites. Despite being born into an Yi family and personally identifying as Yi, the ethnicity marker on his national ID card had recently been changed to 'Han'. When asked why he had not requested that this error be corrected, he remarked that it was easier to do business in Red River as a legal member of China's Han majority. Others found that tourists were frequently indifferent to the nuanced differences between ethnic groups in the area, and that it was easier to participate in selling Huayao Dai culture than to try to create a niche marketing a different identity:

> There is a small souvenir shop next to the halal restaurant where I took most of my meals during the 2017 phase of my fieldwork. It was a modest storefront, less than 200 square feet with a large door that opened out to the main road running through Red River. Shelves lined both side walls and were stocked with dried tea leaves, red sugar, rice paddy eel traps woven from reeds, and small earthenware cups and tea pots made in one of the surrounding villages. The narrow back wall of the store had a large desk and computer where the proprietor of the store, Bai Yi, spent much of the day playing games. Bai is a Hani woman in her early 40s. She married into the village after growing up in […] Sandy Crest, the next town over. Despite being Hani, all of the wares she sold were associated with Huayao Dai culture. We ask why she—or anyone—isn't selling souvenirs associated with Hani culture, to which she responds that no one is interested in the Hani here, local tourism is built on the Dai.
>
> Author's field note, July 2018

Entrepreneurs among the Dai community noticed these divisions as well. Dao Shifu, a Dai man in his late 50s, made his living as a pedicab driver. Red River is too small for bus routes or even automobile taxis, so most people get around by walking, driving electric scooters, or by riding in small trailers pulled by motorcycles. Dao lives in a village close to Orchid Valley close to the Yi communities higher up in the mountains. He notes that much of the inequality between different ethnic groups is fundamentally a question of land quality; when everyone in the region was subsistence farming, standards of living were comparable across groups. However, much of the farmland in the valley areas has been consolidated into plantations and leased out, turning the land into a source of passive income:

> We talk about Qizu. The village is a mixture of Dai and Han; other groups live further up the mountain. He's lived here is whole life and has several daughters who have married and left the village. We talk a little about land distribution—'the Yi have the bad land with no water, the Dai and the Han have the good land'. He gets about [...] [CNY 1,000] per year for each of his 10 *mu*[2] of land from the government; they've planted bamboo on his land to prevent erosion. The village of Qizu isn't slated to move down the mountain, perhaps because it's accessible by road and there isn't a risk of landslides here. Dao Shifu seems to know little about China outside of this region—he hasn't heard of several Eastern provinces and is amazed that my home state [the US state of Mississippi] is very flat—'This sounds like good land'.
>
> Author's field note, July 2017

In short, development in Red River had meant change; the flood of outside investment has raised living standards in obvious ways. The highways connecting Red River to the provincial capital, Kunming, have improved every year, and the town now has a modern hospital. However, this development has created forms of inequality that were neither necessary nor expected by the locals hoping to participate in this growth. Inequality among the region's diverse ethnic groups has been especially marked; the Han majority has occupied much of the new, semi-urban growth area in the town centre, while the Huayao Dai have enjoyed subsidies to build accommodation offerings in the surrounding villages. The Yi, Hui, and Hani, especially those living in more remote mountain villages, have been marginalised or ignored.

Inequalities along categorical lines like ethnicity serve important purposes; creating and entrenching gender, ethnic, and other categorical divides provides a means by which urban elites can consolidate (and hoard) opportunities and function as gatekeepers (Tilly, 1999). This growing ethnic and racial inequality is a noted feature of internal colonialism-style development (Hechter, 1999), but the increased complexity of Red River's ethnic dynamics and the valorisation of certain cultural practices have made this inequality a pronounced feature of post-extraction development as well. Indeed, this pattern, in which a single ethnic group is chosen as the 'winner' of a development agenda, is common throughout Yunnan (Kolås, 2004; Sofield and Li, 1998). This repositioning and solidification of the ethnic hierarchy further serves the purpose of reinforcing Han supremacy in China's ethnic landscape (Gladney, 1994; 2004).

2 A Chinese unit of area measurement equivalent to approximately 0.066 hectares.

7 Discussion and Conclusion

The emerging tourist sector in Red River displays many of the relational and ideological features of natural resource extractivism. Both eras of the region's recent development trajectory are marked by a core–periphery dynamic reminiscent of internal colonial models of national development and state formation, both in their orientation towards resource extraction and in their treatment of ethnic and racial inequality. Culture—namely, the performable and commodifiable dimensions of culture—is viewed as an unprocessed resource ready for consumption by Han ethnic majority tourists, who in turn return to China's urban cores enriched and refreshed. The success of such a tourist industry requires that the culture to be extracted remain consumable, predictable, and legible. As a strong, core-centric state acts to create such an industry, the relevant dimensions of culture become flattened and ossified. The process further creates new forms of inequality; differential opportunities emerge along gender and ethnic boundaries. The net result is that while rural spaces experience economic development—Red River has grown and absolute standards of living have risen—underlying structural relationships are largely unchanged from an era marked by reliance on iron extraction. Economic life is directed by powerful, external actors, and sources of wealth in Red River are conceptualised as unprocessed, natural resources that attain value as they leave the region. The fieldwork used in this study, spread out over a three-year period, highlights the trajectory that these developments follow. In this case, that has meant growing opportunities for Han 'in-migrants', the professionalisation and standardisation of tourist states, and continued marginalisation of ethnic groups other than the Huayao Dai. The tendency towards ossified or new forms of inequality is not, however, indicative of a complete lack of agency on the part of minoritised or subaltern groups. The growth of a tourism industry has allowed for entrepreneurship, employment in better-paying service sector positions, and other opportunities that lead to higher absolute standards of living. Grappling with the tension between development and widening relative inequality in post-extractive tourist spaces will be an important concern for future work.

This case suggests several implications for development policy and development studies. A central concern is the role of transitions out of extractivism in creating, solidifying, and legitimising new forms of inequality. These new forms of inequality point to one embodiment of extraction's afterlife—Gasa is not a post-extractivist economy per se because the emergence of tourism in the region has simply reshaped extractivist logic and allowed it to continue. In situations where powerful state or private sector actors have the capacity to finance and develop a new service industry ex nihilo, the relations embedded in that new industry are likely to reproduce early social patterns: the periphery remains peripheral and stuck in place. Specific policy solutions will be highly context dependent and will require adapting to local state capacity and interests, but in general multinational organisations investing in tourism or cultural development should ensure broad stakeholder participation in planning for transitions out of extractive economies. This case also extends discussions around (post-)extractivism beyond Latin American and other sites seen as especially vulnerable to international financial institutions and neo-liberal policy agendas. While analysis of the specific architectures of development in contemporary China is beyond the scope of this chapter, the Chinese context is certainly far different from cases marked by International Monetary Fund and World Bank intervention. This chapter highlights the need for further work on the near futures of rural development in China, particularly in ethnic minority communities and regions marked by primary resource extraction. The chapter has approached these questions from an ethnographic, grassroots perspective; future work should assess official discourses around development in China.

References

Bourdieu, P., L.J.D. Wacquant and S. Farage (1994) 'Rethinking the State: Genesis and Structure of the Bureaucratic Field', *Sociological Theory*, 12(1), pp. 1–18, DOI: 10.2307/202032.

Burawoy, M. (1998) 'The Extended Case Method', *Sociological Theory*, 16(1), pp. 4–33, DOI: 10.1111/0735-2751.00040.

Burawoy, M., J.A. Blum, S. George, Z. Gille, M. Thayer, T. Gowan, L. Haney, M. Klawiter, S. Lopez and S. O'Rian (eds.) (2000) *Global Ethnography: Forces, Connections, and Imaginations in a Postmodern World* (Oakland: University of California Press).

Calvão, F. and M. Archer (2021) 'Digital Extraction: Blockchain Traceability in Mineral Supply Chains', *Political Geography*, 87, DOI: 10.1016/j.polgeo.2021.102381.

Calvão F., M. Archer and A. Benya (eds.) (2023) *The Lives of Extraction. Identities, Communities and the Politics of Place*, International Development Policy | Revue internationale de politique de développement, 15 (Geneva, Boston: Graduate Institute Publications, Brill-Nijhoff), DOI: 10.4000/poldev.5226.

Chassagne, N. and P. Everingham (2019) 'Buen Vivir: Degrowing Extractivism and Growing Wellbeing through Tourism', *Journal of Sustainable Tourism*, 27(12), pp. 1909–1925, DOI: 10.1080/09669582.2019.1660668.

Clark, K.B. (1989) *Dark Ghetto: Dilemmas of Social Power* (1st Wesleyan ed) (Middletown: Wesleyan University Press).

Cohen, E. (1988) 'Authenticity and Commoditization in Tourism', *Annals of Tourism Research*, 15(3), pp. 371–386, DOI: 10.1016/0160-7383(88)90028-X.

De Haes, J. and M. Archer (2017) 'Nostalgia for the Way Things Never Were: Ambivalence and Ambiguity in the Mississippi Delta', *Lo Squaderno*, 43, pp. 9–13.

Devine, J. and D. Ojeda (2017) 'Violence and Dispossession in Tourism Development: a Critical Geographical Approach', *Journal of Sustainable Tourism*, 25(5), pp. 605–617, DOI: 10.1080/09669582.2017.1293401.

Donaldson, J.A. (2011) *Small Works: Poverty and Economic Development in Southwestern China* (Ithaca: Cornell University Press).

Gago, V. and S. Mezzadra (2017) 'A Critique of the Extractive Operations of Capital: toward an Expanded Concept of Extractivism', *Rethinking Marxism*, 29(4), pp. 574–591, DOI: 10.1080/08935696.2017.1417087.

Gladney, D.C. (2004) *Dislocating China: Reflections on Muslims, Minorities, and Other Subaltern Subjects* (Chicago: University of Chicago Press).

Gladney, D.C. (1994) 'Representing Nationality in China: Refiguring Majority/Minority Identities', *The Journal of Asian Studies*, 53(1), pp. 92–123, DOI: 10.2307/2059528.

Hechter, M. (1999) *Internal Colonialism: the Celtic Fringe in British National Development* (Oxfordshire: Routledge).

Katz, J. (1997) 'Ethnography's Warrants', *Sociological Methods & Research*, 25(4), pp. 391–423, DOI: 10.1177/0049124197025004002.

Kolås, Å. (2004) 'Tourism and the Making of Place in Shangri-La', *Tourism Geographies*, 6(3), pp. 262–278, DOI: 10.1080/1461668042000249610.

Loperena, C.A. (2017) 'Honduras Is Open for Business: Extractivist Tourism as Sustainable Development in the Wake of Disaster?', *Journal of Sustainable Tourism*, 25(5), pp. 618–633, DOI: 10.1080/09669582.2016.1231808.

Mezzadra, S. and B. Neilson (2017) 'On the Multiple Frontiers of Extraction: Excavating Contemporary Capitalism', *Cultural Studies*, 31(2–3), pp. 185–204, DOI: 10.1080/09502386.2017.1303425.

Park, C.-H. (2014) 'Nongjiale Tourism and Contested Space in Rural China', *Modern China*, 40(5), pp. 519–548, DOI: 10.1177/0097700414534160.

Small, M.L. (2009) '"How many cases do I need?": On Science and the Logic of Case Selection in Field-Based Research', *Ethnography*, 10(1), pp. 5–38, DOI: 10.1177/1466138108099586.

Sofield, T.H.B. and F.M.S. Li (1998) 'Tourism Development and Cultural Policies in China', *Annals of Tourism Research*, 25(2), pp. 362–392, DOI: 10.1016/S0160-7383(97)00092-3.

Tao, G.X., 陶贵学 (ed.) (2003) 中国云南新平花腰傣文化国际学术研讨会文集 = [*Collected works of Xinping Huayao Dai Culture International Academic Seminar, Yunnan, China*], 民族出版社 [National Publishing House].

Tilly, C. (1999) *Durable Inequality* (Oakland: University of California Press).

Urry, J. and J. Larsen (2011) *The Tourist Gaze 3.0* (New York: SAGE Publications Ltd), DOI: 10.4135/9781446251904.

Van Gennep, A. (2004) *The Rites of Passage* (London: Psychology Press).

Walsh, E.R. and M.B. Swain (2004) 'Creating Modernity by Touring Paradise: Domestic Ethnic Tourism in Yunnan, China', *Tourism Recreation Research*, 29(2), pp. 59–68, DOI: 10.1080/02508281.2004.11081444.

Yunnan Provincial Tourism Administration (2018) *Huayao Dai Ethnic Embroideries*, Archived at http://www.yunnanadventure.com/city_list/Jiangchuan-County-Shopping_146_721.html (accessed on 4 November 2022).

CHAPTER 5

Regulating Mine Rehabilitation and Closure on Indigenous Held Lands: Insights from the Regulated Resource States of Australia and Canada

Emille Boulot and Ben Collins

Abstract

Countless environmental, social, and economic issues can stem from poor mine closure and post-mining land use planning practices. Such post-extractive landscapes have a disproportionate effect on local Indigenous communities that continue to live in these often remote areas on their traditional lands, with such peoples only recently being able to document and bring their values and stories to closure, rehabilitation, and post-mining land use policy. A strong regulatory environment is the often suggested response to such concerns, and this chapter examines the regulation of mine rehabilitation and closure (MR&C) practices in the developed resource states of Canada and Australia. Analysis of current regulation and policy along with examples from MR&C practice demonstrate that the regulatory state is failing to ensure social, economic, cultural, and environmentally safe landscapes for local Indigenous people on whose lands these mines were situated. This research highlights recent reform in both jurisdictions, primarily designed to limit state liability for abandoned mines, and the impact of that reform upon the influence and inclusion of Indigenous peoples' interests and rights in MR&C. The chapter highlights the common structural, institutional, political and resource challenges that Indigenous peoples across Australia and Canada face in ensuring that their lands and country are effectively and safely rehabilitated, and argues that having a comprehensive regulatory environment is not enough. Greater Indigenous engagement, management, control and ownership of MR&C processes is required if we are to see better outcomes for local people in post-extractive landscapes.

1 Introduction

Compared to policy 30 or more years ago, mine rehabilitation and closure (MR&C) has come a long way towards ensuring that processes are in place to

© GENEVA GRADUATE INSTITUTE, 2024 | DOI:10.1163/9789004686182_006

minimise environmental risks. Mine rehabilitation,[1] initially concerned with simply re-establishing some form of vegetation cover and post-mine land use, has come to include the restoration of pre-existing ecosystems as well as social elements (Gardner and Bell, 2007; Nichols and Nichols, 2003; Trigger et al., 2008; Unger, Everingham and Bond, 2020). However, in many cases MR&C policy and research has only minimally considered the burden many local and Indigenous communities shoulder when inadequate MR&C occurs on or adjacent to their traditional lands and territories (Campbell et al., 2017; Everingham et al., 2018; Lawrence and O'Faircheallaigh, 2018).

The traditional lands and territories of Indigenous peoples[2] in Canada and Australia are often abundant in natural resources and have been subjected to considerable mineral exploration and extraction since early European settlement (Behrendt and Strelein, 2001; Keeling and Sandlos, 2015). With the increased focus on land and economic rights for Indigenous communities, there has been significant discussion about the role of mining in facilitating the increased social and economic well-being of Indigenous people who live in remote, mineral rich areas (Gibson and Klinck, 2005; Jones and Bradshaw, 2015; Keeling and Sandlos, 2015; Langton et al., 2004; 2006; Missens, Dana and Anderson, 2007; Scambary, 2013). Despite significant concerns regarding mine legacy issues, including MR&C failure, abandoned mines, and mines in 'care and maintenance' (see Owen and Kemp, 2018), only limited attention in policy and regulation has been paid to the rights and concerns of Indigenous people who continue to live in these mined regions during and post mine closure (Annandale, Meadows and Erskine, 2021; O'Faircheallaigh, 2013).

Considering Indigenous peoples always have 'more to lose and significantly less to gain' from the erosion of their natural capital (Stoeckl et al., 2013, 214), ensuring the ongoing social, economic and environmental well-being of such communities should be the priority of MR&C regulation. This chapter will discuss and compare MR&C regulation in both Canada and Australia, with the discussion grounded with examples from MR&C practice, to explore common political and structural challenges for Indigenous communities in MR&C, before identifying areas ripe for regulatory reform.

---

1 Also referred to as reclamation, more commonly in Canada.

2 In this chapter, the word 'Indigenous', where not restricted by a specific qualifier, is used as an inclusive term to include Canadian First Nations, Aboriginal, and Métis communities, as well as communities in Australia and the Torres Strait that designate themselves as Aboriginal, First Nations, or Indigenous peoples. 'Traditional owners' is a more specific term used to refer to the Indigenous descent groups who are the owners of particular areas of land or of a country.

It is not our intention to speak for Indigenous and local communities, but rather to highlight the ongoing challenges, both social and ecological, that such peoples face in post-extractive landscapes. Our suggestions for reform in this space are guided by such principles as self-determination and free, prior and informed consent. It is not our role nor our intention to provide specific social and ecological reform proposals, as only local communities can do that in line with their place-specific needs and interests, but rather to identify areas where settler colonial regulatory systems can create space for Indigenous engagement, participation, and control of the MR&C process with the aim of improving MR&C outcomes for local communities. We acknowledge of course that each Indigenous community is different, with different capacities, resources and opportunities to engage with mining companies and regulators. Our discussion is therefore more general in nature when we refer to Indigenous and traditional owners, and more concerned with the regulatory landscape.

The chapter was informed by the previous and ongoing research of the authors. Both have undertaken qualitative research regarding MR&C, in Australia and Canada, respectively. The Canadian case study was part of a collaborative research project with the Stk'emlupsemc te Secwepemc Nation and the University of British Columbia (Collins, 2015). It involved interviews and environmental surveys alongside First Nations traditional knowledge keepers of the Skeetchestn and Tk'emlúps te Secwepemc Indian Bands, as well as photographic and documentary analysis (Collins, 2015). The Australian research is from a larger doctoral research project on the regulation of restoration (see Boulot and Akhtar-Khavari (2020) for an overview). This research has included qualitative interviews with restoration practitioners, scholars and regulatory experts and is also informed by document and policy analysis, as well as participant surveys. In addition to the independent research of the authors, a comprehensive literature review of mine rehabilitation and closure in Australia and Canada was undertaken to inform our analysis of MR&C regulation across the two jurisdictions.

2 MR&C in Australia and Canada

2.1 *Key Definitions*

Multiple definitions of MR&C can be found across the mining sector. The International Council on Mining and Metals (ICMM) has defined MR&C as a process of planning and managing the decommissioning of a mine, the environmental rehabilitation of a mine including mitigating mining impacts to the landscape, and other legacy issues with the eventual relinquishment of the mining lease (ICMM, 2019). Closure in both Canada and Australia occurs when the government regulator releases the mine operator or owner from any liabilities and responsibilities associated with the mine.

The same plethora of definitions exists for regulation. For the purposes of this chapter, we consider regulation to be 'an authoritative set of rules, accompanied by some mechanism, typically a public agency, for monitoring and promoting compliance with these rules' (Baldwin et al., 1998, 3, in Vivoda, Kemp and Owen, 2019, 410). Regulation in liberal market states is therefore a balance between facilitating economic development, in this case resource extraction, and simultaneously ensuring environmental and social outcomes for the state's citizens as well as protecting them from the negative impacts of mining (Ioris, 2015; Vivoda, Kemp and Owen, 2019).

2.2 *MR&C Practice, Policy and Regulation*

Mineral extraction has been a significant contributor to economic growth and liberal capitalism in both Australia and Canada (MacDonald and Sloman, 2020). The mining industry has made significant efforts to brand its activities in language that associates mineral extraction with 'frontier development', 'prosperity' and 'nation building', equating resource extraction with bringing wealth and civilisation to 'undeveloped areas' and thus with a moral imperative (Trigger, 1997; 1998; Nuttall, 2010). With the rise of environmentalism in the 1970s and 1980s came a growing recognition that mining had serious environmental and social consequences, resulting in attempts to incorporate 'sustainable development' within the mining industry (ICMM, 2022; World Bank Group and International Finance Corporation, 2002). The mining industry and mine regulators began to consider the impact of MR&C as well as future land use activities for mined lands (see, e.g., Department of Industry, Tourism and Resources, Australia (2006) and in Canada the 'Towards Sustainable Mining' (TSM) initiative and framework (MAC, 2004)).

Improvements in MR&C practices have also stemmed from mine sites becoming major environmental risks after closure. An estimated 60,000 abandoned mines exist in Australia (Unger et al., 2012) and at least 18,000 in Canada (NOAMI, 2015). Campbell et al. (2017, 2) write in relation to the Australian context that '[m]ine closure, complete rehabilitation and relinquishment of the former mine site is almost unknown', with many mines entering a phase called 'care and maintenance', where, following active extraction, the company—not being obligated to close the mine—will 'mothball' the mine site with minimal investment in rehabilitation and resulting in the deferral of mine closure (Vivoda, Kemp and Owen, 2019). In addition, many companies have divested their mines that are reaching the end of their productive lives to less capitalised companies, often resulting in the purchasing company declaring insolvency and the liability transferring to the state (Owen and Kemp, 2018). The liability of poor closure practices can be significant. In northern Canada for example, the Faro and Giant mines have grown to become billion-dollar environmental liabilities after years of poor environmental practices and environmental planning (Government of Canada, 2018; Sandlos and Keeling, 2016). Stringent regulatory frameworks and the adoption of sustainable development practices have materialised in an attempt to reduce the environmental risk and costs of mine closure sites.

Unfortunately, there is a long history of local Indigenous peoples being largely excluded from the environmental management of their traditional lands (Bowie, 2013; O'Faircheallaigh and Corbett, 2005). Environmental management has often viewed nature as a space to be 'protected or plundered', effectively barring Indigenous people from a stakeholder's role (Kinnane, 2005; Godden, 2012). As a result of this systemic exclusion, significant efforts have been made by Indigenous peoples worldwide to have their environmental rights recognised as interdependent with their cultural and economic rights so that they may undertake their custodial obligations to their country (O'Faircheallaigh and Corbett, 2005). Recognition of these rights has occurred in international law (with the International Labour Office's ILO Convention 169 Concerning Indigenous and Tribal Peoples in Independent Countries, 1991, and the United Nations Declaration on the Rights of Indigenous Peoples, 2007). However, there has been limited recognition of these rights from a national perspective in both Australia and Canada despite acknowledgement that effective environmental management cannot occur without the involvement and support of local and Indigenous people (Langton et al., 2006; Mascia et al., 2003; O'Faircheallaigh and Corbett, 2005; Robertson et al., 2000).

Indigenous communities have been strongly advocating for better MR&C practice and regulation for many years (Annandale, Meadows and Erskine, 2021; Meadows, Annandale and Ota, 2019) and those who have seen their communities severely impacted by poorly managed mine sites are, on occasion, starting to have their voices heard during negotiations. In Canada, the Supreme Court Decisions of Delgamuukw in 1997[3] and Tsilhqot'in in 2014[4] have changed the landscape of Indigenous consultation requirements for resource development negotiations with Indigenous communities, recognising Indigenous communities as rights-holders rather than stakeholders, and there is a duty

3 Delgamuukw v. British Columbia [1997] 3 S.C.R. 1010.

4 Tsilhqot'in Nation v. British Columbia [2014] 2 S.C.R. 256.

to consult with Indigenous communities on resource development matters. This is not the case in Australia, where Indigenous communities are still considered stakeholders, which means that they are considered an interest group and their legal entitlements regarding decision-making and participation are less than those of rights-holders. There remain, however, ongoing barriers to Indigenous engagement and to management and control of MR&C in both jurisdictions. These barriers, and some possible opportunities, are explored in the following.

3 MR&C Regulation and Its Application to Indigenous Communities in Australia and Canada

In order to ground the discussion, we present here a brief overview of MR&C regulation in Australia and Canada before providing examples of the regulatory frameworks in action through the use of brief case study examples. The focus of this regulatory review is first to provide a general summary of the MR&C regulatory frameworks and identify the key regulators in the jurisdictions concerned. We then provide a more detailed review of the elements of the regulatory frameworks that are of particular importance in relation to local communities and their social, economic and environmental interests and futures as they grapple with mine legacies. Our focus here is upon the engagement, participation and decision-making power and control of local communities as well as on land rights and agreement made between local communities and mine operators. We provide case studies from the two jurisdictions to illustrate regulation in practice.

3.1 *Australia*

Resource extraction in Australia was initially subject to few environmental constraints (Bartle and Slessar, 1989). It is now recognised as temporary land use, with MR&C constituting an essential requirement to allow for future land use (Unger, Everingham and Bond, 2020). State and territory governments, the primary regulators of resource development, have developed more stringent MR&C regulation. Environmental and Social Impact Assessments (ESIAs) and Mine Closure Plans (MCPs) are now common requirements across Australia. This section will first examine the Commonwealth regulations before considering the regulatory arrangements in two significant resource states, Queensland and Western Australia.

At the federal level, the mining industry is regulated only where it concerns protected matters of national environmental significance[5] under the Environment Protection and Biodiversity Conservation Act 1999 (Cth) (EPBC Act) or where the national Native Title Act 1993 (NTA) provides for the negotiation of agreements on access to the Indigenous native title estate. Since the EPBC Act was enacted, 118 mining and resource projects have been approved under the Act (Parliament of Australia, 2017); however, no MR&C conditions have ever been applied to an approved mining and resource project (SECRC, 2019). Under the NTA, potential mines are assessed for their impact upon native title rights and interests. Native title claimants are not allowed to refuse proposed projects, thus placing them in a poor bargaining position and negating the possibility of free, prior and informed consent (O'Faircheallaigh and Lawrence, 2019). A recent Commonwealth inquiry noted the impact of insufficient MR&C on Indigenous communities (SECRC, 2019), but not much is known about most negotiated access agreements under the NTA as they are usually confidential (O'Faircheallaigh, 2007; 2008; Bond and Kelly, 2020). A recent analysis of 50 such agreements by O'Faircheallaigh and Lawrence (2019), however, found very little discussion or agreement regarding MR&C conditions.

At the state level in Queensland, the Department of Resources (DR) is responsible for mine licencing compliance, land access and abandoned mines, with mining authorised under the Mineral Resources Act 1989. The Department of Environment and Science (DES) is responsible for the environmental management of operating mines and overseeing MR&C under the Environmental Protection Act 1994 (Qld) (EP Act Qld). Prospective mine operators must apply for an environmental authority to conduct mining activities (EP Act (Qld) s. 125(1)) with the application detailing the proposed rehabilitation of the site post operation with a Progressive Rehabilitation and Closure Plan (PRCP).[6]

5 Matters of national environmental significance protected under the EPBC Act include listed threatened species and communities, listed migratory species, Ramsar wetlands of international importance, Commonwealth marine environment, World Heritage properties, national heritage places, the Great Barrier Reef Marine Park, nuclear actions, and water as a resource in relation to coal seam gas development and large coal mining development (EPBC Act, Part 3).

6 The Queensland Audit Office's (2013) review of Queensland's environmental regulation found that the environmental remediation of mines was 'an unrealised aspiration' with serious mine legacy concerns. State liability for MR&C failure was estimated to be USD 6.7 billion (AUD 8.7 billion) in 2017 (Queensland Treasury Corporation, 2017). Following this review, the Mineral and Energy Resources (Financial Provisioning) Act 2018 (Qld) amended the Qld EP Act and introduced the requirement for PRCPs. Ongoing concerns regarding

The DES assesses the PRCP and the MR&C for part of or the whole of a surrendered mining project (EP Act (Qld) ss. 318Z, 264) and signs off on mine closure certificates.

Rehabilitation is informed by departmental guidelines and policy which require the identification of 'suitable post-mining land uses having regard to the surrounding landscape, community views and the objectives of any local and regional planning strategies' (Department of Environment and Heritage Protection, Department of Natural Resources and Mines, and Queensland Treasury (n.d.), 2). Mine operators are required to achieve the highest practicable rehabilitation level and identify post-mining land uses that are acceptable to the community, local government and other relevant stakeholders. The Strong and Sustainable Resource Communities Act 2017 (Qld) (SSRC Act) also requires that mine operators undertake a 'Social Impact Assessment' in order to ensure that communities located near mines benefit from extractive projects and that ongoing engagement is detailed.

Across the regulatory framework, Indigenous traditional owners are recognised only as stakeholders. The economic and cultural concerns of Indigenous traditional owners and communities are rarely considered, with MR&C primarily concerned with meeting environmental indicators (Annandale, Meadows and Erskine, 2021; State of Queensland, 2018).

One example of the regulatory system in practice is that of bauxite mining in Weipa, Queensland, where the publicly available rehabilitation management plan for the Weipa operations (ML7024) concerns itself largely with the environmental authority conditions, aiming—following mine closure—to establish a sustainable native ecosystem similar to that which predated the mine. The overall objective is to 'return the land to a post-mining land use that will be stable, self-sustaining, requires minimal maintenance, and protects downstream water quality' while recognising the post-mine landform will be considerably altered (Rio Tinto, 2019, 25). Social, cultural and economic considerations in MR&C for the region can be found in other agreements between the mine operator and traditional owners. Traditional owners may, for example, request alternative land rehabilitation forms under the Western Capes Communities Co-existence Agreement (Rio Tinto, 2019); Rio Tinto does not, however, have to concede to such requests, and additional costs may be borne by the traditional owners. The Communities, Heritage and Environmental Management Plan (CHEMP) envisions that Rio Tinto and the traditional

mine rehabilitation and closure have also seen the recent appointment of the Queensland Rehabilitation Commissioner, an independent statutory position to assist in developing best practice mine rehabilitation management.

owners will work together to manage community, heritage and environmental values of the project area (South of the Embley Communities, Heritage and Environment Working Group, 2014). In line with the rehabilitation management plan, the CHEMP aims to establish viable ecosystems similar to surrounding ecosystems but recognises that rehabilitation is both an environmental and a cultural process, acknowledging 'the aspirations of Traditional Owners to be actively involved in caring for country' (South of the Embley Communities, Heritage and Environment Working Group, 2014, 37). There are concerns that there continues to be a lack of consideration of the interests of local communities in developing integrated economic opportunities through the MR&C process (Annandale, Meadows and Erskine, 2021).

In Western Australia, the Mining Act 1978 (WA) (Mining Act) requires all applications for a mining lease after June 30, 2011 be accompanied by an MCP. Such plans must be in accordance with statutory guidelines prepared by the Department of Mines, Industry Regulation and Safety (DMIRS, 2020). Prospective mine operators are required to pay upfront rehabilitation bonds and progressive rehabilitation is promoted, with approval required before land subject to MR&C is relinquished. Where it appears that a mine proposal is a significant proposal as defined under the Environmental Protection Act 1986 (EP Act (WA)), DMIRS must refer it to the Environmental Protection Authority (EPA) to determine whether the proposal requires a formal Environmental Impact Assessment (EIA). The EIA process requires the prospective mine operator to document environmental impacts and its environmental management controls. The EPA will also formally assess mine closure under Part IV of the EP Act (WA) where projects are not subject to the Mining Act or in cases where the EPA considers there to be a significant impact or risk and identifies rehabilitation and closure as a key environmental factor. The EPA will consider the prospective mine operator's proposal, alongside public input and expert advice, before making a recommendation to the relevant Minister. Over 70 per cent of mines in Western Australia have rehabilitation and or closure conditions applied through a Ministerial Statement in addition to requirements for an MCP under the Mining Act.

The guidelines are concerned primarily with environmental indicators, stating that rehabilitation aims to return 'disturbed land to a safe, stable, non-polluting/non-contaminating landform in an ecologically sustainable manner that is productive and/or self-sustaining and is consistent with the agreed post-mining land use' (DMIRS, 2020, 13). Indigenous peoples are not directly identified in the guidelines but can be assumed to be key stakeholders (if identified as post-mining landowners and managers), with no consideration of traditional owners' economic, cultural and environmental rights.

One example of the application of the framework can be found in the Thunderbird Mineral Sands Project, located on the Dampier Peninsula in the west Kimberley region of Western Australia. The MCP for the project states that following mine closure the land is to be returned to pastoral land use in a condition similar to surrounding land at the time of closure. The mine operator aims to close the mine 'in a cost-effective and efficient manner' with MR&C to be undertaken commensurate with the value of the land for post-closure uses (MBS Environmental, 2016, 30). In addition to the MCP, a Native Title Mining Agreement has supplementary rehabilitation requirements regarding the visual amenity of the post-mine landscape, the storage of topsoil for revegetation and the collection of local seed. The Agreement also identifies requirements as to the protection of heritage sites, visual impact requirements post-mining, post-mine land use and management, as well as employment and other financial benefits (MBS Environmental, 2016; 2017). The key focus of the miner in relation to MR&C, however, is financial cost and efficiency.

3.2 *Canada*

Canada's policies and decisions on MR&C largely fall within the portfolios of provincial governments and territorial governments. Each province establishes closure codes and rehabilitation requirements. As mines go through permitting and consultation, the federal government oversees Indigenous relations through an Intergovernmental Working Group, which is a group of community members, community leaders, and regulators. The federal government also oversees 'fisheries, fish habitat, and ocean-related activities', with projects potentially affecting Canada's waterways reviewed by the Department of Fisheries and Oceans (DFO).

Federal Environmental Assessments (EAs) may be conducted along with provincial EAs if 'in the Minister's opinion, either the carrying out of physical activity may cause adverse environmental effects or public concerns related to those effects may warrant the designation' (Government of Canada, 2012). For mining projects (other than uranium mines), a project requires a federal EA if it has a high potential for environmental impacts or requires significant consultation with Indigenous communities. The potential risk and impacts of a mine depend on its size, the mining method, water use, and mine waste management practices, as well as the area's mineralisation, hydrology, climate, and Indigenous traditional land use.

Closure guidelines often used by Canadian mining companies—such as the Mining Association of Canada (MAC, 2004) and ICMM (2008)—provide a high-level discussion of what is needed in a reclamation and closure plan. This includes reclamation objectives, progressive reclamation, removal of structures, standards for tailings and waste rock disposal, water resources, revegetation 'wherever practicable', and ongoing monitoring plans. They discuss the consideration of scientific, traditional, and local knowledge in MR&C and provide that 'feasible and practical' closure activities should benefit local communities and First Nations.

At a provincial level, British Columbian (BC) legislation requires every mine to be responsible for preparing a closure and reclamation plan in advance of receiving permission to start mine construction (BC Ministry of Energy and Mines, 2017). Through the Major Mine Permitting Office (MMPO) applications are reviewed by either the regional Mine Development Review Committee (MDRC) or a project-specific committee, which is comprised of technical staff from federal and provincial regulatory agencies and chaired by the district inspector of mines (Government of British Columbia, 2019; Schmitt, Ames and Stoopnikoff, 2008). Local governments, Indigenous community members, and public representatives are invited to provide input. The MDRCs establish requirements, as specified in the regulations, for land use objectives, water quality, productivity, stability of structures, baseline studies, and environmental impact studies. Mine closure and reclamation plans are required to be updated at least every five years.

The Health, Safety, and Reclamation Code for Mines in British Columbia establishes the MR&C requirements for each area of the mine site. The code details what information needs to be provided to the chief inspector to ensure the physical and chemical stability of the mine. Reclamation requirements, including revegetation, soil cover, water courses, etc., are based upon the agreed post-mining land use approved by the chief inspector (BC Ministry of Energy and Mines, 2017). This all leads to potential cost estimates for MR&C. As per the BC Mines Act (1996) the Lieutenant Governor in Council may require the establishment of a fund (commonly in the form of a bond) to ensure there is adequate money to close a mine.

Understanding and collecting Indigenous traditional knowledge is a key step in BC's provincial EA and feeds into the final land use, closure, and reclamation plans. Engagement with communities is often through chief and council, but is expanded to town halls, community forums or larger meetings when EA applications and information becomes more established.

This inclusion of Indigenous interests and post-mine land use desires is not without its conflicts. Indigenous governance systems can be more diverse than envisioned by the regulation of Indigenous engagement (Ford and Rowse, 2013; Law Commission of Canada, 2008). The chief and council jurisdictions were set up by colonial legislatures who for a long time ignored and overruled Indigenous governance. MR&C regulation can therefore fail to consider the diversity of Indigenous governance by not fully considering hereditary chiefs, family leaders, and other community leaders who have a long history of involvement in their nation's decisions (Menzies, 2006). Unfortunately, processes like EAs do not necessarily ensure that the culture, knowledge, wants, needs and values of Indigenous communities are protected. Such processes often use technocratic approaches that may not coincide with how Indigenous communities make decisions, and such processes may not provide the resources and support required for communities with lower capacities to engage (Myette, 2022).

In addition, MR&C processes can fail to adequately communicate post-mine landscape options to Indigenous communities or to fully integrate a community's vision for a post-mine landscape. In the case of the New Afton Mine, located in Kamloops, BC, in the traditional territory of the Skeetchestn and Tk'emlúps te Secwepemc nations, MR&C struggles to adequately address all the interests and concerns of the local Indigenous people.

The New Afton Mine is an underground copper–gold mine with a long history of operation and of considerable disturbance from many years of mining (SSN, 2017). The current mining permit discusses closure requirements including wildlife protection, vegetation management, soil salvage and storage, cultural heritage resources and air quality. During the permitting process, environmental concerns were raised by First Nations chiefs, particularly in relation to surface and subsurface water resources, the protection of cultural heritage, wildlife, and vegetation, reclamation of roads, mine waste piles and tailings, geotechnical stability, fuel or reagent spills and air quality (Permit M-229 New Afton, 2007). The permit outlines post-mine land use objectives as livestock grazing, wildlife habitat, and traditional land use where appropriate.

In 2015, interviews were conducted with traditional knowledge keepers of the Skeetchestn and Tk'emlúps te Secwepemc nations to understand the traditional land use of the area and to discuss their MR&C objectives for the New Afton Mine site (Collins, 2015). The list of traditional knowledge keepers was selected and approved by the Skeetchestn and Tk'emlúps te Secwepemc leadership. The traditional knowledge keepers were typically elders whose families had lived in the territory for generations.

The research found a significant disconnect between what the community wanted for a post-mine land use plan and what was technically feasible. For example, the subsidence zone, caused by the block caving mining method, is fenced off and access will be restricted in perpetuity. Access was one of the most important requests from the community and the permanent closure of part of their land was unacceptable to the local community, but considered an issue of safety for the mining company and regulators due to the risk of collapse.

Many traditional knowledge keepers also wanted the mine site area to be returned to native grassland. However, grasslands in the Kamloops region have changed significantly in the last 100 years due to grazing, climate change, forestry, water usage and general development in the area. To return the already heavily disturbed land to native grassland would take many decades and is almost impossible with currently available technologies.

Despite significant engagement and input from First Nations peoples throughout the planning phase, the inherent impacts of the mining method selected resulted in an unacceptable post-mine landscape. Ensuring that Indigenous communities are included in mine planning and are effectively consulted is an ongoing concern in BC. Finding and communicating realistic post mine solutions as well as aligning mining methods with desired post-closure landforms and use remains an ongoing challenge for regulators and Indigenous communities.

In the Yukon, a northern Canadian territory, mining has a long history starting with the Klondike Goldrush of the late nineteenth century (Coates and Morrison, 2017). In April of 2003, the Yukon became the first of Canada's three territories to take control of its land from the federal government. The requirements, principles, and guidelines for closure and reclamation are set out in the Yukon's Quartz Mining Act and the Yukon Mine Site Reclamation and Closure Policy. These documents allocate responsibility to the mine operator to develop a robust closure plan and ensure adequate funds are in place for MR&C. The principles promote the use of progressive reclamation and adaptive management, and encourage an understanding of the views of 'all relevant Yukon government departments, affected First Nations, local communities, and stakeholders' (Government of Yukon, 2006). Certificates of Closure are issued only once the Yukon government has consulted with the mine operator, affected First Nations, and local communities, as well as interested stakeholders (Government of Yukon, 2006).

Despite mining contributing to the shift towards a mixed wage–based economy in the Canadian North, away from a traditional land-based economy (Rixen and Blangy, 2016), many Indigenous community members have struggled with this shift, preferring traditionally based lifestyles (Carter, 2013). This is one key reason why Indigenous employment and retention, despite significant policy development, can be very low, resulting in less economic benefits from mining for the region (Collins and Kumral, 2021). MR&C is therefore essential to ensuring that traditional practices such as hunting, trapping and fishing can continue long after mining operations end, and that community members are able to maintain their traditional practices during the entire mine life cycle. As LeClerc and Keeling (2015) and Rixen and Blangy (2016) have shown, however, MR&C planning has failed to produce long-lasting benefits, both social and economic, for these northern communities.

Consultation with Indigenous communities is a requirement in all MR&C regulation across Canada, but these regulations do not ensure the incorporation of the local community's interests into final decisions. Overall, local community engagement and collaboration is improving, but outcomes can be drastically different depending on the region, regulator, community and mining company. When there are disagreements, our decision-making and regulation processes can struggle to allow differing perspectives into a final decision (Collins and Kumral, 2022). Moreover, there are limited mechanisms via which a community might refuse the closure plan if the inspector feels all requirements have been met by the company.

4 Discussion

There follow some key findings that emerge from the regulatory case studies identified in Section 3. Regulatory similarities and differences across the two jurisdictions were identified and inform these findings. Despite differences between the regulatory systems, we find that MR&C failure is a significant risk to Indigenous and local communities across both jurisdictions and that the regulatory frameworks, while much improved, are not comprehensively delivering secure ecological, social and economic afterlives for post-mine communities.

4.1 *'Toxic Legacies': MR&C Regulation is Failing to Ensure Viable Post-extractive Landscapes for Indigenous Peoples*

With much of Australia and Canada's mining activities neighbouring Indigenous communities (see Hunter, Howlett and Gray (2015) for example), Indigenous peoples have more to lose from poor mine rehabilitation and closure than the majority of Australians or Canadians as they do not leave when the mines close (O'Faircheallaigh and Lawrence, 2019). In cases of failed closure and reclamation, future local generations will continue to bear the often significant social, ecological, health, economic and cultural costs, or what Keeling and Sandlos (2015) call 'toxic legacies'. Despite this very real issue of environmental justice, Indigenous communities continue to face structural, political and institutional barriers to involvement in MR&C regulatory processes. Indigenous interests continue to be largely devalued and rendered invisible by other interests that coexist on their traditional lands, where invariably water and natural resource rights are granted to mining companies and more prominent systems of values—upheld by engineers, planners and environmental scientists—take precedence (Lane and Cowell, 2001).

Recent reforms of MR&C across Canada and Australia indicate that these resource states are largely concerned from a regulatory perspective with ensuring mining companies have sufficient financial capacity to ensure mine closure for post-mine land use and that the state is not left with the liability of mine rehabilitation (Mills, 2022). Regulation largely seeks to ensure viable post-mine land use using environmental/biophysical indicators that are singularly focused upon ecosystem responses with fine spatial scales. This regime asserts it is possible to 'borrow' temporarily from nature and to return it to a form similar to that of its previous ecology or to a system that will facilitate future economic use (Trigger, 1997). Successful MR&C is, however, very rare. Challenges, including changes in geomorphology and ecosystem function resulting from what can be decades of mine operation, may result in an inability to support a similar ecosystem or suitable post-mine land use (Collins, 2015; Lamb, Erskine and Fletcher, 2015) and can also result in extensive 'novel' ecosystems with limited social or ecological value (Erskine, Vickers and Mulligan, 2008). The variation in mine closure planning and costing can be immense due to variability in orebody estimation, environmental baseline studies and variable estimations in construction costs. Funding for contingencies can be the largest line item for MR&C, potentially making up 20 per cent of the total projected MR&C cost (Brodie 2013). Many mines close prematurely or in an unplanned way, increasing the likelihood of MR&C failure (Laurence, 2006). MR&C failure has the potential to far outweigh any positive economic and social benefits that Indigenous people might receive from mining on their traditional lands (Lawrence and O'Faircheallaigh, 2018). Furthermore, successful ecosystem recovery can take decades if not centuries (Nilsson et al., 2016), raising the question of whether mining can really be considered temporary land use. In both Canada and Australia, MR&C is often completed in short time frames, often resulting in poor recovery outcomes. Participant interviewees raised concerns that the regulators do not have the capacity, resources and expertise to ensure that MR&C delivers resilient native ecosystems or even viable agricultural land.

MR&C regulation across both Australia and Canada is inconsistent from state to state, province to province, nation to nation and company to company. The different levels of governance within both countries generally function cooperatively but at times can work separately, creating a confusing and overly bureaucratic environment for Indigenous engagement and collaboration. Our analysis of the regulatory frameworks across both jurisdictions suggests that these resource states are failing to prevent the negative social, cultural, economic and environmental impacts of MR&C and are placing Indigenous peoples at risk of intergenerational environmental injustice.

4.2 *Improving MR&C Regulation*

4.2.1 Long-Term Regulation

Much of MR&C assessment, as well as Indigenous stakeholder engagement and inclusion, is concentrated within the front-end assessment and approval phase (O'Faircheallaigh and Lawrence, 2019). Involvement in this process can be costly for local communities and they may not have the expertise to engage in these administrative and legal avenues. Much MR&C regulation with respect to social engagement and participation is—Vivoda, Kemp and Owen (2019, 422) argue—'enabling', with few regulatory restrictions or opportunities for local communities to intervene in the later phases of mine projects. O'Faircheallaigh and Corbett (2005) note that the opportunities for involvement by local communities are primarily predicated upon the project operator's discretion in providing traditional owners with the space to make decisions and engage with the project operator (see the bauxite mining example from Weipa, above). Considering many mines operate over long time periods, often upwards of 30 years, this lack of ongoing participation can result in the long-term exclusion of traditional owners from the management of their own territories. It can also result in monitoring, compliance and enforcement issues, a lack of both medium-to long-term stakeholder engagement and input and opportunities for traditional owner reassessment of MR&C objectives throughout the often decades long resource extraction project (Vivoda, Kemp and Owen, 2019). Exceptions can be found, however, in BC, where mine closure plans must be updated every five years, and in recent reforms that require progressive rehabilitation (for example, in Queensland, Australia) and ongoing review (for example, five-yearly reviews of mine closure plans in BC). These reforms were substantially motivated by concerns regarding state liability for MR&C failure (Mills, 2022), and initial observations from interview participants suggest that they show signs of increasing positive MR&C outcomes. Effective long-term active management and long-term funding of MR&C remain, however, live issues. Mining companies often seek to relinquish mine leases only five to ten years after mines cease production, which shifts the responsibility for the management of threats to recovery—such as weeds, feral animal control, and fire—to the landholder (often the state or communities) and can compromise recovery outcomes (Annandale, Meadows and Erskine, 2021), especially as ecosystems can take centuries to recover (Nilsson et al., 2016).

Such long-term management should not, however, be limited to just biophysical indicators. Certainly, ensuring the ecosystem recovery of a post-mine landscape is necessary to ensuring positive MR&C outcomes, but it is not enough. To ensure just post-extractive landscapes, increased regulatory attention to the ongoing social and cultural elements of MR&C is required (O'Faircheallaigh and Lawrence, 2019). This means that long-term management requires the long-term engagement and participation of local communities. Post-mine landscapes should be principally guided and developed with local Indigenous people, who have both environmental and social expectations of the post-mine landscape (Annandale, Meadows and Erskine, 2021; Collins, 2015). Social and ecological management of mine legacies requires adaptive, active management, stakeholder engagement and decision-making, monitoring, enforcement and assessment if it is to effectively deliver successful MR&C (Annandale, Meadows and Erskine, 2021; Bainton and Holcombe, 2018).

4.2.2 Valuing Indigenous Input

Regulation that is adaptive and responsive to local communities also requires the incorporation and valuing of multiple sources of knowledge (Gómez-Baggethun, Corbera and Reyes-García, 2013). MR&C policy and practice across Canada and Australia is largely concerned with meeting environmental and health indicators and ensuring future land use. There has been a recent push from mining regulators in Canada to protect and use traditional knowledge, but the manner in which it is expressed is often neither consistent nor appropriate, as noted by Sandlos and Keeling (2016). The usual technocratic, biophysical approach to management of MR&C is not in agreement with the manner in which many traditional owners conceptualise their relationship to land. Many traditional owners view their relationship to land as one that does not differentiate between culture and environment (de Castro, 2004; Descola, 2014; Wik Projects Ltd., 2009). Thus, MR&C regulation should include not only the biophysical sciences, but also social and economic sciences, and local 'factual' information. This combination of information contributes to an overall information database with linkages between the data collected, the geographic and spatial context, and the motivational value of the project (Annandale, Meadows and Erskine, 2021; Mascia et al., 2003; Robertson et al., 2000; Unger, Everingham and Bond, 2020). While strong Indigenous engagement may result in higher complexity and higher transaction costs, the effective engagement, consultation and knowledge of local communities along with their beliefs, values, norms and rules will likely increase the success rate of MR&C and help to avoid potential community backlash and social risk (Mascia et al., 2003; O'Faircheallaigh, 2008). Further empirical research is required to assess the potential of MR&C that envisions the restoration of biocultural landscapes (see Annandale, Meadows and Erskine 2021), but initial indicators suggest it may result in better collaboration, recognition of traditional owners' rights, and a certain economic potential for traditional owners who remain on 'country' (as Indigenous Australians commonly refer to their local homelands). To date, however, MR&C regulation largely remains focused on undertaking rehabilitation and closure in a cost-effective and efficient manner that meets environmental indicators and does not result in mining legacies for the state (Joyce and Thomson, 2000; MBS Environmental, 2016; O'Faircheallaigh, 2008; Prno and Slocombe, 2012). Matters of Indigenous input, engagement and participation are left to the discretion of mining companies.

4.2.3 Developing Community Control

While there has been a de-emphasising of Indigenous rights in favour of an examination and quantification of equality indicators (Scambary, 2013), traditional owners are rights-holders. Mining companies working within the sustainable development paradigm of corporate social responsibility should be engaging with them as such, not just as a stakeholders—as should MR&C regulation and policy (Lawrence and O'Faircheallaigh, 2018; The Mining Association of Canada, 2017). The regulatory landscape on this issue differs across Australia and Canada, and is an interesting point for comparison as Canada has made some significant progress in engaging First Nations members as rights-holders.

In Australia, mining companies do not have to, and often do not, engage and consult with Indigenous peoples before preparing mine closure plans (MBS Environmental, 2016; O'Faircheallaigh, 2013). Traditional owners rarely have significant decision-making roles in MR&C and there is limited articulation of Indigenous interests (Wik Projects Ltd., 2009; Lawrence and O'Faircheallaigh, 2018; Rum Jungle Traditional Owner Liaison Committee, 2018). Indeed, the Queensland government's mine rehabilitation policy and the discussion paper *Better Mine Rehabilitation for Queensland* do not mention native title or Indigenous persons at all (State of Queensland, 2017). At the federal level in Australia, guidelines acknowledge the benefit of engaging and working with Indigenous communities on MR&C planning but do not detail what should be communicated to traditional owners, the level of engagement and collaboration that should occur, or how Indigenous objectives can be achieved (Commonwealth of Australia, 2016a; 2016b). Mining industry guidelines are similarly deficient (ANZMEC and MCA, 2000). Despite its ubiquitous use, the sustainable development mantra as adopted by the mining industry has thus been criticised as a conceptual and political position 'explicitly conceived as a strategy for sustaining "development", not for supporting the flourishing and enduring of an infinitely diverse natural and social life' (Esteva, 2005, 16; see also Lanzano (2022) for a review of the mining/sustainability relationship in anthropology).

All this differs from the approach in Canada, where—relatively recently—provincial governments have attempted to include Indigenous communities during environmental assessment and permitting stages (Boiral, Heras-Saizarbitoria and Brotherton, 2020). The process and success of collaboration can differ drastically depending on the policies of the mining company, the expertise of the regulators, and the capacity of the community (Warhurst and Noronha, 2000). It is difficult to determine from the outset whether a collaboration process will be successful and consider the interests of different groups within a community. Additionally, it remains to be seen whether the process will be able to provide the community not only with short-term economic opportunities, but also with long-term sustainable value.

Land rights and economic rights can significantly improve the bargaining power of a community, rights to refuse resource extraction, for example, sometimes leading to better socio-economic outcomes for communities (Adebay and Werker, 2019). Such rights should also include the right to be fully informed of post-closure landscape feasibility, something that mining companies have sought to avoid (Lamb and Coakes, 2012). It is often not possible to restore mined areas completely due to the nature of the landscape degradation and the mine type (Collins, 2015). As the example of the New Afton mine indicates, communities (and government regulators for that matter) sometimes have little understanding of the technical constraints of rehabilitation. Failure to communicate the full extent of environmental issues that might exist post closure, such as those associated with the Faro and Giant mines in northern Canada (Government of Canada, 2018; Fawcett et al., 2015; Sandlos and Keeling, 2016) raises the issue of whether communities have been able to fully provide free, prior and informed consent to mining on their traditional lands. Bona fide engagement with traditional owners and the local community should be required in order to identify appropriate and possible post-mine land use options, and local communities should have the authority and the right to refuse mine closure certificates if closure does not meet their expectations of the post-mine landscape. More regular engagement with communities is also needed, all the way up to, and throughout, MR&C (Unger, Everingham and Bond, 2020). Such engagement is essential for meeting the environmental and economic MR&C expectations of local communities and acknowledging that these expectations are likely to change over the long life of the mine (Annandale, Meadows and Erskine, 2021).

Independent, community-led social and environmental assessments could help provide a better way for communities to discuss and communicate their concerns regarding major projects; unfortunately there are few examples of this being facilitated. Boulot (2017), meanwhile, suggests that traditional owners should be involved in mine operations as operators, stakeholders and equity owners, with mandatory positions on the board of the mining operator and exerting control over MR&C in order to preclude mine legacy concerns. An example of an Indigenously owned mine can be found in the Gulkula bauxite mine in northern Australia, with initial reports suggesting positive rehabilitation processes (Menon et al., 2021).

5 Conclusion

Indigenous communities continue to face significant barriers to their environmental management of their own lands, particularly when these lands are subject to mineral extraction. Regulation aimed at facilitating their involvement is often discretionary, with policy and guidelines (some prepared by the industry itself) giving only minimal direction as to best practice when engaging and collaborating with Indigenous traditional owners in the preparation of MCPs as well as regarding ongoing environmental management. Indigenous communities are still marginalised by regulators in the narratives of sustainable development and sustainable mining despite their specific vulnerability to MR&C failure and the significant and increasing risk of cultural, environmental and economic losses.

Traditional owners must therefore have more regulatory opportunities for involvement, and more decision-making powers, from the very beginning to the very end of mine projects, with opportunities to reconsider rehabilitation/ restoration outcomes over the mine life cycle. Their stories, culture and aspirations for future land use can help frame MR&C goals and ensure effective, ongoing cultural connections to landscape and country. Exactly how much consideration and engagement is required is place-, community-and mine-specific, and requires careful support from regulators.

In addition, Indigenous communities that border on or own mining sites should be recognised as rights-holders and enjoy appropriate regulatory avenues for involvement and decision-making. Such rights should include, at the very least, the opportunity to refuse mining on their ancestral lands. Free, prior and informed consent is impossible when refusing mining development is not an option (Bond and Kelly, 2020). The right to refuse also places Indigenous peoples in a better bargaining position and potentially improves their economic, social, environmental and cultural outcomes (O'Faircheallaigh and Corbett, 2005).

Ensuring better MR&C outcomes may also require financial bonds to be paid directly to communities and traditional owner groups. This process, supported and facilitated by regulatory bodies with appropriate enabling regulatory frameworks, would not only support Indigenous peoples' right to self-determination, it could also protect local communities against the risk of failed MR&C. Such community bonds might provide communities with the financial security to meet some of the social costs of mine closure and constitute economic opportunities from MR&C other than those offered by simple mine royalties. Such a process would necessarily require the involvement of traditional owners throughout the entire mine life cycle.

References

Adebay, E. and E. Werker (2019) *Estimating the Value of Benefits in Benefit-Sharing Agreements*, Conference Proceedings, presented at The 9th International Conference on Sustainable Development in the Minerals Industry (Sydney: Australasian Institute of Mining and Metallurgy), https://www.ausimm.com/publications/conference-proceedings/sdimi-2019/estimating-the-value-of-benefits-in-benefit-sharing-agreements/ (accessed on 3 September 2022).

Annandale, M., J. Meadows and P. Erskine (2021) 'Indigenous forest livelihoods and bauxite mining: a case-study from northern Australia', *Journal of Environmental Management*, 294(113014), DOI: 10.1016/j.jenvman.2021.113014.

ANZMEC (Australian and New Zealand Minerals and Energy Council) and MCA (Minerals Council of Australia) (2000) *Strategic Framework for Mine Closure*, National Library of Australia Catalogue Data, https://www.sernageomin.cl/wp-content/uploads/2017/11/Strategic-Framework-Mine-Closure.pdf (accessed on 3 September 2022).

Bainton, N. and S. Holcombe (2018) 'A Critical Review of the Social Aspects of Mine Closure', *Resources Policy*, 59, pp. 468–478, DOI: 10.1016/j.resourpol.2018.08.020.

Baldwin, R., C. Scott and C. Hood (eds.) (1998) *A Reader on Regulation* (Oxford: Oxford University Press).

Bartle, J. and C. Slessar (1989) 'Mining and Rehabilitation', in B. Dell, J.J. Havel and N. Malajczuk (eds.) *The Jarrah forest: a Complex Mediterranean Ecosystem* (Dordrecht: Kluwer Academic Publishers), pp. 357–377.

BC Mines Act (1996) *RSBC* (Victoria, BC: King's Printer), http://www.bclaws.ca/civix/document/id/complete/statreg/96293_01 (accessed on 3 September 2022).

BC Ministry of Energy and Mines (2017) *Health, Safety and Reclamation Code for Mines in British Columbia* (Victoria, BC: Ministry of Energy and Mines), www2.gov.bc.ca/gov/content/industry/mineral-exploration-mining/health-safety/health-safety-and-reclamation-code-for-mines-in-british-columbia (accessed on 3 September 2022).

Behrendt, L. and L. Strelein (2001) 'Old Habits Die Hard: Indigenous Land Rights and Mining in Australia', *Cultural Survival Quarterly Magazine*, March, https://www.culturalsurvival.org/publications/cultural-survival-quarterly/old-habits-die-hard-indigenous-land-rights-and-mining (accessed on 3 September 2022).

Boiral, O., I. Heras-Saizarbitoria and M.-C. Brotherton (2020) 'Improving Environmental Management Through Indigenous Peoples' Involvement', *Environmental Science & Policy*, 103, pp. 10–20, DOI: 10.1016/j.envsci.2019.10.006.

Bond, C. and L. Kelly (2020) 'Returning Land to Country: Indigenous Engagement in Mined Land Closure and Rehabilitation', *Australian Journal of Management*, 46(1), pp. 174–192, DOI: 10.1177/0312896220919136.

Boulot, E. and A. Akhtar-Khavari (2020) 'Law, Restoration and Ontologies for a More Ecologically Complex World!', *The University of Queensland Law Journal*, 39(3), pp. 450–473, DOI: 10.38127/uqlj.v39i3.5657.

Boulot, P. (2017) 'The Common Law Crisis of Perception and the Wik People's Tender for Cape York Mining', *Alternative Law Journal*, 42(3), pp. 206–210, DOI: 10.1177/1037969X17730198.

Bowie, R. (2013) 'Indigenous Self-Governance and the Deployment of Knowledge in Collaborative Environmental Management in Canada', *Journal of Canadian Studies*, 47(1), pp. 91–121, DOI: 10.3138/jcs.47.1.91.

Brodie, J. (2013) 'Considerations in Mine Reclamation Costing', *B.C. Mine Reclamation Symposium*, DOI: 10.14288/1.0056600.

Campbell, R., J. Linqvist, B. Browne, T. Swann and M. Grudnoff (2017) 'Dark Side of the Boom: What We Do and Don't Know About Mines, Closures and Rehabilitation', *The Australia Institute* (Canberra: the Australia Institute), https://australiainstitute.org.au/wp-content/uploads/2020/12/P192-Dark-side-of-the-boom-web.pdf (accessed on 3 September 2022)..

Carter, T.I. (2013) *When Mining Comes (Back) to Town: Exploring Historical and Contemporary Mining Encounters in the Kivalliq Region, Nunavut*, Master's Thesis (St. John's, NL: Memorial University), https://www.academia.edu/11644852/WHEN_MINING_COMES_BACK_TO_TOWN_EXPLORING_HISTORICAL_AND_CONTEMPORARY_MINING_ENCOUNTERS_IN_THE_KIVALLIQ_REGION_NUNAVUT (accessed on 3 September 2022).

Coates, K.S. and W.R. Morrison (2017) *Land of the Midnight Sun: a History of the Yukon, Third Edition* (Montreal, QC: McGill-Queen's University Press).

Collins, B.C. (2015) *Mine Closure Planning with First Nations Communities: the Stk'emlupsemc te Secwepemc Nation and the New Afton Mine*, B.C. Mine Reclamation

Symposium (Vancouver, BC: University of British Columbia), DOI: 10.14288/1.0135530.

Collins, B.C. and M. Kumral (2022) 'Examining impact and benefit agreements in mineral extraction using game theory and multiple-criteria decision making', *The Extractive Industries and Society*, 10(101094), DOI: 10.1016/j.exis.2022.101094.

Collins, B.C. and M. Kumral (2021) 'A Critical Perspective on Social License to Operate Terminology for Canada's Most Vulnerable Mining Communities', *The Extractive Industries and Society*, 8(2), DOI: 10.1016/j.exis.2020.11.002.

Commonwealth of Australia (2016a) *Leading Practice Sustainable Development Program for the Mining Industry: Mine Closure* (Canberra, ACT: Australian Government) www.industry.gov.au/data-and-publications/leading-practice-handbook-mine-closure (accessed on 3 September 2022).

Commonwealth of Australia (2016b) *Leading Practice Sustainable Development Program for the Mining Industry: Mine Rehabilitation* (Canberra, ACT: Australian Government) www.industry.gov.au/sites/default/files/2019-04/lpsdp-mine-rehabilitation-handbook-english.pdf (accessed on 3 September 2022).

de Castro, E.V. (2004) 'Exchanging Perspectives: the Transformation of Objects into Subjects in Amerindian Ontologies', *Common Knowledge*, 10(3), pp. 463–484, DOI: 10.1215/0961754X-10-3-463.

Department of Environment and Heritage Protection, Department of Natural Resources and Mines, and Queensland Treasury (n.d.) *Mined Land Rehabilitation* (Queensland: Queensland Government), https://environment.des.qld.gov.au/__data/assets/pdf_file/0035/87659/mined-land-rehabilitation-policy.pdf (accessed on 4 November 2022).

Department of Industry, Tourism and Resources, Australia (2006) *Leading Practice Sustainable Development Program: Mine Closure and Completion* (Canberra, ACT: Australian Government), https://nt.gov.au/__data/assets/pdf_file/0015/203415/mine-closure-and-completion.pdf (accessed on 3 September 2022).

Descola, P. (2014) *Beyond Nature and Culture* (Chicago: University of Chicago Press).

DMIRS (Department of Mines, Industry Regulation and Safety) (2020) *Statutory Guidelines for Mine Closure Plans* (Perth, WA: Government of Western Australia), http://www.dmp.wa.gov.au/Documents/Environment/REC-EC-111D.pdf (accessed on 3 September 2022).

Erskine, P., H. Vickers and D. Mulligan (2008) *Completion Criteria for Native Ecosystem Rehabilitation at RTA Weipa—Report to Rio Tinto Alcan—Weipa Operations* (Brisbane: Centre for Mined Land Rehabilitation).

Esteva, G. (2005) 'Development', in W. Sachs (ed.) *The Development Dictionary. A Guide to Knowledge as Power* (London: Zed Books Ltd), pp. 1–23.

Everingham, J.-A., J. Rolfe, A.M. Lechner, S. Kinnear and D. Akbar (2018) 'A Proposal for Engaging a Stakeholder Panel in Planning Post-Mining Land Uses in Australia's

Coal-Rich Tropical Savannahs', *Land Use Policy*, 79, pp. 397–406, DOI: 10.1016/j.landusepol.2018.08.038.

Fawcett, S.E., H.E. Jamieson, D.K. Nordstrom and R.B. McCleskey (2015) 'Arsenic and Antimony Geochemistry of Mine Wastes, Associated Waters and Sediments at the Giant Mine, Yellowknife, Northwest Territories, Canada', *Applied Geochemistry*, 62, pp. 3–17, DOI: 10.1016/j.apgeochem.2014.12.012.

Ford, L. and T. Rowse (2013) *Between Indigenous and Settler Governance* (London, New York: Routledge).

Gardner, J. and D. Bell (2007) 'Bauxite Mining Restoration by Alcoa World Alumina Australia in Western Australia: Social, Political, Historical, and Environmental Contexts', *Restoration Ecology*, 15(s4), pp. S3–S10, DOI: 10.1111/j.1526-100X.2007.00287.x.

Gibson, G. and J. Klinck (2005) 'Canada's Resilient North: the Impact of Mining on Aboriginal Communities', *Pimatisiwin: a Journal of Aboriginal and Indigenous Community Health*, 3(1), pp. 115–139.

Godden, L. (2012) 'Native Title and Ecology: Agreement-making in an Era of Market Environmentalism', in J.K. Weir (ed.) *Country, Native Title and Ecology* (Canberra: ANU Press and Aboriginal History Inc.), pp. 105–134.

Gómez-Baggethun, E., E. Corbera and V. Reyes-García (2013) 'Traditional Ecological Knowledge and Global Environmental Change: Research findings and policy implications', *Ecology and Society*, 18(4), pp. 72, DOI: 10.5751/ES-06288-180472.

Government of British Columbia (2019) *Mine Permitting* (Ottawa: Government of Canada), https://www2.gov.bc.ca/gov/content/industry/mineral-exploration-mining/permitting (accessed on 3 September 2022).

Government of Canada (2018) *Faro Mine Remediation Project: Yukon*, (Ottawa: Government of Canada), https://www.rcaanc-cirnac.gc.ca/eng/1480019546952/1537554989037 (accessed on 3 September 2022).

Government of Canada (2012) *Canadian Environmental Assessment Act, S.C. 2012, c. 19, s. 52*, (Ottawa: Government of Canada), https://laws-lois.justice.gc.ca/eng/acts/c-15.21/ (accessed on 3 September 2022).

Government of Yukon (2006) *Yukon Mine Site Reclamation and Closure Policy* (Yukon: Energy, Mines & Resources, Government of Yukon) https://yukon.ca/sites/yukon.ca/files/emr/emr-forms/emr-yukon-mine-site-reclamation-closure-policy.pdf (accessed on 3 September 2022).

Hunter, B., M. Howlett and M. Gray (2015) 'The Economic Impacts of the Mining Boom on Indigenous and Non-Indigenous Australians', *Asia & the Pacific Policy Studies*, 2(3), pp. 517–30, DOI: 10.1002/app5.99.

ICMM (International Council on Mining & Metals) (2022) *ICMM Principles* (London: ICMM), www.icmm.com/en-gb/our-principles (accessed on 3 September 2022).

ICMM (2019) *Integrated Mine Closure: Good Practice Guide,* 2nd ed (London: ICMM), https://www.icmm.com/website/publications/pdfs/environmental-stewardship/2019/guidance_integrated-mine-closure.pdf (accessed on 3 September 2022).

ICMM (2008) *Planning for Integrated Mine Closure: Toolkit* (London: ICMM), https://www.socialimpactassessment.com/documents/ICMM%20Closure%20Toolkit.pdf (accessed on 3 September 2022).

Ioris, A.A.R. (2015) 'Theorizing State-Environment Relationships: Antinomies of Flexibility and Legitimacy', *Progress in Human Geography*, 39(2), pp. 167–184, DOI: 10.1177/0309132513516893.

Jones, J. and B. Bradshaw (2015) 'Addressing Historical Impacts Through Impact and Benefit Agreements and Health Impact Assessment: Why it Matters for Indigenous Well-Being', *The Northern Review*, 41, pp. 81–109, DOI: 10.22584/nr41.2015.004.

Joyce, S. and I. Thomson (2000) 'Earning a Social Licence to Operate: Social Acceptability and Resource Development in Latin America', *Canadian Institute of Mining, Metallurgy and Petroleum* (CIM Bulletin), 93(1037), pp. 1–9.

Keeling, A. and J. Sandlos (eds.) (2015) *Mining and Communities in Northern Canada: History, Politics, and Memory* (Canada: University of Calgary Press).

Kinnane, S. (2005) 'Indigenous Sustainability: Rights, Obligations and a Collective Commitment to Country', in J. Castellino and N. Walsh (eds.) *International Law and Indigenous Peoples* (Leiden and Boston: Kluwer Law International), pp. 159–194.

Lamb, D., P.D. Erskine and A. Fletcher (2015) 'Widening Gap Between Expectations and Practice in Australian Minesite Rehabilitation', *Ecological Management & Restoration*, 16(3), pp. 186–195, DOI: 10.1111/emr.12179.

Lamb, K. and S. Coakes (2012) 'Effective Social Planning for Mine Closure', in A.B. Fourie and M. Tibbett (eds.) *Mine closure 2012: Proceedings of the seventh International Conference on Mine Closure* (Perth: Australian Centre for Geomechanics), pp. 627–640, DOI: 10.36487/ACG_rep/1208_53_Lamb.

Lane, M. and S. Cowell (2001) 'Land and Resource Planning and Indigenous Interests: Reproducing or transforming the social relations of resource use', in O. Yiftachel, J. Little, D. Hedgcock and I. Alexander (eds.) *The Power of Planning: Spaces of Control and Transformation* (Dordrecht: Springer), pp. 155–169.

Langton, M., M. Tehan, L. Palmer and K. Shain (eds.) (2004) *Honour Among Nations? Treaties and Agreements with Indigenous People* (Melbourne: Melbourne University Press).

Langton, M., O. Mazel, L.R. Palmer, K. Shain and M. Tehan (eds.) (2006) *Settling with Indigenous People: Modern Treaty and Agreement-making* (Sydney: Federation Press)..

Lanzano, C. (2022) 'Sustainability', in L. D'Angelo and R.J. Pijpers (eds.) *The Anthropology of Resource Extraction* (Taylor and Francis), pp. 149–166.

Laurence, D. (2006) 'Optimisation of the Mine Closure Process', *Journal of Cleaner Production*, 14(3–4), pp. 285–298, DOI: 10.1016/j.jclepro.2004.04.011.

Law Commission of Canada (2008) *Indigenous Legal Traditions* (Vancouver: UBC Press).

Lawrence, R. and C. O'Faircheallaigh (2018) *Submission 82*, on Rehabilitation of Mining and Resources Projects as it Relates to Commonwealth Responsibilities, Submissions received by the Committee (Canberra: Commonwealth of Australia)..

LeClerc, E. and A. Keeling (2015) 'From Cutlines to Traplines: Post-Industrial Land Use at the Pine Point Mine', *The Extractive Industries and Society*, 2(1), pp. 7–18, DOI: 10.1016/j.exis.2014.09.001.

MAC (The Mining Association of Canada) (2017) *TSM Aboriginal and Community Outreach Protocol* (Ottawa: MAC), https://mining.ca/resources/guides-manuals/tsm-aboriginal-and-community-outreach-protocol-2017/ (accessed on 3 September 2022)..

MAC (2004) *Towards Sustainable Mining* (Ottawa: MAC), http://mining.ca/towards-sustainable-mining (accessed on 3 September 2022).

MacDonald, C. and P. Sloman (2020) 'Resource Extraction, Economic Growth, and the Climate Dilemma in Canada and Australia', *The Political Quarterly*, 91(4), pp. 780–785, DOI: 10.1111/1467-923X.12902.

Mascia, M.B., J.P. Brosius, T.A. Dobson, B.C. Forbes, L. Horowitz, M.A. McKean and N.J. Turner (2003) 'Conservation and the Social Sciences', *Conservation Biology*, 17(3), pp. 649–650, DOI: 10.1046/j.1523-1739.2003.01738.x.

MBS Environmental (2017) *Public Environmental Review—Thunderbird Mineral Sands Project* (Perth: Sheffield Resources).

MBS Environmental (2016) *Mine Closure Plan; Thunderbird Mineral Sands Project M04/459, L04/82, L04/83, L04/85 and L04/86* (Perth: Sheffield Resources).

Meadows, J., M. Annandale and L. Ota (2019) 'Indigenous Peoples' Participation in Sustainability Standards for Extractives', *Land Use Policy*, 88, pp. 1–13, DOI: 10.1016/j.landusepol.2019.104118.

Menon, T., M. Annandale, J. Meadows and P. Diallo (2021) *Gulkula—The Indigenous Mine Pioneering Sustainability in the Aluminium Supply Chain*, report (Australia: University of the Sunshine Coast for the Aluminium Stewardship Initiative), https://static1.squarespace.com/static/6082baaa0a18ee3263b36a45/t/609d3f9a2ec66c3e98fab506/1620918190125/Gulkula+Case+Study_USC.pdf (accessed on 3 September 2022).

Menzies, C.R. (2006) *Traditional Ecological Knowledge and Natural Resource Management* (Lincoln: University of Nebraska Press).

Mills, L.N. (2022) 'Getting closure? Mining rehabilitation reform in Queensland and Western Australia', *The Extractive Industries and Society*, 101097, DOI: 10.1016/j.exis.2022.101097.

Missens, R., L.P. Dana and R. Anderson (2007) 'Aboriginal Partnerships in Canada: Focus on the Diavik Diamond Mine', *Journal of Enterprising Communities: People and Places in the Global Economy*, 1(1), pp. 54–76, DOI: 10.1108/17506200710736267.

Myette, E. (2022) *Unearthing the discursive politics of mining on Indigenous lands: knowledge, health, contestation, and power in contemporary Canadian regulatory infrastructures*, Master's Thesis (Montreal, QC: McGill University).

Nichols, O.G. and F.M. Nichols (2003) 'Long-term Trends in Faunal Recolonization After Bauxite Mining in the Jarrah Forest of Southwestern Australia', *Restoration Ecology*, 11(3), pp. 261–272, DOI: 10.1046/j.1526-100X.2003.00190.x.

Nilsson, C., A.L. Aradottir, D. Hagen, G. Halldórsson, K. Høegh, R.J. Mitchell, K. Raulund-Rasmussen, K. Svavarsdóttir, A. Tolvanen and S.D. Wilson (2016) 'Evaluating the Process of Ecological Restoration', *Ecology and Society*, 21(1), pp. 41, DOI: 10.5751/ES-08289-210141.

NOAMI (National Orphaned/Abandoned Mines Initiative) (2015) *NOAMI performance update 2009–2015* (Ottawa: National Orphaned/Abandoned Mines Initiative), https://abandoned-mines.org/wp/wp-content/uploads/2015/08/NOAMI-2015-UPDATE-ENG-WEB.pdf (accessed on 3 September 2022).

Nuttall, M. (2010) *Pipeline Dreams: People, Environment, and the Arctic Energy Frontier* (Copenhagen: IWGIA, International Work Group for Indigenous Affairs).

O'Faircheallaigh, C. (2013) 'Extractive Industries and Indigenous Peoples: a Changing Dynamic?', *Journal of Rural Studies*, 30, pp. 20–30, DOI: 10.1016/j.jrurstud.2012.11.003.

O'Faircheallaigh, C. (2008) 'Negotiating Cultural Heritage? Aboriginal–Mining Company Agreements in Australia', *Development and Change*, 39(1), pp. 25–51, DOI: 10.1111/j.1467-7660.2008.00467.x.

O'Faircheallaigh, C. (2007) 'Native Title and Mining Negotiations: a Seat at the Table, But No Guarantee of Success', *Indigenous Law Bulletin*, 21(6), pp. 18–20, http://classic.austlii.edu.au/au/journals/IndigLawB/2007/21.html (accessed on 3 September 2022).

O'Faircheallaigh, C. and R. Lawrence (2019) 'Mine Closure and the Aboriginal Estate', *Australian Aboriginal Studies Journal*, 1, pp. 65–81.

O'Faircheallaigh, C. and T. Corbett (2005) 'Indigenous Participation in Environmental Management of Mining Projects: the Role of Negotiated Agreements', *Environmental Politics*, 14(5), pp. 629–647, DOI: 10.1080/09644010500257912.

Owen, J. and D. Kemp (2018) *Mine Closure and Social Performance: an Industry Discussion Paper*, Centre for Social Responsibility in Mining, Sustainable Minerals Institute (Brisbane: The University of Queensland).

Parliament of Australia (2017) *Rehabilitation of Mining and Resources Projects as it Relates to Commonwealth Responsibilities* (Canberra, ACT: Commonwealth of Australia), https://www.aph.gov.au/Parliamentary_Business/Committees/Senate/Environment_and_Communications/MiningandResources (accessed on 3 September 2022).

Permit M-229 New Afton (2007) https://mines.nrs.gov.bc.ca/p/new-afton/authorizations (accessed on 3 September 2022).

Prno, J. and D.S. Slocombe (2014) 'A Systems-based Conceptual Framework for Assessing the Determinants of a Social License to Operate in the Mining Industry', *Environmental Management*, 53(3), pp. 672–689, DOI: 10.1007/s00267-013-0221-7.

Queensland Audit Office (2013) *Environmental Regulation of the Resources and Waste Industries*, Report 15–14 (Brisbane, QLD: State of Queensland).

Queensland Treasury Corporation (2017) *Review of Queensland's Financial Assurance Framework*, (State of Queensland) https://s3.treasury.qld.gov.au/files/review-of-queenslands-financial-assurance-framework.pdf (accessed on 3 October 2023).

Rio Tinto (2019) *Rio Tinto Weipa Rehabilitation Management Plan* (London: Rio Tinto Pty Ltd.).

Rixen, A. and S. Blangy (2016) 'Life After Meadowbank: Exploring Gold Mine Closure Scenarios with the Residents of Qamini'tuaq (Baker Lake), Nunavut', *The Extractive Industries and Society*, 3(2), pp. 297–312, DOI: 10.1016/j.exis.2015.09.003.

Robertson, M., P. Nichols, P. Horwitz, K. Bradby and D. MacKintosh (2000) 'Environmental Narratives and the Need for Multiple Perspectives to Restore Degraded Landscapes in Australia', *Ecosystem Health*, 6(2), pp. 119–133, DOI: 10.1046/j.1526-0992.2000.00013.x.

Rum Jungle Traditional Owner Liaison Committee (2018) *Submission 90*, on Rehabilitation of Mining and Resources Projects as it Relates to Commonwealth Responsibilities, Submissions received by the Committee (Canberra: Commonwealth of Australia).

Sandlos, J. and A. Keeling (2016) 'Toxic Legacies, Slow Violence, and Environmental Injustice at Giant Mine, Northwest Territories', *The Northern Review*, 42, pp. 7–21, DOI: 10.22584/nr42.2016.002.

Scambary, B. (2013) *My Country, Mine Country: Indigenous People, Mining and Development Contestation in Remote Australia*, Centre for Aboriginal Economic Policy Research (CAEPR), CAEPR Monograph No. 33 (Canberra: ANU E-Press), DOI: 10.22459/CAEPR33.05.2013.

Schmitt, R., S.E. Ames and D. Stoopnikoff (2008) 'Development of the New Afton Copper Gold Mine on a Former Minesite in the Agricultural Land Reserve, Kamloops, BC', *British Columbia Mine Reclamation* Symposium, DOI: 10.14288/1.0042547.

SECRC (The Senate Environment and Communications References Committee) (2019) *Rehabilitation of Mining and Resources Projects and Power Station Ash Dams as it Relates to Commonwealth Responsibilities* (Canberra, ACT: Environment and Communications References Committee), https://apo.org.au/sites/default/files/resource-files/2019-03/apo-nid226336.pdf (accessed on 3 September 2022).

South of the Embley Communities, Heritage and Environment Working Group (2014) *South of the Embley: Communities, Heritage and Environment Management Plan*

(London: Rio Tinto Alcan and WCCCA, Western Cape Communities Coexistence Agreement), https://capeyorknrm.com.au/sites/default/files/2020-05/rta_chemp_report_0914_south_embley.pdf (accessed on 3 September 2022).

State of Queensland (2018) *Achieving Improved Rehabilitation for Queensland: Other Associated Risks and Proposed Solutions,* Discussion Paper (Brisbane: Queensland Government), https://s3.treasury.qld.gov.au/files/8244_Associated-Risks-discussion-paper-V61.pdf (accessed on 3 September 2022).

State of Queensland (2017) *Better Mine Rehabilitation for Queensland,* Discussion Paper (Brisbane: Queensland Government), https://s3.treasury.qld.gov.au/files/better-mine-rehabilitation-in-qld-discussion-paper.pdf (accessed on 3 September 2022).

SSN (Stk'emlupsemc te Secwepemc Nation) (2017) *Decision of the SSN Joint Council on the Proposed KGHM Ajax,* stkemlups.ca/wp-content/uploads/2013/11/3-2017.03.04-SSN-Joint-Council-Decision-Document-.pdf (accessed on 3 September 2022).

Stoeckl, N., S. Jackson, F. Pantus, M. Finn, M.J. Kennard and B.J. Pusey (2013) 'An Integrated Assessment of Financial, Hydrological, Ecological and Social Impacts of "Development" on Indigenous and Non-Indigenous People in Northern Australia', *Biological Conservation,* 159, pp. 214–221, DOI: 10.1016/j.biocon.2012.12.007.

Trigger, D. (1998) 'Citizenship and Indigenous Responses to Mining in the Gulf Country', in N. Peterson and W. Sanders (eds.) *Citizenship and Indigenous Australians: Changing Conceptions and Possibilities* (Cambridge: Cambridge University Press).

Trigger, D. (1997) 'Mining, Landscape and the Culture of Development Ideology in Australia', *Ecumene,* 4(2), pp. 161–180, https://www.jstor.org/stable/44251910 (accessed on 6 February 2023).

Trigger, D., J. Mulcock, A. Gaynor and Y. Toussaint (2008) 'Ecological Restoration, Cultural Preferences and the Negotiation of "Nativeness" in Australia', *Geoforum,* 39(3), pp. 1273–1283, DOI: 10.1016/j.geoforum.2007.05.010.

Unger, C.J., A. Lechner, V. Glenn, M. Edraki and D.R. Mulligan (2012) 'Mapping and Prioritising Rehabilitation of Abandoned Mines in Australia', paper presented to Life-of-Mine Conference, Brisbane, 10-12 July.

Unger, C.J., J.-A. Everingham and C.J. Bond (2020) 'Transition or Transformation: Shifting Priorities and Stakeholders in Australian Mined Land Rehabilitation and Closure', *Australasian Journal of Environmental Management,* 27(1), pp. 84–113, DOI: 10.1080/14486563.2020.1719440.

Vivoda, V., D. Kemp and J. Owen (2019) 'Regulating the Social Aspects of Mine Closure in Three Australian States', *Journal of Energy & Natural Resources,* 37(4), pp. 405–424, DOI: 10.1080/02646811.2019.1608030.

Warhurst, A. and L. Noronha (2000) 'Corporate Strategy and Viable Future Land Use: Planning for Closure from the Outset of Mining', *Natural Resources Forum,* 24(2), pp. 153–164, DOI: 10.1111/j.1477-8947.2000.tb00939.x.

Wik Projects Ltd. (2009) *Towards a Rehabilitation Plan for Bauxite Mines on Wik Waya Country, Draft Report* [(Personal communication]).

World Bank Group and International Finance Corporation (2002) *It's Not Over When It's Over: Mine Closure Around the World*, report (Washington, D.C.: World Bank Group's Mining Department).

PART 2

Resilience, Contestation and Resistance

CHAPTER 6

Aluminium in Suriname (1898–2020): an Industry Came and Went, But Its Impacts on the Maroon Communities Remain

Simon Lobach

Abstract

Suriname was one of the first countries in the global South to produce aluminium. The establishment of this industry, including the hydroelectric dam that was meant to power it, was the key idea upon which Suriname's entire dream of modernity and independence was constructed. Negotiations with the Aluminum Company of America (Alcoa) resulted in Suriname accepting a treaty under which hardly any benefits accumulated in the country itself, while the establishment of the industry caused loss of land, environmental damage and the deculturation of the Surinamese Maroon communities. After these revolted against the state, Alcoa left the country, leaving behind an 'aluminium landscape' where aluminium is no longer produced, but where the original population, insofar as its members have not moved to the cities, is still heavily affected by the changes caused by the Surinamese aluminium boom.

1 Introduction

The twentieth century history of Suriname, a small republic and former Dutch colony on South America's northern shore, is closely tied to the extraction of bauxite and its transformation into aluminium. Ever since the element was identified in 1898 in the 'red soil' that is abundant in the country's interior, it has fuelled hopes of economic growth, political independence, and employment—in short, hopes of 'development'. Having become the world's main exporter of bauxite in the 1940s, Suriname was, by the 1970s, one of the first countries in the global South to have built an entire infrastructure to transform bauxite into aluminium, including the hydroelectric dam that would power that infrastructure.

Today, the aluminium factories of Suriname are closed. Investors retreated from the country 20 years earlier than the date they had agreed upon, leaving behind a landscape rationalised for bauxite extraction but inhabited by the

 | DOI:10.1163/9789004686182_007

same Maroon communities that already lived there a century earlier. Amidst industrial structures, in company towns, and on the shores of the artificial lake created by the flooding of their ancestral lands, these Afro-descendent populations are faced with the challenge of finding new livelihoods and sources of income, now that large tracts of their land have changed beyond recognition.

The Surinamese aluminium industry and its impacts on Maroon communities share many commonalities with other neo-extractivist 'resource booms' that we can observe around the world. The discovery of a valuable resource is often perceived as a promise of human and social development, but cases abound in which the expansion of extractive activities has not matched such expectations, and rather has exacerbated inequality, insecurity, corruption and environmental degradation (as described, for example, by Acosta (2013), Kirsch (2014) and several of the contributions in this volume). Moreover, extractive activities play an important role in the expropriation, marginalisation and deculturation of indigenous and tribal communities living in resource-rich areas.

At the end of the Second World War, Suriname embarked on a pathway to independence, adopting industrialisation as its main strategy for progress, echoing similar strategies that at the time were being implemented in other, much larger South American countries. A major source of inspiration for these strategies was dependency theorists like the Argentinian economist Raúl Prebisch, who encouraged Latin American countries to industrialise in order to break with the role that the international division of labour had 'bestowed' on them as providers of food and raw materials for industrial centres (Prebisch, 1950). These post-war industrialisation policies may have increased employment, economic growth and levels of specialisation in certain countries, but as this chapter shows they often failed to generate improved living conditions for the broader population. Whether an industry-based pathway can generate a development pathway that can be inclusive of a country's entire population in the long run, or even one that includes that country's population at all, depends on a range of factors.

The Surinamese bauxite and aluminium industry provides a unique opportunity to evaluate a resource development cycle already completed, from discovery to resource fever, and from industrial development to eventual decay and closure. I aim to show how the development of this mineral-based industry in the global South contained a promise of development, but already created winners and losers in the short term, and ended up benefiting almost no one in the long term. I identify the factors that were responsible for the failure of the aluminium industry in Suriname, offering reflections not only on the heyday of a mineral and industrial bonanza, but especially on the period that followed it. Such lessons could be valuable for other countries who find themselves in an earlier stage of an extractivist or neo-extractivist resource boom (as in the examples described by Gudynas, 2009; Acosta, 2013; and Svampa, 2015), and ironically also for Suriname itself, which discovered large offshore oil reserves in 2020. Amid new hopes of a resource-fuelled windfall, we may actually be looking at a repetition of history.

The history of Suriname's bauxite and aluminium sector has been described by economic historians such as Westermann (1971), Lamur (1983) and especially Pollack (2016). Several authors have highlighted a number of perspectives on Maroon history in the context of an expanding mining sector (Thoden van Velzen and Van Wetering, 1988; Scholtens, 1994; De Theije and Heemskerk, 2009; Price, 2011; De Koning, 2011a; 2011b; Gomes da Cunha, 2018). The present contribution aims to combine these two strands of scholarship, showing how the chemical and industrial processes used to produce aluminium have shaped physical, social, cultural and environmental landscapes in Suriname, and how Surinamese Maroons have been involuntary players in a narrative of industrialisation and development. Thus, it discusses the supply chains of bauxite and aluminium, the emergence and downfall of Suriname's bauxite and aluminium industries, the changes set in motion by these developments, and the impacts they had on the livelihoods and ways of living of the traditional populations of the area.

The chapter uses a mix of methods. It relies on the available literature on the history of aluminium and bauxite extraction as well as on Maroon history, complemented with original research in the national archives of Suriname and the Netherlands. It also relies on interviews and observations from a field trip I undertook early in 2020—a trip unfortunately cut short due to the COVID-19 pandemic.

2 Suriname and the 'Invention' of Aluminium

Suriname is located on the Guiana Shield, a geologically old area that contains, besides its bauxite cover, significant amounts of gold and gemstones. A Dutch colony since 1667, Suriname's coast was developed into a slavery-based plantation economy exporting several tropical commodities. But this 'plantation of Suriname' (Van Lier, 1949) was only a tiny piece of the colony's territory. The remainder of the country, the interior, only accessible by travelling up one of the mighty rivers with their swirling *soela's* (rapids), was covered by dense forests (still today, forests cover over 80 per cent of Suriname, making it the most forested country in the world (FAO, 2015)) that formed an ideal refuge and hideout for those fleeing slavery on the coast. Over time, these fugitives—referred to as Maroons or, in the colonial terminology, Bush Negroes—created several communities with more or less fixed territories in Suriname's interior: the Ndyuka, Saamaka, Matawai, Paamaka, Aluku and Kwinti.

Over the course of the eighteenth and nineteenth centuries, the Dutch waged several wars against the 'rebellious Negroes' (Stedman, 1796), but the disease-infested, mosquito-ridden forest environment, as well as the guerrilla tactics employed by the Maroons, caused most of the colony's military expeditions to fail miserably. In the meantime, the 'enemy' never ceased to attack or burn down plantations to obtain food items, tools, and new recruits, especially women. For this reason, the colonial government changed its strategy, and started 'pacifying' the Maroon communities through peace treaties. These treaties recognised Maroon autonomy in the lands controlled by them and even entitled the Maroons to receive yearly packages of tools and foodstuffs from the government. After gold was discovered in Suriname's interior in the 1880s, Maroons played an important role in the lucrative business of rowing and guiding miners to the sites where the metal was found—which were mostly located in areas controlled by them, in an environment where any outsider would get easily lost or would not be able to survive.

Omnipresent at the surface in many localities in Suriname, including in those of many Maroon communities, was a reddish material called '*ston*', which was used to pave roads. Only after a similar material present in the French village of Les Baux was, in 1821, shown to be composed of aluminium and iron oxides did the mineral become known, internationally as in Suriname, as 'bauxite'. Even though methods for chemically extracting aluminium from bauxite existed, these processes were so costly that any large-scale exploitation of aluminium was impossible.

Two inventions, both from the 1880s, revolutionised aluminium production. The first process was developed by Carl Joseph Bayer, the second simultaneously by Charles Martin Hall and Paul Héroult. The Bayer process involves the treatment of raw bauxite with caustic soda and other substances at high temperatures to 'clean' it. It produces a white powder known as alumina or aluminium oxide, as well as leftover materials: the infamous, toxic 'red mud'. The purified alumina is then ready for the next step, the Hall–Héroult process, which is based on electrolysis. With the help of very significant amounts of electricity, this process deoxidises the alumina to produce aluminium[1] (and CO_2).

1 'Aluminium' is the name used in Commonwealth English for the same metal that in North America is referred to as 'aluminum'. Both terms refer to the pure metal and should not be confused with 'alumina', the term used for aluminium oxide (Al_2O_3).

After Hall had patented the Hall–Héroult process in the United States, he sought and found investors to create the Pittsburgh Reduction Company, which in 1907 would be renamed Aluminum Company of America (Alcoa). The industrial production of aluminium was limited by two factors: the availability of bauxite and the ability to generate enough electricity to perform electrolysis at a commercial scale, for which hydroelectricity was the cheapest, most stable, and therefore preferred option. The perfect location for aluminium production is thus one that combines bauxite reserves with watercourses with sufficient potential (water run-off and drop) to power a hydroelectric plant. Such locations were to be found in North America as well as in Europe. The early supply chains of the aluminium industries often involved several countries from these two regions.

3 Moengo: an American Company Town on Maroon Lands

The First World War caused significant disruptions in the supply chains of the aluminium industry. In Europe, commercial ties were cut due to opposing alliances, causing countries such as Britain to turn to the United States for supplies. At the same time, the war industry, and especially its new use of warplanes, made aluminium an indispensable material. It was in this context that Alcoa started looking for bauxite reserves in the Caribbean and South America, particularly turning to British Guiana and Suriname, lending these former colonial backwaters strategic importance (Baptiste, 1988).

Alcoa's acquisition of bauxite reserves in Suriname was particularly enabled by the then Dutch Governor of Suriname, Willem Baron van Asbeck (in post 1911–16). Convinced that a completely open market would lead to development and ultimately benefit the colony, he set aside the existing regulation that prohibited the 'concessioning' of land to non-residents of Suriname, first by actively facilitating the settlement of Alcoa agents on Surinamese soil, and second by changing the regulation altogether. In *The American Take-Over* (1983), historian Carlo Lamur concludes that this proved possible due to general institutional weakness and cumbersome communication between the Dutch government and the colonial government in Suriname, as well as naivety regarding the value and importance of the new mineral. The favourable conditions that the colonial authorities in Suriname granted to Alcoa, including a near exemption from taxes, were also the result of an international deal between the Netherlands and the United States, in exchange for US Standard Oil's departure from Sumatra in the Dutch East Indies (present-day Indonesia), which benefitted Royal Dutch Shell (Buddingh', 1995). While this may have been a positive outcome for the Kingdom of the Netherlands as a whole, it deprived Suriname of the potential benefits of its bauxite endowments, even after its independence. Alcoa's revenues from Surinamese bauxite quickly outstripped the Surinamese government budget, but little of the former ended up with the local population.

Alcoa chose Moengo, an abandoned Ndyuka village on the banks of the Cottica River, as the centre of its mining activities. Between 1916 and 1920, Moengo was transformed into a model company town, an 'enclave', with a hospital (Figure 6.1), sports facilities and hygienic conditions (drinking water, sewage disposal, anti-malaria measures) far superior to those in Paramaribo, the capital of the colony. Its seemingly democratic grid of rectangular housing blocks obscured, however, a built-in inequality between different ethnic groups. Moengo had separate neighbourhoods for the American and Dutch expatriates (Figure 2), for skilled Surinamese workers, for unskilled Surinamese workers, and for the contract labourers from the Dutch East Indies, who were referred to as 'Javanese'.

As Moengo was surrounded by Maroon villages, the town's economy has, since its construction, relied on Maroon labour for different kinds of services. Alcoa's subsidiary the Surinaamsche Bauxiet Maatschappij (SBM), however, did not formally recruit any Maroon workers until the 1950s. Still, Maroon men were preferred as informal labourers for felling trees and clearing forested land, while Maroon women frequently came to Moengo to sell agricultural produce or wash clothes. They were required to leave Moengo and go 'down the river' before five o'clock every day (De Koning, 2011a), but eventually started building informal housing just outside the town.

During the early years, Moengo could only be reached by ship after a ten-hour journey on the Cottica River. Then, in 1929 the town was connected by road to Albina, at the French Guiana border, and finally, in 1965, to Suriname's capital Paramaribo (Pollack, 2016).

4 Building an Aluminium Industry

As a rule of thumb, one could state that at the time of Suriname's bauxite boom alumina had a value five times that of bauxite, while aluminium was eight times as valuable as alumina (Kruijer, 1973; World Bank, 1981). There was thus an enormous potential for countries with bauxite reserves to increase their profits if they were able to vertically integrate their industries and instead of exporting bauxite produce aluminium themselves. Ideas of building facilities for the Bayer or even the Hall–Héroult process in Suriname were being floated

FIGURE 6.1 Moengo's hospital, currently in a state of disrepair and used as an art exhibition space
SOURCE: AUTHOR 2020

FIGURE 6.2.1 The Casa Blanca, Moengo's guesthouse, pictured in 1930 by Agusta Curiel
SOURCE: COLLECTION STICHTING SURINAAMS MUSEUM

FIGURE 6.2.2 The Casa Blanca, Moengo's guesthouse, pictured in 2020 in a state of disrepair
SOURCE: AUTHOR, 2020

even in the early days of bauxite mining in the country. In 1925, Alcoa proposed building a dam on the Maroni River at the Surinamese–French Guianese border to generate the necessary hydroelectricity. In return for this investment, the corporation would receive the exploitation rights to all bauxite reserves, identified and unidentified, in Suriname. The Dutch authorities took this option into consideration as they thought that the prospect of producing aluminium in Suriname itself could be beneficial to the colony's economy. They even reached an agreement with the French government regarding a possible dam across the border river, but Alcoa eventually pulled out, building extra Hall–Héroult capacity in North America instead (Pollack, 2016). It is telling, however, that Alcoa expected to be compensated with bauxite concessions for the costs of building the dam. Apparently, the company regarded the construction of an aluminium industry in Suriname not as an investment in its own productive capacity, but as a favour to the colony, for which it could ask for something in return.

Demand for aluminium kept rising over the course of the 1930s. Tensions in Europe that would eventually lead to the Second World War were a reason for the United States to expand its stock of military equipment, especially warplanes, for which it sought reliable bauxite supplies. Suriname was unlikely to be directly affected by the war, but still the reliance on Moengo as the only centre of production could be problematic, due both to its single means of access—via the narrow Cottica River—and to the risk of labour unrest in the town. For this reason, Alcoa opened a second bauxite mine in Suriname, at the location where, in 1938, the company town of Paranam would spring up, not far from the capital, Paramaribo. In order to balance American dominance in the sector, the colonial authorities granted a mining concession not only to Alcoa but also to the Dutch company Billiton,[2] which now started operations in Onverdacht, a few kilometres distant from Paranam.

The capacity to carry out the Hall–Héroult process remained unattainable, but Suriname did embark on efforts to carry out the Bayer process, which would enable it to export alumina instead of bauxite. For this purpose, in 1938 Alcoa started planning the construction of an alumina plant in Paranam, serving both the Alcoa and the Billiton concessions. The outbreak of the Second World War spurred Surinamese exports of bauxite and alumina as well as the country's economic reliance on this single industry. Suriname was now responsible for 60 per cent of US imports of bauxite, and soon enough the US government stationed military personnel in Suriname to secure the mines and their access routes. In order to satisfy the quickly rising demand, working hours were increased, and mining operations in Moengo were now running seven days a week. This, in combination with the fact that the economic downturn of the 1930s and 1940s had caused the cost of living to rise in Suriname while wages had stagnated, led to the outbreak of a series of strikes in Moengo and Paranam in 1941 and 1942. In a radio address aired on 18 January 1942, the district commissioner of Marowijne, J. Postma, called the strikers 'traitor[s] to our cause; fifth columnist[s]' (De Koning, 2011b). Clearly he recognised what the Moengo strikers knew all too well: that they had unique bargaining power due to the geopolitical game that they had become a part of.

But the US would not be reliant on Suriname for long. Suriname's share of international bauxite exports already started falling as of 1943, as known bauxite stockpiles and domestic production capacity in the US had grown, and the ships used for the trade were now needed to transport troops and military supplies to the front lines in Europe (Pollack, 2016).

Nonetheless, Suriname's '15 minutes of fame' during the Second World War, during which its 'mother country', the Netherlands, was subdued by Nazi

2 In 2001, Billiton merged with BHP to form BHP Billiton, which today is once more known simply as BHP.

Germany, led to a new self-confidence and a wave of nationalism in the colony. In 1942, the Dutch Queen, Wilhelmina, broadcast a radio address from exile in London, mentioning the need for a 'restructured Kingdom' after the war, in which the colonies would gain more autonomy. This statement was primarily directed at audiences in the Dutch East Indies under Japanese occupation, but was received with enthusiasm in Suriname (Buddingh', 1995). Shortly after the end of the Second World War, a process began that would, in 1954, make Suriname an autonomous country within the Kingdom of the Netherlands.

In 1951, the Stichting Planbureau Suriname (Planning Office Suriname) was founded to accompany this shift from colony to country. The Planbureau presented the first draft of its *Ten-Year Plan for the Development of Suriname* in 1952. Its authors argued that:

> [Since] the middle of the 19th century an uncontainable process of decay has turned Suriname into an indigent community, but currently there are indications that forces in the country are active that—as long as they are directed and supported from outside—can constitute a more prosperous society in Suriname.
>
> Stichting Planbureau Suriname, 1952, 15

The authors considered Suriname an 'indigent community' due to the decline of the agricultural sector that Suriname had once relied upon, while the forces they suggested could lead to prosperity were associated with Suriname's bauxite reserves. While putting all its hope in the mining sector, the Planbureau also observed that the rising wages in the sector, unmatched by increases in other sectors, were leading to growing inequality. The decline in agriculture also augmented the gap in income levels between city and countryside, fuelling a movement of rural flight.

In order to reinvest bauxite revenues in other sectors, the Ten-Year Plan contained a series of policies for the agricultural, forestry and industrial sectors. The highlight of the Plan, however, was a project in which several of Suriname's identified needs would come together: the Brokopondo Plan. The construction of a hydroelectric dam, this time across the Suriname River close to the Saamaka village of Brokopondo (Figure 6.3), would lead to the generation of 1 billion kilowatt hours of electricity per year, 90 per cent of which was intended to power the Hall–Héroult process in an aluminium smelter that would also be built under the Plan. According to the authors, there would also be many helpful side benefits: *en passant*, Suriname's electricity problem would be solved,

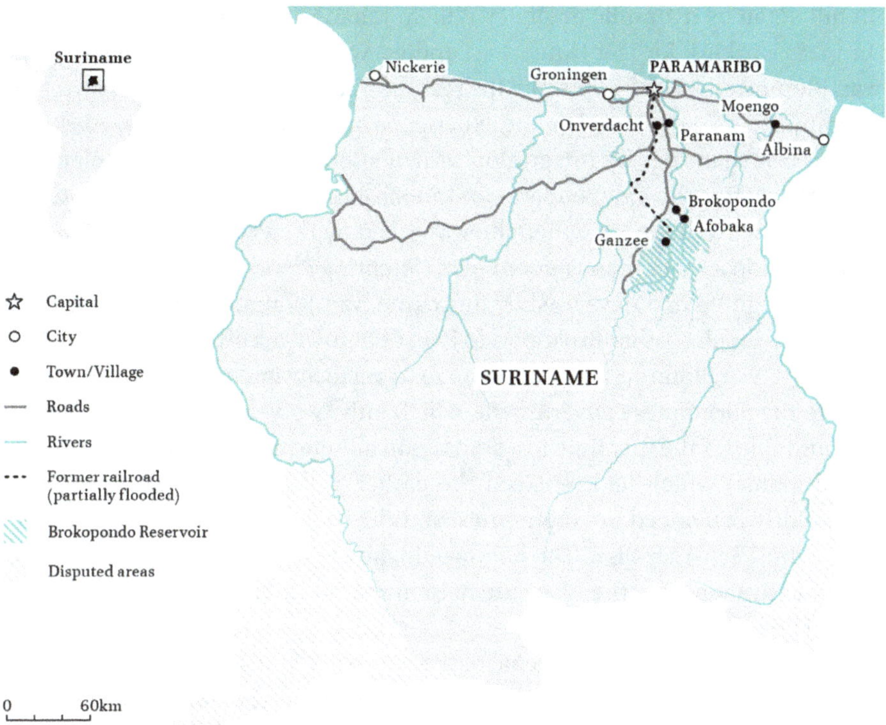

FIGURE 6.3 Map of Suriname, showing the capital Paramaribo and the mining towns Moengo and Paranam
SOURCE: AUTHOR

while a new road and train line[3] from Paramaribo to Brokopondo would allow for the exploitation of forest and mineral resources alongside it, and the regularisation of the river's water stream in all seasons would end siltation problems during the dry season, which would allegedly be beneficial for agriculture. The many Maroon communities upstream of Brokopondo were only mentioned once in the Plan: the authors stressed that the lake would create opportunities for fish farming, which could form an additional source of income for the 10,000 'Bush Negroes' in the area (Stichting Planbureau Suriname, 1952, 113).

Even though the original idea for the Brokopondo Plan may have come from civil engineer Willem Eysvoogel (Pollack, 2016), it would be developed

3 Not to be confused with the previously existing 'Lawa train line' from Paramaribo to the gold fields in central Suriname. The Lawa train line was eventually flooded by the Brokopondo Dam, and the new train line proposed in 1952 was never built.

in full detail by hydraulic engineer Willem Johan van Blommestein (1905–85). In 1948, working for the Dutch East Indies' water management department, van Blommestein had published his *Federal Welfare Plan for Western Java* (Van Blommestein, 1949), based on the experience of the Tennessee Valley Authority in the US regarding the integration of irrigation and hydroelectric planning. Soon thereafter, the independence of Indonesia prompted van Blommestein to move to the Netherlands, where he was asked by the Planbureau Suriname to help develop a water management plan (Stichting Planbureau Suriname, 1952). Even though he had never visited Suriname, van Blommestein promptly proposed the much costlier Brokopondo Plan of his own accord (Ravesteijn, 2002).

In 1951, van Blommestein was asked to travel to Suriname to defend his ideas before the Surinamese government, which only two years earlier had become accountable for the first time to a democratically elected parliament: the 'States of Suriname', which had replaced the earlier 'Colonial States'. The engineer apparently convinced the dignitaries, and the Brokopondo Plan was included in the draft Ten-Year Plan. The dam would, however, not fall under the budget that was available for the Planbureau to invest, so external sources of funding would be needed.

First, Suriname turned to Alcoa for the necessary funds, but Alcoa responded in the negative. It considered the enterprise risky, at the margin of making a loss, and it had enough aluminium smelting capacity in the US (Loeff, 1960). A World Bank mission, visiting Suriname on the invitation of the Dutch government in 1952, came to the conclusion that the project was feasible, but stressed that more data on both the physical environment and sales markets would be necessary. Billiton launched its own research, and warned that the geological conditions had not been sufficiently investigated, and moreover that carrying out the Hall–Héroult process in Suriname would—given the cost at which the Brokopondo Plan envisaged generating electricity—cause Surinamese aluminium to be too expensive for international markets (Pollack, 2016). Nonetheless, Suriname asked the French company Société Anonyme de Grands Travaux de Marseille to deliver a technical report leading to a detailed plan for the building of the dam. This report was, in turn, submitted to Dutch consultancy firm Nedeco, which concluded that 1) the potential electricity output of the dam was too optimistic, 2) the geological conditions had not been adequately researched, and 3) there was a lack of articulation between the technical report and the business case. The Dutch government showed itself to be increasingly annoyed with the Surinamese government, not having been consulted during the entire process, and made clear that it would not be providing any financial guarantees were Suriname prove able to secure a loan for the project—which was exactly what Suriname was planning to ask for (Pollack, 2016).

In 1957, a deal suddenly emerged nonetheless. Alcoa had identified a loophole in US law. Under the Western Hemisphere Trade Corporation, a company's US taxes could be greatly reduced if it obtained at least 95 per cent of its income from activities elsewhere in the Americas. To comply with this condition, Alcoa set up a secondary company: the Suriname Aluminum Company (Suralco), which would undertake all of Alcoa's activities in Suriname, but which was legally and fiscally based in Delaware. As this option reduced the investment required, the project had become more commercially attractive in Alcoa's eyes—or so it said. Alcoa showed itself willing to fund the aluminium smelter and, in 1958, also the dam's construction and that of the road leading to it—but in return it demanded ownership of these structures for 75 years and an additional concession of 20,000 square kilometres for bauxite exploration in Suriname, of which 200 square kilometres could be used as actual mining areas once reserves had been found. When Prime Minister Johan Ferrier defended the deal in Parliament, some parliamentarians expressed the suspicion that these concessions were the true reason for Alcoa's sudden enthusiasm (cited in Pollack (2016)).

The Brokopondo Agreement was signed on 27 January 1958, and construction of the dam started the same year. On 1 February 1964, the dam was finished and the 'Prof.dr.ir. W.J. van Blommestein Lake', commonly referred to as 'Brokopondo Lake', started filling up. Seeing that the plan was going ahead in spite of its initial warnings, Billiton now also joined the project, allowing for an expansion of the aluminium smelter. Queen Juliana opened the smelter in 1965, and by the early 1970s Brokopondo Lake had reached its current water level (Pollack, 2016) (Figure 6.4).

5 But ... What about the Population?

Let us now return to the Maroons, whom we had almost forgotten amidst the festivities. On 16 August 1958, an advisor reminded Prime Minister Ferrier that under the Brokopondo Agreement Suriname was responsible for the 'removal of the population, the buildings and other property from the area of the artificial lake'.[4] Upstream of the location of the dam, but below the intended water

4 'Stukken betreffende de bouw van de stuwdam bij Brokopondo, 1957–1961'. Dutch National Archives, The Hague: Gouverneur van Suriname, Kabinet, number 2.10.26, folder 1364, p. 128.

FIGURE 6.4 The Brokopondo Dam
SOURCE: AUTHOR, 2020

level, lived approximately 6,000 Maroons, mostly Saamaka along the Suriname River, but also some Ndyuka along Sara Creek. In 1956, a representative of the government in the area had been asked not to discuss the Brokopondo plans with the population. Only in 1959, over a year after the Brokopondo Agreement was signed, was *gaamá* (Chief) Agbagó Abóikóni (in post 1951–89) of the Saamaka officially informed of the project—even though he stated he had been hearing rumours about the plans for ten years already. Agbagó demanded that the Maroons be included in plans for the development of the area, simultaneously deploring that any promises made to the Maroons were never fulfilled anyway in this new 'economic slavery' (cited in Scholtens (1994)).

The construction of the dam itself required around 2,100 workers, of which 1,800 would be recruited from local communities.[5] A common observation is that many of the Maroons who were helping to build the dam never themselves believed that it would actually cause their lands to flood. District Commissioner Jan Michels, the public authority in the area, stated during an interview with anthropologist Richard Price, 'They were too much like children'. Saamaka author Carlo Hoop said the same, from a slightly different

5 Or at least this was originally envisaged. 'Stukken betreffende de bouw', p. 128.

perspective: 'The government treated the forest dwellers … as primitive and childlike'. *Gaamá* Agbagó referred, in an interview with Price, to the peace treaties struck between the Dutch colony and the Saamaka people from the eighteenth century: 'From Mawási to Adjámina and on up on the headwaters of this river, that's for us Saramakas'. If they wanted the land back, he said, they would have to pay for it. But the 'Americans' simply arrived, with all their heavy equipment. 'They'd simply taken it away from us—our own land!' (all cited in Price, 2011).

In January 2020, I interviewed the retired schoolteacher Berry Vrede, born in 1943 in the now flooded Saamaka village of Ganzee, and currently residing in the outskirts of Paramaribo. Before the construction of the Brokopondo Dam, Ganzee used to be the largest Saamaka village, with 1,500 inhabitants (Figure 6.5). Given the long history of the missionary activities of the Moravian Church (Evangelische Broedergemeente (EBG)), the village had the most developed school system in the whole 'land of Saamaka'. Boys from Ganzee, like Berry Vrede, were trained as schoolteachers to work in the other villages. However, as they were required to teach in Dutch rather than *Saamaka Tongu*,

FIGURE 6.5 School children of the Saamaka Maroon community
SOURCE: WILLEM VAN DE POL (1948)

Berry Vrede stated that 'the level of development was not such that we could talk about [the consequences of building a dam]. People thought: What God has built, how can they dam it? A river that we couldn't even swim across!'

The immediate impact of the construction activities was, according to Berry Vrede, a different one. 'Young people earned money building the dam; you could see the clothing change; you could hear other types of music; they could buy new items. Now they were Suralco employees, they obtained a diploma to operate a bulldozer! They could even find employment in Paramaribo'. The new wealth of the young people, while 'village elders earned a mere trifle in comparison', started eroding the authority of the traditional leadership. In the old times, Berry Vrede says, conflicts occurred mostly within relationships, marriages, families—there was hardly any crime, and all problems were solved by the village elders. 'Today, you need the police'.

As the Saamaka did not believe the dam would actually flood the area, they were not planning to leave. As Michels told Price: 'Village elders would tell me they weren't going anywhere—this was their land'. The longer the situation lasted, the more concerned the government officials responsible for the 'transmigration' became, as it was increasingly unlikely that the evacuation would occur in an orderly fashion. Eventually, the Saamaka only got ready to leave after the water started flooding the villages, and by then it was too late to take all their belongings with them. Saamaka author Dorus Vrede (1949–2020, not a close relative of Berry Vrede) remembered, in his short story *I won't leave until the water touches my feet*:

> The storm blew the water into the huts, of which the doors had been torn out by the inhabitants, as they had left the village in a great hurry. […] An event like this had seldom been witnessed by the Bush Negroes and their ancestors. The water had never come this high, and never had it threatened them in this way. But it wasn't a surprise. […] They had been warned years ago already of the big dam that would be built in the river, and of what would happen if the water would be trapped behind it. But how could someone believe in water that would come till your doorstep? As long as the *obyas* [forest spirits] were alive, how could such a thing be possible? But the *obyas* didn't perform any miracles, although they had not abandoned their people. Their power was not without limits. […] That's why the Bush Negroes rushed to leave the place where they had sworn they would stay even if the ocean invaded it.
>
> VREDE, 1986

In his story, Dorus Vrede had an explanation for the *obyas* not coming to the rescue—but Price (2011, 37) cites an informant according to whom

> the forced relocation led to a crisis of the beliefs of the Maroon society. The gods and the ancestors, who are expected to protect the community, were unable to prevent the disasters. Traditional leaders who had assured their people that the water would not swallow their villages were proven wrong.

But what had the government in mind for the 6,000 displaced people? The Planbureau had created a separate entity to answer this question: the Brokopondo Bureau. A 1958 brochure from this office, entitled *Light and Power from the Jungles of Suriname*,[6] boasted about the improvements for the local population that would result from the project: 'A piece of wilderness will be taken away from them and their needless isolation will come to an end. […] Also for them, the Brokopondo Project is therefore of great value'. It was promised that new, better houses would be built, new employment generated, and that the displaced population would receive compensation for lost lands and fruit trees, free distribution of food during one year, and a coop with chickens per family. Twenty-five new villages sprang up: 12 smaller ones south of the lake, deeper into the country's interior—where the newcomers would have to compete for scarce resources with the existing Saamaka villages of the Upper Suriname River basin—and 13 north and north-east of the lake, including Brownsweg, the largest conglomerate of villages of all, which gathered together the populations of six to eight flooded villages, all of which came with their traditional leaders, leading to new conflicts.

Berry Vrede remembers that the 'huts', with their palm-thatched roofs in the original villages, were, in the so-called transmigration villages, replaced by 'real houses: so we should be very happy'. The size of each house was based on the size of the original hut that each family had owned. But, Berry Vrede states, in the original villages there had been much more space. Apart from the 'big house' (*gaan wosu*), where the family would sleep, they used to have another, 'small house' (*pikin wosu*), where they could store their provisions, and sometimes some family members would also sleep there. Then there was the *gangasá*, the cooking hut, with a palm-thatched roof on stilts and without walls—here, you could cook, eat, talk and more. Sometimes, families would

6 Brokopondo Bureau, 1958. *Licht en kracht uit de oerwouden van Suriname*. Dutch National Archives, The Hague: Archief van de Vertegenwoordiger van de STICUSA in Suriname 1956–1975, number 3.1, folder 660.

even have a second *gangasá* for the preparation of foodstuffs. But most importantly, all these structures and the trees offered plenty of shade. Now, in the transmigration villages, only the size of the *gaan wosu* was taken into account, and your neighbour was living two metres away from you, and as soon as you stepped out of the house, you left all shade behind you.

The process of determining each family's compensation suffered from similar issues. For what was the value of a hut that was now under water? Monetary compensation offered to families finally equalled roughly 10 Surinamese guilders,[7] according to Berry Vrede, or 3 US dollars, according to Richard Price (2011). It was known that families had also owned fruit trees, scattered all over the forest, but how many? Families were asked to give an estimate, but, as Berry Vrede remarked, it could not be too high, 'otherwise they thought you were gambling'.

Maroons usually lived off their own land, with each family cultivating roughly 1.5 hectares for a year or two—then, the soil exhausted, they moved on to cut a new piece of forest. Maroon agriculture traditionally took place without tilling the soil, so that the tree roots stayed intact and the forest was allowed to grow back. In their new locations, they did not proceed differently: they cut a piece of forest and started cultivating crops. Berry Vrede remembers that this occurred 'around Brownsweg, along the Atjoni Road—but these areas had already been given in concession, and then someone would show up and say: Nice to see that you've planted; you can harvest your rice and your cassava, but you shouldn't plant again'. The displaced population was not compensated for the land it had lost, nor was it provided with new lands to cultivate as its property structures functioned in ways that the Surinamese authorities could not understand—in the same way that the colonial authorities before them had not grasped or registered them. Within the communities, everyone knew which forest areas belonged to which family or *lö* (subtribe), but now the government was claiming that the flooded lands had no known owner. Only a Guyanese man who had lived in Ganzee—a *balata* banker (who provided loans to local rubber tappers and would buy up their harvest)—received full compensation, as he owned a fenced garden containing fruit trees, which was easy to recognise and measure. And, according to Berry Vrede, 'because the responsible inspectors were staying in his house'.

Particularly painful was the fact that the Maroons had been removed from their villages in order to generate electricity, but that the transmigration

7 Contemporary US dollar value difficult to ascertain.

villages themselves had not been connected to the grid. Thus, the Maroons lacked both electricity and clean water in their new homes.[8]

It was clear that the transmigration created a lot of anger among the Maroons. The Dutch Army realised this: a series of helicopters was put on standby during the operation, to be used if there were protests. In an internal note, the responsible commander informed the Governor of Suriname (the highest Dutch representative) that irregularities could occur, as the population 'on mere personal and religious grounds' resented their resettlement.[9]

In the end, active resistance to the transmigration was limited, not least because the rising water left no time for collective action. Maroons did, however, express their discontent after the event, including in a letter to Queen Juliana indicating the deterioration of their situation due to their displacement (Figure 6.6). They requested fair compensation for what they had lost, referring to their rights under the 1762 peace treaties.

When Queen Juliana visited the area once more for the opening of the aluminium smelter, she was handed a pamphlet authored by a certain Toelingha Martin, who claimed to represent 'Saamaka popular committees' in which 5,000 Saamaka were united. It stated that 'the Saamaka are currently living in disgraceful conditions in their new places of residence, which are concentration camps'. Martin's note announced that any representative of the Surinamese government was henceforward forbidden from entering Saamaka land. To ensure compliance with this unilaterally established rule, and recalling the eighteenth-century treaties, Martin requested support from the Dutch Army. The Dutch Army formally answered that it could not offer support, and advised Martin to send his request to the Surinamese authorities instead.[10] The Surinamese authorities, however, told the elders of the different villages to

8 And then there was Operation Gwamba, launched by the International Society for the Protection of Animals and led by 23-year-old American John Walsh, to save the animals trapped by the rising water. District Commissioner Michels, even though he belonged to the government team that was implementing the Brokopondo project, expressed support for the private operation, as he could not 'passively see the drowning of thousands of animals without taking any action' (Walsh and Gannon, 1967). But while Walsh took most of the credit for the work, pictures of the operation clearly show that he was aided by a team of Maroons in saving the more than 9,000 animals. Some of these helpers would later bitterly complain that more effort had been made to save the animals than to save the people.

9 'Stukken betreffende de transmigratie van Bosnegers uit het gebied van het geplande Brokopondo-stuwmeer en de opvang van deze transmigranten in het kamp Brownsweg'. Dutch National Archives, The Hague. Digitaal Duplicaat: Gouverneur van Suriname, Kabinet, number 2.10.26, folder 2661, pp. 24–35.

10 Dutch National Archives, The Hague. Digitaal Duplicaat: Gouverneur van Suriname, Kabinet, number 2.10.26, folder 2661, pp. 45–58.

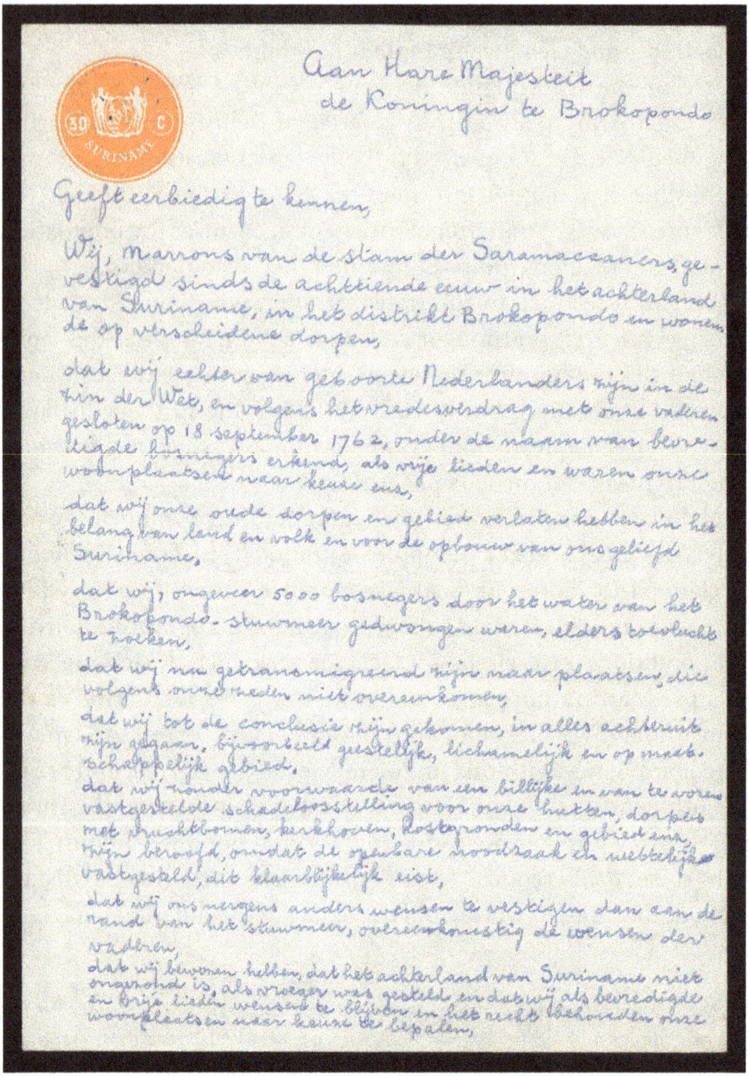
Aan Hare Majesteit
de Koningin te Brokopondo

Geeft eerbiedig te kennen,

Wij, marrons van de stam der Saramaccaners, ge-
vestigd sinds de achttiende eeuw in het achterland
van Suriname, in het distrikt Brokopondo en wonen-
de op verscheidene dorpen,

dat wij echter van geboorte Nederlanders zijn in de
zin der Wet, en volgens het vredesverdrag met onze vaderen
gesloten op 18 september 1762, onder de naam van bevre-
digde bosnegers erkend, als vrije lieden en waren onze
woonplaatsen naar keuze ons,

dat wij onze oude dorpen en gebied verlaten hebben in het
belang van land en volk en voor de opbouw van ons geliefd
Suriname,

dat wij, ongeveer 5000 bosnegers door het water van het
Brokopondo-stuwmeer gedwongen waren, elders toevlucht
te zoeken,

dat wij nu getransmigreerd zijn naar plaatsen, die
volgens onze zeden niet overeenkomen,

dat wij tot de conclusie zijn gekomen, in alles achteruit
zijn gegaan, bijvoorbeeld geestelijk, lichamelijk en op maat-
schappelijk gebied,

dat wij zonder voorwaarde van een billijke en van te voren
vastgestelde schadeloosstelling voor onze hutten, dorpen
met vruchtbomen, kerkhoven, kostgronden en gebied enz.
zijn beroofd, omdat de openbare noodzaak en wettelijk
vastgesteld, dit klaarblijkelijk eist,

dat wij ons nergens anders wensen te vestigen dan aan de
rand van het stuwmeer, overeenkomstig de wensen der
vaderen,

dat wij bevonden hebben, dat het achterland van Suriname niet
onbewoond is, als vroeger was gesteld en dat wij als bevredigde
en vrije lieden wensen te blijven in het recht behouden onze
woonplaatsen naar keuze te bepalen,

FIGURE 6.6 First page of the letter from the Saamaka community to Queen Juliana, 1965
SOURCE: 'STUKKEN BETREFFENDE DE TRANSMIGRATIE VAN BOSNEGERS'

dissolve the popular committees. The elders refused. *Gaamá* Agbagó declared his solidarity with the committees. The complainants in Brownsweg referred to a 'revolution' that had just begun, and said that any representative of the Surinamese government would be welcomed with gunfire, as plenty of weapons had been delivered to them by Brazilian smugglers. They threatened to burn down the police station, because 'the Bushland Creoles desire complete separation, for which they, if necessary, can rely upon support from outside'.[11] A long struggle lay ahead of them, in which ultimately there would be no winners.

6 Independence, War, and the Closure of the Mines and Factories

Flash forward. In the year 2022, looking back at the history of bauxite and alumina and aluminium production in Suriname, we can see that the government's expectations regarding modernisation through bauxite-based industrialisation have remained a vision unfulfilled. Yes, Suriname managed to perform all the steps of the value chain from bauxite to aluminium on national soil, but it paid a high price.

After the country became independent in 1975, it raised its own armed forces—a faction of which, only five years after independence, committed a coup d'état and installed a military government under Sergeant Dési Bouterse. Under his regime, the conflict with the Maroons reached boiling point in the so-called War of the Interior ('*Binnenlandse Oorlog*'), which lasted from 1986 to 1992 and greatly impacted the Maroon communities. The conflict caused one out of three inhabitants of the interior to flee their villages—25,000 people in total. Today, 83,000 Maroons reside in and around Paramaribo, while the French-Guianese town of Saint-Laurent-du-Maroni, just across the Maroni River, which forms the border with Suriname, has a Maroon population of 31,000, mostly Surinamese refugees and their descendants (Price, 2018). Contrasting this with the 57,000 Maroons who still reside in Suriname's interior (the '*binnenland*'), including semi-urban areas like Moengo and Brownsweg, we can safely conclude that Maroons in their majority have shifted from a rural to an urban setting in only a few decades.

The War of the Interior also established the position of the guerrilla fighter turned politician Ronnie Brunswijk. A Ndyuka Maroon born in 1961 in a village close to Moengo, Brunswijk, with his 'Jungle Commando', unleashed the Maroon guerrillas against Bouterse in spite of express objections from the traditional Maroon leadership, including the Saamaka *gaamá* Agbagó and his Ndyuka counterpart *gaanman* Gazon Matodya (in post 1965–2011). Thus, Brunswijk effectively sidelined these leadership structures, replacing them

11 Dutch National Archives, The Hague. Digitaal Duplicaat: Gouverneur van Suriname, Kabinet, number 2.10.26, folder 2661, pp. 59–64.

with a new authority based on military might. Brunswijk's Jungle Commando came to control large parts of Maroon lands, and extracted surplus resources from them, requesting a share of the proceeds of the illegal activities that were increasingly undertaken in the interior by smugglers, Brazilian goldminers (*garimpeiros*), and the prostitutes catering to them (Hoogbergen and Kruijt, 2005). The war ended when Brunswijk and Bouterse announced their reconciliation, and the two men have since collaborated on numerous occasions. Brunswijk is currently the vice president of Suriname, heading the Party for General Liberation and Development (ABOP), which is especially popular among Maroons.

The various events that have uprooted the Maroon communities have caused them to suffer from an overall erosion of authority. Berry Vrede describes how in the old times people refrained from violent crime out of fear of the *kunu*, the revenge spirit. The War of the Interior changed this, as young men joined the guerrilla movement and saw that nothing happened after they had killed government soldiers. As such, the traditional norms of the Maroons started to change, and their armed youth became more powerful than their village elders.

During a trip I undertook in the first months of 2020 to certain mining sites, I was able to observe (and confirm with interviewees) that former company towns like Moengo and Paranam are today inhabited by a Maroon majority. Many Maroons settled in these towns when the War of the Interior made it increasingly unsafe for them to remain in their villages of origin, while at the same time the employees of the bauxite and aluminium industries started to abandon the towns. The Maroons have mostly settled in the neighbourhoods where Surinamese workers used to live. The former expatriate dwellings, the 'staff villages' with their nice bungalows and swimming pools, are in a state of decay and surrounded by 'No entry' signs. No industrial activity is to be found. How can this demise of the sector be explained?

Immediately after the construction of the Brokopondo Dam, Suriname experienced an episode of considerable economic growth, mainly due to the expansion of aluminium exports. Other sectors did not reflect this growth, causing the Surinamese economy to become increasingly tied to the international aluminium market. Whereas the original Brokopondo Plan had envisaged local development in the area affected by the lake, in the final (and only) offer of financing that Suriname received the regional development component was much less important, and ownership of the dam was transferred to Suralco, hence to Alcoa. Creating jobs, attracting new investments, reinvesting in the Surinamese economy: these were not priorities for Suralco, and most of the revenue from the sector flowed abroad (Pollack, 2016).

Over the course of the 1970s, new bauxite reserves were identified in other countries, notably Australia, Brazil and Guinea. While Guinea mostly supplied European and North American smelters, Australia and Brazil quickly developed their own aluminium smelters, relying on locally developed hydroelectric potential. Just a few years after the completion of the Brokopondo Dam, Suriname was already struggling to keep up with other aluminium producers, mostly due to economies of scale and the low profit margins of the Paranam smelter. Moreover, as Suriname's economy was almost exclusively based on aluminium, its imports of all other goods were heavily dependent on the price of aluminium. When the oil price started rising while aluminium prices remained stable, Suriname introduced an aluminium levy to allow it to maintain its level of imports. The country did not consider currency devaluation, and remained unwilling to unpeg its currency from the US dollar. And at the same time the labour unions in Suriname were strong, and effective in preventing any erosion of their members' salaries (Pollack, 2016). While the price of Surinamese aluminium was thus particularly inflexible, the large aluminium producers (such as Alcoa) lost their price-setting power over the course of the 1970s. The exploding supply of bauxite and aluminium worldwide transferred this price-setting power to aluminium consumers, united in the London Metal Exchange (LME) (Barjot, 2019). Aluminium from Suriname, one of the only 'developing' countries to have an aluminium industry, had become simply too expensive for the international market. Moreover, bauxite reserves started to become exhausted, but no investments were made to exploit new resources.

The War of the Interior did the rest: The mining facilities in the Moengo area became a target for the actions of the Jungle Commando (classified as 'terrorist attacks' and 'sabotage and vandalism'—both classifications cited in Pollack, 2016). Bauxite mining came to a halt, and in order to keep the smelter going, bauxite had to be imported from Brazil. When the power lines linking the Brokopondo Dam to the smelter in Paranam were blown up in 1987, aluminium production was interrupted altogether. Several attempts to restart the sector were undertaken, during and after the war, but to no avail. While significant investments were made to repair the damaged infrastructure, world aluminium prices kept falling. In 1999, Suralco announced the closure of the smelter (Pollack, 2016), and in 2015 the refinery that used to produce alumina was also closed (Boselovic and Lord, 2018). Ultimately, Suralco had only one asset left: electricity from the Brokopondo Dam, of which only a small portion had been sufficient to power all of Paramaribo. Therefore, before turning off the lights in its facilities, Suralco needed a deal with the government to sell the electricity generated (Pollack, 2016).

The deal defining the terms under which Suralco would leave Suriname has been the subject of controversy. The company was allegedly willing to make a significant investment in the environmental clean-up of the area where its operations had taken place. According to Hugo Blanker, retired teacher, union leader, journalist and TV personality, this has not materialised: 'They have only buried the polluted soil under 2 metres of sand: would that be sufficient?' Blanker was born in 1950 and grew up in the village of Onverdacht, 5 kilometres from the Paranam aluminium smelter, where his father worked. In August 2019, while the 'Alcoa affair' was being discussed in parliament, Blanker showed up in the press box with a sizable Surinamese flag, protesting against the plundering of the Surinamese economy. Security escorted him to the exit, but his action attracted some media attention (*Suriname Nieuws*, 2019).

I spent an enjoyable afternoon with Blanker in a house in the Billiton staff village near Paranam, which he squatted in 2019. After Billiton ceased its operations in Suriname, the 'expat village' was supposed to be demolished, but 17 years later the jungle had overtaken it. Now Blanker and his new neighbours are making it inhabitable again. 'I had hoped the whole nation would work together to negotiate a good deal with Alcoa, but from left to right, I haven't heard anything from them', he says, while hammering on what should become an outdoor bar in his new garden—'the people have not been heard on this'.

Since 2015, there have been discussions in the country's parliament and in the media about a mysterious Memorandum of Understanding (MoU) between Alcoa and Suriname. The government was said to have signed this agreement, while the parliament rejected it. Whether or not parliament's approval is necessary, however, is subject to debate among lawyers—as a result of which it remains unclear whether the MoU is valid or not (Essed, 2018). According to energy consultant and lawyer Viren Ajodhia, the signed text of the MoU cannot be found anywhere online. Apart from the environmental clean-up, the deal must, surely, have contained provisions regarding the price that Suriname would pay Suralco for the electricity (tied to the oil price, rather than the much cheaper cost price of hydroelectricity), as well as the date on which the Brokopondo Dam would be transferred to Suriname. According to Ajodhia, Suriname had, under the Brokopondo Agreement with its duration of 75 years, expected to reap benefits from Alcoa's presence in the country until 2033. Now that the company has left much earlier, with the mines closed, a sizable piece of land flooded, and a lot of environmental damage, Suriname even has to pay for the electricity, whereas 'Suriname should have told them to pay compensation!' Ajodhia estimates that the outcome of the negotiations has been very negative for Suriname, and 'the suspicion, of course, is of corruption'.

Suriname created the Brokopondo Dam to obtain cheap electricity and to modernise the country through aluminium exports. It currently does not export even bauxite, and is paying oil prices for its electricity. Brokopondo Lake was expected to have numerous side benefits, such as opportunities for fish breeding. However, since the area was not stripped of its forest cover prior to its flooding, dead trees both above and below the water still obstruct navigation today (Figure 6.7), and eutrophication severely affects the fish stocks. In several areas of Suriname's interior, gold mining is the only sector offering employment to a population that can no longer rely on its traditional livelihoods. The Rosebel gold mine employs a significant proportion of the population of nearby Brownsweg, but even more Maroons are involved in artisanal gold mining, alongside immigrants from Brazil (De Theije and Heemskerk, 2009). The expanding gold mining activities have led to mercury pollution in the Maroni River and in Brokopondo Lake, leading to health problems related to consuming fish from these waters. The story of Suriname's bauxite boom is definitely over. But the boom's ecological impacts remain.

FIGURE 6.7 A branch of Lake Brokopondo with its dead trees
SOURCE: TED SUN, 2020

7 Conclusion

The case of the bauxite and aluminium industries of Suriname is illustrative of how dreams of modernity (Sheller, 2014) can go wrong. Countries in the global South have often used industrialisation and import substitution as strategies for development, but only occasionally do these help lift them out of poverty and improve the living conditions of the majority of the population. Often, the process of decolonisation has transferred power to particular groups in society, who take decisions based on the colonial model of the capitalisation of resources, to the detriment of those who in colonial society are generally looked down upon: the 'primitive', the 'untamed', the 'unmodern'.

In the case of Suriname, the idea of bringing an entire value chain into the country and thus becoming an aluminium producer had been floated a long time before it finally became a reality. The plan for the Brokopondo Dam, originally a one-size-fits-all solution copy-pasted from the Dutch East Indies, did not appeal to international investors, who considered it commercially unattractive. Several companies had turned down invitations to become involved in the project, but the Surinamese government, fuelled by its Planbureau, insisted—its entire vision of development depended on it. When Alcoa finally stepped aboard, the entire plan was executed with respect to its conditions, which ultimately turned out to be unfavourable for the majority of Suriname's population. The project did provide benefits for certain groups in society, and may even have helped to speed up the process of independence, but the economic heyday was short-lived as the profit margins were slim and Suriname quickly lost the market to its much bigger competitors.

Suriname apparently failed to recognise a series of challenges to its aluminium-based industrialisation plan. It disregarded reports that showed how small the profit margin was, and thus how vulnerable the sector would be if aluminium prices were to fall. Second, the country relied exclusively on one commodity, and gave no support to other sectors during the heyday of aluminium exportation. Third, it entrusted its economic future to a single, foreign company, which could easily shift production to other countries. But most importantly, it underestimated how the industry would uproot the local Maroon communities, eventually leading to political disruption at the national level.

The Maroon population of the sites where bauxite mining and hydroelectricity generation took place was mostly seen as a nuisance by development advocates. When it was no longer possible to keep the Maroons out of the picture of Suriname's industrial dream, and a solution had to be found for their presence in the area, aspects of their identity that were especially 'unmodern' were accentuated: their irrationality, primitivity, religiosity—their otherness. In this way, they could be easily framed as 'opposed to development', and therefore not worthy of consideration. The alternative livelihoods offered to them were inadequate, and the process led to significant movements of migration and deculturation. Not only did the bauxite and aluminium sectors flood, pollute and deforest ancestral Maroon lands, they also set in motion a process that would change their traditional lifestyles, which for centuries had kept Suriname's rainforest landscapes in check. Now, the Maroon population is a young and urban one, looking for new livelihood opportunities, while its traditional leadership has been side-lined by its new political representatives, who are themselves heavily involved in illegal activities. The Maroons are the new urban poor, dwelling in newly emerging slums, or crafting out a living in the artisanal gold mines of the interior. Ultimately, aluminium has not delivered on its promises of development and modernity.

References

Acosta, A. (2013) 'Extractivism and neoextractivism: two sides of the same curse', in M. Land and D. Mokrani (eds.) *Beyond Development: Alternative Visions from Latin America*, Permanent Working Group on Alternatives to Development (Quito, Amsterdam: Fundación Rosa Luxemburg / Transnational Institute), pp. 61–82, www.tni.org/files/download/beyonddevelopment_extractivism.pdf (accessed on 25 September 2022).

Baptiste, F.A. (1988) 'The exploitation of Caribbean bauxite and petroleum, 1914–1945', *Social and Economic Studies*, 37(1–2), pp. 107–142.

Barjot, D. (2019) 'Alcan et Pechiney: Une comparaison des processus de multinationalisation en période de croissance instable des marchés (de 1971 à la première moitié des années 1990)', *Cahiers d'histoire de l'aluminium*, 63(2), pp. 56–75, DOI: 10.3917/cha.063.0056.

Blommenstein, W.J. (1949) *Federaal welvaartsplan voor het westelijk gedeelte van Java door prof.dr.ir. W.J. Blommenstein, hoofd van de Afdeling Irrigatie en Assainering van het Departement van Waterstaat en Wederopbouw*, Dutch National Archives, The Hague: Inventaris van de collectie archieven Strijdkrachten in Nederlands-Indië, (1938–1939) 1941–1957 [1960], number 2.13.132, folder 776.

Boselovic, L. and R. Lord (2018) 'A century after arriving in Suriname, Alcoa negotiates exit with the South American country', *Pittsburgh Post-Gazette*, 31 August, www.post-gazette.com/business/pittsburgh-company-news/2018/08/31/alcoa-leaves-suriname-afobaka-dam-bauxite-alumina-production-desi-bouterse-suralco/stories/201808300031 (accessed on 2 September 2022).

Buddingh', H. (1995) *De geschiedenis van Suriname*, 1999 edition (Amsterdam: Rainbow).

De Koning, A. (2011a) 'Shadows of the plantation? A social history of Suriname's bauxite town Moengo', *New West Indian Guide*, 85(3–4), pp. 215–246, DOI: 10.1163/13822373-90002430.

De Koning, A. (2011b) 'Moengo on strike: the politics of labour in Suriname's bauxite industry', *European Review of Latin American and Caribbean Studies*, 91, pp. 31–47, DOI: 10.18352/erlacs.9241.

De Theije, M. and M. Heemskerk (2009) 'Moving frontiers in the Amazon: Brazilian small-scale gold miners in Suriname', *European Review of Latin American and Caribbean Studies*, 87, pp. 5–25, DOI: 10.18352/erlacs.9600.

Essed, S.N. (2018) 'De Alcoa affaire', *Surinaams Juristen Blad*, 56(3), www.sris.sr/wp-content/uploads/2019/07/De-Alcoa-affaire-Mr.-Serena-N.-Essed-NJB-December-2018-no.-3.pdf?fbclid=IwAR0brSmUzgPSeyB0r1z9bP-VrdD2qvh2uSjdOMkD0MbC52AL_ariNmnNJO0 (accessed on 2 September 2022).

FAO (Food and Agriculture Organization) (2015) *Global Forest Resources Assessment 2015. Desk Reference* (Rome: FAO), www.fao.org/3/i4808e/i4808e.pdf (accessed on 2 September 2022).

Gomes da Cunha, O.M. (2018) 'Making things for living, and living a life with things', in M.A. Crichlow, P. Northover and J. Giusti-Cordero (eds.) *Race and Rurality in the Global Economy* (Albany: State University of New York Press), pp. 93–124.

Gudynas, E. (2009) 'Diez tesis urgentes sobre el nuevo extractivismo: Contextos y demandas bajo el progresismo sudamericano actual', *Extractivismo, política y sociedad* (Quito: Centro Andino de Acción Popular; Centro Latinoamericano de Ecología Social), pp. 187–225.

Hoogbergen, W. and D. Kruijt (2005) *De oorlog van de sergeanten: Surinaamse militairen in de politiek* (Amsterdam: Bakker).

Kirsch, S. (2014) *Mining Capitalism: the Relationship between Corporations and Their Critics* (Oakland: University of California Press).

Kruijer, G.J. (1973) *Suriname, neokolonie in rijksverband* (Meppel: Boom).

Lamur, C. (1983) *The American Take-Over: Industrial Emergence and ALCOA's Expansion in Guyana and Suriname (with Special Reference to Suriname 1914–1921)*, PhD dissertation (The Hague: Haagse Drukkerij en Uitgeversmaatschappij).

Loeff, J.A.L.M. (1960) 'Pleitnota voor het Rijksdeel Suriname in het geding voor scheidslieden tegen Société des Grands Travaux de Marseille, en Compagnie de Fives-Lilles', 2–3 February 1961, Dutch National Archives, The Hague, Gouverneur van Suriname, Kabinet, number 2.10.26, folder 1364.

Pollack, H.R. (2016) *Suriname's Bauxite Industry (1898–2009) and the Brokopondo Agreement* (Paramaribo: Vaco).

Prebisch, R. (1950) *The Economic Development of Latin America, and its Principal Problems* (Lake Success, New York: United Nations Department of Economic

Affairs), https://repositorio.cepal.org/bitstream/handle/11362/30088/S4900192_en.pdf (accessed on 2 September 2022).

Price, R. (2018) 'Maroons in Guyane: Getting the numbers right', *New West Indian Guide*, 92(3–4), pp. 275–283, DOI: 1163/22134360-09203001.

Price, R. (2011) *Rainforest Warriors: Human Rights on Trial* (Philadelphia: University of Pennsylvania Press).

Ravesteijn, W. (2002) 'Een ingenieur met visie: Prof.dr.ir. Willem Johan van Blommestein (1905–1985)', *Tijdschrift voor Waterstaatsgeschiedenis*, 11(1), pp. 6–11, www.jvdn.nl/Downloads/WG/2002/TWG2002_006-011.pdf (accessed on 2 September 2022).

Scholtens, B. (1994) *Bosnegers en overheid in Suriname: De ontwikkeling van de politieke verhouding 1651–1992*, PhD dissertation (Paramaribo: Afdeling Cultuurstudies/Minov).

Sheller, M. (2014) *Aluminum Dreams: the Making of Light Modernity* (Cambridge: MIT Press).

Stedman, J.G. (1796) *Expedition to Surinam: Being the Narrative of a Five Years Expedition against the Revolted Negroes of Surinam in Guiana, on the Wild Coast of South America, from the Year 1772 to 1777, Elucidating that Country and Describing its Productions, with an Account of Indians of Guiana and Negroes of Guinea*, 1963 edition (London: Folio Society).

Stichting Planbureau Suriname (1952) *De grondslagen van een Tienjarenplan voor Suriname*, Dutch National Archives, The Hague: Gouverneur van Suriname, Kabinet, number 2.10.26, folder 1305.

Suriname Nieuws (2019) 'Hugo Blanker uit DNA gebouw gezet door beveiliging', *Suriname Nieuws*, 27 August, http://www.srnieuws.com/suriname/270454/hugo-blanker-uit-dna-gebouw-gezet-door-beveiliging/ (accessed on 30 September 2022).

Svampa, M. (2015) 'Commodities consensus: Neoextractivism and enclosure of the commons in Latin America', *South Atlantic Quarterly*, 114(1), pp. 65–82, DOI: 10.1215/00382876-2831290.

Thoden van Velzen, H.U.E. and W. van Wetering (1988) *The Great Father and the Danger: Religious Cults, Material Forces, and Collective Fantasies in the World of the Surinamese Maroons*, 1991 edition (Leiden: KITLV Press).

Van Lier, R. (1949) *Samenleving in een grensgebied: Een sociaal-historische studie van de maatschappij in Suriname*, 4th (revised) edition, 2013 (Paramaribo: Vaco).

Vrede, D. (1986) *Rond het sterfbed van mijn dorp* (Paramaribo: PAS).

Walsh, J. and R. Gannon (1967) *Time Is Short and the Water Rises, Operation Gwamba: the Story of the Rescue of 10,000 Animals from Certain Death in a South American Rain Forest* (New York: E. P. Dutton).

Westermann, J.H. (1971) 'Historisch overzicht van de wording en het onderzoek van het Brokopondo-stuwmeer', *New West Indian Guide*, 48(1), pp. 1–55, https://brill.com/view/journals/nwig/48/1/article-p1_3.xml?language=en (accessed on 2 September 2022).

World Bank (1981) *Bauxite and Aluminum Handbook* (Washington D.C.: Commodities and Export Projections Division, Economic Analysis and Projections Department, World Bank), https://documents1.worldbank.org/curated/en/657851492545150840/pdf/multi-page.pdf (accessed on 2 September 2022).

CHAPTER 7

Contesting Extraction: Challenges for Coalition Building between Agrarian and Anti-mining Movements

Louisa Prause

Abstract

In the context of a global expansion of the extractive frontier, building broad protest coalitions is key for emancipatory and non-extractive future transformations of the countryside. Yet even though movements in both the agrarian and the mining sector struggle against the enclosure of land and the loss of livelihoods in rural areas, inter-sectoral coalitions remain scarce. This chapter therefore aims to identify challenges to inter-sectoral coalition building between movements struggling against extractive projects in the agrarian and the mining sector. Based on a case study of Senegal it shows that mutually exclusive identities, missing 'bridge builders', and different policy spaces constitute key challenges for the building of coalitions. Furthermore, extraction plays out differently in the agrarian and in the mining sector. Different regulations and economic histories as well as distinct impacts of extractive activities on land and nature provide different incentives and challenges for claim making in the two sectors. In order to understand resistance to extraction, it is therefore key to stay attuned to the different impacts extractive investments have on the ground.

1 Introduction[1]

This chapter analyses the challenges faced in the building of inter-sectoral coalitions between social movements that struggle against the expansion of the extractive frontier in the mining and the agrarian sectors. Extractive activities have become a core feature of many economies in the global South in recent decades (Greco, 2020; Burchardt and Dietz, 2014). The extractivist logic

1 The author declares no conflict of interest. The work that contributes to this chapter was supported by the German Federal Ministry of Education and Research as part of two funding lines: 'Bioeconomy as Societal Change' [FKZ 031B0750] and 'Global Change' [Grant Number FKZ 01LN1302A].

 | DOI:10.1163/9789004686182_008

of 'operating through depletion' (Durante, Kröger and LaFleur, 2021, 20) is thereby no longer only a characteristic feature of mining investments alone, but has also become prominent in large-scale investments in agricultural land (Mezzadra and Neilson, 2017). These latter investments, often referred to as land grabbing, not only change control and ownership of land, but also introduce a 'green revolution' and more recently digital technologies (Prause, Hackfort and Lindgren, 2021) into areas that have previously been dominated by smallholder agriculture. This involves an industrialisation, specialisation, and intensification of farming, based on the extraction of soil fertility and water reserves, alongside a loss of biodiversity and often the deforestation of large areas of land. Furthermore, industrialised agriculture extracts large volumes of materials that are destined for export, usually with little or no processing (McKay, 2017). Agro-industrial and mining projects are thus characterised by 'value generation that is necessarily temporary and generally followed by barrenness and an inability to sustainably reproduce livelihoods in the affected habitat' (Ye et al., 2020, 155).

As a reaction to the expansion of extractive agro-industrial and mining projects, numerous protest movements have sprung up throughout many countries in the global South since the mid-2000s (Sändig, 2021; Conde, 2017; Engels, 2022). Protest movements regarding both agro-industrial and mining projects are similarly concerned with issues of land and land use, questions of access and control, and the challenge of sustaining land-based livelihoods in the context of an expanding extractivist frontier, as well as with broader emancipatory developmental pathways for the countryside (Prause and Le Billon, 2021; Kapoor, 2022). However, despite these similarities in motives and goals, coalitions between movements in the agrarian and the mining sectors have, to the best of my knowledge, so far not been reported and analysed in the literature. While this does not necessarily mean that they are non-existent, such coalitions seem to be at least rare (see Borras, 2016).

This lack of inter-sectoral coalitions is problematic for movements that struggle for a non-extractivist development path for the countryside, since coalitions are among the most important tactical tools available to social movements (Gawerc, 2021). They enable the sharing of networks, resources, expertise, and information, and strengthen abilities to mobilise (McCammon and Moon, 2015). Coalitions can act as 'transformative encounters' that produce or induce wider social change or provide an opportunity for learning and knowledge exchange (Berriane and Duboc, 2019). In particular, coalitions between diverse groups and transnational or translocal coalitions can lead to broader-based mobilisations, which can heighten movements' visibility and legitimacy (Gawerc, 2021; Tarrow, 2005; Temper, 2019). The literature stresses how important coalitions are for the success of struggles against extractivist projects, but the contributions focus on coalitions between organisations and movements contesting the same form of extractive project, either industrial mines or agro-industrial projects, in the same country or across countries (e.g. Walter and Urkidi, 2017; Gingembre, 2015), or on transnational coalitions linking protest actors in the global South to organisations in the global North (e.g. Anyidoho and Crawford, 2014; Renauld, 2016; Kapoor, 2022).

At the same time, the broader debate on the expansion of the extractive frontier in agriculture and in mining shows that both sectors are increasingly entangled. There are growing spatial overlaps between both industries and they often compete over access to key input resources, in particular water (Le Billon and Sommerville, 2017). Large mining projects also often endanger local subsistence and small-scale food production because of the land they use, the water resources they need, and their often negative environmental consequences. Such 'colliding ecologies' (Kirsch, 2014, 15) are not limited to the vicinity of the mine. Polluted waterways can also have negative impacts on agricultural production in regions that lie downstream. Finally, several contributions have shown the close interlinkages between artisanal mining and small-scale farming as often complementary and sometimes contradictory rural livelihoods strategies (Pijpers, 2014; Mkodzongi and Spiegel, 2019).

In view of the similarities between agrarian extractivist projects and mining projects and of the interlinkages between both sectors, forming cross-sectoral coalitions between agrarian and non-agrarian actors might be a key tactical tool for social movements that are struggling against dispossessions and for the protection of local livelihoods and emancipatory development paths for the countryside (Borras, 2016). Thus, activists as well as critical academics need to pay more attention to the potential and challenges of horizontal alliances and the 'coalitional politics of resistance to dispossession' (Kapoor, 2022, 346) on extractive frontiers. This chapter therefore aims to put forward a first exploratory attempt at explaining why such inter-sectoral coalitions are, despite the many similarities between movements in the agrarian and the mining sector, difficult to establish. Drawing on my own field research in Senegal, I investigate two movements, one struggling against large-scale land transformations for agro-industrial projects, the other contesting large-scale mining operations. I use this case study to gain insights into the challenges faced when building coalitions between movements that are struggling against different types of extractive projects, and thereby show what hinders the scaling up of political struggles in a way that would transcend a sectoral logic and tackle the development vision of extractivism more broadly.

I chose Senegal as my case study context since investment in extractive projects in both the agrarian and the mining sector have increased significantly since the turn of the millennium (Anseeuw et al., 2012; Nolte, Chamberlain and Giger, 2016; ITIE Senegal, 2019) and new movements have formed to contest these projects. In the agrarian sector, the Cadre de Réflexion et d'Action sur le Foncier au Sénégal (Reflection and Action Network on Land in Senegal (CRAFS)) was formed by organisations active in the agrarian sector in 2011. In the mining sector, the coalition Publish What You Pay (PWYP) Senegal was formed in 2015. I chose these two movements as they are the only two actively opposing land appropriations for agro-industrial and mining projects at the national level in Senegal. Furthermore, each was formed by bringing together a larger number of organisations, and each had excellent ties to international partner organisations. PWYP Senegal specifically is part of an international movement, thus demonstrating its willingness and ability to forge large coalitions and networks.

My analysis of these two movements is based on 65 interviews and seven focus group discussions that I conducted during four field trips in Senegal in April–May 2014, February–April 2015, March–May 2016 and November 2021. In 2020, I also conducted two interviews using teleconferencing tools. Many interviewees were members of movements active in conflicts regarding agro-industrial projects and industrial mines in Senegal. They included members of local communities that were engaged in resistance actions against agro-industrial and mining projects, and representatives of national and international non-governmental organisations (NGOs) and the national peasant federation. I also conducted interviews with state representatives and representatives of corporations active in mining and agro-industrial projects. The case study is also based on a thorough review of national Senegalese press reports on land and mining conflicts in the country and on the reform processes of the land and mining law, as well as of documents published by PWYP and by CRAFS and of these movements' social media accounts.

The chapter is structured as follows. I first develop my theoretical framework based on approaches from social movement studies and critical agrarian studies to identify factors that impede coalition building between different movements. In the empirical section, I then introduce the two main protest movements in the agrarian and the mining sector in Senegal—CRAFS and PWYP—and show that they struggle to attain similar goals and use comparable protest strategies. In subsequent sections, I identify factors that, despite these similarities between the movements, hinder closer collaboration and coalition building in Senegal. I conclude by highlighting key challenges for coalition building, and reflect upon the necessity to acknowledge the specific impacts of different extractive projects on local communities if such challenges are to be overcome.

2 Analytical Framework: Building Coalitions in the Countryside

To understand the challenges faced by efforts to build inter-sectoral movement coalitions in the countryside, I draw on approaches from social movement studies and critical agrarian studies. While the former offers a general understanding of the factors facilitating and impeding coalition building, its approaches have mainly been developed drawing on urban social movements in the global North and lack the analytical tools necessary to grasp the agrarian and rural structures in which movements engaged in struggles centred on extractive projects in the global South are embedded. Approaches from critical agrarian studies allow us to understand the structural changes that are induced by an expansion of capitalist relations and extractivist logics in the countryside.

I understand coalitions as a 'kind of coordination within and between movements that entails closer activist relationships than networks but looser ties than mergers' (Daphi, Anderl and Deitelhoff, 2019, 2). The identities of the groups involved as well as their organisational structures remain separate, but they do engage in cooperative joint action (Tarrow, 2005; McCammon and Moon, 2015). With the term inter-sectoral coalitions, I refer to coalitions between movements that are active with regard to (partially) different issues, but are united by shared goals and seek to engage in joint planning and actions (Beamish and Luebbers, 2009). These include, for example, coalitions between environmental and labour movements (Obach, 2004), between peasant and indigenous organisations (Brent, 2015) and, in the case of this chapter, between agrarian and anti-mining movements. With the term 'social movement', I refer to collectivities acting with some degree of organisation and continuity outside of institutional channels for the purpose of challenging or defending extant authority (Snow, Soule and Kriesi, 2004, 11). I use the terms 'movement', 'protest movement' and 'social movement' interchangeably throughout the chapter.

The literature on social movements has shown that inter-sectoral movement coalitions are often brought about by critical issues that affect various movements (Veltmeyer, 2004), and are facilitated by shared goals and protest strategies (Van Dyke and McCammon, 2010). Hindering factors for inter-sectoral coalitions (and coalitions more generally) include distinct and narrow beliefs and identities. These might inhibit coalition building even if broad goals are shared (Gerhards and Rucht, 1992; Lichterman, 1995). Whether or not divergences in terms of ideology and collective identities between different movements can be at least temporarily overcome depends to a great extent on existing social ties and direct interpersonal connections between activists across organisations (Rose, 2000; Van Dyke and Amos, 2017). Social ties provide knowledge of past actions and commitments, which can help foster trust (Gawerk, 2021). Here, so-called bridge builders or brokers can be key to establishing contact and to facilitating the formation of social ties in the first place (Tarrow, 2005). Multi-issue organisations that work from a broad ideological base on a variety of issues may act as important bridge builders, particularly for inter-sectoral coalitions (Van Dyke, 2003). Negative social ties in the form of personal differences might, meanwhile, impede coalition building or increase tensions in existing coalitions (Borras, Edelman and Kay, 2008). Whether positive or negative social ties exist depends partly on the histories of struggle and the previous interactions of different resistance groups (Martiniello, 2015). Furthermore, different geographies of struggle might prevent social movements' members from forming social ties. If a group is spatially isolated and has limited opportunities to interact then coalition formation with actors from other regions will be difficult (Bandy and Smith, 2005). Limitations to interaction are not, however, linked only to differences in geographical spatial locations, but also to differences in political spaces or arenas. The state and particularly its policy apparatus serve as a focal point of much movement activity. In the policy process, however, the state creates policy subsystems—such as specific agencies or committees that are responsible for certain policy areas—which movements must address with their actions. Thus, the state creates important opportunities for interaction among particular groups of movement actors operating in the same policy area, which may facilitate the establishment of social bonds between movements. At the same time, these state-defined policy spheres also serve to separate protest actors, since they create very little opportunity for interaction between actors in policy-distinct movements, even if these actors' goals might be similar (Obach, 2004).

Studies from the field of critical agrarian studies stress the social class origin of social movements as another key factor influencing coalition building between different movements (Borras, Edelman and Kay, 2008; Borras, 2010). Different class affiliations shape the interests, goals and identities of various social groups when it comes to land-based extractivist projects . Land means different things to different groups of people, depending on their social class. For small-scale land users, it is a means of production and reproduction and a central source of livelihoods; for investors or large-scale landholders, it constitutes a commodity and a site of investment (Dietz and Engels, 2020). Social movements with different class bases, such as peasants and large-scale landholders, might therefore take different positions vis-à-vis the changes that are induced through extractivist projects(Borras, Edelman and Kay, 2008).

Furthermore, while the rural poor have long been perceived as being mainly peasants; this perception does not adequately reflect the complex and diverse livelihoods of people in the countryside, who combine different activities such as fishery, pastoralism, artisanal mining or wage labour in both the agricultural and the non-agricultural sector. Henry Bernstein (2010) therefore talks about 'classes of labor' that encompass those who have to pursue their reproduction through increasingly scarce wage employment or a range of precarious small-scale and insecure survival activities. These 'classes of labor' do not have a pre-existing form of class consciousness or a sense of collective identity, especially since class relations intersect and combine with other social differences and divisions, such as gender, race, or ethnicity (Bernstein, 2010). Thus, even if the class affiliations of two movements are not as different from each other as are, for example, those of peasants and of large-scale landholders, movement actors nevertheless need to actively shape a collective identity if their aim is to mobilise the diverse groups belonging to these classes of labour (Borras, Edelman and Kay, 2008).

These approaches from social movement studies and critical agrarian studies have shown us key facilitating and hindering factors with regard to coalition building. Shared goals, broad, cross-cutting issues, and similar protest strategies as well as social ties and shared geographical and policy spaces of movement action all facilitate coalition building. Their absence, in turn, makes coalition building more difficult. Distinct and narrow beliefs and identities as well as different class origins of movements' bases can also hinder successful coalition building.

3 Protest Movements Contesting Extractive Projects in Senegal

In response to rising investment in extractive agro-industrial and mining projects in Senegal, two new national movements formed, bringing together a variety of actors that were already active in the agrarian and the mining sector but that had not yet formed a formal network. The agrarian movement CRAFS was formed on April 28, 2011 (CRAFS, 2016). The roughly 20 organisations that participate in CRAFS include associations of land users who were affected by and opposed to large-scale agrarian extractivist projects, national organisations (mainly NGOs and think tanks), and the national peasant association the Conseil National de Concertation et de coopération des Ruraux (National

Council for Consultation and Cooperation of the Rural Population (CNCR)), which brings together a large variety of associations of peasants, pastoralists, and fishermen. In addition, some regional organisations active in West Africa and the national sections of certain international NGOs are also part of the alliance (Prause, 2019). CRAFS acted on the national level, for example by organising demonstrations in Dakar that addressed the Senegalese government and by engaging in the national land reform process and lobbying national decision makers. It was also was involved in many local struggles at the sites of large-scale land transactions, mainly in the Senegal River valley in the department of St-Louis in the north of Senegal as well as in the area of Ndiaye in the department of Thiès.

In the mining sector, meanwhile, 25 civil society organisations came together in 2015 to establish the national chapter of PWYP. In Senegal, PWYP is mainly comprised of local and national NGOs and the national sections of international NGOs such as Amnesty International. The most influential national mining-related NGO in the early years of the movement has been La Lumière, whose president also served as the president of PWYP. Unlike CRAFS, PWYP Senegal is part of an international network. This network promotes transparency and environmental protection in the mining sector and the fair transfer of mining levies to the local communities concerned (PWYP, 2017). Like CRAFS, PWYP is active at the national level and is also involved in local actions, in this case with regard to specific mines. These are located mainly in the region of Kédougou in the south-east of the country and to a lesser degree in the area of Ndiaye, in the region of Thiès.

Even though these two movements developed in a similar time frame and both came together in reaction to the expansion of the extractive frontier, formal inter-sectoral coalitions between the movements and their member organisations—or even lengthy periods of collaboration—have yet to be realised. The following sections aim to answer why closer collaboration between the two movements has not occurred.

3.1 *Goals and Strategies*

The literature on social movements highlights shared goals and protest strategies as being key for the facilitation of coalitions. CRAFS formulated two central goals for its struggle. The first was to stop or downsize large-scale land transactions to international and national investors. CRAFS did not reject land transactions outright. Rather, it criticised the size, non-inclusivity, and negative impacts on local communities of the larger land deals and aimed to secure access to land for local communities.[2] It thus advocated a vision whereby local land users could use land more productively and sustainably than multinational investors and in a way that would safeguard their own livelihoods and contribute to food sovereignty (ENDA Pronat, 2019; Prause, 2019). The CRAFS movement's second goal was related to the land law reform process that President Macky Sall initiated in 2012 following his election. CRAFS saw its struggles against large-scale land investments as closely related to this project. The movement aimed to make the reform process inclusive so that the voices of family farmers would be heard, and to guarantee that a new land law would protect access to and control over land for smallholders and rural communities.

PWYP formulated similar goals to CRAFS in some respects, but there were also some important differences. Like CRAFS, PWYP does not reject investments in large-scale mining projects outright. Rather, its main concern is to protect local communities from adverse impacts such as pollution or resettlement, and to secure access to land for rural communities.[3] PWYP's goals differ from those of CRAFS, however, in that the former movement does not propose an alternative vision of how to use the land now mined by the mining companies. Instead, PWYP aims to ensure that local communities derive some form of benefit from these mining activities and receive other lands by way of compensation. Regarding the process of reforming mining law, there were yet again strong similarities between the respective goals of the two movements. PWYP also struggled for a more participatory reform process—this time with respect to the reform of mining law, a process from which civil society actors had initially been excluded—and for a mining law that would guarantee access to and control over land for communities affected by large-scale mining. PWYP, though, went further than CRAFS, stressing the importance of financial benefits for these communities—in the form of a community fund that would distribute a part of mining revenues among them—and of higher mining revenues for the state in general (Agence de Presse Sénégalaise, 2015; La Lumière, 2008).

CRAFS used four core strategies in its struggle. First, it organised a large-scale, bottom-up process including workshops with peasants and pastoralists in all regions of Senegal in order to develop propositions for the land reform, which it was to bring to the negotiating table in 2016. Second, CRAFS organised and supported several demonstrations against large-scale land allocations

2 Source: interview with representatives of a member organisation of CRAFS, Dakar, 4 February 2015.

3 Source: interviews with the president of PWYP Senegal—Tambacounda, 6 March 2015; 8 April 2016.

for agro-industrial purposes. The most prominent of these was related to the Senhuile-Senethanol project in the region of St-Louis, which demonstrations successfully brought to a temporary halt (Benegiamo, 2020; Gagné 2021). Third, CRAFS attempted to build bottom-up networks of land user collectives, bringing together users threatened by land loss. In 2020, CRAFS member organisations began to form a network of peasant collectives active in conflicts centred on agro-industrial projects in different regions of Senegal, as well as those mobilising with regard to industrial phosphate mines in the region of Thiès (ENDA Pronat, 2020). Fourth, CRAFS lobbied key decision makers regarding both the land law reform and the allocation of land to agro-industrial projects.

PWYP strategies were very similar, if generally less inclusive of local land users. First, PWYP also developed its own proposals for the reform process and struggled for the right to be heard by the commission in question—a demand that was finally granted in 2015. PWYP's development of civil society proposals was, however, expert based and thus far less participatory, and it did not have the same mobilising effect for rural communities as was the case in the agrarian sector. Second, PWYP supported local community struggles centred on industrial mines, mainly on gold mines in the region of Kédougou and phosphate and zircon mines in the area of Niayes, where its member organisations mounted protests, lobbying, and media campaigns (EJ Atlas, 2018a; 2018b). Unlike CRAFS, PWYP did not systematically attempt to connect collectives of local land users; it did, however, engage in lobbying, contacting politicians and traditional authorities.

This brief overview of the two movements and their involvement in struggles regarding the expansion of extractive projects in the mining and the agricultural sector has revealed many commonalities: both aimed to secure land access for smallholders, using similar strategies of engaging with community struggles and becoming active in the national law reform process. Despite some clear overlap in goals and strategies there are, however, important differences between PWYP and CRAFS that might impede the building of coalitions between them. In terms of goals, PWYP invests more in securing local communities' access to and control over the benefits and revenues generated by extractive projects. While this point is a core aspect of struggles in the mining sector, it barely plays any role in its agrarian counterpart. CRAFS, meanwhile, has developed a vision of alternative land use based on smallholder agriculture, while PWYP has not. In terms of strategies, it is important to note that the CRAFS approach has a stronger bottom-up character regarding both engagement in the reform process and the organisation of protests against specific land transactions.

3.2 *Class and Collective Identities*

Differences in class positions has been identified in the critical agrarian studies literature as a key challenge to coalition building. While a systematic sociological analysis of the social bases and class composition of both the movements being examined is beyond the scope of this chapter, the claims, in this regard, of PWYP and CRAFS show that each aims to represent groups of land users that have similar class positions but that practice partially different land-based livelihoods. Members of CRAFS claim that the movement represents mainly poor peasants and family and smallholder farmers, as well as pastoralists engaged in family-based, often semi-nomadic cattle breeding and milk production. The interests of medium-sized or large-scale farming or large-scale, industrial cattle breeders or dairy producers, as well as those of workers who are formally or informally employed in the agricultural sector, are not prominently represented bythe movement (CRAFS, 2016).

In order to bring pastoralists and peasants, two groups that often have conflicting interests when it comes to land use, together in the struggle against large-scale land transactions, CRAFS used the term 'rural producers'. This term was originally developed by the national peasant federation, CNCR. The idea of rural producers was proposed with the aim of expanding a purely peasant-based identity to include other agrarian and food-producing activities (CNCR, 2018). The term encompasses pastoralists, peasants, and fishers.[4] While this collective identity of rural producers does succeed in grouping together a broad range of food producers and agriculturalists, it nevertheless tends to exclude other forms of rural livelihoods, and such exclusion is a frequent issue for agrarian movements (see Borras, Edelman and Kay, 2008).

In Senegal, one of the key land-based livelihoods excluded from this collective identity is that of artisanal miners. Next to small-scale farming and pastoralism, artisanal mining is one of the key livelihood activities practiced in the gold mining region of Senegal. It has traditionally been practiced to generate additional household income in the dry season, alongside small-scale agriculture (Niang, 2014). Since the rise in gold prices in the mid-2000s, artisanal gold mining has become the primary household income generating activity in many communities living in the area of the two industrial gold mines in Kédougou (Persaud et al., 2017; Prause, 2016). Artisanal gold miners occupy

4 Fisher communities in certain villages on the coastal strip between Dakar and St-Louis have started to organise resistance to the offshore exploitation of gas and oil, which is supposed to begin within the next several years. These same communities have, however, so far not been concerned either with large-scale land transformations for agro-industrial purposes or with the land reform process, and have not been a prominent force within CRAFS.

a similar class position as peasants and pastoralists (Engels and Dietz, 2018). Artisanal miners are generally informally employed by 'big men' who own the mine shafts, and are paid in shares of the material mined, or they collectively mine easy-to-access gold deposits (Diallo, Diouf and Ngom, 2016).

In Kédougou artisanal miners make up an important constituency of the PWYP member organisations active in the region[5] and thus it was important that they be included in the collective identity of the movement. Rather than constructing its collective identity around the land-based livelihood activities of its constituency, PWYP opted to construct it around the external factor of large-scale mining. PWYP describes itself as a coalition representing the interests of communities affected by industrial mines, and tends to depict these communities as victims of large transnational corporations.[6] This collective identity is more inclusive, in terms of the land-based activities that local community members are engaged in, than the 'rural producers' identity of CRAFS. It still, however, excludes communities that suffer from the adverse effects of other kinds of land investment. So, while the differences in class bases between PWYP and CRAFS do not necessarily constitute a challenge to intersectoral coalition building, the respective collective identities constructed by the two organisations are divisive as each excludes key constituencies of the other movement.

3.3 *A Lack of Social Ties*

An important element of any effort to overcome differences in identities, strategies, or goals between movements are the social ties and inter-movement familiarity that enable a collaborative negotiation process to take place (Obach, 2010). Such social ties between PWYP and CRAFS were largely lacking. Even though one organisation, Rencontre Africaine pour la Défense des Droits de l'Homme (African Assembly for the Defence of Human Rights (RADDHO)), was a member of both movements, and Oxfam was a donor to both coalitions, there are no records of official meetings between CRAFS and PWYP. Some representatives of organisations involved in either CRAFS and PWYP that I interviewed stated that they did know by name some of their counterparts in the other movement, and a few reported having briefly come across one another at conferences or workshops. Regular meetings, though, were not reported, and

5 Source: interviews with representatives of PWYP member organisations, 19 April 2016, 5 March 2015, and 14 April 2016.

6 Source: interviews with PWYP representatives, Tambacounda, 06 March 2015 and 08 April 2016, and with representatives of a PWYP member organisation, Kédougou, 05 March 2015 and 12 April 2016.

other representatives interviewed stated that they did not know any of their peers from organisations active in the other of the two fields.[7] So neither RADDHO nor OXFAM seems to have acted as an effective bridge builder with regard to the two movements.

One explanation for the overall lack of social ties between the organisations active in CRAFS and in PWYP is the different geographies of struggle in the mining and the agrarian sector. Some key organisations active in struggles over mines do not have their offices in the capital, Dakar, but in the cities of Tambacounda and Kédougou, which are located in Senegal's gold mining region. These regions are only poorly connected by road infrastructure with Dakar, where most of the member organisations of CRAFS have their offices. Furthermore, community-based struggles regarding mining were, at least until 2016, concentrated in the gold mining area of Kédougou. Only in recent years have conflicts over industrial mines intensified in the phosphate mining region of Thiès, north of the captial. Struggles regarding agro-industrial projects are largely located in the region of St-Louis along the Senegal River delta and in Thiès in the area of Niayes, since these are the areas with the best conditions for agro-industrial production, with easy access to water and infrastructure (Benegiamo, 2020; Bourgoin et al., 2019).

Thus, personal meetings between representatives of NGOs from each sector, as well as between those of the grassroots collectives active in struggles with regard to local agro-industrial and mining projects, respectively, are difficult to arrange due to the different geographical locations of the struggles themselves and the different locations of these organisations' headquarters. This might change though. In the past few years there has been increasing overlap between industrial phosphate and zircon mining and agro-industrial activities in the area of Niayes. This spatial overlap might provide fertile ground for closer inter-sectoral collaboration. It is thus also in Niayes that the CRAFS member organisations CICODEV (The Pan-African Institute for Citizenship, Consumers, and Development), ENDA Pronat (Association pour l'Environnement et Developpement Action pour une Protection Naturelle des Terroirs–Association for the Environment and Development Action for the Natural Protection of Lands) and CNCR have become active in struggles regarding mines—thus far, however, without building longer-term coalitions with the PWYP member organisations that are also involved in these struggles.

---

7 Source: interviews with representatives of a CRAFS member organisation, Dakar, 12 February 2016 and by telephone on 24 October 2020, and with representatives of a PWYP member organisation, Tambacounda, 8 April 2016.

The lack of social ties between PWYP and CRAFS is also a result of the different histories of struggle in each of the two sectors. Senegal's colonial and postcolonial economy was built around agrarian production. Thus, the political organisation of peasants and pastoralists and political struggles led by peasant organisations have a long history in the country (McKeon, Watts and Wolford, 2004). The mining sector in Senegal is, by comparison, relatively young. Even though phosphate mining dates back to colonial times, industrial mining has only substantially expanded since the turn of the millennium (Coderre et al., 2019). Many grassroots organisations—including collectives and networks of land users and communities active in conflicts centred on mines—have only formed as a reaction to this recent expansion of the mining sector (Prause and Le Billon, 2021). Similarly, many of the NGOs active in the mining sector were founded only in the late 1990s or early 2000s, when mining investments were on the rise in Senegal (KEOH, 2018; La Lumière, 2008; SADEV, 2018). Since both struggles focusing on mining and the political organisations engaged in these struggles are a comparatively recent phenomenon, CRAFS and PWYP have no common previous struggles, which might have established inter-sectoral social ties and relationships between them, to draw upon.

Finally, each movement operates in different policy spaces. The use of land for agricultural or for mining purposes is regulated in Senegal by different laws, and governed by different institutions. This is not unique to Senegal. In fact, it is the norm in most countries (Le Billon and Sommerville, 2017). In Senegal, the mining code regulates land use and land transactions for mining purposes, and the leading bureaucratic and regulatory agency is the Ministry for Industries and Mining. The land law regulates land use and transactions for agro-industrial purposes, and the leading agency is the Ministry for Agriculture and Rural Development. This means that the activities of PWYP and of CRAFS take place in different policy spaces and are directed at different state agencies. This division became most apparent in each organisation's engagement with the processes of reforming the land law and the mining code, respectively. For both movements, these reform processes constituted important institutional opportunities to bring their demands to the policy arena, and they sparked significant activity and mobilisation from each movement. Even though these processes took place in a similar time frame, there was, however, no overlap between the activities of PWYP and of CRAFS. Instead, each movement struggled for access to the respective law reform commissions and fought to have its own suggestions included in the discussions and their results, which once again left few opportunities for exchange and the formation of social ties.

4 Discussion

Building inter-sectoral coalitions between movements contesting extractive projects in the mining and the agrarian sector might be key to the success of struggles for an emancipatory transformation of the countryside. Not only do many governments pursue parallel extractivist development paths in the agrarian and in the mining sector that threaten rural livelihoods and risk deepening social inequalities in the countryside, both sectors are also closely intertwined. Mining activities often impact (both small-and large-scale) agricultural activities negatively because of their need for resources, mainly water, and their negative environmental impacts, including water and soil pollution. Furthermore, small-scale mining and small-scale farming are strongly interdependent as livelihood strategies for rural households.

My analysis has revealed some key challenges for such coalitions: First, even though investments in mining and in agriculture are both characterised by an extractivist logic, the consequences of these respective activities for land and nature differ, which provides different incentives for movements active in the respective sectors. While open-pit gold mining, as it is practiced in Senegal, makes it virtually impossible to use the land for agriculture in the future, the negative consequences, for the environment and for soil fertility, of agro-industrial extractivist projects are, over time, at least partially reversable. Agriculture, even in its extractive form, is still based on cultivation, and its physical effects on nature thus differ from those of mining (Boyd, Prudham and Schurman, 2001). Thus, when Ye et al. (2020, 155) define extraction as value generation that is followed by barrenness and an inability to sustainably reproduce livelihoods, it is important to note that this inability can have very different time frames in the agrarian and the mining sector. Second, state income generated by mining through taxes and royalty payments is not comparable to the considerably lower amounts paid by agricultural businesses for lease agreements. Thus, different regulation and different amounts in rents in each sector as well as the different impacts on land and nature set different incentives for movements and their formulation of demands and goals. In Senegal, the agrarian movement emphasised alternative, non-extractive visions for future land use. While the anti-mining movement stressed access to mining rents, compensation payments, and access to alternative land.

The literature on social movements' coalitions clearly shows that social ties between movements are key to any efforts to overcome such differences regarding goals, ideologies, or identities. In Senegal, the establishment of these ties was hampered by the different histories and geographies of struggle in the mining and the agrarian sector. Social movements' activities with respect to large-scale extractivist projects are, on the ground, bound by the locations of the investments in question. In Senegal, investments in large-scale mining and agro industry projects have only begun to geographically overlap in the past five years, in the region of Thiès. Finally, the agrarian and the mining sector are governed by distinct laws, and their struggles with regard to extraction are thus negotiated in different policy spaces, which contributes to the separation of the two movements that are the subjects of the present study.

This points to certain particularities of struggles centred on agriculture and mining. Investments in these sectors are place-bound (Le Billon and Sommerville, 2017). Thus, different geographies of struggle might be a more important hinderance to the establishment of coalitions than it is in other areas of political struggle. Furthermore, it is not only differing policy spaces that prove challenging for attempts at coalition building. The different regulations of the agrarian and the mining sector also provide different incentives for movements' claim-making activities from the outset. Policies thus not only structure the spaces of negotiation as Obach (2004) argues, but also influence what is negotiated in the first place.

This, in turn, points to an important debate within the literature on extraction. Many authors currently emphasise how extractive logic is now characteristic of global capitalism as a whole, and that it is no longer specific to the extractive industries (Yen et al., 2020; Mezzadra and Neilson, 2017). However, in order to understand resistance to and struggles against extractive projects it is important to pay close attention to differences regarding political regulation, economic histories, place, and impacts on land and nature across a range of extractive projects. Rather than only focusing upon the commonalities of extractive projects, it is necessary to also look at their specificities, and to acknowledge that extractive logics can, on the ground, play out quite differently, and that they therefore also provide very particular challenges for acts of political struggle. Only by acknowledging such differences can we understand what hampers coalition building between movements struggling against extraction, and identify avenues via which these hampering elements might be overcome. In order to strengthen future attempts at coalition building, a focus on shared policy spaces relevant across sectors, such as environmental or water-related policies, the construction of more inclusive collective identities for rural land users and communities, and a broader vision of non-extractive rural development might all constitute important starting points.

5 Conclusion

In the context of an expanding extractive frontier in the mining and the agricultural sector, particularly in the global South, building coalitions that span both sectors is a key challenge for social movements' attempts to successfully prevent dispossessions, protect local livelihoods, and foster non-extractivist developmental paths for the future countryside. This chapter has investigated the factors hindering closer inter-sectoral collaboration and coalition building through a case study of two movements, CRAFS and PWYP, in Senegal. CRAFS and PWYP share broad goals such as the protection of access to and control over land for local land users vis-à-vis extractive projects, and similar types of organisational structures, similar protest strategies, and similar class bases. So why have they not formed a coalition against land dispossessions?

The analysis presented here has shown that some of the goals espoused by CRAFS and by PWYP were none the less different between the two movements, and that the social ties necessary for each to overcome such differences were lacking due to their different histories and geographies of struggle as well as to the different policy spaces the two movements operated in. The analysis has also shown that the collective identities constructed by each movement with the aim of bringing together the classes of labour each represents were mutually exclusive. The agrarian movement built an identity based on the notion of food producers; the anti-mining movement one built around the fact of being a victim of industrial multinational mining corporations. This echoes challenges faced by other agrarian movements—including the transnational movement La Via Campesina—in their efforts to extend their identities to groups of rural poor who do not fit the notion of agrarian and food producers, including rural workers, or, in the case of Senegal, artisanal miners (see also Borras, 2016).

The analysis in this chapter has also highlighted the usefulness of bringing approaches from social movement studies together with approaches from critical agrarian studies when studying anti-extractivist movements in the countryside. Only by combining both these theoretical traditions can we understand the specific conditions and constituencies that social movements work with in rural spaces in the global South.

My analysis also points to some more practical implications, particularly for international, multi-issue NGOs, but also for sympathetic development agencies. These often support and work with movements in both the mining and the agrarian sector, and thus could play an important role in facilitating coalition building. In view of the separate policy spaces movements in the agrarian and the mining sector usually engage in, such organisations and agencies could provide neutral spaces for open and respectful dialog between movements, facilitate ongoing interactions between different groups and movements, and act as bridge builders. They also could enable conversations about constructing a non-extractivist vision of future development. Here, the international agrarian movement La Via Campesina already offers many starting points, with its vision of food sovereignty that could also be relevant to struggles centred on mining. For future research on the lives and afterlives of extraction, I believe it is important to go beyond identifying the extractivist logic that governs rural spaces through the mining industry and the agro industry, and its consequences. Development studies also need to provide pointers for concrete transformation paths that lead towards a non-extractivist countryside if they are to support both engaged policy makers and social movements.

Acknowledgements

I am very grateful to Jan Brunner, Sarah Kirst and Mario Schenk for their valuable comments on an earlier draft of this chapter. I would also like to thank the Initiative Prospective Agricole et Rural (IPAR) particularly Dr Aminata Niang, the West Africa office of the Rosa-Luxemburg-Stiftung, ENDA Pronat, the Collectif de Ndiael, and Dr Lamine Diallo for support during my fieldwork.

References

Agence de Presse Sénégalaise (2015) 'Sénégal: « Publiez ce que vous payez » veut être impliquée dans le processus de réforme du Code Minier', http://fr.allafrica.com/stories/201506011340.html (accessed on 4 October 2017).

Anseeuw, W., M. Boche, T. Breu, M. Giger, J. Lay, P. Messerli and K. Nolte (2012) *Transnational Land Deals for Agriculture in the Global South. Analytical Report Based on the Land Matrix Database* (Bern, Montpellier and Hamburg: CDE/CIRAD/GIGA).

Anyidoho, N.A. and G. Crawford (2014) 'Leveraging National and Global Links for Local Rights Advocacy: WACAM's Challenge to the Power of Transnational Gold Mining in Ghana', *Canadian Journal of Development Studies*, 35(4), pp. 483–502, DOI: 10.1080/02255189.2014.936369.

Bandy, J. and J. Smith (2005) *Coalitions Across Borders: Transnational Protest and the Neoliberal Order* (Lanham: Rowman & Littlefield).

Beamish, T.D. and A.J. Luebbers (2009) 'Alliance Building across Social Movements: Bridging Difference in a Peace and Justice Coalition', *Social Problems*, 56(4), pp. 647–676, DOI: 10.1525/sp.2009.56.4.647.

Benegiamo, M. (2020) 'Extractivism, Exclusion and Conflicts in Senegal's Agro-Industrial Transformation', *Review of African Political Economy*, 47(166), pp. 522–544, DOI: 10.1080/03056244.2020.1794661.

Bernstein, H. (2010) *Class Dynamics of Agrarian Change* (Halifax NS; Fernwood/ Sterling VA: Kumarian Press).

Berriane, Y. and M. Duboc (2019) 'Allying beyond social divides: an introduction to contentious politics and coalitions in the Middle East and North Africa', *Mediterranean Politics*, 24(4), pp. 399–419, DOI: 10.1080/13629395.2019.1639022.

Borras, S.M. (2016) *Land Politics, Agrarian Movements and Scholar-Activism*, Inaugural Lecture 14 April 2016 (Den Haag: International Institute of Social Studies).

Borras, S.M. (2010) 'The Politics of Transnational Agrarian Movements', *Development and Change*, 41(5), pp. 771–803, DOI: 10.1111/j.1467-7660.2010.01661.x.

Borras, S.M., M. Edelman and C. Kay (2008) 'Transnational Agrarian Movements: Origins and Politics, Campaigns and Impact', *Journal of Agrarian Change*, 8(2–3), pp. 169–204, DOI: 10.1111/j.1471-0366.2008.00167.x.

Bourgoin, J., E. Valette, S. Guillouet, D. Diop and D. Dia (2019) 'Improving Transparency and Reliability of Tenure Information for Improved Land Governance in Senegal', *Land*, 8(3), DOI: 10.3390/land8030042.

Boyd, W., W.S. Prudham and R.A. Schurman (2001) 'Industrial Dynamics and the Problem of Nature', *Society & Natural Resources*, 14(7), pp. 555–570, DOI: 10.1080/ 08941920120686.

Brent, Z.W. (2015) 'Territorial Restructuring and Resistance in Argentina', *The Journal of Peasant Studies*, 42(3–4), pp. 671–94, DOI: 10.1080/03066150.2015.1013100.

Burchardt, H.-J. and K. Dietz (2014) '(Neo-)extractivism—a new challenge for development theory from Latin America', *Third World Quarterly*, 35(3), pp. 468–486, DOI: 10.1080/01436597.2014.893488.

CNCR (Conseil National de Concertation et de Coopération des Ruraux) (2018) 'Présentation CNCR', https://cncr.org/qui-sommes-nous/ (accessed on 3 January 2023).

Coderre, M., M.L. Diallo, A. Diawara and B. Campbell (2019) 'La Vision minière pour l'Afrique et les transformations des cadres règlementaires miniers: les expériences du Mali et du Sénégal', *Canadian Journal of Development Studies*, 40(4), pp. 464–81, DOI: 10.1080/02255189.2019.165033.

Conde, M. (2017) 'Resistance to Mining: a Review', *Ecological Economics*, 132, pp. 80–90, DOI: 10.1016/j.ecolecon.2016.08.025.

CRAFS (Cadre de Réflexion et d'Action sur le Foncier sur la réforme foncière au Sénégal) (2016) *Document de position du Cadre de Réflexion et d'Action sur le Foncier sur la réforme foncière au Sénégal* ['Position Paper of the Reflection and Action Network on Land in Senegal'] (Dakar: CRAFS), http://hubrural.org/IMG/pdf/crafs_doc_de_position_reforme_fonciere_v.finale.pdf (accessed on 11 June 2020).

Daphi, P., F. Anderl and N. Deitelhoff (2019) 'Bridges or Divides? Conflicts and Synergies of Coalition Building across Countries and Sectors in the Global Justice Movement', *Social Movement Studies*, 21(1–2), pp. 8–24, DOI: 10.1080/14742837.2019.1676223.

Diallo, M.L., N.C. Diouf and N.M. Ngom (2016) *Étude sur l'exploitation artisanale des mines à Kédougou: Nouvelle réorganisation, migrations, et différentes implications* ['Study on artisanal mining in Kédougou: reorganisation, migrations, and different implications'], (Dakar: IPAR).

Dietz, K. and B. Engels (2020) 'Analysing Land Conflicts in Times of Global Crises', *Geoforum*, 111, pp. 208–217, DOI: 10.1016/j.geoforum.2020.02.019.

Durante, F., M. Kröger, and W. LaFleur (2021) 'Extraction and Extractivism. Definitions and Concepts', in J. Shapiro, and J.-A. McNeish (eds.) *Our Extractive Age. Expressions of Violence and Resistance* (Oxon and New York: Routledge), pp. 19–30.

EJ Atlas (Environmental Justice Atlas) (2018a) *Projet Grande Côte for Zircon and Ilmenite Mining, Senegal*, https://ejatlas.org/conflict/diogo-zircon-mining-niayes-senegal (accessed on 1 October 2020).

EJ Atlas (2018b) *Taïba Phosphates Mine in the Fertile Gardening Area of Niayes, Senegal*, https://ejatlas.org/conflict/phosphates-mining-in-the-gardening-zone-of-niayes-mboro-senegal (accessed on 1 October 2020).

ENDA Pronat (Association pour l'Environnement et Developpement Action pour une Protection Naturelle des Terroirs) (2020) *Déclaration Commune du Collectif des 16* [Common Declaration of the Collective of the 16], May 27, https://www.endapronat.org/declaration-commune-du-collectif-des-16/ (accessed on 19 October 2020).

ENDA Pronat (2019) *La résistance paysanne à l'accaparement des terres et le processus de la réforme foncière au Sénégal* ['Peasant resistance against land grabbing and the land reform in Senegal'], July 29, https://farmlandgrab.org/post/view/29069 (accessed on 1 October 2020).

Engels, B. (2022) 'African Anti-mining Movements', in D.A. Snow, D. Della Porta, D.J. McAdam and B. Klandermans (eds.) *The Wiley Blackwell Encyclopedia of Social and Political Movements 2e* (Blackwell: Wiley), DOI: 10.1002/9780470674871.wbespm667.

Engels, B. and K. Dietz (2018) 'Structural Transformation in the Countryside', *Review of African Political Economy / ROAPE Online*, 9 May, http://roape.net/2018/05/09/structural-transformation-in-the-countryside/ (accessed on 1 October 2020).

Gagné, M. (2021) 'Analysing the constraints to corporate land control: the influence of local power dynamics on a large-scale land deal in Senegal', *Canadian Journal of African Studies*, 56(2), pp. 239–259, DOI: 10.1080/00083968.2021.1890628.

Gawerc, M.I. (2021) 'Coalition-building and the forging of solidarity across difference and inequality', *Sociology Compass*, 15(3), DOI: 10.1111/soc4.12858.

Gerhards, J. and D. Rucht (1992) 'Mesomobilization: Organizing and Framing in Two Protest Campaigns in West Germany', *American Journal of Sociology*, 98(3), pp. 555–596, DOI: 10.1086/230049.

Gingembre, M. (2015) 'Resistance or Participation? Fighting Against Corporate Land Access amid Political Uncertainty In Madagascar', *The Journal of Peasant Studies*, 42(3–4), pp. 561–584, DOI: 10.1080/03066150.2015.1022867.

Greco, E. (2020) 'Africa, Extractivism and the Crisis This Time', *Review of African Political Economy*, 47(166), pp. 511–521, DOI: 10.1080/03056244.2020.1859839.

ITIE Senegal (Initiative pour la transparence dans les Industries Extractives du Sénégal) (2019) *Rapport de Conciliation 2018* (Dakar: ITIE).

Kapoor, D. (2022) 'Rural dispossession and resistance in Asia and Africa', in H. Veltmeyer, and P. Bowles (eds.) *The Essential Guide to Critical Development Studies* (Oxon and New York: Routledge), pp. 341–349.

Kirsch, S. (2014) *Mining Capitalism. The Relationship between Corporations and Their Critics* (Berkeley: University of California Press).

KEOH (L'association Kédougou Encadrement Orientation et Développement Humain) (2018) Mission, Vision, Valeur, http://associationkeoh.org/keoh.php (accessed on 19 January 2018).

Lichterman, P. (1995) 'Piecing Together Multicultural Community: Cultural Differences in Community Building among Grass-Roots Environmentalists', *Social Problems*, 42(4), pp. 513–534, DOI: 10.2307/3097044.

La Lumière (2008) *Transparence et gestion durables des ressources naturelles au Sénégal: experience de l'ONG La Lumière* ['Transparancy and sustainable administration of natural ressources in Senegal. Experiences of the NGO La Lumière'], http://siteresources.worldbank.org/EXTSOCIALDEVELOPMENT/Resources/DIALLO.pdf (accessed on 8 May 2018).

Le Billon, P. and M. Sommerville (2017) 'Landing Capital and Assembling "Investable Land" in the Extractive and Agricultural Sectors', *Geoforum*, 82, pp. 212–224, DOI: 10.1016/j.geoforum.2016.08.011.

Martiniello, G. (2015) 'Social Struggles in Uganda's Acholiland: Understanding Responses and Resistance to Amuru Sugar Works', *The Journal of Peasant Studies*, 42(3–4), pp. 653–669, DOI: 10.1142/9789813208162_0020.

McCammon, H.J. and M. Moon (2015) 'Social Movement Coalitions', in D. Della Porta and M. Diani (eds.) *The Oxford Handbook of Social Movements* (Oxford: Oxford University Press), DOI: 10.1093/oxfordhb/9780199678402.013.38.

McKay, B.M. (2017) 'Agrarian Extractivism in Bolivia', *World Development*, 97, pp. 199–211, DOI: 10.1016/j.worlddev.2017.04.007.

McKeon, N., M. Watts and W. Wolford (2004) 'Peasant Associations in Theory and Practice', *Civil Society and Social Movements*, Programme Paper No. 8 (Geneva: United Nations Research Institute for Social Development).

Mezzadra, S. and B. Neilson (2017) 'On the multiple frontiers of extraction: excavating contemporary capitalism', *Cultural Studies*, 31(2–3), pp. 185–204, DOI: 10.1080/09502386.2017.1303425.

Mkodzongi, G. and S. Spiegel (2019) 'Artisanal Gold Mining and Farming: Livelihood Linkages and Labour Dynamics after Land Reforms in Zimbabwe', *The Journal of Development Studies*, 55(10), pp. 2145–2161, DOI: 10.1080/00220388.2018.1516867.

Niang, K. (2014) *Dans les mines d'or du Sénégal oriental. La fin de l'orpaillage* [In the Goldmines of oriental Senegal. The end of artisanal mining] (Paris: L'Harmattan).

Nolte, K., W. Chamberlain and M. Giger (2016) *International Land Deals for Agriculture. Fresh Insights from the Land Matrix: Analytical Report II* (Bern, Montpellier, Hamburg and Pretoria: Centre for Development and Environment (CDE), University of Bern; Centre de coopération internationale en recherche agronomique pour le développement (CIRAD); German Institute of Global and Area Studies (GIGA); University of Pretoria, Bern Open Publishing).

Obach, B. (2010) 'Political Opportunity and Social Movement Coalitions. The Role of Policy Segmentation and Nonprofit Tax Law', in N. Van Dyke and H.J. McCammon (eds.) *Strategic Alliances*, (Minneapolis: University of Minnesota Press), pp. 197–218.

Obach, B. (2004) *Labor and the Environmental Movement: the Quest for Common Ground* (Cambridge: MIT Press).

Persaud, A.W., K.H. Telmer, M. Costa and M.L. Moore (2017) 'Artisanal and Small-Scale Gold Mining in Senegal: Livelihoods, Customary Authority, and Formalization', *Society & Natural Resources*, 30(8), pp. 980–993, DOI: 10.1080/08941920.2016.1273417.

Pijpers, R. (2014) 'Crops and carats: Exploring the interconnectedness of mining and agriculture in Sub-Saharan Africa', *Futures*, 62, pp. 32–39, DOI: 10.1016/j.futures.2014.01.012.

Prause L. (2019) 'Success and Failure of Protest Actors' Framing Strategies in Conflicts Over Land and Mining in Senegal', *Canadian Journal of Development Studies*, 40(3), pp. 387–403, DOI: 10.1080/02255189.2018.1479633.

Prause, L. (2016) 'West Africa's Golden Future? Conflicts around gold mining in Senegal', *Natural Resources Series* (Dakar: Rosa-Luxemburg Stiftung Westafrika).

Prause, L. and P. Le Billon (2021) 'Struggles for Land: Comparing Resistance Movements against Agro-Industrial and Mining Investment Projects', *The Journal of Peasant Studies*, 48(5), pp. 1100–1123, DOI: 10.1080/03066150.2020.1762181.

Prause, L., S. Hackfort, and M. Lindgren (2021) 'Digitalization and the Third Food Regime', *Agriculture and Human Values*, 38(2), pp. 641–655, DOI: 10.1007/s10460-020-10161-2.

PWYP (Publish What You Say) (2017) *Publish What You Pay Senegal*, https://www.pwyp.org/pwyp_members/senegal/ (accessed on 3 January 2023).

Renauld, M. (2016) 'The Esquel Effect: Political Opportunity Structure and Adaptation Mechanisms in Anti-Mining Mobilisation in Argentine Patagonia', *Canadian Journal of Development Studies*, 37(4), pp. 524–540, DOI: 10.1080/02255189.2016.1202102.

Rose, F. (2000) *Coalitions across the Class Divide: Lessons from the Labor, Peace, and Environmental Movements* (London: Cornell University Press).

SADEV (Solidarité Action Développement) (2018) *SADEV*, http://sadevsenegal.blogspot.de/ (accessed on 19 January 2018).

Sändig, J. (2021) 'Contesting large-scale land acquisitions in the Global South', *World Development*, 146, DOI: 10.1016/j.worlddev.2021.105581.

Snow, D., S. Soule and H. Kriesi (2004) 'Mapping the Terrain', in *The Blackwell Companion to Social Movements* (Malden, MA: Blackwell Pub), pp. 3–16.

Tarrow, S. (2005) *The New Transnational Activism* (Cambridge: Cambridge University Press).

Temper, L. (2019) 'From boomerangs to minefields and catapults: dynamics of trans-local resistance to land-grabs', *The Journal of Peasant Studies*, 46(1), pp. 188–216, DOI: 10.1080/03066150.2017.1398144.

Van Dyke, N. (2003) 'Crossing Movement Boundaries: Factors that Facilitate Coalition Protest by American College Students 1930–1990', *Social Problems*, 50(2), pp. 226–250, DOI: 10.1525/sp.2003.50.2.226.

Van Dyke, N. and B. Amos (2017) 'Social Movement Coalitions: Formation, Longevity, and Success', *Sociology Compass*, 11(7), DOI: 10.1111/soc4.12489.

Van Dyke, N. and H.J. McCammon (2010) 'Introduction: Social Movement Coalition Formation', in *Strategic Alliances* (Minneapolis: University of Minnesota Press), pp. XI–XXVIII.

Veltmeyer, H. (2004) *Civil Society and Social Movements. The Dynamics of Intersectoral Alliances and Urban-Rural Linkages in Latin America* (Geneva: United Nations Research Institute for Social Development).

Walter, M. and L. Urkidi (2017) 'Community Mining Consultations in Latin America (2002–2012): the Contested Emergence of a Hybrid Institution for Participation', *Geoforum*, 84, pp. 265–279, DOI: 10.1016/j.geoforum.2015.09.007.

Ye, J., J.D. van der Ploeg, S. Schneider and T. Shanin (2020) 'The incursions of extractivism: moving from dispersed places to global capitalism', *The Journal of Peasant Studies*, 47(1), pp. 155–183, DOI: 10.1080/03066150.2018.1559834.

CHAPTER 8

'We Are Nature Defending Itself': the Forest of Dannenrod Occupation as an Example of Contested Extractivism in the Global North

Dorothea Hamilton and Sina Trölenberg

Abstract

Extractive activity is not limited to mining; it also occurs in the other forms of large-scale landscape destruction, including the deforestation involved in extensive infrastructure projects. Yet while resistance to activities such as fracking and coal mining has been intensively investigated within the extractivism debate under the collective term 'contested extractivism', resistance to the extraction of renewable parts of nature such as woodland has, by comparison, been somewhat neglected. Likewise, the academic debate has focused mostly on case studies from the global South. We argue that opposition to the felling of more than 85 hectares of woodland in the Forest of Dannenrod (Germany) for the construction of a highway is an example of contested extractivism in the global North. We portray the protest as a clash between extractivist and anti-extractivist notions in Europe, the latter partly transitioning into post-extractivist imaginaries. And although the area was felled in 2020, we argue that this opposition marked a turning point for the German environmental justice movement and sparked a national debate, despite persistent support mechanisms for wood extraction and negative media reports.

1 Introduction

In academic literature, extractivist practices are often described as contested. Investigating environmental protests against such practices has a long history in the field of political ecology, yet the literature shows that there has been a strong emphasis on research in the global South (e.g., Dietz and Engels, 2017, on gold mining in Colombia; Ghosh, 2016, on coal mining in India; and Bebbington, 2013, on mining in the Andean region). Comparatively few investigations take into account contestation of extractivism in the global North. Furthermore, the focus has been on movements that oppose non-regenerative resource extraction (e.g., Brock and Dunlap, 2018, on coal mining), making

© GENEVA GRADUATE INSTITUTE, 2024 | DOI:10.1163/9789004686182_009

extractivism and the act of contesting it resemble a phenomenon of the global South, and one limited to mineral or hydrocarbon extraction. We, however, argue that the partial logging of the Forest of Dannenrod in central Germany for road infrastructure expansion is an example of a European site of extractivist practice that has been similarly contested. Much like in other parts of the world, this environmental conflict manifests fundamentally different perceptions of human–nature interaction and distinct extractivist, anti-extractivist and post-extractivist imaginaries (see Boulot and Collins; Post, both in this volume and Nikolaeva, 2023). Further, we argue that even though the section of forest in question was eventually felled the protest constitutes a success, as it sparked a national debate on how anti-extractivist positions can develop into post-extractivist imaginaries. To explore these assumptions, this chapter draws on several theories and presents a mixed-method approach. Building on this, it outlines the evolution of the contestation as well as the role of the stakeholders involved in an attempt to make sense of different local imaginaries that developed during the protest. The chapter concludes with proposals for concrete policy measures.

The woodland in question was situated in the Forest of Dannenrod in the central German federal state of Hesse. The site is near the village of Dannenrod (160 inhabitants) in a peripheral and economically weak region close to the university towns of Marburg and Giessen. An aisle of trees approximately 100 metres in width was felled in the winter of 2020 in order to allow for the completion of an interstate highway (*autobahn*)—the 'A49', a road of major national and supranational importance due to the desire to increase connectivity between logistical sites throughout Germany and Europe (see Figure 8.1). It is also argued that the highway will improve the infrastructural connectivity of two other major highways, thereby reducing traffic in nearby villages currently suffering the effects of traffic noise and congestion. The chosen route, though, dissects several areas of forest, of which the Forest of Dannenrod is the most biodiverse. The more than 85 hectares of woodland that needed to be cleared for the project to go ahead included 250-year-old oak and beech trees and was characterised as a biodiverse ecosystem that connected ecological corridors important for threatened species. The affected forest also forms part of a large water protection area with critical importance to half a million people in the region which depend on the drinking water. Opponents to the highway expect severe pollution of the groundwater from construction as well as from contaminated sites in the area.

The protesters oppose the building of the highway due to one or more of its negative impacts: For some, the ecological integrity of the forest and of the endemic local species is crucial. Others refer to the threat to water quality in

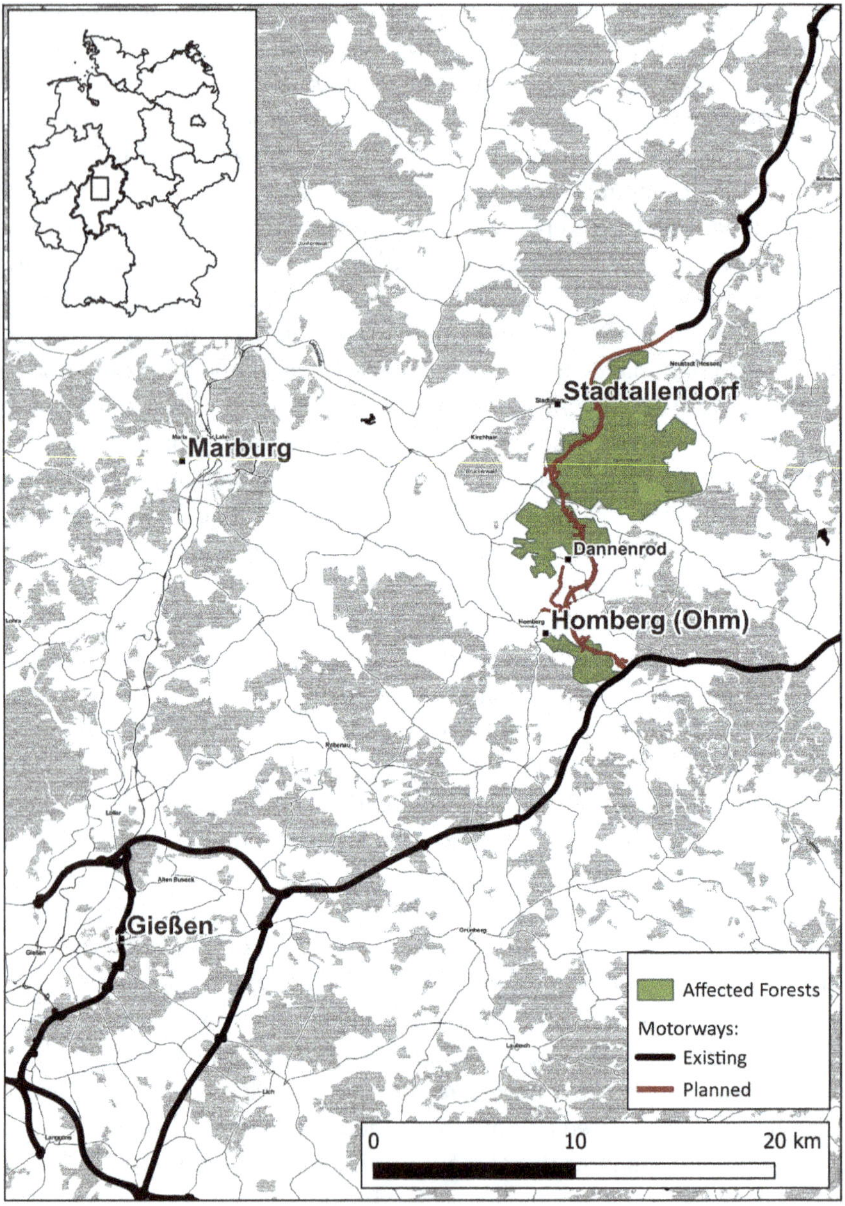

FIGURE 8.1 Location of the Forest of Dannenrod and the planned highway A49
SOURCE: IGNATIUS PERERA (2022B)

the region. Locals fear the negative effects of noise pollution, and a lessened quality of life in their village. For others, it is a symbol of absurdity that, amid a climate crisis and with global temperatures rising, the felling of a forest for the sake of increased individual mobility is being permitted despite the adverse effects on promises to reduce carbon dioxide emissions.

2 Research Purpose and Methodological Approach to the Argumentation

In this chapter, we argue that the conflict around tree felling in the Forest of Dannenrod is a clash between extractivist and post-extractivist imaginaries, specifically emphasising the heterogenous protest movement that has formed over recent decades. Traditional approaches in the field of political ecology focus on access to nature as a central point of conflict (Robbins, 2020; Neumann, 2005). We, meanwhile, argue that extractivist practices in the realm of above-ground woodland extraction are likewise contested, as seen in several cases in the global south. And, although the area of the forest in question was eventually cut down, the protest still represents a success. In order to look beyond the unifying effect that the joint opposition to the A49 had on various environmental initiatives, we aim to explore the consequential dynamics present within the movement.

We recognise the need to highlight our personal and geographical proximity to the protest. We were, at all times, highly biased in our studies as we were personally involved in the protest we were trying to understand as researchers. This resulted in different approaches to the object of study during the research process, which lasted for over a year. We found it a methodological and epistemological challenge to observe a protest from the inside while drawing objectifiable conclusions from that observation. In fact, we do not consider ourselves outsiders investigating a faraway phenomenon, but rather position ourselves among the affected groups, as the construction of the highway might affect future access to water and aggravate local effects of the climate crisis.

Our range of methodological approaches reflect our attempt to strike a balance between objectivity and involvement. Over the time of observation (October 2019—March 2021) we employed what could be called a mix of methods, consisting of participatory observation, quantitative techniques, a literature review, focus groups and critical discourse analysis. Such a description would, however, be an oversimplification—the main challenge of investigating something we were physically and emotionally involved in was to find appropriate approaches under changing circumstances. We combined perspectives and techniques from critical anthropogeography, political ecology, sociology and ethnology. In doing so, we were striving for a multifaceted picture that would help us understand the complexity of the contestation.

Our first contact with the contestation of this act of woodland extraction saw us in the role of participatory observers. This was in September 2019, when we attended events related to the upcoming clearing season, such as weekly forest walks and demonstrations in the region. Later the same year, when the first tree houses were built, we attended a cultural and educational programme on the site of the camp, and talked to locals and to the so-called activists living temporarily or permanently in the tree houses. In October 2020, we saw the need to include an 'objective' observation method and, embedded in a Master's seminar, conducted semi-structured interviews with their attendant questionnaire to get an insight into the protesters' standpoints, experiences and motivations. This laid the grounds for a quantitative approach (N=127) in order to obtain representative results. Since we were highly entangled in an emotional protest, our aim was to concentrate on the preconditions that make contestation possible. At all times we were aware of the diversity and heterogeneity of the participants, yet we categorised them into subgroups to get a clearer picture of different tendencies.

In the analysis, we found our initial outcomes highly biased as we had homogenised the protesters and attributed to them monodimensional characteristics. Consequently, we decided to complement our results with an analysis of the related media discourse, which had been growing in intensity in the course of our investigation. Based on the approach employed by Siegfried Jäger (2015), we carried out a critical discourse analysis, aiming to dissect the media coverage and make better sense of it. To this end, we documented and visualised the main discursive events and analysed representative newspaper articles.

Three months after the last tree was cut down, we sought to contrast the 'internal' with the 'external' view in an interactive manner. In the context of the 'Camp for Climate Action' held in Dannenrod in April 2021, we aimed to elicit participants' perspectives.

3 Theoretical Embedding: Contested Extractivism in the Global North?

Traditionally, extractivism is considered a model of development based on the exploitation of generally non-renewable and subterranean resources for export (Gudynas, 2009). The academic discourse on extractivism and on protests against practices such as mining, large-scale infrastructure projects or extensive monocultures—often referred to as contested extractivism—mainly stems from the global South, with a strong emphasis on Latin America (e.g., Dietz and Engels, 2017; Gudynas, 2013; Bebbington, 2013). Explanations for this can be found in a greater economic dependency on the extraction of natural resources, the more frequent and more violent persecution of environmental activists in the region, and the traditional geographic focus of political ecology (Bailey and Bryant, 1997).

In the current academic debate, meanwhile, the idea of extractivism is increasingly being expanded to encompass a wider critique of extractive practices that require the exploitation of humans and of non-human species in the context of a growth-based economy (Mezzadra and Neilson, 2017; Bresnihan and Brodie, 2020). Thereby, extractivism is interpreted as a practice that involves profound landscape changes for the sake of extracting one element of nature, usually referred to as a 'resource'. Generally this involves large-scale projects in peripheral areas and economic profit for powerful stakeholders, alongside long-term ecological costs that considerably impact local livelihoods (Hamilton, 2022). Most of the time this goes hand in hand with centralised decision-making at both a geographical and contextual distance from the site of extraction, resulting in the externalisation of ecological costs to the local community, which remains invisible.

In the political ecology discourse, it is often argued that struggles around nature are a product of unequal 'access to nature' (Ahlborg and Nightingale, 2018). Linking this thought to extractivism, it is often contended that the necessary control that implies a certain use of nature is a direct reflection of power relations. Different groups are said to enjoy unequal access to nature and so-called resources (Bauriedl, 2016). However, studying the protest centred on the Forest of Dannenrod reveals that this particular contestation cannot be explained by this theory of access to nature. In order to understand the protest's dynamics, we prefer to deploy the territory approach used by Maristella Svampa, who highlights that extractivism is based on 'the exploitation of increasingly scarce, mostly non-renewable, natural resources and the expansion of these resources into territories that were previously considered "unproductive"' (Svampa, 2012, 14). Territory becomes a central term in her approach. It involves more than just the access to nature, instead proposing a fundamentally different idea of human–nature interaction and 'good living' (Quechuan: '*sumaq kawsay*'; Spanish: '*buen vivir*'). The ideais based on a 'paradigm shift from an anthropocentric to an eco-centric perception of nature, from hyper-individualism to a community-focus responsibility, from a […] growth-fetish to a needs-based regenerative lifestyle' (Gomes, 2018, 150).

Rooted in Latin American ontology, '*buen vivir*' proposes that a harmonious and peaceful relationship between humans and non-humans is the foundation of a 'good' life. This is contrary to the conventional dualistic view found in Western approaches, which places humankind above nature in an exploitative manner. '*Buen vivir*' thwarts the fundamentals of extractivism, which are directly tied to an anthropocentric world view wherein a non-human environment is only appreciated, if at all, for its (economic) value to humans. Nature has to be 'put into value' (Altvater and Mahnkopf, 1997); otherwise it is considered unproductive. Extractivist practices tend to expand into 'unproductive' territories, producing contestation with the local population (Ulloa, 2016). In Latin America many of the groups contesting extractivism argue from a post-extractivist or anti-extractivist point of view, based on the idea of 'good living' and opposed to a growth-oriented, centralised idea of development. We understand anti-extractivist views oppose to extractivism from a rather conservative standpoint with the aim of maintaining the status quo within the existing system. Post-extractivist motivations, meanwhile, involve the idea of necessary systemic changes in order to achieve a 'good life'.

Building on these thoughts, extractivism can be applied to examples outside the global South. In the case of 'the Danni'—as the forest was nicknamed by the protesters, thus giving it an identity that it does not possess according to German law—the infrastructure project is considered more valuable than the forest. The forest can be understood as one of Svampa's 'unproductive territories' as it adds no additional monetary value to the region. Much like various other cases, the destruction of the ecosystem is justified by enforcing more 'productive' use of the land. Large-scale projects are discursively justified by linking them to growth-oriented 'progress', wherein the prospect of improved connectivity and economic benefits has been described as a major driving force, particularly for the realisation of infrastructural projects (Harvey and Knox, 2015). In this way, valid critique is delegitimised and alternative proposals for regional development beyond the anthropocentric and the growth-oriented remain unheard or are actively suppressed.

Looking at the Danni movement from this angle, we see that contestation of extractivism does not only occur because of inequalities with regard to access. Rather, it is based on a radically different conceptualisation of the nature–human relationship and on a post-extractivist idea of a 'good life'. In what follows, we attempt to understand both the different emic concepts of good living that are at the basis of the protest as well as the ideas of post-extractivist movements in the global North.

4 'The Danni' as an Example of Contested Extractivism in the Global North

In order that readers comprehend our conceptual approach, we will briefly describe the history of the Danni protest and present the actors involved as well as their anti-and post-extractivist imaginaries.

The discussion between local, regional and national actors on how to improve the regions infrastructure connectivity dates back more than 40 years. The decision to choose the variant that dissects the Forest of Dannenrod was backed by the CDU, the conservative party and the "green party", nearby industries, and by the initiative 'JA49' ('Yes A49'), which claims that the closure of this particular gap in the region's road infrastructure will deliver both better logistical links and noise alleviation measures in the surrounding villages. Resistance to the highway extension, meanwhile, centres around residents of the village of Dannenrod—later taking form as the citizen's initiative 'Keine A49' ('No A49')—and is as old as the construction plans themselves. Initial legal action aimed at stopping the extension failed and suggestions for alternate routes remained mostly unheard. But the issue only attracted supra-regional attention late in 2019 when activists from all over Germany and beyond joined local protesters. Encouraged by the Naturschutzbund (NABU), a national environmental protection body, protesters initially built five tree houses 25 metres above ground level, and defence structures, including wooden barricades, to protect the trees marked for felling. As a result, clearance of the area was postponed, and what gradually became tree house villages kept growing (Figure 8.2), right up until the following possible clearing season, in October 2020. Throughout that year, engagement in and knowledge of the matter accumulated, the former ranging from weekly demonstrations such as the so-called Sunday forest walks through infrastructural and logistical support from residents of the village of Dannenrod and the participation of NABU to more radical forms of environmental protest by activist groups.

A self-organised protest camp was set up between the edge of the forest and the village with the help of local residents, landowners and environmental groups, creating a bridge between the tree house villages and their supporters. Not all villagers supported the growing number of protesters in their village. But the camp did gain allies from the nearby university towns of Giessen and Marburg, bringing additional support by raising awareness of the matter in a middle-class, academic setting and pointing to the ecological value of the forest and the threat the highway expansion would pose to neighbouring towns.

During the first COVID-19-related lockdown period, in March 2020, the number of tree house villages grew, as did the number of protesters. With the

FIGURE 8.2 Tree house seen during one of the guided forest walks
SOURCE: AUTHOR, 2020

logging season approaching, by September 2020 an unknown number of so-called activists had built more than 50 tree house–like structures, in approximately ten 'neighbourhoods' in the area of trees that were to be cut down (see Figure 8.3). In June 2020, the last legal avenue for halting the clearance had been closed by the Federal Administrative Court logging, and felling operations were expected for October 2020.

Inspired by other successful forest protection campaigns, especially the Hambacher Forest occupation (Liersch and Stegmaier, 2022), the protestors in the Forest of Dannenrod prepared for the threat of eviction. They joined a larger movement, which used the slogan '*Wald statt Asphalt*' ('Forest instead of asphalt') as a political rhetorical phrase to raise awareness of the necessity for a general change in transport policy (*Verkehrswende*). Thus, the Danni evolved as a national symbol of the necessity of a mobility transition within Germany—a

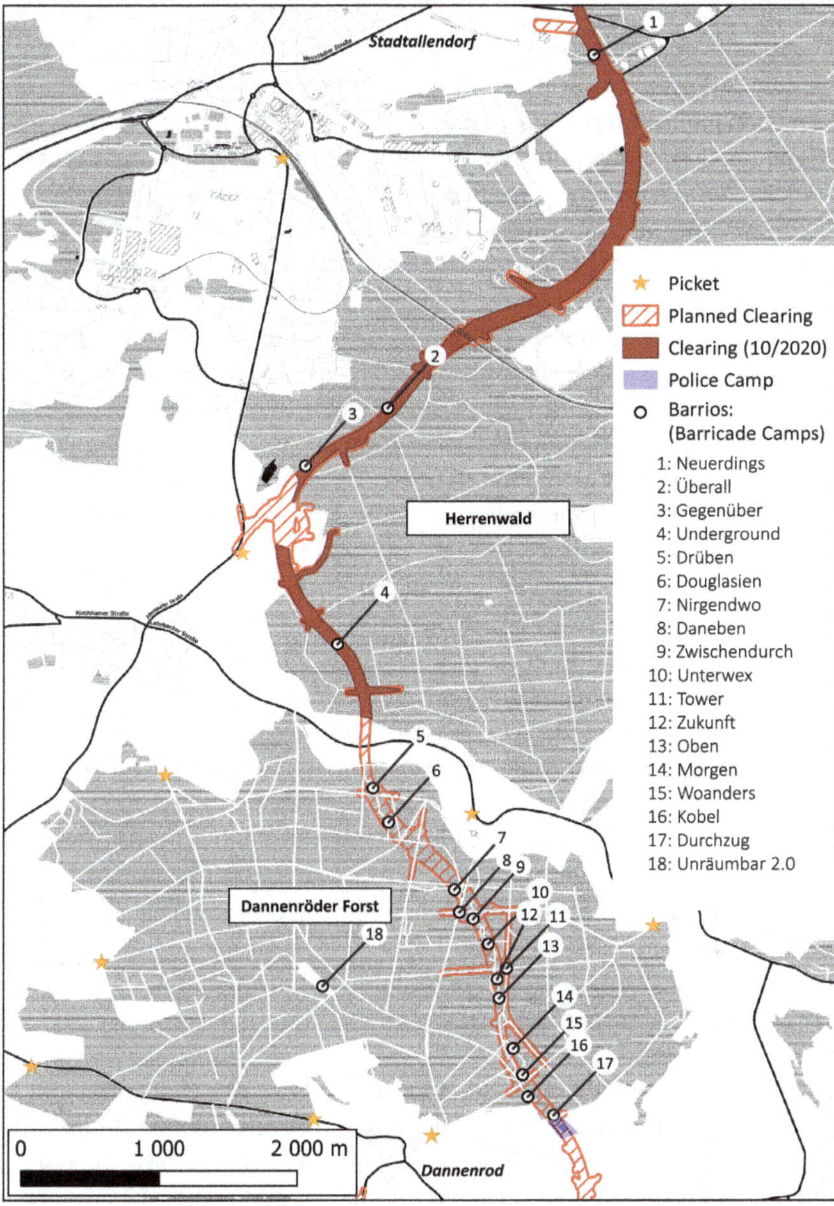

FIGURE 8.3 Barrios A49 (Map of tree house village in the Forest of Dannenrod in October 2020)
SOURCE: IGNATIUS PERERA (2022A)

crucial adaptation measure given the alarming situation of climate crisis. As a self-organised counter project to local and national politics, the protest camp at Dannenrod hosted political events, concerts, and workshops about alternatives to an extractive lifestyle. The camp included a community kitchen, and functioned as a meeting point for the regular Sunday walk that continued, even during the eviction stage, in a family-oriented, educational manner, hosting up to 5,000 participants a day.

On 1 October 2020, the evictions began, with a major police presence. After some initial failures, police tactics changed, employing counter-insurgency methods. The following month, with up to 2,000 police officers in attendance each day, all the tree house villages were subjected to evictions, and the trees were immediately logged, all of which attracted major media attention. At this time, the contestation was joined by other climate activist groups, such as *Ende Gelände* ('End of the [construction] site'), a European alliance of movements that opposes coal mining and gas extraction and uses non-violent and subversive methods of environmental protection (Kinna and Gordon, 2019). The collaboration with *Ende Gelände* marked the confluence of the two sides of the same coin of post-extractivist imaginaries: On the one hand, there were objections to the extraction of natural resources. On the other, a critique of the fossil fuel–based transport system. Both extraction and transportation contribute significantly to the climate crisis. The contested extractivism of the Danni therefore created a space for exchanging ideas about post-extractivist and post-carbon lifestyles.

During the felling, protesters used increasingly radical methods to protect the forest, including chaining themselves to trees, occupying excavators and harvesters, and abseiling from bridges spanning highways, causing major traffic jams all over Germany. Thus, the protest evoked strong opposition in the general population. And while certain prominent individuals who showed solidarity with the cause brought it further national attention, others accused the protesters of terrorism.

As described, the Danni manifested a clash of imaginaries of what a 'good life' should imply. Protesters fought for every meter of vegetation in order to reinforce the protection of the forest and a post-extractivist view. The police, for its part, enabled felling and logging in line with official decision-making and following an extractivist norm. The last tree of the aisle was cut down in December 2020 (Figure 8.4). By then, police had, according to media reports, made more than 1,000 temporary arrests, destroyed more than 500 barricades, and left at least three activists with major injuries.

FIGURE 8.4 Cleared and fenced-off forest area
SOURCE: JULIA MANEK, 2021

Even though the movement did not achieve its original goal of stopping the felling of the forest, we argue that it was a success. The protest camp has continued to host events on the subject of post-extractivist imaginaries, including the 'Climate Camp in 2021', with participants from all over Germany and a large number of workshops and discussion groups on post-extractive lifestyles in times of climate crisis.

4.1 *Ramifications of Imaginaries from a Discursive Viewpoint*

Based on the following analysis of media perceptions, we show that this conflict can be interpreted as a clash between extractivist and post-extractivist views. In the literature, extractivism is portrayed as going hand in hand with the appropriation of territory and the oppression of human and non-human livelihoods. The pro-extractivist media argues against other forms of development and criminalises contestation (Santisteban, 2016). The rights of nature and of locals are to be subdued in the name of a common good often portrayed as 'progress' or 'economic growth'—paradigms that are often attributed to the expected beneficial outcomes of infrastructure (Harvey and Knox, 2015).

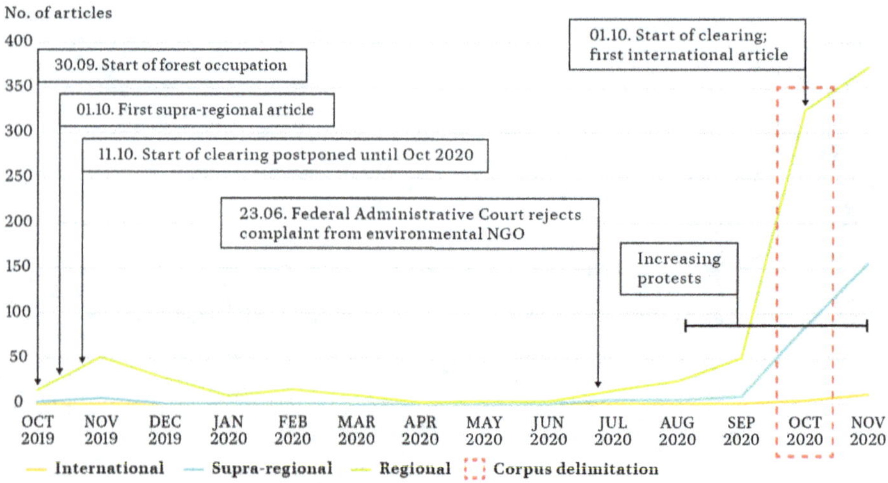

FIGURE 8.5 Media coverage during the occupation of the Dannenrod Forest (start of forest occupation–start of clearing)
SOURCE: AUTHORS, BASED ON DATA FROM WISO-NET AND GOOGLE NEWS, 2021

Our cross-sectional examination of the environmental discourse regarding the contested extractivism in the Forest of Dannenrod at the level of the media focused—based on the work of Mattissek and of Jäger—on linguistic text elements that are understood as socially established rules and their discontinuities (Mattissek, 2021, 365–378). As can be seen in Figure 8.5, a total of 1,198 articles were recovered from German online newspapers, showing the entire media coverage over the investigated time. The contestation clearly remained an unrecognised, regional phenomenon until the point of the planned eviction in November 2019, and certainly until the eviction was actually conducted, one year later. The exponential increase in media attention sees the matter attract even international coverage at the peak of the confrontation between the protesters and the police. We posit that the media coverage rises in parallel with the number of violent incidents, as peaceful gatherings of 5,000 protesters attracted no national media attention while single acts of violence attracted the most coverage. While both police and protesters used different degrees of violence media responded mainly to the use of different kind of violence like sabotaging machines and blocking highways by abseiling from bridges which protesters were accused of.

One piece, in the popular national newspaper *Welt* even states, 'They call themselves activists. But in fact, they're engaging in terrorism'[1] (Welt/ Schwilden, 2020). This draws attention to questions of whether protesters turned violent because of a lack of media attention and whether the portrayal of tree squatters as terrorists—and the overall notable use of military language in media coverage—was proportionate to the reality of the conflict. A general media analysis reveals that the protesters were often described as a homogenous group and denied any individuality, but were generally attributed a uniform propensity for violence. Through 'othering', a sharp distinction is drawn between the law-abiding police 'arming themselves/gearing up for a large-scale operation' (Welt, 2020a), on the one hand, and 'massively resisting' activists using 'extreme force' (Welt, 2020a; 2020b), on the other, thereby implying that an encounter between these two groups is virtually expected to turn violent. Overall, patterns of thought prevail whereby activists are not to be taken seriously as a social movement but merely as a threat to general security, as they are not perceived as representative of the general public's interests.

In order to understand how public opinion was shaped, we will now take an in-depth look at two representative articles from the last and most contested period, that between the first forest occupation and the start of felling (October 2019–November 2020). The articles, respectively from influential newspapers from the left (*Süddeutsche Zeitung*, SZ) and the conservative spectrum (*Frankfurter Allgemeine Zeitung*, FAZ), were analysed for discursive elements that shaped perceptions of the contestation and the representation of the actors involved. Elements and perspectives that were left out of reporting (non-mentions) or that were especially highlighted were of particular interest as they represented narratives and counter-narratives around the conflict.

4.2 *Conceptualisation of Stakeholders in the Media*

A closer look at the two representative articles shows that the constitutional state that enforces the extractivist view is presented as infallible and unquestionable. According to them, supporters of the highway are described to be limited in their right to demonstrate, while activists and their reasons for protesting are implicitly located on the fringes of society and associated with far left movements only, not reflecting popular opinion.

For example, the term 'silent majority' (FAZ, 2020) is used to describe supporters of the highway to portray them as overlooked in the debate and to

1 All terms and passages quoted from German-language news outlets and interviews are the authors' translations.

create a counter discourse to the hegemonic discourse of the A49's opponents, associated with social–ecological movements such as Fridays for Future. This notion puts economic well-being above the conservation of livelihoods and devalues the intentions of the protesters. This may be due to the press' perception of climate activism as a threat to established economic and political norms as it challenges the industrial and imperial lifestyle. This threat is countered by the paradigm of economic growth, in which mega infrastructure projects are given positive connotations, while climate science and policy discourse remain completely ignored. The underlying implication is that the highway serves a common good by enhancing the regional economy through an act of infrastructural 'gap closure' (FAZ, 2020). Ecological effects are justified as containable and therefore harmless; scientific findings as irrelevant. Political ecology's understanding is that this creates an objectification of nature as an element that is subservient to humans even in the context of its supposed protection. The role of activists is largely described as negatively impacting and harmful to societal security by using the power of framing and othering through a demarcation of the own and known from the foreign and unknown.

Terms from transportation and economics, such as 'economically underdeveloped' and 'relief for the congested federal highway' (SZ, 2020) are consistently used positively and the highway's expansion is portrayed as inevitable. This is especially made visible by highlighting that all past court decisions have ruled in favour of the construction project (SZ, 2020). This undermines both the progressive nature of science and the potential of current climate and environmental research as a fundamental indicator that could constitute a power-exerting, decision-making force and set premises for the adaptation and revision of legal decisions.

4.3 *Discursive Exclusions*

4.3.1 The Anti-extractivist Imaginaries of Locals

Returning to our broader media review, although some of the articles retrieved and analysed provide a comparatively differentiated overview of the discourse around, and aim for a detailed description of the varying positions within, the conflict, they contain several phrasings that accentuate only certain characteristics, thus influencing the interpretation of what is read and what is not (Matthes, 2007, 18). Ongoing opposition by locals, for example, remains unmentioned, and the voices of those protesters that are not engaged specifically in the forest occupation remain mostly unheard, leaving almost no room for an understanding of anti-extractivist imaginaries as a motivation for protest. According to responses to our questionnaire, the residents of Dannenrod were not involved in non-legal actions, yet they supported the movement in other crucial ways, including by hanging banners or taking part in protest walks. Others supported the so-called activists by providing access to showers and hot food, or employed more clandestine types of support, taking medicine and building materials to the forest or supporting the camp financially even though they might have had less radical political ideas. The reasons they supported the movements with different political ideals are apparent in the following statement from an anonymous interviewee:

> The tree squatters transformed the movement [...]—probably in a decisive way. But it is wrong to reduce discussion of the resistance to the A49 (or the 'car madness') to this action alone. [...] citizen groups have been fighting the project in different ways for 40 years. And if we have the chance today to stop the A49 for the sake of the Forest of Dannenrod, then [this is] only because these long-term protests and legal proceedings have at least delayed the planning and construction.

Reasons for engagement that remained unheard in the media discourse included the following:

> Just as there is no second world, there will be no second Forest of Dannenrod. My father is probably the oldest demonstrator. With almost 94 years and more than 50 years of activity as a forester in Dannenrod, hardly anyone knows the Forest of Dannenrod as well as he does.

We observe a highly emotional and personal connection between some protesters and the forest. The position with regard to the highway project is not, however, unanimous, and that there is a certain ambiguity within the local community, as, for example, the slogan 'Do we need the A49?' (Figure 8.6) demonstrates. The unwillingness to give up the comfort of individual motorised transport might be seen as a reason for the objection to the highway as much as the lack of reasonable transport alternatives, especially in remote areas. Ultimately, this anti-extractivist way of thinking rather seems to be based on individual rather than collective needs, contrary to the idea of '*buen vivir*'. It also avoids the question 'Do we need the Forest of Dannenrod?' and therefore represents the view of the anti-A49 movement rather than a general post-extractive or post-carbon imaginary. Only due to the protest were many of the residents confronted with more general questions regarding the ideals of 'good life' and changes in individual habits.

FIGURE 8.6 Bumper sticker asking, 'Do we need the A49?'
SOURCE: AUTHOR, 2020

4.3.2 The Post-extractivist Imaginaries of Activists

Contrary to the locals' perspective, those actually engaged in the forest occupation had no emotional connection to the forest prior to the occupation, nor would they be directly affected in their daily lives by the impact of the highway. For this group, the felling served as indicative of the absurdity of clearing healthy, ecologically relevant forests in times of climate crisis for the sake of creating more traffic. One said:

> For me personally, it's not so much about the A49 [highway], but about a general system change that makes ecological sense. For me, it's not that important that this [the forest occupation] takes place here in this region; I could also sit in the trees 100 km away because of another highway route.

For these mostly younger protesters willing to engage in non-legal actions, the Dannenrod Forest served as a symbol of capitalist approaches to nature as also seen in other anti-extractivist movements around the globe. Their view is deeply rooted in a belief in the necessity of a transformation of transport policy that would only become reality if radical action were taken. We were able to observe that this group showed high mobility and adaptability to external circumstances over the course of the occupation. Many students lived temporarily in the forest during the lock-down period, the semester break, or weekends.

They criticised the extractivist politics that they understand to be the driver of the collapse of climatic and ecological conditions. Their vision of post-extractivism goes beyond the local imaginaries based as they were on emotional attachment. This vision goes hand in hand with a post-carbon lifestyle, and requires a change in personal lives—and in national politics based on growth and the exploitation of nature—if the climate crisis is to be combatted effectively.

4.3.3 View of Nature as Part of a Post-extractivist Imaginary

In the media reports, the underlying questions of whether non-human nature should itself have rights and whether in times of a climate crisis past decisions might respect the law but at the same time be inappropriate for the current moment remain undiscussed. The fact that the importance of the forest goes unmentioned in media reports, alongside their presentation of an economic importance that supposedly outweighs the needs of ecosystems, reflects arguments from the pro-extractivist discourse. This is contrary to the protesters' notion that 'we are nature defending itself', a phrase commonly used in the protest, which creates a counter narrative that aligns with post-extractivist ideals, pointing beyond an anthropocentric view and exhibiting similarities to the '*buen vivir*' debate. Protesters criticised the anthropocentric distinction between humans and nature and the implicit hierarchy that places humankind above non-human nature. The phrase 'we are nature defending itself' is compatible with the territorial approach borrowed from indigenous protests in Latin America, studied by Svampa (2012). The place of extraction is no longer 'empty' as portrayed by the media but is a place of living organisms functioning according to their own roles.

An extractive understanding of nature is the foundation for large-scale destruction and the suppression of alternative forms of development and 'good life'. It reframes the philosophical question of whether humans are to 'subdue the earth' as stated in the Bible. It also sheds light on current, mostly Westernised, human–nature relationships and challenges the assumption that economically non-productive spaces have to be 'put into value'. In the case of the Forest of Dannenrod, the clearance of the forest was based on decisions made in the past rather than being a reaction to the current situation vis-à-vis the climate and the role of forests for mitigation. The latter, as a decisional foundation, would require recognition of the need to protect forests given their role as a crucial factor for mitigating climate change effects, prioritising such protection over economic 'necessity', and revising past democratic decisions accordingly.

Among other demands, the protesters ask for a vision of a 'good life' in which nature has a value of its own as opposed to having its role reduced to that of something that is useful for humans alone. In the Forest of Dannenrod, this was also expressed by the name given to the forest: Within the protester community and some media reports, the forest was named Danni, as though referring to an individual. Some ancient trees were named 'grandma' or 'grandpa', and once felled were given funerals. This personalisation of the forest questions the view that humans and nature are to be seen as separate entities, and such questioning arguably the basis of post-extractivist views on life. Solidarity is shown with indigenous principles, wherein non-human actors are not merely seen as external factors to human existence. A post-extractivist view of a 'good life' cannot reduce nature to something for human use alone. Nature is thus to be respected as an essential part of existence that cannot be easily separated from the human sphere.

4.4 *The 'Danni' Movement—a Success?*

Even though the last tree of the forest aisle was felled in December 2020, and despite the negative opinions formed by media, we argue that the contested extractivism of the Forest of Dannenrod was a success as it changed the debate in Germany. Firstly, several analogue and online networks were created or strengthened, which laid the foundations for further tree house villages in other parts of Germany whenever a forest or even individual trees were threatened by a similar infrastructure project. The number of temporarily 'protected forests' rose to 35 according to media reports (TAZ, 2021), making the felling of trees to make way for economic expansion a risky option for decision makers. Several occupied spaces have led—on a regional level—at least to the payment of compensation and the planting of new trees. On the local level, a house was bought in Dannenrod with the aim of creating an 'environmental school' to maintain the place's function as a post-extractivist exchange. Also at the local level the Greens lost credibility, making way for the emergence of a new party, the 'Climate List'. Whether the protest marked a sea change via which decision-making will move in the direction of a post-extractivist imaginary in terms of policy on a national level, meanwhile, is a matter for further investigation. But despite this open question, we argue that the protest should nevertheless be considered a success, as it shaped public discourse around the meaningfulness of the destruction of ecosystems for the benefit of highways in times of climate crisis and species loss.

Further, from our research we deduce that the contested extractivism on the proposed route of the A49 had a unifying effect on the various environmental initiatives involved, and one that reached across different age groups, political ideals, and regional connections. We were able to show the convergence of post-extractivist and anti-extractivist imaginaries in the protest camp as a place of exchange.

5 Conclusions and Policy Implications

Opposition to woodland extraction in the Forest of Dannenrod is an example of a form of contested extractivism that concerns renewable parts of nature in the global North.

We argue that in the extractivist view a hierarchical system verbally separates a specific group (humans) from a larger system (nature). The counter argument advanced by the Dannenrod protesters reunites these two elements, thereby shaping different post-extractivist and anti-extractivist imaginaries. By conceptualising environmental protest through this lens, political ecology evolves into the investigation of power structures manifested in the territory of the global North that do not differ so much from those of the global South. Following this line of thought, the Danni represents a clash of understandings of 'good life': The protesters pursue an understanding of 'good life' that is comparable with '*buen vivir*', arguing that extraction is an outdated model. Local anti-extractivist movements argue for maintaining the status quo based on an emotional attachment to the forest and the fear of noise pollution. Decision makers, meanwhile, understand economic growth—expressed by the construction of so-called efficient infrastructure—to be a precondition of prosperity. In contrast, an understanding of the 'good life' inspired by Latin American movements rather than measuring 'good life' by economic growth highlights the question of how harmony with non-human beings can be achieved. We propose further research on entanglements with environmental protests in the global North and emic concepts of '*buen vivir*'.

In terms of anti-extractivist imaginaries, we conclude that there was a certain ambivalence among locals with regard to the argument for joining the protest, while non-locals tended to be driven by post-extractivist motivations that are tied to a systematic transformation that goes beyond the protection of one local forest. Collective resistance, however, brought protesters and environmental entities closer to one another. And even though the protest failed in its original aims and was mainly disregarded in the discourse of the media, it still succeeded, by sparking debate and by bringing different kinds of post-extractivist and post-carbon imaginaries together. As a result, these were able to emerge stronger, in the form of a more connected, resilient network.

How did a local protest in a small German village turn into a larger movement? We deduce that in order for small-scale resistance dynamics to become larger, a close and interdependent connection between protesters and the local community is necessary, the latter providing a foundation for active, long-term engagement in various manners against, in this case, the destruction of woodland. In Dannenrod, locals, contrary to other examples of contested extractivism, were not, however, willing to participate in non-legal actions. The presence of more radical individuals seems to be a prerequisite for gaining the necessary media attention.

Our analysis of the media's perception of the issue showed that much of the media portrays activists as violent and a threat to society due to their unwillingness to accept democratic decisions. Yet many of the protesters were young people who had not had the chance to participate in those very democratic decisions concerning the A49 highway as they were taken 40 years ago. What these protesters are asking for is that we discuss anew the idea of a 'good life', this time going beyond purely economic prioritisations. Within their vision, we find a relationship to nature similar to that to be found in many struggles in Latin America. The definition of a 'good life' and who is to decide how to deal with nature are, then, above all questions of power. The environmental protest movement in the Forest of Dannenrod galvanised public discourse, which we consider a powerful tool for efforts to turn around the 'productive spaces' narrative of nature and to question the purpose of large-scale woodland extraction.

There are multiple practical lessons to be learnt from this case study, and in what follows, we translate our research outcomes into **policy implications:**

(1) Contested extractivism in the global North must be taken seriously. If downplayed, criminalised or ignored, the protesters involved will most likely turn to more radical measures as this seems to be the only way to gain media attention. Our analysis shows that protestors felt left out of the decision-making process, and participatory strategies that directly involve groups from civil society are thus strongly recommended.

(2) On a legislative level we should question whether decisions taken in the past should remain valid in times of climate crisis or should be re-evaluated. Young people argue that the legal basis for the building of the highway was established under different conditions, and that they had no opportunities to object to this. Policy makers should consider

questioning decisions taken in the past with regard to their possible noxious effects vis-à-vis climate change. To effectively recognise and protect the role of woodland in climate change mitigation, we could learn from Latin American countries wherein elements of nature can be assigned an identity in order to assure their protection. Examples of this include the Ecuadorian Constitution and the case of the Atrato river in Colombia. As this requires in-depth reflection on our anthropocentric views on nature, we strongly recommend further transdisciplinary research.

(3) Post-extractivist thought needs a public space in which it can be discussed if we wish to avoid a hegemony of self-organised spaces, which tend to ally themselves with more radical forces. In order to prevent violent clashes between extractivist and post-extractivist views, platforms for the exchange and discussion of post-extractivist imaginaries should be established and the debate on post-carbon lifestyles and pluralistic views of the 'good life' should include academia, politics and civil society. Therein, the basic assumption of a growth-based economy should also be the subject of debate.

References

Altvater, E. and B. Mahnkopf (1997) *Grenzen der Globalisierung: Ökonomie, Ökologie und Politik in der Weltgesellschaft* (Münster: Westfälisches Dampfboot).

Ahlborg, H. and A.J. Nightingale (2018) 'Theorizing power in political ecology: the 'where' of power in resource governance projects', *Journal of Political Ecology*, 25(1), pp. 381–401, DOI: 10.2458/v25i1.22804.

Bailey, S. and R. Bryant (1997) *Third World Political Ecology* (Abingdon: Routledge).

Bauriedl, S. (2016) 'Politische Ökologie: Nicht-deterministische, globale und materielle Dimensionen von Natur/Gesellschaft-Verhältnissen', *Geographica Helvetica*, 71(4), pp. 341–351, DOI: 10.5194/gh-71-341-2016.

Bebbington, A. (2013) *Industrias extractivas, Conflicto social y dinámicas institucionales en la Región Andina* (Lima: IEP; CEPES; GPC Grupo Propuesta Ciudadana, América problema, 36).

Bresnihan, P. and P. Brodie (2020) 'New extractive frontiers in Ireland and the moebius strip of wind/data', *Environment and Planning E: Nature and Space*, 4(4), pp. 1645–1664, DOI: 10.1177/2514848620970121.

Brock, A. and A. Dunlap (2018) 'Normalising corporate counterinsurgency: engineering consent, managing resistance and greening destruction around the Hambach coal mine and beyond', *Political Geography*, 62, pp. 33–47, DOI: 10.1016/j.polgeo.2017.09.018.

Dietz, K. and B. Engels (2017) 'Contested extractivism: actors and strategies in conflicts over mining', *Die Erde—Journal of the Geographical Society of Berlin*, 148(2–3), pp. 111–120, DOI: 10.12854/erde-148-42.

FAZ (Frankfurter Allgemeine Zeitung) (2020) 'Demonstrieren dürfen beide Seiten', https://www.faz.net/-gzl-a3w3w (accessed on 06 May 2021).

Ghosh, D. (2016) '"We don't want to eat coal": Development and its Discontents in a Chhattisgarh district in India', *Energy Policy*, 99, pp. 252–260, DOI: 10.1016/j.enpol.2016.05.046.

Gomes, A. (2018) 'Lessons from the Margin. Indigenous Peace Ecology', *Organicom* 15(28), pp. 149–166.

Gudynas, E. (2013) *Extracciones, extractivismos y extrahecciones—Un marco conceptual sobre la apropiación de recursos naturales* (Montevideo: CLAES).

Gudynas, E. (2009) 'El buen vivir más allá del extractivismo', in A. Acosta (ed.) *La maldición de la abundancia* (Quito: Abya-Yala; Comité Ecuménico de Proyectos), pp. 15–20.

Hamilton, D. (2022) 'Andengold. Bergbaufluch in (Post-)Bürgerkriegsländern Lateinamerikas', in W. Gieler and M. Novak (eds.) *(Re-)konstruktionen—Internationale und Globale Studien*, Vol.3. (Berlin: Springer).

Harvey, P. and H. Knox (2015) *Roads. An anthropology of Infrastructure and Expertise* (New York: Cornell University Press).

Jäger, S. (2015) *Kritische Diskursanalyse. Eine Einführung* (Münster: Edition DISS, Bd. 3).

Kinna, R. and U. Gordon (2019) *Routledge Handbook of Radical Politics* (Abingdon: Routledge).

Liersch, C. and P. Stegmaier (2022) 'Keeping the forest above to phase out the coal below: the discursive politics and contested meaning of the Hambach Forest', *Energy Research and Social Science*, 89, pp. 1–15, DOI: 10.1016/j.erss.2022.102537.

Manek, J. (2021) *Cleared and fenced-off forest area*, 14th April, *Twitter* (https://twitter.com/ju_manek/status/1382387165011832836/photo/1).

Matthes, J. (2007) *Framing-Effekte. Zum Einfluss der Politikberichterstattung auf die Einstellungen der Rezipienten* (Baden-Baden: Reihe Rezeptionsforschung, Bd. 13).

Mattissek, A. (2021) 'Die Aussagenanalyse als Mikromethode der Diskursforschung', in G. Glasze and A. Mattissek (eds.) *Handbuch Diskurs und Raum. Theorien und Methoden für die Humangeographie sowie die sozial-und kulturwissenschaftliche Raumforschung*, Sozial-und Kulturgeographie (Bielefeld: transcript, Bd. 11), pp. 365–378.

Mezzadra, S. and B. Neilson (2017) 'On the multiple frontiers of extraction: excavating contemporary capitalism', *Cultural Studies*, 31(2–3), pp. 185–204, DOI: 10.1080/09502386.2017.1303425.

Neumann, R. P. (2005) *Making Political Ecology* (Oxfordshire: Routledge), DOI: 10.4324/9780203764206.

Nikolaeva, S. (2023) 'Anti-Extractive Rumouring in the Russian North-East' in F. Calvão, M. Archer and A. Benya (eds.) *The Lives of Extraction. Identities, Communities and the Politics of Place,* International Development Policy | Revue internationale de politique de développement, 15 (Geneva, Boston: Graduate Institute Publications, Brill-Nijhoff), DOI: 10.4000/poldev.5226.

Perera, I. (2022a) *Barrios A49*, unpublished digital map, 19 July.

Perera, I. (2022b) *Overview A49*, unpublished digital map, 19 July.

Robbins, R. (2020) *Political Ecology: a Critical Introduction*, 3rd Edition (Hoboken: John Wiley & Sons).

Santisteban, R.S. (2016) 'Perros y antimineros: discursos extractivistas y prácticas represivas en el Perú', *Tabula Rasa*, (24), DOI: 10.25058/20112742.58.

SZ (*Süddeutsche Zeitung*) (2020) 'Räumfahrzeuge vorm Jahrhundertwald', https://www.sueddeutsche.de/politik/dannenroeder-forst-raeumfahrzeuge-vorm-jahrhundertwald-1.5050295 (accessed on 06 May 2021).

Svampa, M. (2012) 'Bergbau und Neo-Extraktivismus in Lateinamerika', in Forschungs- und Dokumentationszentrum Chile-Lateinamerika e.V. (FDCL) (eds.) (2012) Der Neue Extraktivismus—Eine Debatte über die Grenzen des Rohstoffmodells in Lateinamerika (Berlin: FDCL-Verlag), pp. 14–23.

TAZ (*Tageszeitung*) (2021) 'Das Halbjahr auf den Bäumen', https://taz.de/Waldbesetzungen-in-Deutschland/!5776091/ (accessed on 20 March 2021).

Ulloa, A. (2016) 'Feminismos territoriales en América Latina. Defensa a la vida frente a los extractivismos', *Nómadas*, (45), pp. 123–139.

Welt (2020a) 'Weiterbau der A49: Polizei wappnet sich für Großeinsatz', https://www.welt.de/regionales/hessen/article216903634/Weiterbau-der-A49-Polizei-wappnet-sich-fuer-Grosseinsatz.html (accessed on 6 May 2021).

Welt (2020b) 'Die Grünen lassen sich von der Aktivistenszene treiben', https://www.welt.de/debatte/kommentare/article217176354/Dannenroeder-Wald-Die-Gruenen-lassen-sich-von-der-Aktivistenszene-treiben.html (accessed on 6 May 2021).

Welt/Schwilden, F. (2020) 'Sie nennen sich Aktivisten. Aber tatsächlich betreiben sie Terrorismus', https://www.welt.de/debatte/kommentare/article218717380/Dannenroeder-Wald-Selbst-ernannte-Aktivisten-betreiben-Terrorismus.html (accessed on 23 June 2022).

CHAPTER 9

National Resources, Resistance, and the Afterlives of the New International Economic Order in Bangladesh

Paul Robert Gilbert

Abstract

Over the last two decades in Bangladesh, a well-organised resistance to coal mining in the north-west, and to onshore and offshore gas exploration, has been animated by concerns over dispossession of land, and plans to export much of the coal and gas to be extracted in the name of financial viability. As such, these movements might be read as resistance to 'extractivism' in a 'literal sense'. In scholarship on resistance to resource extraction in Bangladesh, significant attention has been given to the tensions that appear to arise between 'resource nationalist' opposition to foreign-owned or export-oriented extractive operations, and (some) supposed resource nationalists' accommodation of fossil fuel extraction in the name of energy sovereignty and development. In this chapter, I argue that this apparent tension in understanding resistance to extractivism dissolves when the New International Economic Order (NIEO)—which centred on attempts to assert permanent sovereignty over natural resources and empower postcolonial states to negotiate with extractive corporations—is foregrounded. In Bangladesh, sovereignty over natural resources and the primacy of domestic courts in disputes over resource extraction are frequently enacted, much to the displeasure of international extractive industry corporations. Focusing on attempts to enact the spirit of the NIEO by Bangladeshi courts, and arbitrators locking horns with extractive industry corporations, I suggest that 'resource nationalist' mobilisation against unjust forms of resource extraction can at times be understood as resistance to the international legal architecture that frames extractive corporations' relationships with postcolonial states, rather than to extractivism in the 'literal sense'.

 | DOI:10.1163/9789004686182_010

1 'Global Extractivism' and the Afterlives of the New International Economic Order[1]

Analytical and political concern with 'extractivism' has rapidly intensified over the last decade.[2] Scholarly and activist concern with extractivism can be traced initially to Latin American political ecology/political economy analyses of economic models that involve the extraction of raw materials for export. In this context, the term 'neo-extractivism' has been used to describe the model of development adopted particularly in Bolivia and Ecuador in response to a 'commodity supercycle' or price boom between 2004–2014, where export earnings from expanding extractive frontiers have been used to fund redistributive social policy (Bowles and Veltmeyer, 2020). Notwithstanding the redistributive ambition underlying neo-extractivist social policy, the attendant expansion of resource frontiers has been accompanied by privatised and state-supported violence against land and environmental defenders (Orellana López, 2021) and the contamination of water sources, with particular impacts on Indigenous women (Rodriguez Fernandez, 2020).

Yet a concern with extractivism in academic literature is no longer centred on Latin America. For Marcus Kröger, 'extractivism became the dominant political-economic model of many governments around the globe' during the late 2000s, and extractivism here means 'accelerated natural resource extraction' (Kröger, 2020, 3–4). For Kröger, extractivism is still a model of rapid extraction that responded to a commodity price boom even if it can be found beyond Latin America. For other scholars, however, extractivism can be detached from a specific historical context and becomes an economic mode that 'predated industrial capitalism' (Bowles and Veltmeyer, 2020, 103), which 'in its most literal sense, is the pursuit of primary resource extraction' with a view to export (Grinspun and Mills, 2015, 133; Gago and Mezzadra, 2017, 576). Political ecologists concerned with resistance to fossil fuel extraction in Europe have identified contemporary forms of fracking and coal mining as extractivism, while also arguing that the 'British imperial state has historically relied on extractivism in its colonies and at home' (Brock, 2020, 2). Manifestos for degrowth

---

1 The research presented in this chapter draws on fieldwork funded by an ESRC/Sussex DTC +3 Doctoral Scholarship (2011–14), as well as by the Sussex Research Opportunities Fund (2019).

2 As of 15 November 2021, a Web of Science citation report for 'extractivism' shows a rapid upswing in mentions and citations from 2013 to 2020. Prior to 2013, there were fewer than five publications a year mentioning extractivism, and citations were below 30 (apart from a brief spike in 2011 and 2012). Publications mentioning extractivism ballooned after 2013, rapidly rising to 172 in 2020, and citations followed suit rising to 1,073 in the same year.

rooted in the European policy milieu identify extractivism as that by which the global North has the global South in its grip; extractivism is here figured not only as a political economic structure involving commodity exports but as an ideology or theology (Gudynas, 2018, 74) of hierarchical domination over non-human nature, where such nature is seen as a set of passive objects to be exploited (Hickel, 2021; Brock, 2020, 3–5).[3]

Perhaps this expansion of extractivism reflects a productive linguistic plasticity that allows coalitions of scholars and activists concerned with expanding fossil fuel extraction, dispossession of Indigenous people and peasants from their lands, and hybrid state–capital violence at the extractive frontier to foster global solidarities. But we may equally want to ask what do we mean—or more importantly, 'take as given, leave unspoken—when we talk about extractivism? And just why are we talking about extractivism *now*?' (Szeman and Wenzel, 2021, 506). Does the broader analytical conception of extractivism—especially the reduction of extractivism simply to resource extraction (sometimes) for export in any historical period—not undermine our ability to think about the global political economic structures and colonial dependencies through which contemporary extractive industries operate? Do some critics of extractivism perhaps 'confuse *technical system* with *mode of production*, and from this confusion [do] they go on to associate extractivism with capitalism, forgetting that there are non-extractivist, industrial, societies that are completely capitalist' (García Linera, 2013)—even if they are implicated in processes of resource-making and extraction elsewhere?[4]

In collapsing extractivism into either an ahistorical technical system or a transhistorical form of colonial domination, we may lose the opportunity to examine the different ways in which extractivism as 'ruthless looting of the environment for the benefit of a distant few—in short, colonialism' comes into awkward alignment with extractivism as 'a developmentalist ideology of social welfare premised on the extraction of natural resources' (Szeman and Wenzel, 2021, 507). To ask about these alignments is not in any way to minimise the

3 See Abraham (2021) for a review of Hickel (2021) situating it within a European environmental policy milieu.

4 It is perhaps also worth noting that in framing extractivism as an *ideology* through which non-human nature is rendered an inert object, ready for exploitation and extraction, some scholars and critics of extractivism (e.g. Brock, 2020; Hickel, 2021) overlook the considerable body of work on the *making of resources*, and the processes through which specific geological features can become valuable and worthy of extraction at different times (see, e.g., Kama, 2020). Minimising the sociotechnical processes of resource-making in favour of a generalised ideology of extractivism risks reducing possibilities for intervening in the politics of extractivism. See Section 3, below.

destruction, violence and dispossession that expansion of extractive industry frontiers entails. Instead, it is to ask whether we can look behind expansive uses of the term extractivism to consider the political economic structures and colonial inheritances that today shape aspects of resource extraction in the global South.

In particular, this chapter is concerned with resource extraction in contemporary Bangladesh. Specifically, it aims to show how extractive politics in Bangladesh hinge on conflicts between durable colonial forms of international investment law and the vestiges of the New International Economic Order (NIEO) as they can be detected in legal and 'resource nationalist' activism in Dhaka. This resource nationalist activism, and the activism of public interest lawyers in Bangladesh, can be understood as speaking to one pole of extractivism: the postcolonial developmentalist ideology of social welfare that has been advocated by some in Latin America (García Linera, 2013), and subjected to significant criticism by those who see in this model an 'evident albeit surprising' siding of progressive national elites with extractive capital, against local communities (between 2004–2014'). As I show here, it is not always the case that national elites side with extractive capital (even if they do not necessarily side with local communities affected by resource extraction), and to understand their alignments we need to attend to the unfinished history of the NIEO, and avoid dislocating the study of 'global extractivisms' from particular postcolonial histories. One particularly useful site for understanding how the durable remnants of the NIEO come into conflict with international extractive capital is investor-state arbitration, and the final section of this chapter involves a sustained engagement with one particular dispute between Bangladesh and a foreign extractive industry corporation.

The chapter proceeds by first introducing the history of the New International Economic Order, its relationship to developmentalist models of resource extraction, and the need to attend to this history in order to understand global extractivisms more fully (Section 1.1). Subsequently, in Section 2, the landscape of resource exploration and extraction in Bangladesh is sketched out, and I introduce the forms of 'resource nationalist' opposition to foreign extractive industries that have been organised by middle-class professional activists in Dhaka, and highlight Bangladesh's history of legal disputes with foreign extractive corporations. In Section 3, I turn to one particular case that reveals the relationship between colonial extractivism (the ruthless looting of the environment for the benefit of a distant few) and postcolonial extractivism (the developmentalist ideologies of social welfare that seek to keep the vestiges of the NIEO alive): the case of Niko Resources and the Chhatak and Feni gas blowouts. In the conclusion, I argue that in order to understand the political economic structures in which global South states engage with extractive industry corporations, and the possibilities for alternatives to extractive-led development, proper attention needs to be given to the durable colonial structures that shape investor-state relations today, and the postcolonial developmentalist projects that have often brought national elites into conflict with Indigenous people and peasants affected by extractive expansion, but which do not always entail an alliance between national elites and foreign extractive interests.

Methodologically, the chapter draws on a series of interviews and participation in industry events conducted with engineers, geologists and lawyers working in the extractive industries in Dhaka in 2013, follow-up interviews in 2019, the analysis of Bangladeshi court filings and judgements, and ongoing conversations with members of groups including the Bangladesh Environmental Lawyers' Association (BELA) and National Committee to Protect Oil, Gas, Port-Power and Mineral Resources in Bangladesh (NCBD). Since the initial period of fieldwork in 2013, I have been following the progression of one particular case—Niko vs. Bangladesh—through the International Centre for the Settlement of Investment Disputes (ICSID). This chapter thus draws on an analysis of the rulings made in ISCID documents, as well as dissenting evaluations of those rulings in the international law literature. The final methodological strand running through this chapter is a focus on the intellectual biographies of key persons implicated in the Niko v. Bangladesh case, and their involvement in historical efforts to craft a New International Economic Order (NIEO), as well as contemporary contributions to literature and practice in international investment law. These intellectual biographies and 'scholactivist' careers have provided the scaffolding through which to both historicise Niko v. Bangladesh in relation to the legacy of the NIEO and durable colonial legal structures, and interrogate contemporary analysis of extractivism in relation to Niko v. Bangladesh set in historical context.

1.1 *Extraction, Resource Sovereignty and the NIEO*

In 1974, the UN General Assembly adopted the Declaration on the Establishment of a New International Economic Order. Building on a number of previous resolutions, and on rights and demands articulated by the G77 and Non-Aligned Movement, the Declaration asserted the rights of newly independent, postcolonial, developing nations to determine their own form of economic organisation, to participate in international trade on an equitable footing, and to declare Permanent Sovereignty over Natural Resources (PSNR). A later report to the United Nations General Assembly (UNGA) drafted by Georges Abi-Saab (UNGA, 1984) argued clearly that both the right to determine one's own economic organisation (including nationalisation where necessary for social welfare) and PSNR arose straightforwardly from basic, structural principles of sovereign equality and the duty of states to cooperate. Reflecting on his role as a 'ghostwriter' to the UN, Abi-Saab later argued that 'the report is still there as a feasible blueprint of the NIEO, if and when there is sufficient will to transform it into living law' (Abi-Saab, 2016, 1966). Abi-Saab understands his work on this document as a matter of transmuting deconstructive critique into ideas and reconstructive practice where possible, as part of his contribution to 'TWAIL', or the Third World Approach to International Law.

The TWAIL network emerged in the 1960s and 1970s among lawyers from newly independent postcolonial states concerned with challenging the notion that postcolonial states entered on an equal footing into an international legal order that was 'universal' or 'legitimate'. TWAIL scholars have argued that international law—especially international investment law—is a product of a European concern to ensure the right of colonising agents to carry out commerce and secure property ownership. As such, the sovereignty of 'less civilised' nations has long been treated as *conditional,* recognised only when it does not pose an impediment to the right of entities from the global North to trade (Anghie, 2004). More specifically, as TWAILers like S.K.B. Asante have argued, investment law has had a clear concern with protecting Northern property in 'alien' lands, and these norms were established 'without [postcolonial nations'] participation and consent' (Asante, 1988, 627). State responsibility has, through the decisions made by global North nations, without the participation of former colonies, been configured in international investment law as 'primarily preoccupied with the protection of foreign investment against the legitimate sovereign interests of the host state' (Asante, 1988).

The organisation of the G77 and Non-Aligned Movement created anxieties for transnational corporations operating in states keen to assert PSNR or their right to nationalise where necessary for social welfare. These anxieties have been partially assuaged by the proliferation of Bilateral Investment Treaties (BITS) since the 1960s. These treaties contain provisions for arbitration should it be found that host states are not doing their utmost to protect 'alien property', even if this comes at the expense of public interest regulation. While the number of BITS signed in the 1960s was low (in the single figures apart from 1964–65), the 1970s oil shocks and Third World Debt crisis undermined the capacity of Southern states to push for the NIEO and to resist Northern standards for protecting alien property (Asante, 1988, 591; Sornarajah, 2016, 1976).[5]

5 Prior to 1977, most Latin American states adhered to the Calvo doctrine, whereby state sovereignty was considered primary, and 'national treatment' took precedent over the US-led 'international minimum standard' of treatment of alien property.

The number of BITs being signed annually increased rapidly, remaining in the double figures through the 1980s. This pace of BIT expansion accelerated even faster through the 1990s when more than 100 new BITs were signed most years (and more than 200 were signed in 1996). The result is a meshwork of treaties designed to ensure the protection of alien property at the expense of Southern states' right to regulate in the public interest, and that frequently allow claimants to bypass national courts and move straight to investor-state dispute settlement (ISDS) at a forum like the World Bank's ICSID. The number of ICSID cases being brought has expanded at pace, closely following the expansion of BIT coverage. While between zero and four cases were brought a year up until 1996, cases jumped into the double figures from 1997 to 2002 and there were between 21 and 37 cases a year during the 2000s and between 38 and 58 cases per year during the 2010s. The extractive industries figure prominently in these cases.

TWAIL scholars have been unsurprisingly critical of theses BITs and the ISDS system, arguing that the system means 'the state is pressed to avoid measures that are needed to prevent poverty and encourage sustainable social development through distributive methods of taxation, environmental measures, and observance of human rights standards where those might impact on the foreign investors' profits' (Linarelli, Salomon and Sornarajah, 2018, 161). A number of Southern states have renegotiated BITs in recent years, following concerns that public interest regulation designed to redress racial and economic injustice could be undermined (Mossallam, 2015), or following concerns that ISDS arbitration tribunals were making unfairly punitive awards. Even analytical legal scholars unconnected to TWAIL have noted that there are plenty of 'unreasoned awards [and] awards with only extremely succinct reasons' where precedents are used selectively and unsystematically (Schultz, 2014, 636). The lack of an appeal mechanism or systematic use of precedent means that even where recently negotiated 'balanced' BITs concerned with sustainable development are in force, 'the ingrained tendency of the arbitrators' is to interpret state liability in a narrow manner, prioritising alien property over developmental concerns (Sornarajah, 2020, 2). Arbitrators' ingrained tendencies have resulted in an expansive interpretation of investors' 'legitimate expectations', such that the protection of investors' legitimate expectations (of profit, ongoing asset ownership) is no longer balanced against public interest regulation in many rulings (Ortino, 2022; see also Gilbert, 2020).

In the remainder of this chapter, I build on this review of the NIEO, TWAIL, and its relationship to contemporary investor-state dispute settlement and arbitral practice. In Section 2, I show that putative resource nationalist politics that does not reflect the concerns of those most directly affected by extractive expansion should not be understood as a siding of developmentalist elites or middle classes with transnational extractive capital, but as a residue of the NIEO. In Bangladesh, this is particularly potent given the role played by Bangladeshi lawyer, constitutional architect and arbitrator (briefly associated with the Niko case) Kamal Hossain in the TWAIL movement (Hossain, 1979; 1980), but also because of the continued commitment to PSNR in Article 143 of the Bangladeshi Constitution, which vests all minerals in the Republic. While Venzke (2018, 296) notes that much contemporary interest in a return to the NIEO rests on an 'exaggeration of the possibilities of the past', the focus in this chapter is on durable remnants of the NIEO that still act as leverage points for contemporary social and legal activists. As TWAIL lawyer Muthucumaraswamy Sornarajah (2016, 1976) observes, the 'NIEO cannot be erased as it forms a part of the constitutions of many Third World states'. This is true of Bangladesh, and informs resource nationalist mobilisation as well as middle-class or elite public interest litigation around extractive industry development. In Section 3, I show that this clash between the durable remnants of the NIEO and neo-colonial extractive industry corporations can be read most clearly in the investor-state dispute settlement proceedings that have taken place between Bangladesh and transnational extractive corporations in recent years. Focusing on these disputes, and the tension between vestiges of the NIEO and the colonial extractive economy can shed insight on the political economic structures underpinning contemporary resource extraction and avoid the risk of ahistorical and deterritorialised engagements with 'global extractivism'.

2 Energy Futures and the Afterlives of Extraction in Bangladesh

Bangladesh does not extract resources for export at any great scale. In fact, it is precisely the *threat* of exporting fossil fuels extracted from Bangladesh's subsoil that has mobilised many so-called resource nationalist activists in the last two decades. As such, questions can be raised regarding how far an understanding of extractivism based on extracting raw materials for export (Grinspun and Mills, 2015) can be globalised in this case. Yet if extractivism speaks to situations in which expanded extractive frontiers are accompanied by threats to land and environmental defenders carried out in tandem by state and private security forces (Bowles and Veltmeyer, 2020; Orellana López, 2021), it can perhaps be identified in Bangladesh where a number of protestors and landowners have lost their lives protesting against coal mines and coal power plans in recent years (Gilbert and Khan, 2021). The political economy of resource extraction in Bangladesh has less, however, to do with extraction of raw materials for export, in order to fund redistributive social welfare, and more to do with developmentalist attempts to solve a persistent energy crisis.

Bangladesh's export-oriented ready-made garments sector is frequently plagued by power outages and load-shedding, and multilateral investment banks have prioritised power infrastructure development given its saliency as a concern for potential investors in Bangladesh's export-oriented industries. Historically, Bangladesh has been gas-dependent, following the first commercial discoveries in Titas (1957) and Chhatak (1959) during the Pakistan era. In 1961, a parastatal oil and gas development corporation was formed with Soviet assistance, and after Independence in 1971 this became Petrobangla (1974), which subsequently spun off an exploration wing, the Bangladesh Petroleum Exploration and Production Company Limited (BAPEX) in 1989. Between 1974 and 1977, the first Production Sharing Contracts (PSCs) were written up in Bangladesh, under the auspices of constitutional architect and TWAIL lawyer Kamal Hossain, based on the Indonesian template. PSCs were established to deal with a central concern of the NIEO and TWAIL: the granting of *concessions* to extractive industry firms that allowed them to gain windfalls and pay minimal tax and royalties when commodity prices boomed (Hossain, 1979). This was a particular problem where favourable concessions had been granted during the colonial period, and the retrospective sovereignty of postcolonial states was not recognised, preventing renegotiation of these concessions (Anghie, 2004). The PSCs also contained provisions for sale to the host state and non-market rates, and contractor contribution to national 'capacity building'. At all times, resources remained vested in the Republic.

It was precisely the attempt of Southern states to renegotiate royalty and taxation rates following the commodities boom in the 2000s that led Northern political risk analysts to stoke anxieties about resource nationalism, and 'resource-drunk' politicians posing threats to alien property (Bremmer and Johnston, 2009, 150). The history of the NIEO, the legal foundations for PSNR (Abi-Saab, 2016; UNGA, 1984), and the possibility of Southern states legitimately curtailing the profitability of extractive operations for redistributive (or other developmental) purposes was rendered a non-question in this industry-academic discourse. In Bangladesh, while a number of multinationals established onshore gas operations in Sylhet, most notably Chevron (Gardner, 2012), exploration declined and effectively dried up after 2012. This was because of a provision in the 2012 PSC that reversed investor-friendly terms from the 2008 PSC, setting limits on the price at which Bangladesh would purchase gas from multinational producers, and prohibiting natural gas export (in 2008, prices were uncapped and export unrestricted). These progressive, developmental provisions were reversed yet again in 2016 following an exploration strike and objections by firms including Norway's Statoil that the terms were too hostile to extractive industry.

During this period of low to no exploration, and declining gas reserve estimates, successive Bangladeshi governments embarked, responding to World Bank advice, on a plan to provide quick-rental power plant contracts to make up for energy generation shortfalls and the forecast of declining gas availability. The result has been multiple contracts being awarded to firms close to the Awami League government since 2009, USD 744 million in subsidies being paid between 2008 and 2014 for importing fuel oil for this power plan, and massive capacity payments paid to power plants who cannot feed in to an inadequate transmission grid (Mirza, 2020). In the 2016 Power System Master Plan, Bangladesh, guided by Japan's International Cooperation Agency (JICA), set out plans to compensate for declining gas reserves by increasing domestic coal reliance from 0.7 to 11 megatonnes (Mt) per annum, and imported coal from 0 to 60 Mt per annum, though an upcoming Integrated Energy and Power Master Plan looks likely to make more room for renewables in the energy development strategy.

Energy experts and policymakers aligned with transnational extractive corporations in Bangladesh have often blamed the exploration strike in 2012 on 'resource nationalist' activists. Those activists, drawn mostly from professional and academic cadres in Dhaka, have also been criticised for supporting (domestically owned) extractive industry despite opposition from Indigenous and peasant communities impacted by planned resource extraction—appearing perhaps to be the developmentalist elites, who appear in many critiques of extractivism. Notwithstanding the gap between these elite activists' concerns and those of the dispossessed (or soon-to-be-dispossessed) living on the edge of the extractive frontier, their 'resource nationalism' can perhaps be better understood by thinking about the vestiges of the NIEO, in Bangladesh's constitution, public interest litigation, and left-wing political organisation. The remainder of this section examines critiques of these resource nationalist activists, and their disputes with experts on either side of investor-state dispute settlement cases brought by foreign extractive firms against Bangladesh. In Section 3, I go on to examine one of these cases, Niko vs. Bangladesh, in more detail.

2.1 *Nationalist Resistance to (Foreign) Resource Extraction*

The NCBD was founded by left-leaning organisations and intellectuals (predominantly economists and engineers) in 1998, initially in response to plans for the privatisation of Chittagong port and its transfer to foreign owners. Subsequent campaigns focused on the Magurchara gas blowout (1997), where an Occidental operated well burned for 17 days, destroying 250 billion cubic feet of gas and causing untold damage to Lawachara National Park and an estimated USD 12 billion in economic damage to surrounding plantations (Deb, 2020). Despite numerous safety and technical failures, no compensation or redress was secured by Bangladesh from Occidental (or Unocal, to whom the field was transferred in 1999, or Chevron, who purchased the well in 2005). Subsequent campaigns have focused on the planned Phulbari coal mine, which has been stalled since 2006 when three local residents were killed by police during a *gherao*, or sit-in. The Phulbari mine is owned by Asia Energy, a subsidiary of UK-listed GCM Resources. GCM currently has a framework agreement in place with China's state-owned NFC construction company and state-owned PowerChina, and has advised shareholders of an understanding that GCM's partners will lobby for the Phulbari mine and 1,000 MW of mine-mouth power plant, as part of both the Belt and Road Initiative and Bangladesh's 2016 Power Sector Master Plan. The mine has nonetheless remained stalled since the killings, when a symbolic moratorium was signed by NCBD representatives and the local mayor—based also on the understanding that the project would not be feasible unless coal could be exported, something the NCBD and others were firmly against given Bangladesh's energy shortages (Chowdhury, 2020).

The NCBD's nationalist-developmentalist orientation has been highlighted by a number of scholars of local resistance to mining in Phulbari, and to gas extraction in Sylhet. Gardner notes that 'the narratives of the dispossessed are rarely heard and are generally dismissed' but that the well-connected NCBD in Dhaka, for whom 'national sovereignty rather than global warming is the rallying cry against coal mining or gas extraction', is frequently heard (Gardner, 2012, 216–224).[6] Nuremowla's (2016) detailed ethnographic study of opposition to mining in townships around Phulbari highlights the disjunct between NCBD concerns and those of local people who migrated to Phulbari following erosion elsewhere, settling on *khas* (government) land. Narratives from nearby Boropukuria, where compensation has not been paid, or has been paid in instalments (foreclosing the opportunity to resettle), leads to Phulbari residents being rightly suspicious of any compensation and resettlement scheme. The NCBD's leaflets in Phulbari, reading 'No to foreign company. No to coal export. Yes to the extraction of coal by a state-owned body for the best interest

6 It should be noted, however, that as of 2017 the NCBD has been promoting renewable energy expansion as part of an alternative People's Masterplan that responded to the Government of Bangladesh/JICA 2016 Power System Master Plan. In addition, NCBD spokespeople have welcomed the cancellation of ten planned coal power plants which was announced by the Government of Bangladesh in June 2021.

of the nation. No to open-pit coal mining' (Nuremowla, 2016, 2), are clearly at odds with local resistance, for which mining should not happen, at any cost. Resource nationalist activism that draws upon the remnants of the NIEO and other resources to counter extractive operations bolstered by colonial international investment law can certainly come into alignment with socially and environmentally harmful forms of mining of the kind that is rightly emphasised by critics of extractivism and neo-extractivism.

The NCBD has been criticised for this position elsewhere, in relation to their opposition to the Rampal power plant, a part-Indian parastatal–funded power plant in the Sundarbans, which has been opposed by a network of Bangladeshi (including the NCBD and BELA) and international campaigners. Here again, the NCBD's 'professed official positions are deeply contradictory, opposing the Rampal project on environmental grounds and yet supporting coal power generally on nationalist ones' (Mookerjea and Misra, 2017, 174). Rampal's disappeared have 'slipped through the cracks of the NCBD's capacities to mobilize a broad based "multitude" to protest the Rampal development' (Mookerjea and Misra, 2017, 79). It would be naive to claim that the NCBD is unproblematically aligned with local concerns, and the concerns of the most vulnerable: it is clear it is not. In aligning with developmentalist extraction for redistributive or social welfare purposes, there are seeming parallels between the NCBD and the Latin American political-economic models that critics of extractivism or neo-extractivism oppose. But the story does not end there: the developmentalist, middle-class activists in the NCBD and other organisations involved in opposing Rampal (and to a degree, Phulbari), such as BELA, are by no means aligned straightforwardly with the state, or with extractive capital. In their opposition to extractive industry firms, and engagements with the state and the constitution of Bangladesh, we can detect durable remnants of the NIEO and shed light on the political economic structures within which extraction—not necessarily extractivism—takes place in the contemporary global South.

In the next section, I highlight in detail the legal proceedings surrounding the Chhatak blowouts, and the subsequent disputes between Niko Resources and the Government of Bangladesh. It is worth noting that this dispute was infused with the conflict between 'resource nationalist' experts and those who allied themselves more closely to foreign extractive industry corporations. Following the blowouts at Chhatak in 2005 (detailed more fully below, in Section 3), a series of commissions was set up. The Tamim commission, headed by an eminent petroleum geologist and advisor to the military caretaker government, determined that 8.9 billion cubic feet had been lost in the Chhatak blowouts. An alternative commission established by the Bangladesh Economic Association disputed this, arguing 115 billion cubic feet of gas had been lost and that USD 228 million—243 million[7] (BDT 1,500–1,600 *crore*)[8] in compensation was owed (The Daily Star, 2005). NCBD spokesperson Professor Anu Muhammad linked the blowouts at Magurchara and the Chhatak blowouts, arguing for compensation from both companies involved and linking the destruction of national resources to energy access: 'The volume of natural gas damaged in the two fields would have been enough for generating electricity for two years in the country' (Tribune Desk, 2013).

I interviewed a number of Dhaka-based geologists and economists involved on each of the competing commissions, who positioned themselves differently in relation to the 'resource nationalist' politics of the NCBD, during 2013 when the Niko arbitration was frequently in the headlines. For one NCBD-aligned geologist, the Niko blowouts were an opportunity to question the idea that BAPEX lacked 'capacity'. In its 40 years of drilling it had produced no blowouts, he argued. The same could not be said for a number of foreign exploration firms:

> BAPEX is not like the international oil companies, it cannot explore at sea, but is good enough onshore. They have been producing for forty years now. There is no problem in BAPEX drilling wells [...] Chhatak was producing under BAPEX. Then production stopped. Instead of sending a new BAPEX team, they sent the unknown, Niko. There was no bidding, no competition, then two blowouts in 2005.[9]

Another geologist, who did not support the NCBD, was still frustrated by the extent to which national *technical* capacity was superior to that of the 'unknown' (in fact, rather long established) Canadian explorer. By contrast, one Niko executive informed me that he would 'sell everything we had in Bangladesh in a heartbeat if we could'—in part because of the 'adversarial approach' of the government, and in part because of the 'lack of support service companies set up with resources in Bangladesh (like Schlumberger, Weatherford, etc.) making any drilling, workover, facilities construction exercise a monumental effort in importing personnel and equipment'.[10] Technical 'capacity' became an additional fault line in disputes between Niko and Bangladeshi subsurface experts, with Niko's (disputed) claims about a *lack* of Bangladeshi capacity forming an

7 Based on 1 September 2005 exchange rates of USD 1 = BDT 65.69.
8 A *crore* is a unit of measure denoting ten million in the Indian numbering system.
9 Interview, November 2013.
10 Interview, December 2013.

important part of their claims that they ought to be treated less adversarially by the government. It is worth noting that this frustration at a lack of external capacity could be read as an inversion of the discourse that normally accompanies 'local content policies': that such policies are designed to encourage the transfer of skills and expertise to domestic industries. While Bangladesh has experimented with limited local content policies in the garment-export sector, there has been little in the way of sustained local content promotion in the extractive sector. Were such policies in place, and given repeated arbitration cases brought against Bangladesh by foreign oil and gas firms, it would be likely that further ISDS cases might ensue. Even if many BITs make no mention of the 'performance requirements' that many local content policies involve, it is not unusual to find widely discussed local content approaches that have in fact been direct triggers of ISDS disputes.[11]

A third geologist, this time involved in the Tamim committee (see Section 3, below), initially charged by the government with investigating the blowouts, was less convinced by the capacity of BAPEX. The NCBD was putting their faith in BAPEX, he noted, but BAPEX had only found one field, of 50 billion cubic feet, in the last four years. Such a find, he said, 'can never be declared as a commercial discovery but they, the National Committee, have declared it as a commercial discovery'. As for the blowouts, the drilling plans, he said, had been perfect, and the accident could not have been foreseen. His original estimate for lost gas was almost twenty times lower than that of a second committee whose compensation claim became the basis for legal action against Niko (see Section 3.1, below). The official in charge at Petrobangla was, he said, 'some kind of resource nationalist, and he was not able to separate the technical and legal issues'. He continued:

> Nowhere in the world do you pay for gas that has been destroyed. All that with BP in the USA—that is about compensation for the farmers. Otherwise how would you work? If you had an accident and gas leaks out and it will be worth ten times your company? How will you work?

11 For example, IISD and IGF (2019) give broad-based black economic empowerment (B-BBEE) as an example of an ownership-driven local content policy in South Africa. Tellingly, the Foresti et al. v. Republic of South Africa case brought under the Italy-South Africa BIT, and that seems to have triggered South Africa's retreat from a number of BITs (Mossallam, 2015), was brought precisely on the basis that B-BBEE could be tantamount to discrimination against Foresti et al. As such, local content policies can be seen to open states up to challenge via ISDS.

But he did grant that what had been wrong in the Niko case was the rendering of the fields 'marginal' rather than 'suspended' in Petrobangla's classification, in order to allow a joint venture between BAPEX and Niko. The classification matters, and is in fact part of what made the field a viable asset (Wood, 2016). Niko was given access to fields that were *suspended* full-production fields, rather than *exhausted* marginal fields, and for which BAPEX had already paid the development costs. It is never really possible to separate the 'technical and legal issues' in matters of resource ownership and value, given the degree to which geological categories and classifications of resource value are co-produced (Hughes, 2017; Nystrom, 2014). The degree to which resources are 'made' or 'made valuable' through technical and legal classification risks being missed by approaches to extractivism that transform extractivism into an 'ideology' that entails the treatment of non-human nature as a ready-made inert resource (Brock, 2020; Hickel, 2021). In addition, these contested processes of resource-making are opportunities for engineers and geologists to recraft the bases of their authority and tie that authority to larger structures of power (Ottinger, 2013, 27), in relation either to claims over national resources grounded in remnants of the NIEO, or accusations of 'resource nationalism' that draw on industry anxieties about greedy and reckless Southern governments.

3 The Niko Case: Blowouts at Chhatak and Feni

In 1999, BAPEX entered into a framework of understanding with Canadian oil and gas firm Niko Resources for the development of the Feni and Chhatak gas fields. The fields had been declared 'marginal/abandoned' following a period of production from 1960 to 1985 (Chhatak) and 1988 to 1998 (Feni), and as such Niko was able to enter into a joint venture with BAPEX on seemingly favourable terms in 2003. The Joint Venture Agreement restates the extent to which all minerals were vested in the Republic, and that the government had the 'exclusive right and authority to explore, develop, exploit, produce, process, refine & market Petroleum resources'.[12] While the joint venture negotiations appeared to go fairly smoothly, a separate Gas Price Sale Agreement negotiation proved more problematic. Gas price negotiations went on from May 2004 to December 2006, with Niko asking for USD 2.75 per thousand cubic feet (MCF), and the Gas Pricing Committee offering USD 1.75/MCF. The same tensions that were

12 Joint Venture Agreement, 16 October 2003. As quoted in ICSID Case Nos. ARB/10/11 and ARB/10/18: Decision on Jurisdiction (19 August 2013), para 44–45.

subsequently seen in successive rounds of bidding under the 2008, 2012 and 2016 PSCs (see above) were visible here: between the affordability of energy provisioning for the energy-starved Bangladeshi state, and the relative profitability of particular extractive operations.

By November 2005, there was still no gas pricing agreement, but Petrobangla (the parent company of BAPEX) made a USD 4 million holding payment to Niko for gas delivered thus far, on the understanding this would not prejudice the outcome of the pricing negotiations. Niko threatened to withdraw, but Petrobangla noted that this 'will be seriously prejudicial to our national interest and we shall be constrained to act accordingly'.[13] On 16 November 2005, the High Court Division of Bangladesh's Supreme Court restrained further payment, and Niko accepted USD 1.75/MCF until final determination by an 'expert'. However, Niko went on to announce a shutdown of the Feni field in January 2006. The response from Petrobangla was that this 'is a violation of [Joint Venture Agreement] article 24.3 since Petrobangla is the only authority and agent of [the Government of Bangladesh] that purchases, sells, monitors and controls the transmission and distribution systems of gas in the country'.[14] The vesting of the subsoil resources in the Republic, as well as the re-assertion of the Republic's control of gas transmission and distribution in the Joint Venture Agreement, were again foregrounded by Petrobangla/BAPEX.

By December 2006, Niko had agreed on USD 1.75/MCF, and on 10 January 2007 invoiced the Government of Bangladesh, but was not paid. The reason given was that in 2005, on 7 January and 24 June, there had been two blowouts at Niko's Chhatak field. A commission of inquiry had concluded that Niko was at fault, and the Government had filed a case with a district court demanding USD 79 million (BDT 746 *crore*) in compensation from Niko for the blowouts. Earlier, in 2005, the High Court Division had constrained the Government and Petrobangla from paying Niko further in response to a writ petition filed by BELA. BELA has frequently been involved in coalitions of activists opposing coal power developments, such as the Rampal coal power plant in the Sundarbans (see Section 2.1), but has also been at the centre of pioneering public interest litigation in Bangladesh. The first public interest litigation case in the country in which *locus standi*[15] was granted to a person not directly aggrieved by a specific rights violation was filed in 1996 (*Dr Mohiuddin Farooque v. Bangladesh*)

---

13 ICSID Case Nos. ARB/10/11 and ARB/10/18: Decision on Jurisdiction (19 August 2013), para 65.

14 ICSID Case Nos. ARB/10/11 and ARB/10/18: Decision on Jurisdiction (19 August 2013), para 72.

15 The position from which one may make a valid legal claim or seek to enforce a right.

by BELA, who was granted standing to challenge flood control projects on the grounds of rights violations (Hoque, 2006). Paralleling the seemingly middle-class/elite orientation of organisations like the NCBD (see Section 2.1), BELA and public interest litigation more broadly in Bangladesh has been 'elitist [...] reflected in virtually the total absence of true epistolary [public interest litigations] or of real victim litigations' (Hoque, 2006, 409), but this does not make it any less significant as a forum for challenging durable colonial structures of extraction, and restating the fragmentary remnants of the NIEO that can be found in Bangladesh's constitution.[16]

Through filing its writ petition,[17] BELA exercised its constitutional right to challenge the Government for an account of why the Niko joint venture should not be declared illegal. BELA made its challenge on the grounds that Niko had been given a productive field on the basis that it was technically 'marginal'. BELA also asked why the joint venture should not be declared illegal, and in violation of Article 143 of the Constitution, which vests in the Republic 'all minerals and other things of value underlying any land of Bangladesh'. Included in the evidence attached to the petition was a letter from Niko in which it petitioned for the Chhatak East field to be included in the joint venture in order to 'mitigate the reserve risk that we face in Chhatak West'.[18] The finding of the petition, given in 2010, and which considered responses from Niko, BAPEX, Petrobangla and the Government of Bangladesh, was that Niko did owe the amount of compensation stated in the Government's 2008 money suit. In addition, Mr Justice Quamrul Islam Siddiqui ruled that the Bangladesh Government and parastatal respondents were 'restrained by an order of injunction from making any payment' to Niko for gas that had already been delivered.[19]

Niko's response to this injunction was to activate the arbitration clause in the Barbados-Bangladesh Bilateral Investment Treaty, given that Niko Resources (Bangladesh Ltd) was in fact incorporated in Bridgetown (and in Cyprus), even if the ultimate control seemed to be in the hands of Canadian executives and the Niko Resources (Ltd) head office in Calgary. Niko filed two requests for arbitration, in April and June 2010, requesting an award for payment of outstanding invoices, and a declaration it was not liable for compensation

16 BELA also successfully filed a writ petition in response to which the High Court Division ruled that the Government should pursue a 100 per cent renewable energy strategy, in June 2021.

17 Writ Petition Number 6911 of 2005.

18 Letter from Niko Vice President South Asia Qasim Sharif to the Managing Director, BAPEX, dated July 8, 2002.

19 Writ Petition Number 6911 of 2005, p. 42.

for the blowouts (ARB/10/11 and ARB/10/18, treated as merged by ICSID). In the final section of this chapter before the conclusion (Section 3.1), I show how the Niko vs. Bangladesh ICSID arbitration seems to typify the 'unreasoned awards' (Schultz, 2014) that are often found in investor-state dispute settlement. Equally, I show that the investor-state arbitration system works to protect 'alien property' at the expense of permanent sovereignty over natural resources—and developmentalist desires of the Bangladeshi state. These conflicts between durable colonial structures of international investment law and fragmentary remnants of the NIEO in Bangladesh's constitution (invoked by both parastatal extractive corporations like Petrobangla and BAPEX and by public interest lawyers at BELA) risk being left unexamined by analyses of extractivism in which developmentalist ambitions are frequently treated as converging with the interests of foreign extractive capital.

3.1 *Corruption, Canada and Arbitrary Decisions*

The BELA writ petition filed with the High Court Division of Bangladesh's Supreme Court, which invoked Article 143 of Bangladesh's constitution and the Republic's PSNR, reflects one fragmentary strand of the NIEO's persistence. As Sornarajah (2016) has noted, the NIEO cannot be entirely erased given its presence in the constitutions of many formerly colonised states. The persistence of the NIEO can also be detected in Bangladesh's nominations for the arbitration tribunal, following Niko's filing of cases at ICSID in April and June 2010. Bangladesh proposed first Georges Abi-Saab, the TWAIL lawyer and 'ghostwriter' of the UNGA (1984) template for enacting PSNR as part of the NIEO, and S. K. B. Asante, another TWAIL lawyer attuned to North-South dependencies and the injustice of investment laws designed to protect (Northern) alien property at the expense of postcolonial sovereignty and public interest regulation (Asante, 1981; 1988). Both proposals were vetoed by Niko, whose proposal of NAFTA negotiator Guillermo Aguilar Alvarez was in turn vetoed by Bangladesh, and a mutually agreed panel of arbitrators chaired by Jan Paulsson was eventually agreed. Paulsson is notable for advancing the case for 'arbitration without privity', and providing the legal justification for investors to initiate arbitration even without breach of contract to which they are a party (Paulsson, 1995), thereby allowing arbitrators to gain authority without the legitimacy that should be derived from the consent of both (investor *and* state) parties (Sornarajah, 2015, 139–141).

This tussle over arbitrators—and Bangladesh's calling upon TWAIL practitioners—reflects the degree to which ICSID arbitrations can be a battleground between durable colonial legal orders and the remnants of the NIEO. Equally, such arbitrations could be seen as a domain in which the two poles of extractivism—brutal colonial extraction, and redistributive postcolonial developmentalism (Szeman and Wenzel, 2021)—are at least partially set against each other. Bangladesh's desire to secure affordable gas supplies (as one alternative to importing fuel oil and subsidising quick rental power plants) runs up against Niko's search for profit at this extractive frontier. The voices of those impacted by extractive operations are admittedly, as is far too common at many ICSID arbitrations, absent from this legal battleground.

The decisions made by the tribunal in the case of Niko v. Bangladesh, in a series of judgements running from 2013 to 2021, have largely not gone in Bangladesh's favour. In September 2014, the arbitrators ruled that Petrobangla owed Niko USD 25,312,747 plus USD 1,483,197 (BDT 139,998,337) for gas invoiced from the Feni field, and in September 2015 it was agreed this would be held in escrow. Petrobangla and the Government of Bangladesh responded, challenging this ruling, arguing that the Joint Venture Agreement and the Gas Purchase Sale Agreement had been the outcome of corruption, and thus could not be considered an 'investment' that would entitle Niko to bring an arbitration claim against them. The High Court Division of Bangladesh's Supreme Court once again filed an injunction against payment to Niko, but in May 2016, the arbitrators ruled once again on the payment claim, adding interest of USD 5,932,833 and USD 524,316 (BDT 49,489,961) to the earlier award. The arbitrators have refused to hear further petitions questioning their jurisdiction (including on the grounds that Canada has not ratified the ICSID treaty, and that the clear owner and authority behind Niko is based in Calgary not Bridgetown), but a number of additional decisions were made on the claim that the Joint Venture and Gas Purchase Sale Agreement were the products of corruption.

The corruption claim is based on the fact that in 2005 Bangladeshi Energy Minister Mosharaf Hossain received a vehicle and expenses for a trip to Canada from Niko *during* the pricing negotiations. The acknowledged corruption in this case, which resulted in Hossain resigning in June 2005, combined with the reclassification of the Feni/Chhatak fields from 'suspended' to 'marginal' (see above) has raised suspicion about the degree to which corruption or malfeasance was involved in the negotiation of the Joint Venture Agreement too. Initially, the arbitral panel dismissed the corruption claim on the grounds that the High Court Division of Bangladesh had ruled the Joint Venture was *not* obtained by flawed means when responding to BELA's 2008 writ petition in 2010. In 2011, Niko was convicted of corruption and fined USD 7.3 million (CAD 9.5 million), the largest fine under Canada's Corruption of Foreign Public Officials Act (1999) to date. The lawyers for Petrobangla/Government of Bangladesh argued that the established legal fact of this corruption, which took place during the negotiation of the Gas Purchase Sale Agreement, should mean that the tribunal declines from deciding on Bangladesh's liabilities to Niko arising from that Agreement (i.e., the payment for the Feni gas). The tribunal has repeatedly rebuffed these requests.[20]

Lawyers for Bangladesh/Petrobangla have subsequently requested materials from the Royal Canadian Mounted Police investigation into Niko, arguing that these may shed light on aspects of corruption material to the Gas Purchase Sale Agreement/Joint Venture Agreement. Upon learning that Deloitte had been asked to audit Niko when Niko was made aware of the impending corruption investigation, Bangladesh/Petrobangla requested Deloitte's audit results for their own scrutiny. However, the arbitration tribunal upheld an aspect of Canadian law, namely that since Niko's *lawyers* had hired Deloitte, Deloitte's actions were covered by litigation privilege.[21] Ultimately, the corruption claim has been treated as resolved, and the tribunal is now considering the compensation claim.[22] Legal fee claims of over USD 2 million have been submitted by Niko, for which Bangladesh is liable. In addition, Bangladesh has been found liable for USD 982,089 of arbitration costs incurred by ICSID.[23] This is not at all unusual in arbitration decisions. Based on an analysis of 292 cases up to 2014, Van Harten (2016) shows that respondent states have lost on average USD 47 million per case, while large companies have made on average USD 136 million per case, and the arbitration/legal industry has made USD 8 million per case.

The degree to which the Niko decisions on corruption might be considered arbitrary or 'unreasoned' (Schultz, 2014) is highlighted by an examination of alternative rulings. There is, for instance, no reason that the tribunal necessarily had to refuse to consider wider corruption investigations into Niko, or refuse to allow Bangladesh access to wider corruption investigations. In earlier cases, tribunals have rejected the notion they are required to defer to local courts in considering whether evidence can be heard about the legality of an 'investment'.[24] Similarly, other high-profile cases have seen arbitrators refuse to consider the merits of a case where bribery was involved, whereas in the Niko case arbitrators insisted on separating specific acts of bribery from related

20 ICSID Case Nos. ARB/10/11 and ARB/10/18: Procedural Order No. 16: Concerning the Respondents' Request for Reconsideration of 30 June 2016 (14 November 2016).

21 ICSID Case Nos. ARB/10/11 and ARB/10/18: Procedural Order No. 22 (Privilege Asserted Against the Production of the Deloitte Documents) (27 July 2017).

22 ICSID Case Nos. ARB/10/11 and ARB/10/18 (Decision on the Corruption Claim) (25 Feb 2019).

23 ICSID Case Nos. ARB/10/11 and ARB/10/18 (Decision on Heads of Recoverable Loss Concerning the Compensation Declaration Proceedings) (18 May 2021).

24 *Inceysa Vallisoletana S.L. v. Republic of El Salvador*, ICSID Case No. ARB/03/26.

contractual agreements that could not specifically be traced to the accepted individual acts of bribery.[25]

Numerous scholars concerned with expanding analyses of extractivism from the Latin American context, and developing conceptualisations of 'global extractivism', have drawn attention to the degree to which the Canadian state supports extractive imperialism abroad, and domestically (Grinspun and Mills, 2015; Veltmeyer and Bowles, 2014). Elsewhere, the work carried out by Canada's development agency CIDA (now incorporated into Global Affairs Canada) on 'building capacity' in mineral rich nations has been understood as being less about serving the citizens of developing states, and more about reworking mineral codes to de-risk Canadian extractive investments (Butler, 2015, 136). In this context, ICSID tribunals seem to work to uphold the colonial endeavours of both Canadian foreign policy and Canada-based (even if via Barbados) extractive industry firms. Bangladesh's attempts to revive the principles of the NIEO, so that the protection of alien property is not seen as the ultimate purpose of international law, have been frustrated here. Bangladeshi sovereignty over its national resources, the pricing of much needed gas, and the control, monitoring and transmission of that gas, has not been considered seriously by the tribunal, any more than the material impact Niko's acknowledged corruption might have had in securing a 'suspended' field under terms reserved for 'marginal' fields. In this case, resource nationalist activists like the NCBD seem somewhat aligned with the Government and Bangladesh, even if they are often at loggerheads domestically. If there is a global extractivism, it does not by any means necessarily align redistributive developmentalism with extractive capital, and may in some cases intensify their opposition.

4 Extractive Futures and Policy Possibilities

In this chapter, I have responded to Szeman and Wenzel's (2021) injunction to ask, what do we leave unspoken when we talk about extractivism? I have suggested that in deterritorialising and even de-historicising the concept of (neo-)extractivism such that it speaks not only to Latin American redistributive policies during the 2000s commodity price boom but also to a general feature of capitalism, we miss much that is important about contemporary resource politics. Framing extractivism as not only a set of political economic structures but as an *ideology* risks detracting attention from the technical and

25 Compare *World Duty Free Company v Republic of Kenya*, ICSID Case No. ARB/00/7.

legal wranglings through which geological deposits become resources and valuable assets—as we have seen from the disputes around the status of the Chhatak gas field, these processes of resource-making have profound implications for host governments and extractive industry firms. Where some 'literal' definitions of extractivism focus on resource extraction for export, extractive frontiers do not only expand in order to fuel exports. In the Bangladeshi case, the possibility of exporting fossil fuels was a prime motivating factor in the organising of a resource nationalist backlash to planned coal and gas projects. Nonetheless, firms operating in Bangladesh and firms involved in export-oriented extractivism are able to avail themselves of the same colonial international investment law should they enter into dispute with host governments.

While critiques of extractivism focusing on Latin America (Veltmeyer and Bowles, 2014) or on the contemporary global North (Brock, 2020) have focused on alignments between extractive capital and violent states, this chapter has highlighted other (partial and temporary) alignments, between states, 'resource nationalist' professionals and academics, and middle-class public interest litigators, *against* extractive capital. BELA, the NCBD and Bangladesh's legal representatives in ICSID tribunals all act in a way that recovers the fragments of the NIEO that can be found in Bangladesh's constitution, in the operations of BAPEX/Petrobangla, and in attempts to secure central figures from the TWAIL movement as Bangladesh's representatives in the Niko arbitration. The NCBD, BELA and indeed some of Bangladesh's eminent TWAIL 'scholactivists' like Kamal Hossain have all been criticised for their 'few engagements with directly dealing with rights of the poor' (Farid, 2016, 76; Mookerjea and Misra, 2017; Hoque, 2006). To question the conceptual efficacy of extractivism is not to deny the violence of extraction, nor the dispossession and deprivation it entails.[26]

Yet the very real injustices of international investment law's colonial durability, and the equally real remnants of the NIEO that can be found in legal and other 'resource nationalist' mobilisation against transnational extractive corporations, need to remain in focus if the injustices of contemporary extraction are to be effectively challenged. To unpick the role of state actors, domestic elites and transnational corporations is not to deny the violence of extractivism. Nor should the argument that state (and other domestic) actors mobilise the remnants of the NIEO against transnational extractive corporations be

26 As noted by@maxajl (Max Ajl) 'The *experiences* of dispossession or deprivation some peoples endure during natural resource extraction are not denied when we place this concept under the microscope'. *Twitter*, 19 Mar 2021, https://twitter.com/maxajl/status/1372838294552203264.

read as a defence of the state violence that frequently accompanies extraction. The possibility of alignments between states and affected communities against extractive corporations should never detract from the realities of state perpetration of and complicity in violence against land and environmental defenders protesting extractive operations in Bangladesh and elsewhere (Gilbert and Khan, 2021). Yet collapsing the interests of developmental elites, Southern states, and extractive capital under the rubric of extractivism runs the risk of disguising as many structures of durable colonial injustice as it reveals.

Numerous challenges remain for advocates of developmentalist attempts to solve the persistent energy crisis in Bangladesh. Groups opposed to foreign-owned extractive operations and the export of fossil fuels, such as the National Committee, have increasingly moved towards advocacy of a renewable-led energy strategy (NCBD, 2017). BELA successfully filed a writ petition in response to which the High Court Division ruled that the Government should pursue a 100 per cent renewable energy strategy, in June 2021, and the cancellation of numerous coal power plants was announced by the Government in 2022. But Bangladesh continues to be heavily reliant on gas. Impacted by the spike in liquid natural gas import prices following Russia's invasion of Ukraine, domestic gas exploration is once again a salient concern. In an echo of the Chhatak case, international drilling firms continue to profit from operations where BAPEX made original discoveries and could seemingly carry out drilling at vastly lower rates (Rahman, 2022).

Globally, the NIEO—as much as it was often a project of domestic elites against transnational corporations—has been eclipsed, not lost,[27] enshrined as it is in numerous constitutions. There is a resurgent global interest in reforming international investment law, in an environment where defences of sovereignty against international law are made not only by postcolonial states seeking independence and development, but by right-wing and nativist regimes in the global North. Ongoing efforts to push for reforms—such as including an appellate body and a code of conduct for arbitrators—through the United Nations Commission on International Trade Law (UNCITRAL)[28] offer what some view as glimmers of hope (Uribe and Danish, 2021), even if the 'ingrained tendency' of the community of arbitrators seems to mitigate the effectiveness of such gradual reforms (Sornarajah, 2020). UNCITRAL's involvement in establishing a programme of work on ISDS reform that privileges states' views over those of arbitrators hints at possible shifts in the regimes

27 With thanks to M. Sornarajah for this phrasing.

28 UNCITRAL's initial programme of work was also focused on the legal implications of the NIEO for the law of international trade.

governing investor-state disputes, and even at the possible 'transnational constitutionalization of the investment regime' (Rodrigues, 2021, 15): a potential re-assertion of multilateralism during a period marked by the dominance of public-private 'multi-stakeholderism'. This too offers hints of a possible pathway via which the dormant and eclipsed NIEO might be revived with a view to disciplining transnational extractive corporations, where fissures between the interests of national elites and transnational corporations might be leveraged against a backdrop of a durable, but perhaps not impregnable, colonial investment law regime.

The importance of leveraging durable remnants of the NIEO, or indeed of recovering the sense of the possibility of an alternative international law that the NIEO seemed to offer, is taking on ever greater policy salience. As noted by Working Group III of the Intergovernmental Panel on Climate Change (IPCC), trade agreements enshrining ISDS provisions have tended to prioritise investor rights and constrain host countries' ability to adopt environmental policies, and may through 'regulatory chill' delay the phase out of fossil fuels (IPCC, 2022, 72).[29] Contemporary, colonially derived international investment law protects the interests of investors from the global North against the legislative imperatives of states of the global South. While at times domestic elites from Southern states come into alignment with international extractive industry capitalists, the potential for activists, experts and legal/judicial elites to utilise remnants of the NIEO to challenge foreign investors should not be dismissed. Recovering the sense of possibility offered by the NIEO in order to curtail the interests of foreign extractive industry investors is increasingly vital not only for the pursuit of developmentalist aims, but also to have the freedom to pursue climate change mitigation policies.

References

Abi-Saab, G. (2016) 'The Third World intellectual in praxis: confrontation, participation, or operation behind enemy lines?', *Third World Quarterly*, 37(11), pp. 1957–1971, DOI: 10.1080/01436597.2016.1212653.

29 Another ongoing site of dispute where the legacies of the NIEO come into conflict with neo-mercantilist ambitions on the part of Northern extractive industry investors is the 'frontier' comprised by deep-sea mining (Zalik, 2018). The area of the seabed categorised as the 'common heritage of mankind' runs up against the ambitions of Canadian and other mining capitalists, against a backdrop of hostility to revenue sharing provisions mandated by the International Seabed Authority.

Abraham, S. (2021) 'Degrowth Remains a Slogan', *Jamhoor,* 9 June, https://www.jamhoor.org/read/degrowth-is-still-but-a-slogan (accessed on 11 November 2021).

Anghie, A. (2004) *Imperialism, Sovereignty and the Making of International Law* (Cambridge: Cambridge University Press).

Asante, S.K.B. (1988) 'International Law and Foreign Investment: a Reappraisal', *The International and Comparative Law Quarterly*, 37(3), pp. 588–628, https://www.jstor.org/stable/760279 (accessed on 3 August 2022).

Asante, S.K.B. (1981) 'Another machinery for updating dependency?', *Intereconomics*, 16(4), pp. 189–191, DOI: 10.1007/BF02924768.

Bowles, P. and H. Veltmeyer (2020) 'Extractivism', in O. Kaltmeier, A. Tittor, D. Hawkins and E. Rohland (eds.) *The Routledge Handbook to the Political Economy and Governance of the Americas* (London: Routledge), pp. 103–112.

Bremmer, I. and R. Johnston (2009) 'The Rise and Fall of Resource Nationalism', *Survival*, 51(2), pp. 149–158, DOI: 10.1080.00396330902860884.

Brock, A. (2020) "Frack off': towards an anarchist political ecology critique of corporate and state responses to anti-fracking resistance in the UK', *Political Geography*, 82, pp. 1–15, DOI: 10.1016/j.polgeo.2020.102246.

Butler, P. (2015) *Colonial Extractions: Race and Canadian Mining in Contemporary Africa* (Toronto: University of Toronto Press).

Chowdhury, N.S. (2020) 'The Taka, Transparency, and an Alternative Politics of Seeing From Phulbari, Bangladesh', in M.T. Khan and M.S. Rahman (eds.) *Neoliberal Development in Bangladesh: People on the Margins* (Dhaka: University Press Limited), pp. 321–350.

Deb, N. (2020) 'Corporate capitalism, environmental damage and the rule of law: the Magurchara gas explosion in Bangladesh', in N. South and A. Brisman (eds.) *Routledge International Handbook of Green Criminology* (London: Routledge), pp. 367–381.

Farid, C. (2016) 'Legal scholactivists in the Third World: between ambition, altruism and access', *The Windsor Yearbook of Access to Justice*, 33(3), pp. 57–86, DOI: 10.22329/wyaj.v33i3.4887.

Gago, V. and S. Mezzadra (2017) 'A Critique of the Extractive Operations of Capital: toward an Expanded Concept of Extractivism', *Rethinking Marxism*, 29(4), pp. 574–591, DOI: 10.1080/08935696.2017.1417087.

García Linera, Á. (2013) 'Once Again on So-called "Extractivism"', *Monthly Review Online*, 29 April, https://mronline.org/2013/04/29/gl290413-html/ (accessed on 11 November 2021).

Gardner, K. (2012) *Discordant Development: Global Capitalism and the Struggle for Connection in Bangladesh* (London: Pluto Press).

Gilbert, P.R. (2020) 'Expropriating the Future: Turning Ore Deposits and Legitimate Expectations Into Assets', in K. Birch and F. Muniesa (eds.) *Assetization: Turning*

Things into Assets in Technoscientific Capitalism (Cambridge, MA: MIT Press), pp. 173–201.

Gilbert, P.R. and M.T. Khan (2021) "Land defenders' and the political ecology of coal power in Bangladesh', in M. Menton and P. Le Billon (eds.) *Environmental Defenders: Deadly Struggles for Life and Territory* (Oxon: Routledge).

Grinspun, R. and J. Mills (2015) 'Canada, extractivism and hemispheric relations', in K. Ervine and G. Fridell (eds.) *Beyond Free Trade: Alternative Approaches to Trade, Politics and Power* (London: Palgrave Macmillan), pp. 133–151.

Gudynas, E. (2018) 'Extractivisms: Tendencies and Consequences', in R. Munck and R.D. Wise (eds.) *Reframing Latin American Development* (London: Routledge), pp. 61–76.

Hickel, J. (2021) *Less is More: How Degrowth will Save the World* (London: Penguin Random House).

Hoque, R. (2006) 'Taking justice seriously: Judicial public interest and constitutional activism in Bangladesh', *Contemporary South Asia*, 15(4), pp. 399–422, DOI: 10.1080/09584930701330006.

Hossain, K. (1980) 'Permanent Sovereignty over Natural Resources', in *Legal Aspects of the New International Economic Order* (London: Bloomsbury Academic Collections), pp. 33–43.

Hossain, K. (1979) *Law and Policy in Petroleum Development: Changing Relations between Transnationals and Governments* (London: Frances Pinter).

Hughes, D. (2017) *Energy without Conscience: Oil, Climate Change, and Complicity* (Durham: Duke University Press).

IISD (International Institute for Sustainable Development) and IGF (Intergovernmental Forum on Mining, Minerals, Metals and Sustainable Development) (2019) *Local Content Policies in the Mining Sector: Scaling up local procurement* (Winnipeg and Ottawa: IISD-IGF), https://www.iisd.org/publications/local-content-policies-mining (accessed on 22 July 2022).

IPCC (Intergovernmental Panel on Climate Change) (2022) *Mitigation of Climate Change: Working Group III contribution to the Sixth Assessment Report to the Intergovernmental Panel on Climate Change* (Geneva: WMO/UNEP), https://www.ipcc.ch/report/ar6/wg3/ (accessed on 22 July 2022).

Kama, K. (2020) 'Resource-making controversies: Knowledge, anticipatory politics and economization of unconventional fossil fuels', *Progress in Human Geography*, 44(2), pp. 333–356, DOI: 10.1177/0309132519829223.

Kröger, M. (2020) *Iron Will: Global Extractivism and Mining Resistance in Brazil and India* (Ann Arbor: University of Michigan Press).

Linarelli, J., M. Salomon and M. Sornarajah (2018) *The Misery of International Law: Confrontations with Injustice in the Global Economy* (Cambridge: Cambridge University Press).

Mirza, M. (2020) 'State-Business Nexus in Bangladesh: Quick Rental Power Plants in Perspective', in M.T. Khan and M.S. Rahman (eds.) *Neoliberal Development in Bangladesh: People on the Margins* (Dhaka: University Press Limited), pp. 113–136.

Mookerjea, S. and M. Misra (2017) 'Coal Power and the Sundarbans in Bangladesh: subaltern resistance and convergent crises', in D. Kapoor (ed.) *Against Colonization and Rural Dispossession: Local Resistance in South and East Asia, the Pacific and Africa* (London: Zed Books), pp. 164–186.

Mossallam, M. (2015) *Process matters: South Africa's experience exiting its BITs*, Global Economic Governance Programme Working Paper No. 2015/97 (Oxford: University of Oxford).

NCBD (National Committee to Protect Oil Gas Mineral Resources Power and Ports, Bangladesh) (2017) *The Alternative Power and Energy Plan for Bangladesh* (Dhaka: NCBD), https://ncbd.org/wp-content/uploads/2018/01/The-Alternative-Power-and-Energy-Plan-for-Bangladesh-by-NCBD.pdf (accessed on 20 June 2022).

Nuremowla, S. (2016) 'Land, Place and Resistance to Displacement in Phulbari', *SAMAJ: South Asia Multidisciplinary Academic Journal*, 13, pp. 1–17. DOI: 10.4000/samaj.4113.

Nystrom, E. (2014) *Seeing Underground: Maps, Models, and Mining Engineering in America* (Reno: University of Nevada Press).

Orellana López, A. (2021) *Neoextractivism and State Violence: Defending the Defenders in Latin America* (Amsterdam: Transnational Institute), https://www.tni.org/files/publication-downloads/tni-sop-2021-neoextractivism.pdf (accessed on 30 September 2021).

Ortino, F. (2022) 'The Public Interest as Part of Legitimate Expectations in Investment Arbitration: Missing in Action?', in C. Brower, J. Donoghue, C. Murphy, C. Payne and E. Shirlow (eds.) *By Peaceful Means: International Adjudication and Arbitration* (Oxford: Oxford University Press).

Ottinger, G. (2013) *Refining Expertise: How Responsible Engineers Subvert Environmental Justice Challenges* (New York: New York University Press).

Paulsson, J. (1995) 'Arbitration without Privity', *Foreign Investment Law Journal ICSID Review*, 10(2), pp. 232–257, https://cdn.arbitration-icca.org/s3fs-public/document/media_document/media012254614477540jasp_article_-_arbitration_without_privity.pdf (accessed on 25 July 2022).

Rahman, M. (2022) 'Ukraine war bans weigh on Bangladesh gas drilling', *Financial Express*, 1 March, https://thefinancialexpress.com.bd/trade/ukraine-war-bans-weigh-on-bangladesh-gas-drilling-1646016853 (accessed on 20 June 2022).

Rodrigues, B.S. (2021) 'UNCITRAL and the Governance of International Investments', in A. Gourgourinis (ed.) *Transnational Actors in International Investment Law* (Cham: Springer Cham), pp. 1–18.

Rodriguez Fernandez, G. (2020) 'Neo-extractivism, the Bolivian state, and indigenous peasant women's struggles for water in the Altiplano', *Human Geography*, 13(1), pp. 27–39, DOI: 10.1177/1942778620910896.

Schultz, T. (2014) *Transnational Legality: Stateless Law and International Arbitration* (Oxford: Oxford University Press).

Sornarajah, M. (2020) 'The Covid-19 Pandemic and Liability under Investment Treaties', *SouthViews*, 204, 11 August 2020, https://www.southcentre.int/southviews-no-204-11-august-2020/ (accessed on 25 July 2022).

Sornarajah, M. (2016) 'On fighting for global justice: the role of a Third World international lawyer', *Third World Quarterly*, 37(11), pp. 1972–1989, DOI: 10.1080/01436597.2016.1180955.

Sornarajah, M. (2015) *Resistance and Change in the International Law on Foreign Investment* (Cambridge: Cambridge University Press).

Szeman, I. and J. Wenzel (2021) 'What do we talk about when we talk about extractivism?', *Textual Practice*, 35(3), pp. 505–523, DOI: 10.1080/0950236X.2021.1889829.

The Daily Star (2005) 'Tengratila Blowout: Real Damage Greater than Estimate; Civic Body Plans to Sue Niko', *The Daily Star*, 09 September.

Tribune Desk (2013) 'Magurchhara blowout: Demand Tk450bn from Chevron and NIKO: Speakers', *Dhaka Tribune*, 15 June, https://www.dhakatribune.com/uncategorized/2013/06/15/magurchhara-blowout-demand-tk450bn-from-chevron-and-niko-speakers (accessed on 14 November 2021).

UNGA (United Nations General Assembly) (1984) *Progressive Development of the Principles and Norms of International Law Relating to the New International Economic Order* (New York: United Nations) https://digitallibrary.un.org/record/71137?ln=en (accessed on 11 Nov 2021).

Uribe, D. and Danish (2021) 'UNCITRAL Working Group III: Moving forward towards consensus or loosing balance?', *South Centre Investment Policy Brief*, 23, https://www.southcentre.int/wp-content/uploads/2021/07/Investment-PB-23.pdf (accessed on 25 July 2022).

Van Harten, G. (2016) 'Who has Benefited Financially from Investment Treaty Arbitration? An Evaluation of the Size and Wealth of Claimants', *Osgood Legal Studies Research Paper Series*, 135.

Veltmeyer, H. and Bowles, P. (2014) 'Extractivist resistance: the case of the Enbridge oil pipeline project in Northern British Columbia', *Extractive Industries and Society*, 1(1), pp. 59–68. DOI: 10.1016/j.exis.2014.02.002.

Venzke, I. (2018) 'Possibilities of the Past: Histories of the NIEO and the Travails of Critique', *Journal of the History of International Law*, 20(3), pp. 263–302, DOI: 10.1163/15718050-20020050.

Wood, C. (2016) 'Inside the halo zone: Geology, finance, and the corporate performance of profit in a deep tight oil formation', *Economic Anthropology*, 3(1), pp. 43–56, DOI: 10.1002/sea2.12043.

Zalik, A. (2018) 'Mining the seabed, enclosing the Area: ocean grabbing, proprietary knowledge and the geopolitics of the extractive frontier beyond national jurisdiction', *International Social Science Journal*, 68(229–230), pp. 343–359, DOI: 10.1111/issj.12159.

PART 3

'Green' Extractivism and Its Discontents

CHAPTER 10

The 'Alterlives' of Green Extractivism: Lithium Mining and Exhausted Ecologies in the Atacama Desert

James J. A. Blair, Ramón M. Balcázar, Javiera Barandiarán and Amanda Maxwell

Abstract

Green technologies designed to mitigate climate change through renewable energy and zero-emissions transportation currently depend on lithium-ion batteries, which require 'critical materials'. Like nickel, graphite, manganese and cobalt, lithium is a key component of batteries that store energy for electric vehicles, smart devices and renewable power plants. Although lithium is present all over the globe, one of the main commercial lithium reserves is in the Puna de Atacama, a desert region at the borders of Chile, Argentina and Bolivia. Resulting from a collaborative study for the Natural Resources Defense Council and the Plurinational Observatory of Andean Salt Flats, this chapter examines how the reliance on brine evaporation as an extraction method for lithium mining exacerbates conditions of ecological 'exhaustion' in the Puna de Atacama. The study is based on ethnographic and historical research primarily conducted in Chile with environmental activists, Indigenous leaders, scientists and policy practitioners. Furthering the concept of 'alterlives' to examine not only exposure to downstream chemicals but also the in situ alteration of life at mining sites upstream in the chemical supply chain, the chapter analyses environmental injustices inherent to green extractivism across multiple scales. It considers under what conditions Indigenous and local participation may contribute new models and standards for monitoring and offers policy recommendations to prevent further social harm and environmental damage.

1 Introduction

A global transition from fossil fuels to renewable energy is underway to mitigate climate change (Bridge and Gailing, 2020; Newell and Mulvaney, 2013). Such climate action policies are centred on electrified transportation and energy storage that currently depend on batteries, which is accelerating the extraction of critical materials. Lithium—in addition to copper, nickel, graphite, manganese and cobalt—is a key component of lithium-ion batteries that store energy for electric vehicles, smart devices and renewable power plants. Lithium is mined from three main sources: (1) hard rock pegmatites, especially in Australia, (2) sedimentary rock, particularly clay, under development in Nevada in the United States and other locales worldwide, and (3) brine pumped from beneath arid salt flats, primarily in Chile and Argentina (USGS, 2021). The last of these three methods, lithium brine evaporation, has become controversial due to legal disputes over water depletion and Indigenous rights violations in South America (Babidge et al., 2019; Blair et al., 2022; Bustos-Gallardo, Bridge and Prieto, 2021; Flexer, Baspineiro and Galli, 2018). Nonetheless, mining companies have tried to greenwash the environmental injustices inherent in lithium extraction by associating solar evaporation with climate change mitigation and disassociating brine from water (Voskoboynik and Andreucci, 2021). This critical conjuncture of global climate action and local environmental injustice has operated under a paradoxical regime of 'green extractivism' that has made the expansion of mining and other extractive industries a prerequisite to sustainable development (Dunlap and Jakobsen, 2019; Jerez, Garcés and Torres, 2021; Riofrancos, 2019).

Drawing on collaborative, engaged and policy-oriented research for the Natural Resources Defense Council (NRDC) and the Plurinational Observatory of Andean Salt Flats (OPSAL), this chapter interrogates how the reliance on brine evaporation as an extraction method for lithium mining has exacerbated conditions of 'ecological exhaustion' and undermined Indigenous sovereignty in South America (Babidge et al., 2019).[1] Our study is primarily based on ethnographic and historical research conducted in the period 2014–19, including participant observation, document analysis and workshops and interviews with environmental activists, Indigenous leaders, international scientists and policy practitioners in the Puna de Atacama from across Chile, Argentina and Bolivia, with a particular focus on northern Chile (see Figure 10.1).[2] Drawing on the interdisciplinary fields of political ecology and science and technology studies, or STS (Bustos-Gallardo, Prieto and Barton, 2015; Goldman, Nadasdy

1 In this study, 'exhaustion' is an emic term from Chilean environmental law and policy declaring that a basin does not have enough surface water to allow additional water rights to be granted. For an exploration of exhaustion from critical Western philosophical perspectives on energy, see Toscano (2018).

2 The Puna de Atacama is a geographical term defined by the characteristics of the ecoregion such as its flora, fauna, elevation and geology (Matteucci, 2012). In contrast to the Puna, the term 'Lithium Triangle' just distils the region to its extractive potential (Jerez Henríquez, 2018).

FIGURE 10.1 Selected salt flats in Argentina, Bolivia, and Chile
SOURCE: AUTHORS, BASED ON BRENDA J. ROJAS (BLAIR ET AL., 2022)

and Turner, 2011; Peet, Robbins and Watts, 2011; Sultana, 2020; 2021), we analyse how the 'slow violence' (Nixon, 2011)—the uneven effects that take place gradually and often invisibly—of lithium brine evaporation has transformed Andean wetland ecologies into what decolonial feminist STS scholar Michelle Murphy (2017) calls 'alterlives', or 'collectivities of life recomposed by the molecular productions of capitalism in our own pasts and the pasts of our ancestors, as well as into the future' (Murphy, 2017, 497). While Murphy developed this concept to refer to the alteration of life through exposures to downstream chemicals in the built environment, here our focus is on the in situ alteration of life at extraction sites upstream in the chemical supply chain.[3] In the instance of intensive lithium mining in the Puna de Atacama, green extractivism has had wide-ranging effects across multiple scales of life in relation to water: from Indigenous agropastoralists who have established irrigation practices and customs based on local knowledge over millennia (Babidge and Bolados, 2018; Prieto, 2016) to charismatic megafauna such as flamingos, and unique biodiverse microorganisms that have adapted to the extreme environments of ancient palaeolakes and are now facing extirpation or extinction (Bonelli and Dorador, 2021; Gutiérrez et al., 2022).

The urgency of confronting hydrosocial impacts that transcend spatio-temporal scales of life has inspired many environmental movements throughout Latin America to protect their territories from immediate threats of development by extractive industries.[4] Here, we consider under what conditions Indigenous and local participation may contribute new models and standards for monitoring ecological exhaustion, and we encourage concrete policy alternatives to lithium brine evaporation—the dominant method of lithium extraction used in the Puna de Atacama. We conducted 41 interviews and organised 13 workshops or public events with Indigenous leaders and those involved in environmental defence and campaigning in the region, from 2014 to 2019. Some community members feel they are benefiting from lithium development; some do not. Some mining operations have the support of local and/or national governments, while others do not. These communities are not monolithic, and relations with the mining industry are complex (Carrasco, 2020; Johnson et al., 2021). Informed by these heterogeneous local experiences with green extractivism, we argue that the intensive use of water and land for lithium mining through brine evaporation has altered life in and around salt flats, and we offer policy recommendations to prevent further social and environmental damage. Before presenting our policy recommendations, in section 2 we provide a historical background of the role of neo-liberal statecraft in resource development, as well as ethnographic and analytical perspectives on the slow violence of lithium brine evaporation and the upstream alterlives of green extractivism in the Puna de Atacama.

3 We thank Philippe Le Billon for pointing out this distinction between Murphy's use of the concept to refer to exposures to chemicals in buildings and its use to refer to alteration of water-and landscapes by extraction.

4 See Acosta (2017); Acuña and Tironi (2022); Blair (2021); Del Bene, Scheidel and Temper (2018); Gudynas (2018); Hernando-Arrese and Tironi (2019); Hommes et al. (2019); Hoogesteger and Verzijl (2015); Li (2015); Lins Ribeiro (1994); Riofrancos (2017); Svampa (2013); Swyngedouw (2004).

FIGURE 10.2 Selected salt flats with lithium resources
SOURCE: AUTHORS, BASED ON BRENDA J. ROJAS (BLAIR ET AL., 2022)

2 Historical, Ethnographic and Analytical Perspectives

2.1 *Neo-liberal Statecraft and Resource Development*

The Puna de Atacama—a high, arid desert region that spans northern Chile, north-western Argentina and south-western Bolivia—is known for vast, mineral-rich salt flats as well as for wetlands.[5] The hypersaline lakes of this

---

5 The Intergovernmental Science-Policy Platform on Biodiversity and Ecosystem Services Global Assessment has identified wetlands as the world's most threatened ecosystems

stretch of the Andes host three of the world's six species of flamingo, an array of endemic mammals, and unique communities of microorganisms (Contador et al., n.d.; Dorador et al., 2018b; Dorador et al., 2013; Gajardo and Redón, 2019; Marambio-Alfaro et al., 2017). Yet, many of these lagoons are adjacent to or overlap with mining projects (see Figure 10.2). Mining has long occurred in Chile's Atacama salt flat, dating back to before the Inca or the Spanish conquests. From the Spanish colonial era and into the twentieth century, the authorities argued that the Atacama Desert was empty and arid, and used this as the rationale for erasing and marginalising Indigenous peoples living there (Mendez, Prieto and Godoy, 2020; Saldivia Maldonado, 2003). This belies the contemporary formation of an Atacameño/Lickanantay ethnopolitical movement (Bustos, 2014; Carrasco, 2020; Gundermann, 2004; Morales Morgado, 2013). After World War II, the United States and other wealthy nations began stockpiling strategic resources like uranium and lithium for the development of nuclear energy and weapons, as policies of resource nationalism became foundational to the consolidation of global power (Black, 2018; Hecht, 2012; Mitchell, 2011). The governments of Chile, Argentina and Bolivia have developed lithium mining by pursuing extractivist and neo-extractivist policies that have at times envisioned lithium as a banal commodity, at times as a strategic resource; more recently, lithium has animated green extractivism as part of a 'sociotechnical imaginary' of future sustainable development (Barandiarán, 2019; Jasanoff and Kim, 2015).

While Chile and Argentina have been exporting lithium for several decades, Bolivia has sizeable reserves that remain largely unexploited due to technical and political hurdles, including higher levels of precipitation, greater concentrations of magnesium and more stringent state intervention (Narins, 2017; Sanchez-Lopez, 2019). Nonetheless, Bolivia has formed new alliances with China, Russia and US entrepreneurs, proposing new global production networks (Bos and Forget, 2021; Perreault, 2020). Argentina's provincial governments have sought to leverage lithium mining as a source of foreign currency and economic growth with limited oversight (Nacif, 2015). The modern Chilean state, meanwhile, was built on revenue from nitrates and copper from this area, and some Indigenous communities welcomed mining (Carrasco, 2020). However, in the 1980s and 1990s when neo-liberalism took hold under the dictatorship of Augusto Pinochet, there was a rapid development of large-scale mining for gold and copper, as well as for brine-based

(IPBES, 2019). Many of the lagoons in this area host migratory and native wildlife, and several are already designated as Ramsar Wetlands of International Importance or nature reserves and/or have some sort of national protected status.

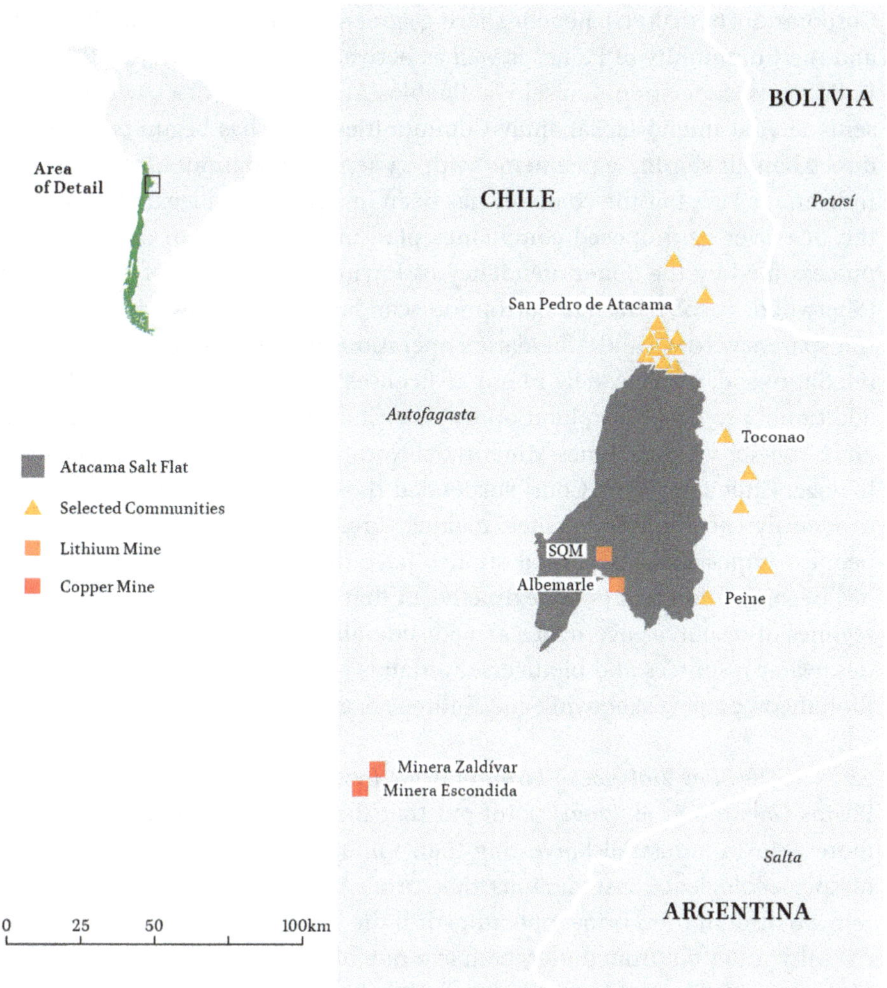

FIGURE 10.3 18 Selected Indigenous communities and the four largest mining operations
SOURCE: AUTHORS, BASED ON BRENDA J. ROJAS (BLAIR ET AL., 2022)

fertiliser and lithium extraction, among other privatised resources (Arboleda, 2020; Barandiaran, 2018; Carrasco, 2020; Fermandois, Bustos and Schneur, 2009; Tironi and Barandiarán, 2014). In the Salar de Atacama basin (see Figure 10.3), two large copper mines from this period, Minera Escondida and Minera Zaldívar, have overused fresh water and devastated the environment (OPSAL, 2020b). Adjacent to these, Chile's two current major lithium mining operations—Sociedad Química y Minera de Chile (SQM) and Albemarle—began operating thanks to contracts brokered by state institutions, specifically the Corporación de Fomento de la Producción (Production Promotion

Corporation, or CORFO). Benefit-sharing agreements exist between Albemarle and the Community of Peine, as well as between Albemarle and the broader Indigenous association, Consejo de Pueblos Atacameños (CPA), which represents 18 Atacameño/Lickanantay Communities. SQM has begun to establish direct benefit-sharing agreements with 23 separate communities under the Indigenous Law, but the company has been in a protracted legal dispute with the CPA over its proposed compliance plan in the context of a sanctioning process filed by the Superintendency of Environment (SMA) of Antofagasta (Sherwood, 2020b). Despite corruption scandals and controversies over data transparency, SQM's and Albemarle's operations have expanded (*CIPER Chile*, nd; Sherwood, 2021). A new round of licenses was issued in 2021, with new, additional projects in exploration by BYD Chile SpA, Cosayach Caliche S.A., and Servicios y Operaciones Mineras del Norte S.A (Balcázar, 2022). However, in 2022, Chile's Supreme Court suspended those licenses because they failed to identify specific mining sites, making timely consultation of Indigenous peoples impossible. As several studies have demonstrated, lithium mining has become a force of green extractivism that has thrived under neo-liberal regimes of resource governance at a considerable cost to front line communities, water resources and biodiverse wetlands (Jerez, Garcés and Torres, 2021; Riofrancos, 2019; Voskoboynik and Andreucci, 2021).

2.2 *The Slow Violence of Lithium Brine Evaporation*

Bustos Gallardo et al. (2021) point out that the lithium extraction process is more akin to industrial harvesting than mining, presenting a particular set of socioecological contradictions that result in overall water depletion. To remove lithium from brine, operators drill the crust of the salt flat and pump the salty water out from underneath at a rate of up to 1,700 litres per second.[6] The subsurface minerals are then distributed into a series of cascading evaporation pools. These vast bodies of mineralized groundwater soak up the desert sun and undergo chemical treatment before separation and transfer to a processing plant to produce lithium carbonate. The evaporation process takes up to 18–24 months, and 95 per cent of water from brine evaporates in the process, exacerbating conditions of 'ecological exhaustion' (Babidge et al., 2019). This water depletion is gradual, cumulative, and difficult to represent, as captured by Nixon's notion of slow violence. It is also enabled by Chile's 1980 Constitution, together with the Mining and Water Codes, which respectively privatised access and use of minerals and water under the then dictatorship

6 This rate is for SQM (Heubl, 2019). In 2016, Albemarle gained approval to increase brine pumping from 142 to 442 litres per second.

(Hervé, 2015; Prieto, 2015b). Chile began to regulate water consumption by copper mines in 2009 (Babidge, 2019). However, regulators only track usage of surface water, freshwater aquifers, and ocean water, and not the extraction of brine in lithium mining because brine is treated as a mineral rather than as water. Permits are required from the environmental authority, but these restrictions do not account for physical conditions and externalised processes such as the hydrogeology of brine, variations in lithium content, or the solar insolation rate (Bustos-Gallardo, Bridge and Prieto, 2021). Lithium mining operates under the assumption that the brine extracted from the salt flat is separate from the adjacent wetlands and aquifers, but scientists are not in full agreement about how fresh groundwater connecting distant wetlands across the region interacts with brine (see Figure 10.4) (Amphos 21, 2018; Frau et al., 2021; Garcés and Alvarez, 2020; Liu, Agusdinata and Myint, 2019; Marazuela et al., 2019; Munk et al., 2021; Riofrancos, 2019).

Resource extraction's stressors with regard to water availability and quality pose a significant threat to the area's wildlife. The most immediately impacted life forms are unique species of microorganisms, including diverse archaeal and bacterial communities that are at risk of extinction due to brine evaporation (Cubillos et al., 2018). Scientists are concerned that this may have knock-on effects for more charismatic megafauna higher up the food chain (Dorador et al., 2018a). The collective memory of local residents suggests that flamingos are disappearing, and this perception is supported by scientific modelling that shows a reduction in two of the three local species of flamingo due to lithium mining and declining surface water (Gutiérrez et al., 2022). At the same time, climate change is hastening the retreat of glaciers and the disappearance of lakes from the landscape (Babidge et al., 2019; Garcés, 2011; Garcés and Alvarez, n.d.; Garcés, Alvarez and Marambio, 2017). As a result, the area has been suffering from the slow violence of 'extractivist droughts' in an ongoing water crisis (Nixon, 2011; Acuña and Tironi, 2022).

2.3 *The Alterlives of Green Extractivism*

Water relations have long been crucial to Atacameño/Lickanantay Indigenous peoples' efforts to adapt to one of the driest deserts in the world (Neville and Coulthard, 2019; Prieto, 2015a; 2016; Yáñez and Molina, 2011). Water from springs allowed the first human settlements to take root perhaps earlier than 10,000 BCE.[7] Atacameño/Lickanantay culture and livelihood adapted to the

7 The R.P. Gustavo Le Paige Archaeological Museum in San Pedro states that archaeologists have found arrowheads or '*colas de pescado*' for hunting large animals that have been extinct for 12,500 years. See also UNESCO (1998).

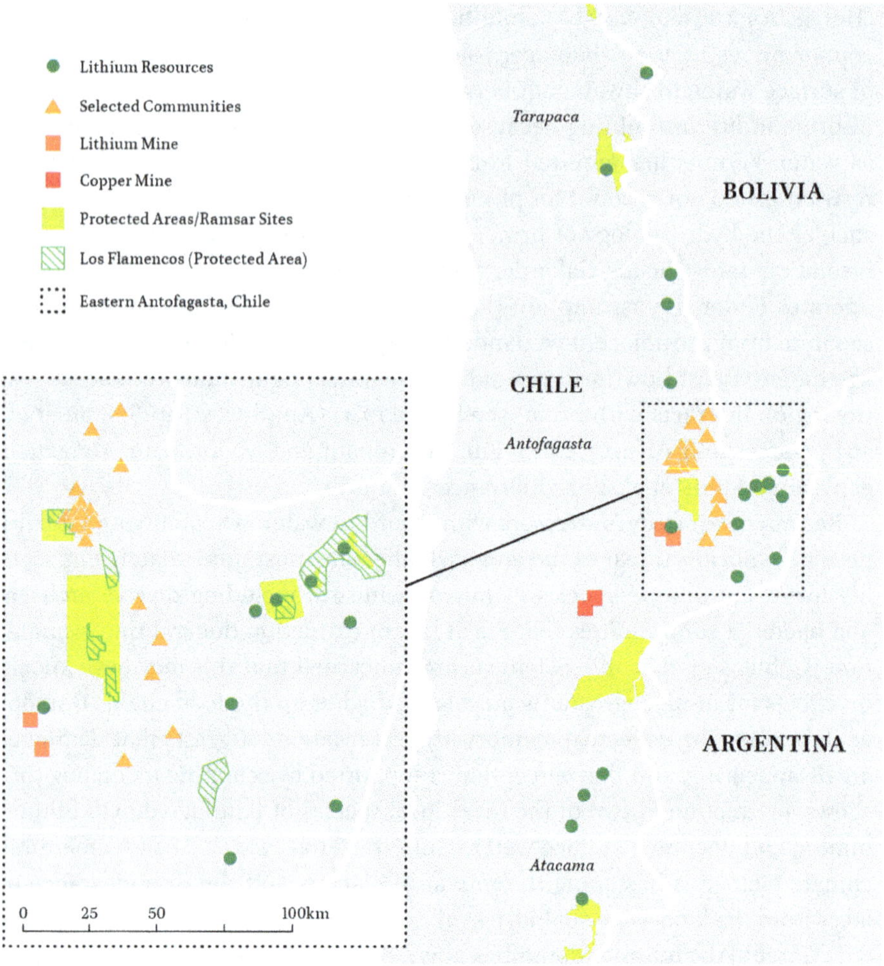

FIGURE 10.4 Mining activities overlapping with salt flats, protected wetlands and communities
SOURCES: AUTHORS, USING BRENDA J. ROJAS WITH DATA FROM ESRI, USGS AND NOAA (BLAIR ET AL., 2022)

seemingly hostile high desert environment through local agropastoral practices such as growing maize, quinoa, alfalfa and fruit, as well as raising llamas and other livestock. 'We are grateful for every drop of water and understand its cycles', said Jorge Muñoz Coca, of the Atacameño/Lickanantay Community of Solcor and member of OPSAL. Much like the emancipatory potential of 'the plot' as an oppositional mode of cultivating alternatives to the racialised oppression of the plantation for Black enslaved people and peasants around the world (Davis et al., 2019; Jegathesan, 2021; McKittrick, 2013; Wynter, 1971), agroecological gardening—an ancient practice threatened by water scarcity (Carrasco, 2020)—is providing Indigenous residents located on the margins of the salt flat a way to assert food sovereignty at the interstices of the lithium harvest (Altieri, 2002; Edelman, 2014; Grey and Patel, 2015; Wit, 2021).

However, in this area the availability of water for irrigation has decreased, in terms of both quantity and quality (Sepúlveda Rivera et al., 2015). This led the irrigation associations that have long stewarded the local San Pedro and Vilama rivers to limit water concessions by requesting a Declaration of Exhaustion (*agotamiento*), which was ratified by the government in 2017 (Ministerio de Obras Públicas, Dirección General de Aguas, 2016; 2017). The decision officially declared the watersheds 'exhausted', with insufficient surface water to allow for additional water rights to be granted. Local communities have received far fewer freshwater rights than mining companies have: about 92 litres per second compared to a combined 2,739 litres per second owned by the mining companies operating in the area (Babidge and Bolados, 2018, 176). In 2018 technical reports indicating ecological exhaustion led the General Water Directorate (DGA) to declare a prohibition on the use for extractive purposes of groundwater from the aquifer of the Atacama salt flat (Ministerio de Obras Públicas, Dirección General de Aguas, 2018). Moreover, in 2022 the government of Chile sued Albemarle as well as the two nearby copper mines for their over-use of the aquifer.[8] Nonetheless, lithium mining has already transformed modes of living and relations within local communities such as Toconao, as Indigenous activist Rudecindo Espíndola[9] explains in his own words:

> Development starts in Toconao, and the agriculture in that area begins to decay; craftwork starts to decay; customs start to go down. This monster is called 'mining with SQM or Albemarle'. It transforms the thoughts and way of life of Native people, in a way that causes division. They tell us lithium is clean. We can offer a way of life. But unfortunately, they're winning over there, and we're losing over here. They're drying up our waters. They're drying up the conscience we're lacking.[10]

---

8 Cecilia Jamasmie, "Chile sues BHP, Albemarle, Antofagasta over water use," *Mining.com*, April 8, 2022 https://www.mining.com/chile-sues-bhp-albemarle-antofagasta-over-water-use/ (accessed on 7 November 2022).

9 Espíndola is a member of the Atacameño/Lickanantay Community of Toconao, the Association of Irrigators and Farmers of Quebrada de Soncor, and OPSAL.

10 Rudecindo Christian Espíndola, 'Proyecto Paloma', Presentation at 2019 workshop, Fundación Tantí, OPSAL, San Pedro de Atacama, transcribed by Bianca Delgado and translated by Amanda Maxwell and Language Divas.

Mining not only alters life directly through mining extraction, as Espíndola indicates, but also through the mining companies' sustainability programmes intended to compensate for impacts in the surrounding territory, such as SQM's Tierra Fértil programme and local wine production project Vino Ayllu. The latter initiative stands out as it has established one of the first Indigenous people's cooperatives dedicated to commercial wine production, making Toconao and other nearby areas the origin of one of the world's few wines produced at high altitude. These new wine production and related activities are, however, highly dependent on external support (Herrera, 2019). Contrary to the company's claims, for some local farmers Vino Ayllu has little to do with traditional practices and culture. To become grape producers, local farmers have altered life near the salt flat by transforming their agroecological plots from biodiverse matrices into small monocultures. Moreover, farmers who join the cooperative must choose between preserving inherited old vines used for the traditional home-made *vino criollo* and opting for more commercial, introduced varietals such as Sauvignon Gris, Chardonnay and Pinot Noir, which are suitable for niche market demands (SQM, 2021, 208).[11] The growing aggregate surface area of vineyards requires even more water, producing new tensions between and among Indigenous farmers within and around the oasis of Toconao. Espíndola stresses how the introduction of commercial practices by SQM's Tierra Fértil is exacerbating conflicts around water, not just with the mining company, but also among Indigenous gardeners and winemakers:

> When we want to use water for our family gardens and see the winemakers are using the water to fill their accumulation tanks, we prefer to wait until the water is back in the canals just to avoid more arguments among farmers. So we don't ask in the WhatsApp group and we instead come every 30 minutes to check it out because this little trickle of water is not enough for us to irrigate our parcels. Anyway, it's better to avoid speaking of SQM or about the vineyards out loud because someone can hear us and that will cause us more problems.[12]

While corporate social responsibility programmes and community benefit agreements may, ironically, alter life and impede monitoring (Peterson St-Laurent and Le Billon, 2015), the CPA Indigenous association and broader

---

11 *Vino criollo* is a local wine produced in Toconao with grapes introduced by the church during the Spanish colonisation for use during Catholic mass. It is also used during other celebrations and ritual processes, such as carnival or the San Lucas celebration.

12 Rudecindo Espíndola, from the fieldnotes of Ramón Balcázar M., 2021.

alliances have not only established their own monitoring programmes but also taken action to regulate and limit mining expansion. The struggle for water resources has been especially contentious between SQM and local residents.[13] In 2020, OPSAL gathered more than 350 signatures from advocates and scientists in support of the CPA's demand that the company's operations be halted (OPSAL, 2020a). Atacameño leaders and community members from across Socaire, Toconao, Camar and Peine engaged in direct action protests, including road blockades and hunger strikes (Jerez Henríquez, 2018). In 2020, in the wake of the COVID-19 pandemic, the CPA sent a report to the United Nations demanding that SQM and Albemarle withdraw their collective workforce of up to 10,000 personnel (Comunidad Indígena Yagán de Bahía de Mejillones de Puerto Williams et al., 2020; Hitchcock Auciello, 2020). The CPA and OPSAL point out that these communities have not been properly consulted, and have not given their free, prior and informed consent as required by the guidelines contained in International Labour Organization Convention 169 (ILO 169) or the United Nations Declaration on the Rights of Indigenous Peoples (UNDRIP). Sergio Cubillos, former CPA president, has added:

> In fact, we have told the state: let's put together a working group through which we can first speed up the handing over of lands, as per the constitutional acknowledgment of our Native people. And then let's take a look at different ideas or interests that may exist regarding the law. But today, ideally, the most important things are those two things I just mentioned. Also much more important is to find solutions for issues as basic and tangible as drinking water, sewage, electricity, accessibility. I mean, right in the middle of the 21st century, a country that has come out to say they're at the threshold of development, of being a 'developed country', still has communities that lack these types of services. That speaks very poorly of an administration. And what's worse, the wealth in which the state lives, the wealth that the state has, which sustains the economy and the economic power of this country, comes precisely out of these communities

13 In 2019, Chile's Superintendency of Environment (SMA) approved SQM's USD 25 million compliance plan for the expansion of its operations, but later that year the CPA filed a successful lawsuit in a regional court that paused the approval process due to the 'particular fragility' of the Atacama salt flat (Sherwood, 2020a). In 2020, the SMA decided instead to develop its own comprehensive management plan, which would assess impacts of all four of the mega mining projects at the Atacama salt flat. Following its successful litigation campaign, the CPA went further, demanding that SQM's environmental permits be revoked (Sherwood, 2020b).

> . . .Chile, unfortunately, is a country that's still unable to see its Native people.[14]

In sum, green extractivism has not only exacerbated ecological exhaustion, it has also limited Indigenous peoples' access to basic necessities and contributed to their erasure due to uneven development in the Puna de Atacama. In addition to such dispossession, mining is also often associated with toxic contamination (Hecht, 2012; Voyles, 2015). Murphy developed the concept of alterlives from their Indigenous feminist perspective, to re-conceptualise chemical pollution's negative impacts in the built environment. Yet there remains a need to develop 'alter-concepts of care and responsibility' (Murphy, 2017, 496) that grapple with other expansive problems across the battery chemical supply chain: from water depletion, land use and underdevelopment at extraction sites to market demand in the global North and China, where the social and ecological costs of individual car ownership may fall only marginally if electric vehicles replace internal combustion engines (Marx, 2022). In what follows, we take 'alterlife as a prompt' (Murphy, 2017, 497) and propose policy recommendations for alternatives that are designed to protect water and regenerate more just, sustainable and equitable conditions of living beyond green extractivism.

3 Policy Recommendations to Support Alterlife in Andean Salt Flats and Wetlands[15]

Lithium-ion batteries may be, in the short and medium term, a critical component of the global strategy to fight climate change and mitigate air pollution by electrifying vehicles and providing storage for intermittent renewable energy (Sanderson, 2022). Yet the ecosystems that contain lithium resources—and the humans and non-humans that live in them—should not be sacrificed to extract this material. Fortunately, there are several ways in which actors throughout the lithium-ion battery supply chain can mitigate or eliminate negative impacts of lithium mining in the Puna de Atacama and other environments (Greim, Solomon and Breyer, 2020).

---

14 James J. A. Blair, personal communication with Sergio Cubillos, 2019, transcribed by Bianca Delgado and translated by Amanda Maxwell and Language Divas.

15 This recommendations section is adapted with permission from Blair et al., 2022.

3.1 *Apply International Human Rights Principles and Adhere to Indigenous-Led Protocols*

While existing benefit-sharing agreements in this region offer a foundation for corporate partnerships with communities, they should be understood as a floor, not a ceiling. Full participation of, and equal distribution of benefits among, Indigenous peoples and local communities have not been ensured in a democratic process because agreements with some communities have left others out, pitting communities against one another. Similar to other impact and benefit agreements, this has resulted in the silencing of dissent, state agencies' non-responsiveness to community needs, and an absence of regulation, monitoring and transparency (Peterson St-Laurent and Le Billon, 2015; Le Billon and Middeldorp, 2021). To operate in a more just, sustainable, and equitable way, the government should require and monitor—and companies should follow—the principles of international conventions such as:

- ILO 169,
- UNDRIP,
- The United Nations Declaration on the Rights of Peasants (UNDROP), and
- The Escazú Regional Agreement on Access to Information, Public Participation and Justice in Environmental Matters in Latin America and the Caribbean.

ILO 169 has already been ratified and in force in Chile since 2009, and Chile's President, Gabriel Boric, signed Escazú on March 18, 2022. Both should henceforth apply to all new mining projects and, ideally, apply retroactively to existing operations. In addition, while state agencies and corporations alike often ignore or only inconsistently adopt them, Indigenous-led protocols such as the Kachi Yupi Protocol, which applies in Salinas Grandes, Argentina, should be benchmarks for both governments and companies.[16] This includes recognising communities' rights to say no to mining proposals and instead continue making a living through established local economies, such as salt extraction, livestock raising and tourism.

3.2 *Strengthen Environmental Standards to Reflect Local Demands and Needs*

In addition to deeper engagement with Indigenous communities, mining activities should respect stronger environmental standards. Many organisations and institutions have produced recommendations that could be used

16 For example, see Comunidades de la Cuenca de Salinas Grandes y Laguna de Guayatayoc (2015); Secretariat of the Convention on Biological Diversity (2004); and Secretariat of the Convention on Biological Diversity (2011).

to address waste streams, water use and contamination, and air pollution (Elkind, Heller and Lamm, 2020; Amnesty International, 2021; Gankhuyag and Gregoire, 2018). A combination of remote sensing, oral history and ethnography could help identify changes to water tables, shifts in the population dynamics of local plants and animals, and other environmental indicators, including climate change—a key variable in the environmental assessment of extractive projects in salt flats and wetlands (Babidge et al., 2019; Flexer, Baspineiro and Galli, 2018). Monitoring should happen in ways that build trust and produce meaningful data that communities and citizens can use to hold mining companies accountable. To this end, funding for monitoring efforts should be transparent and independent of these companies (Barandiaran, 2018). Monitoring practices could be carried out by universities or public agencies, as well as by community members recognised as knowledge producers. Moreover, authorities should reclassify brine as water so they are able to better monitor and safeguard this material. If not already in place, governments around the Puna de Atacama should also adopt legislation and regulations that enable them to study and measure available groundwater and brine resources, and/or provide funding to independent professionals who can do so. Governments should regulate the use of these resources and require companies to disclose data to the public in a transparent and consistent manner.

3.3 *Build Collaborative Monitoring Practices Based on Indigenous Knowledge and Science*

The lithium sector has applied conventional business practices, including flawed Western science-based impact agreements that ignore the millennia of experience gained by communities that have deep knowledge of local ecology (Li, 2015; Lawrence and Kløcker Larsen, 2017; Perreault, 2020). Companies and governments should prioritise learning from local Indigenous peoples and earnestly centre that knowledge at the heart of their practices. Indigenous knowledge of local ecosystems may help with environmental monitoring, building local food production, and safeguarding biodiversity; for example, ethnobiological data on ancestral knowledge of watering sites for livestock herds may help identify monitoring locations and inform models of the area's complex hydrogeological landscape (Geralda Armstrong and McAlvay, 2019). There are several models of Indigenous-led land-use planning, climate adaptation and environmental management to follow when seeking to protect biodiverse areas, and Indigenous knowledge and science may be complementary to the co-management of resources by local communities and governments (Wang et al., 2016; Whyte, 2013).

3.4 *Enforce a Moratorium on Brine Evaporation through the Application of the Precautionary Principle*

According to UNESCO's World Commission on the Ethics of Scientific Knowledge and Technology (COMEST), 'When human activities may lead to morally unacceptable harm that is scientifically plausible but uncertain, actions shall be taken to avoid or diminish that harm' (UNESCO, 2005, 14). This is known as the precautionary principle. Because brine evaporation is thought to exacerbate ecological exhaustion and alter life in the Puna de Atacama, and because the actors responsible for this activity have failed to disclose clear evidence establishing that it does not do so, precautionary measures should be taken. The burden of proof is on the industry to show definitively that water and life are not threatened by brine evaporation, and until it has done so, it is in the public interest to cease this activity in the Puna de Atacama. Following demands from the CPA, as well as the non-binding verdict of the International Rights of Nature Tribunal (2020), a moratorium should be enforced on lithium mining through brine evaporation in the Puna de Atacama.

3.5 *Encourage Battery Recycling and Long-Term Planning for Alternative Transportation*

At the international level, governments and institutions should encourage and invest in reducing the demand for minerals and implement alternative ways of obtaining lithium—other than onshoring more conventional mining to the global North or over-relying on direct lithium extraction technologies, for these approaches may risk increasing water use and waste streams (Riofrancos, 2022). Governments may engage in such efforts through educational programmes, infrastructure development, and industrial policy (e.g. cradle-to-cradle incentives to reconvert gas cars or establish battery recycling programmes). Several circular economy strategies and international standards may lengthen the life duration and life cycle of a lithium-ion battery or its components (Standridge and Corneal, 2014; Mulvaney et al., 2021). Once a lithium-ion car battery can no longer hold a sufficient charge to power a vehicle, it can still serve as an energy storage element in buildings. Recycling the pure chemical lithium contained in old batteries can reduce the need to mine more new materials (Xiong, Ji and Ma, 2020). Recent research for Earthworks found that recycling electric vehicle batteries at the end of their useful life can reduce primary demand for lithium by as much as 25 per cent, for cobalt and nickel by 35 per cent, and for copper by 55 per cent (Dominish et al., 2021). Recycling facilities are not yet focused on recovering the full range of materials in lithium-ion batteries (Gaines, Richa and Spangenberger, 2018). However, this could change with regulation and policy, as has been observed with lead acid batteries: recycling rates for these have climbed to upwards of 90 per cent in many countries, largely in response to regulation (Turner, 2015). Currently, recycling lithium from discarded batteries is more expensive than extracting it from brine via evaporation. But lithium prices have increased and various types of recycling technologies are already in development with the aim of making the process more cost efficient and replicable, particularly in industrialised countries and regions—such as China, the European Union and the United States—where most lithium-ion batteries are currently consumed (Harper et al., 2019).[17]

Pressure to protect the alterlives of extractivism and reduce the long-term costs of lithium mining on salt flats and wetlands should come from downstream in the battery supply chain, including from battery manufacturers and vehicle makers, as well as from policymakers and urban and regional planners. Governments and third parties should support the corporate efforts of lithium purchasers to exert direct pressure on mining companies without letting certification standards amount to greenwashing. Policymakers, private companies, and citizens can help push forward a range of complementary strategies, including: (1) planning and policy tools to allow greater access to public transportation, bicycling, and walking to reduce long-term dependency on single-passenger vehicles; (2) retrofitting or building affordable, energy-efficient, regenerative homes and buildings for all; (3) investing in and adopting long-duration methods of renewable energy storage (e.g. gravity-based or iron flow) that minimise extraction and maximise efficiency over time. Such actions to reduce downstream reliance on lithium-ion batteries may play a critical role in supporting the regeneration of alterlife at extraction sites farther upstream in the global value chain.

4 Conclusion

Green extractivism threatens biodiverse life forms across multiple scales in the Puna de Atacama (Bonelli and Dorador, 2021; Flexer, Baspineiro and Galli, 2018; Gutiérrez et al., 2022). The slow violence of lithium brine evaporation, compounded by over-exploitation of water resources for copper mining, has contributed to conditions of ecological exhaustion. As Murphy suggests, we must go beyond conventional biological categories that separate non-human organisms from individual bodies, and instead 'situate life as a kind of varied

17 See, for example, 116th Congress, 2nd session, S. 3356: To support the Reuse and Recycling of Batteries and Critical Minerals, and for Other Purposes, February 27, 2020, https://www.congress.gov/116/bills/s3356/BILLS-116s3356is.pdf (accessed on 7 November 2022).

enmeshment and enfleshment in infrastructures—as well as in water as a distributed being' (Murphy, 2017, 498). Brine is water. And if water is life, then brine evaporation for the production and distribution of lithium has seriously altered life. Yet, Murphy reminds us that alterlife also entails 'the potential to become something else, to defend and persist, to recompose relations to water and land, to become alter-wise in the aftermath' (Murphy, 2017, 500). Given the urgency of the climate and ecological crisis, this means embracing the possibility that the energy transition may be open to transformation and resistant to maladaptation: not just to be clean and green for consumers, but also for those living at extraction sites.

At Chile's Atacama salt flat and nationwide, activists and advocates have been calling for more just, sustainable and equitable mining policies, including by calls for constitutional reform (Barandiarán, 2021). In a referendum held on September 4, 2022 in Chile, 62 per cent of voters rejected a new Constitution drafted by a democratically elected Constitutional Convention. With regard to the environment, this result postponed potentially transformative changes, and environmental activists are adjusting their work and strategies accordingly. For many advocates—including we, the authors—the proposed Constitution would have deepened democracy due to the process that brought it, and its content, about.

The Constitutional Convention commenced under the presidency of Dr Elisa Loncon, an Indigenous Mapuche linguist, with regional constituent representation of Antofagasta by Dr Cristina Dorador, a microbiologist with expertise in the biodiversity of salt flats. Dr Dorador joined OPSAL in launching the Plurinational Initiative for the Valorisation and Protection of Andean Salt Flats and Wetlands, a community-based participatory project that forms the basis for a bill to recognise the importance of defending these ecosystems against further industrial extraction. According to Dr Dorador, 'The north of Chile has been viewed by the country as an exploitable territory because "there is no life there." Deconstructing that image implies profound changes. The extraction of lithium is like taking the soul out of the salt flats' (OPSAL, 2021). To shift the narrative and raise awareness of overlooked alterlives at extraction sites, Dorador proposed and then led the Commission of Systems of Knowledges, Cultures, and Science—one of seven Commissions within the Constitutional Convention—which introduced articles that promoted epistemic justice, ethics in science, and integration of local knowledge into decision-making. Drawing on recent constitutional reforms in Bolivia and Ecuador, the Constitution would, if accepted, have established Chile as a plurinational, intercultural and ecological state, one that protects both human rights and the rights of nature (Barandiarán et al., 2022; Blair and Balcázar, 2022; Gudynas,

2014). These principles continue to resonate in ongoing debates about constitutional reform, and they remain critical for regenerating the alterlives of green extractivism.

References

Acosta A. (2017) 'Post-Extractivism: from Discourse to Practice—Reflections for Action', *International Development Policy | Revue internationale de politique de développement*, 9, pp. 77–101, DOI: 10.4000/poldev.2356.

Acuña, V. and M. Tironi (2022) 'Extractivist droughts: Indigenous hydrosocial endurance in Quillagua, Chile', *The Extractive Industries and Society*, 9(101027), DOI: 10.1016/j.exis.2021.101027.

Altieri, M.A. (2002) 'Agroecology: the Science of Natural Resource Management for Poor Farmers in Marginal Environments', *Agriculture, Ecosystems & Environment*, 93(1), pp. 1–24, DOI: 10.1016/S0167-8809(02)00085.

Amnesty International (2021) *Powering Change: Principles for Businesses and Governments in the Battery Value Chain*, No. ACT 30/3544/2021 (London: Amnesty International).

Amphos 21 (2018) *Modelo Hidrológico Consolidado Cuenca Salar de Atacama. Estudio de Modelos Hidrológicos Conceptuales Integrados Para Los Salares de Atacama, Maricunga y Pedernales*, Etapa III Informe Final (Chile).

Arboleda, M. (2020) *Planetary Mine. Territories of Extraction under Late Capitalism* (London: Verso).

Babidge, S. (2019) 'Sustaining Ignorance: the Uncertainties of Groundwater and Its Extraction in the Salar de Atacama, Northern Chile', *Journal of the Royal Anthropological Institute*, 25(1), pp. 83–102, DOI: 10.1111/1467-9655.12965.

Babidge, S. and P. Bolados (2018) 'Neoextractivism and Indigenous Water Ritual in Salar de Atacama, Chile', *Latin American Perspectives*, 45(5), pp. 170–185, DOI: 10.1177/0094582X18782673.

Babidge, S., F. Kalazich, M. Prieto and K. Yager (2019) '"That's the Problem with That Lake; It Changes Sides": Mapping Extraction and Ecological Exhaustion in the Atacama', *Journal of Political Ecology*, 26(1), pp. 738–760, DOI: 10.2458/v26i1.23169.

Balcázar, R.M. (2022) 'Licitación del litio: el agua vale más que el Litio', *Revista de Frente*, https://www.revistadefrente.cl/licitacion-del-litio-el-agua-vale-mas-que-el-litio-por-ramon-morales-balcazar/ (accessed on 19 March 2022).

Barandiarán, J. (2021) 'Assessing 30 Years of Neoliberal Environmental Management in Chile: Effective, Democratic or Neither?', in J. Sowers, S. VanDeveer, and E. Weinthal (eds.) *The Oxford Handbook of Comparative Environmental Politics* (Oxford: Oxford University Press).

Barandiarán, J. (2019) 'Lithium and Development Imaginaries in Chile, Argentina and Bolivia', *World Development*, 113, pp. 381–391, DOI: 10.1016/j.worlddev.2018.09.019.

Barandiarán, J. (2018) *Science and Environment in Chile* (Cambridge, MA: The MIT Press).

Barandiarán, J., V. Belemmi, G. Burdiles, and C. Ezio (2022) *Derechos de la Naturaleza en Chile: Argumentos para su desarrollo constitucional* (Santiago, Chile: Ocho Libros).

Black, M. (2018) *The Global Interior* (Cambridge, Massachusetts: Harvard University Press).

Blair, J.J.A. (2021) 'Extractivismo Del Litio y El Problema de La Escala: Acción Climática Global y Justicia Ambiental Local', in B. Jerez Henríquez, S. Uribe Sierra, and R.M. Balcázar (eds.) *Salares Andinos: Ecología de Saberes Por La Protección de Nuestros Salares y Humedales* (Santiago: Fundación Tantí).

Blair, J.J.A. and R.M. Balcázar (2022) 'Plurinational Climate Action: Environmental Governance Beyond Green Extractivism', *Cultural Anthropology-Hot Spots*, 23 June, https://culanth.org/fieldsights/plurinational-climate-action-environmental-governance-beyond-green-extractivism (accessed on 24 June 2022).

Blair, J.J.A., R.M. Balcázar, J. Barandiarán and A. Maxwell (2022) *Exhausted: How We Can Stop Lithium Mining from Depleting Water Resources, Draining Wetlands, and Harming Communities in South America*, No. R: 21-10-A (New York: Natural Resources Defense Council (NRDC)).

Bonelli, C. and C. Dorador (2021) 'Endangered Salares: Micro-Disasters in Northern Chile', *Tapuya: Latin American Science, Technology and Society* (London: Routledge), 4(1), p. 1968634, DOI: 10.1080/25729861.2021.1968634.

Bos V. and M. Forget (2021) 'Global Production Networks and the lithium industry: a Bolivian perspective', *Geoforum*, 125, pp. 168–180, DOI: 10.1016/j.geoforum.2021.06.001.

Bridge, G. and L. Gailing (2020) 'New Energy Spaces: towards a Geographical Political Economy of Energy Transition', *Environment and Planning A: Economy and Space*, 52(6), DOI: 10.1177/0308518X20939570.

Bustos, C. (2014) 'La Producción de "Etnomercancias" En El Contexto Turístico Atacameño', *Revista Lider*, 25, pp. 9–31.

Bustos-Gallardo, B., G. Bridge and M. Prieto (2021) 'Harvesting Lithium: Water, Brine and the Industrial Dynamics of Production in the Salar de Atacama', *Geoforum*, 119, pp. 177–189, DOI: 10.1016/j.geoforum.2021.01.001.

Bustos-Gallardo, B., M. Prieto and J. Barton (2015) *Ecología Política En Chile* (Santiago: Editorial Universitaria).

Carrasco, A. (2020) *Embracing the Anaconda* (Lanham: Lexington Books).

CIPER Chile (Centro de Investigacion Periodística) (n.d.) 'Archivos De SQM', *CIPER Chile*, https://www.ciperchile.cl/tag/sqm/ (accessed on 30 March 2022).

Comunidad Indígena Yagán de Bahía de Mejillones de Puerto Williams, Consejo de Pueblos Atacameños, Mesa de Coordinación de Pueblos Originarios del Budi,

Municipalidad de Saavedra and Observatorio Ciudadano and Plataforma Política Mapuche (2020) *Emergencia Sanitaria En El Contexto de La Pandemia Por COVID-19 En Chile y Su Impacto En Los Derechos de Los Pueblos Originarios* (Santiago, Chile: Observatorio Ciudadano) https://observatorio.cl/wp-content/uploads/2020/06/emergencia-sanitaria-en-el-contexto-de-la-pandemia-por-covid-19-en-chile-y-su-impacto-en-los-derechos-de-los-pueblos-originarios-11.pdf (accessed on 7 November 2022).

Comunidades de la Cuenca de Salinas Grandes y Laguna de Guayatayoc (2015) *Kachi Yupi—Huellas de La Sal: Procedimiento de Consulta y Consentimiento Previo, Libre e Informado Para Las Comunidades Indígenas de Las Salinas Grandes y Laguna de Guayatayoc*, https://cl.boell.org/sites/default/files/protocolo_final.pdf (accessed on 7 November 2022).

Contador, C.A., L. Veas-Castillo, E. Tapia, N. Antipán, B. Miranda, B. Ruiz-Tagle, J. García Araya, B.A. Andrews, M. Marín, C. Dorador and J.A. Asenjo (n.d.) *Atacama Database: a Platform of the Microbiome Diversity of the Atacama Desert* (Santiago: Universidad de Chile), https://www.atacamadb.cl/#/ (accessed on 7 November 2022).

Cubillos, C.F., P. Aguilar, M. Grágeda and C. Dorador (2018) 'Microbial Communities From the World's Largest Lithium Reserve, Salar de Atacama, Chile: Life at High LiCl Concentrations', *Journal of Geophysical Research: Biogeosciences*, 123(12), pp. 3668–3681, DOI: 10.1029/2018JG004621.

Davis, J., A.A. Moulton, L.V. Sant and B. Williams (2019) 'Anthropocene, Capitalocene, … Plantationocene?: a Manifesto for Ecological Justice in an Age of Global Crises', *Geography Compass*, 13(5), e12438, DOI: 10.1111/gec3.12438.

Del Bene, D., A. Scheidel and L. Temper (2018) 'More Dams, More Violence? A Global Analysis on Resistances and Repression around Conflictive Dams through Co-Produced Knowledge', *Sustainability Science*, 13(3), pp. 617–633, DOI: 10.1007/s11625-018-0558-1.

Dominish, E., N. Florin and R. Wakefield-Rann (2021) *Reducing New Mining for Electric Vehicle Battery Metals: Responsible Sourcing Through Demand Reduction Strategies and Recycling* (Sydney: Earthworks and Institute for Sustainable Futures, University of Technology Sydney), https://earthworks.org/assets/uploads/2021/04/UTS-EV-battery-metals-sourcing-20210419-FINAL.pdf (accessed on 7 November 2022).

Dorador, C., P. Fink, M. Hengst, G. Icaza, A.S. Villalobos, D. Vejar, D. Meneses, V. Zadjelovic, L. Burmann, J. Moelzner and C. Harrod (2018a) 'Microbial Community Composition and Trophic Role along a Marked Salinity Gradient in Laguna Puilar, Salar de Atacama, Chile', *Antonie Van Leeuwenhoek*, 111(8), pp. 1361–1374, DOI: 10.1007/s10482-018-1091-z.

Dorador, C., D. Meneses, V. Urtuvia, C. Demergasso, I. Vila, K.-P. Witzel and J.F. Imhoff (2018b) 'Diversity of Bacteroidetes in High-Altitude Saline Evaporitic Basins in

Northern Chile', *Journal of Geophysical Research: Biogeosciences*, DOI: 10.1029/2008JG000837@10.1002/(ISSN)2169-8961.HIGHLAKES1.

Dorador, C., I. Vila, K.-P. Witzel and J. Imhoff (2013) 'Bacterial and Archaeal Diversity in High Altitude Wetlands of the Chilean Altiplano', *Fundamental and Applied Limnology / Archiv Für Hydrobiologie*, 182, pp. 135–159, DOI: 10.1127/1863-9135/2013/0393.

Dunlap, A. and J. Jakobsen (2019) *The Violent Technologies of Extraction* (Cham: Palgrave Pivot).

Edelman, M. (2014) 'Food Sovereignty: Forgotten Genealogies and Future Regulatory Challenges', *The Journal of Peasant Studies*, 41(6), pp. 959–978, DOI: 10.1080/03066150.2013.876998.

Elkind, E.N., P.R.P. Heller and T. Lamm (2020) *Building a Sustainable Electric Vehicle Battery Supply Chain: Frequently Asked Questions* (Berkeley, New York: Natural Resource Governance Institute and Center for Law, Energy and the Environment, UC Berkeley), https://www.law.berkeley.edu/wp-content/uploads/2020/04/Building-A-Sustainable-Electric-Vehicle-Battery-Supply-Chain.pdf (accessed on 7 November 2022).

Fermandois, J., J. Bustos, and M.-J. Schneur (2009) *Historia política del cobre en Chile.* (Santiago, Chile: Centro de Estudios del Bicentenario).

Flexer V., C.F. Baspineiro, C.I. Galli (2018) 'Lithium recovery from brines: a vital raw material for green energies with a potential environmental impact in its mining and processing', *Science of The Total Environment*, 639, pp. 1188–1204, DOI: 10.1016/j.scitotenv.2018.05.223.

Frau D., B.J. Moran, F. Arengo, et al. (2021) 'Hydroclimatological Patterns and Limnological Characteristics of Unique Wetland Systems on the Argentine High Andean Plateau', *Hydrology*, 8(164), DOI: 10.3390/hydrology8040164.

Gaines, L., K. Richa and J. Spangenberger (2018) 'Key Issues for Li-Ion Battery Recycling', *MRS Energy & Sustainability*, 5(1), p. 12, DOI: 10.1557/mre.2018.13.

Gajardo, G. and S. Redón (2019) 'Andean Hypersaline Lakes in the Atacama Desert, Northern Chile: between Lithium Exploitation and Unique Biodiversity Conservation', *Conservation Science and Practice*, 1(9), e94, DOI: 10.1111/csp2.94.

Gankhuyag, U. and F. Gregoire (2018) *Managing Mining for Sustainable Development: a Sourcebook* (Bangkok: United Nations Development Programme), https://www.undp.org/sites/g/files/zskgke326/files/publications/UNDP-MMFSD-HighResolution.pdf (accessed on 7 November 2022).

Garcés, I. (2011) 'Salar de Surire un ecosistema altoandino en peligro, frente a escenario del cambio climático', *Nexo Revista Científica*, 24(1), pp. 43–49.

Garcés, I. and G. Alvarez (2020) 'Water Mining and Extractivism of the Salar de Atacama, Chile', in J. Casares Long (ed.) *Environmental Impact V*, WIT Transactions on Ecology and the Environment (Southampton: WIT Press), pp. 189–199, DOI: 10.2495/EID200181 (accessed on 27 January 2021).

Garcés, I. and G. Alvarez (n.d.) *Implicancias del Cambio Climático Sobre la Biodiversidad del Salar de Aguas Calientes I, Chile*, https://bibliotecadigital.ciren.cl/handle/20.500.13082/26026 (accessed on 7 November 2022).

Garcés, I., G. Alvarez and Y. Marambio (2017) *Relevancia Del Salar de Atacama Frente al Escenario Económico*, non-published.

Geralda Armstrong, C. and A.C. McAlvay (2019) 'Introduction to Special Section on Action Ethnobiology', *Journal of Ethnobiology*, 39(1), p. 3, DOI: 10.2993/0278-0771-39.1.3.

Goldman, M., P. Nadasdy and M. Turner (eds.) (2011) *Knowing Nature* (Chicago: University of Chicago Press).

Greim, P., A.A. Solomon and C. Breyer (2020) 'Assessment of Lithium Criticality in the Global Energy Transition and Addressing Policy Gaps in Transportation', *Nature Communications* (Nature Publishing Group), 11(1), p. 4570, DOI: 10.1038/s41467-020-18402-y.

Grey, S. and R. Patel (2015) 'Food Sovereignty as Decolonization: Some Contributions from Indigenous Movements to Food System and Development Politics', *Agriculture and Human Values*, 32(3), pp. 431–444, DOI: 10.1007/s10460-014-9548-9.

Gudynas, E. (2018) 'Extractivisms', in R. Munck and R. Delgado Wise (eds.) *Reframing Latin American Development* (New York: Routledge Critical Development Studies), pp. 61–76.

Gudynas, E. (2014) *Derechos de La Naturaleza Ética Biocéntrica y Políticas Ambientales*, Primera edición peruana (Lima: Programa Democracia y Transformación Global).

Gundermann K., H. (2004) 'Inicios de Siglo En San Pedro de Atacama: Procesos, Actores e Imaginarios En Una Localidad Andina', *Chungará: Revista de Antropología Chilena*, 36(1), pp. 221–239, DOI: 10.4067/S0717-73562004000100007.

Gutiérrez J.S., J.N. Moore, J.P. Donnelly, et al. (2022) 'Climate change and lithium mining influence flamingo abundance in the Lithium Triangle', *Proceedings of the Royal Society B: Biological Sciences*, 289(1970), pp. 1–11, DOI: 10.1098/rspb.2021.2388.

Harper, G., R. Sommerville, E. Kendrick, L. Driscoll, P. Slater, R. Stolkin, A. Walton, P. Christensen, O. Heidrich, S. Lambert, A. Abbott, K. Ryder, L. Gaines and P. Anderson (2019) 'Recycling Lithium-Ion Batteries from Electric Vehicles', No. 7781, *Nature* (Nature Publishing Group), 575(7781), pp. 75–86, DOI: 10.1038/s41586-019-1682-5.

Hecht, G. (2012) *Being Nuclear* (Cambridge, Mass: The MIT Press).

Hernando-Arrese, M. and M. Tironi (2019) 'Worlding Hydropower: River Realities in the Chilean Patagonia', *Tapuya: Latin American Science, Technology and Society*, 2(1), pp. 295–309, DOI: 10.1080/25729861.2019.1675955.

Herrera, I. (2019) 'De la vinificación a la etnomercancía. Proceso de conversión de actividades agrarias en propuesta turística en Toconao, Norte de Chile', *Antropologías del Sur*, 6(12), pp. 283–305, DOI: 10.25074/rantros.v6i12.1157.

Hervé, D. (2015) *Justicia Ambiental y Recursos Naturales* (Santiago: Ediciones Universitarias de Valparaíso).

Heubl, B. (2019) *Lithium Firms Depleting Vital Water Supplies in Chile, Analysis Suggests*, (Stevenage: E&T Engineering and Teachnology) https://eandt.theiet.org/content/articles/2019/08/lithium-firms-are-depleting-vital-water-supplies-in-chile-according-to-et-analysis (accessed on 22 September 2019).

Hitchcock Auciello, B. (2020) 'Indigenous Communities in Chile Raise Concerns about Public Health Risks Posed by Mining Operations During the COVID-19 Pandemic', *Earthworks*, 28 July, https://www.earthworks.org/blog/indigenous-communities-in-chile-raise-concerns-about-public-health-risks-posed-by-mining-operations-during-the-covid-19-pandemic/ (accessed on 18 January 2021).

Hommes, L., R. Boelens, S. Bleeker, D. Stoltenborg, B. Duarte-Abadía and J. Vos (2019) 'Water Governmentalities: The Shaping of Hydrosocial Territories, Water Transfers and Rural–Urban Subjects in Latin America', *Environment and Planning E: Nature and Space*, p. 2514848619886255, DOI: 10.1177/2514848619886255.

Hoogesteger, J. and A. Verzijl (2015) 'Grassroots Scalar Politics: Insights from Peasant Water Struggles in the Ecuadorian and Peruvian Andes', *Geoforum*, 62, pp. 13–23, DOI: 10.1016/j.geoforum.2015.03.013.

International Rights of Nature Tribunal (2020) 'Launch of the Verdict, 5th International Rights of Nature Tribunal' (Santiago: Global Alliance for the Rights of Nature), https://www.garn.org/press-release-verdict-5th-international-rights-of-nature-tribunal-chile/ (accessed on 29 November 2022).

IPBES (Intergovernmental Science-Policy Platform on Biodiversity and Ecosystem Services) (2019) *Global Assessment Report on Biodiversity and Ecosystem Services of the Intergovernmental Science-Policy Platform on Biodiversity and Ecosystem Services* (Bonn: IPBES secretariat), DOI: 10.5281/zenodo.5517154.

Jasanoff, S. and S.-H. Kim (eds.) (2015) *Dreamscapes of Modernity* (Chicago: University of Chicago).

Jegathesan, M. (2021) 'Black Feminist Plots before the Plantationocene and Anthropology's 'Regional Closets'', *Feminist Anthropology*, 2(1), pp. 78–93, DOI: 10.1002/fea2.12037.

Jerez, B., I. Garcés and R. Torres (2021) 'Lithium Extractivism and Water Injustices in the Salar de Atacama, Chile: the Colonial Shadow of Green Electromobility', *Political Geography*, 87, DOI: 10.1016/j.polgeo.2021.102382.

Jerez Henríquez, B. (2018) *Impacto Socioambiental de La Extracción de Litio En Las Cuencas de Los Salares Altoandinos Del Cono Sur* (Santiago: Observatorio de Conflictos Mineros de América Latina, OCMAL).

Johnson, O.E.A., A. Zalik, C.S. Mollett, F. Sultana, E. Havice, T. Osborne, G. Valdivia, F. Lu and E. Billo (2021) 'Extraction, Entanglements, and (Im)Materialities: Reflections on the Methods and Methodologies of Natural Resource Industries Fieldwork', *Environment and Planning E: Nature and Space*, 4(2), pp. 383–428, DOI: 10.1177/2514848620907470.

Lawrence, R. and R. Kløcker Larsen (2017) 'The Politics of Planning: Assessing the Impacts of Mining on Sami Lands', *Third World Quarterly*, 38(5), pp. 1164–1180.

Le Billon, P. and N. Middeldorp (2021) 'Empowerment or Imposition?: Extractive Violence, Indigenous Peoples, and the Paradox of Prior Consultation', in J. Shapiro and J.-A. McNeish (eds.) *Our Extractive Age: Expressions of Violence and Resistance* (London: Routledge).

Li, F. (2015) *Unearthing Conflict* (Durham: Duke University Press).

Lins Ribeiro, G. (1994) *Transnational Capitalism and Hydropolitics in Argentina* (Gainesville: University of Florida Press).

Liu, W., D.B. Agusdinata and S.W. Myint (2019) 'Spatiotemporal Patterns of Lithium Mining and Environmental Degradation in the Atacama Salt Flat, Chile', *International Journal of Applied Earth Observation and Geoinformation*, 80, pp. 145–156, DOI: 10.1016/j.jag.2019.04.016.

Marambio-Alfaro, Y., G. Álvarez, M.C. Araya and A.E. Serrano (2017) *The Salt Flats Fighter: Agonistic Survival of Liolaemus Fabiani in the Salar de Atacama*, No. e2891v1 (PeerJ Inc.), DOI: 10.7287/peerj.preprints.2891v1.

Marazuela M.A., E. Vázquez-Suñé, C. Ayora, et al. (2019) 'Hydrodynamics of salt flat basins: The Salar de Atacama example', *Science of The Total Environment*, 651, pp. 668–683, DOI: 10.1016/j.scitotenv.2018.09.190.

Marx, P. (2022) *Road to Nowhere: What Silicon Valley Gets Wrong about the Future of Transportation* (London, Brooklyn: Verso).

Matteucci, S. (2012) 'Ecorregión Puna', in J. Morello, S.D. Matteucci, A. Rodriguez, and M. Silvia (eds.) *Ecorregiones y Complejos Ecosistémicos Argentinos* (Orientación Gráfica Editora S.R.L.), pp. 87–127.

McKittrick, K. (2013) 'Plantation Futures', *Small Axe*, 17(3), pp. 1–15.

Mendez, M., M. Prieto and M. Godoy (2020) 'Production of Subterranean Resources in the Atacama Desert: 19th and Early 20th Century Mining/Water Extraction in The Taltal District, Northern Chile', *Political Geography*, 81, p. 102194, DOI: 10.1016/j.polgeo.2020.102194.

Ministerio de Obras Públicas, Dirección General de Aguas (2018) Resolución 13: Declara Como Zona de Prohibición Para Nuevas Explotaciones de Aguas Subterráneas en el Sector Hidrogeológico de Aprovechamiento Común Denominado C2 de la Cuenca del Salar de Atacama, Región de Antofagasta, August (Santiago: Gobierno de Chile), https://www.leychile.cl/Navegar?idNorma=1121804&idVersion=2018-08-16 (accessed on 7 November 2022).

Ministerio de Obras Públicas, Dirección General de Aguas (2017) Resolución 3: Declara el Agotamiento de la Cuenca del Río Vilama y sus afluentes, Provincia de El Loa, Región de Antofagasta, June (Santiago: Gobierno de Chile), https://www.leychile.cl/Navegar?idNorma=1103421 (accessed on 7 November 2022).

Ministerio de Obras Públicas, Dirección General de Aguas (2016) Resolución 44: Declara el Agotamiento de Cuenca del Río San Pedro y Sus Efluentes, Provincia de El Loa, Región de Antofagasta, July (Santiago: Gobierno de Chile), https://www.leychile.cl/Navegar?idNorma=1092006 (accessed on 7 November 2022).

Mitchell, T. (2011) *Carbon Democracy* (New York: Verso).

Morales Morgado, H. (2013) 'Génesis, Formación y Desarrollo Del Movimiento Atacameño (Norte de Chile)', *Estudios Atacameños*, 1, pp. 110–128, DOI: 10.4067/S0718-10432014000300007.

Mulvaney, D., R.M. Richards, M.D. Bazilian, E. Hensley, G. Clough and S. Sridhar (2021) 'Progress towards a Circular Economy in Materials to Decarbonize Electricity and Mobility', *Renewable and Sustainable Energy Reviews*, 137, p. 110604, DOI: 10.1016/j.rser.2020.110604.

Munk L.A., D.F. Boutt, B.J. Moran, et al. (2021) 'Hydrogeologic and Geochemical Distinctions in Freshwater-Brine Systems of an Andean Salar', *Geochemistry, Geophysics, Geosystems*, 22(3), DOI: 10.1029/2020GC009345.

Murphy, M. (2017) 'Alterlife and Decolonial Chemical Relations', *Cultural Anthropology*, 32(4), pp. 494–503, DOI: 10.14506/ca32.4.02.

Nacif, F. (2015) 'El Litio En Argentina: De Insumo Crítico a Commodity Minero', in *El ABC Del Litio Sudaméricano* (Quilmes: Universidad Nacional de Quilmes Editorial), pp. 219–92.

Narins, T.P. (2017) 'The Battery Business: Lithium Availability and the Growth of the Global Electric Car Industry', *The Extractive Industries and Society*, 4(2), pp. 321–328, DOI: 10.1016/j.exis.2017.01.013.

Neville, K.J. and G. Coulthard (2019) 'Transformative Water Relations: Indigenous Interventions in Global Political Economies', *Global Environmental Politics*, 19(3), pp. 1–15.

Newell, P. and D. Mulvaney (2013) 'The Political Economy of the 'Just Transition'', *The Geographical Journal*, 179(2), pp. 132–140, DOI: 10.1111/geoj.12008.

Nixon, R. (2011) *Slow Violence and the Environmentalism of the Poor* (Cambridge: Harvard University Press).

OPSAL (Observatorio Plurinacional de Salares Andinos) (2021) 'OPSAL invitó a definir cómo avanzar en protección de salares y humedales andinos en el nuevo contexto constituyente—Salares Andinos', *Salares Andinos*, 14 July, https://salares.org/2021/07/14/opsal-invito-a-definir-como-avanzar-en-proteccion-de-salares-y-humedales-andinos-en-el-nuevo-contexto-constituyente (accessed on 25 October 2021).

OPSAL (2020a) 'Declaración por el Salar de Atacama y los Humedales Altoandinos de Chile frente al Avance del Extractivismo Minero', *Observatorio Plurinacional de Salares Andinos*, 26 August, https://observatoriosalares.wordpress.com/2020/08/26/declaracion-por-el-salar-de-atacama-y-los-humedales-altoandinos-de-chile-frente-al-avance-del-extractivismo-minero/ (accessed on 8 September 2020).

OPSAL (2020b) 'Minera Escondida / BHP Billiton, un 'buen vecino' en el Salar de Atacama', *Observatorio Plurinacional de Salares Andinos*, 14 January, https://observatoriosalares.wordpress.com/2020/01/14/minera-escondida-bhp-billiton-un-buen-vecino-en-el-salar-de-atacama/ (accessed on 8 September 2020).

Peet, R., P. Robbins and M. Watts (eds.) (2011) *Global Political Ecology* (London and New York: Routledge).

Perreault, T. (2020) 'Bolivia's High Stakes Lithium Gamble', *NACLA Report on the Americas*, 52, pp. 165–172, DOI: 10.1080/10714839.2020.1768739.

Peterson St-Laurent, G.P. and P. Le Billon (2015) 'Staking claims and shaking hands: Impact and benefit agreements as a technology of government in the mining sector', *The Extractive Industries and Society*, 2(3), pp. 590–602.

Prieto, M. (2016) 'Practicing Costumbres and the Decommodification of Nature: the Chilean Water Markets and the Atacameño People', *Geoforum*, 77, pp. 28–39.

Prieto, M. (2015a) 'Privatizing Water in the Chilean Andes: the Case of Las Vegas de Chiu-Chiu', *Mountain Research and Development*, 35(3), pp. 220–229.

Prieto, M. (2015b) 'La Ecología (a)Política Del Modelo de Aguas Chileno', in B. Bustos-Gallardo, M. Prieto and J. Barton (eds.) *Ecología Política En Chile* (Santiago: Editorial Universitaria), pp. 143–164.

Riofrancos, T. (2022) 'The Security–Sustainability Nexus: Lithium Onshoring in the Global North', *Global Environmental Politics*, pp. 1–22, DOI: 10.1162/glep_a_00668.

Riofrancos, T. (2019) 'What Green Costs', *Logic Magazine*, https://logicmag.io/nature/what-green-costs/ (accessed on 20 January 2020).

Riofrancos, T. (2017) 'Scaling Democracy: Participation and Resource Extraction in Latin America', *Perspectives on Politics*, 15(3), pp. 678–696, DOI: 10.1017/S1537592717000901.

Saldivia Maldonado, Z. (2003) *La Visión de La Naturaleza En Tres Científicos Del Siglo XIX En Chile: Gay, Domeyko y Philippi.* (Santiago, Chile: Universidad de Santiago de Chile).

Sanchez-Lopez, M.D. (2019) 'From a White Desert to the Largest World Deposit of Lithium: Symbolic Meanings and Materialities of the Uyuni Salt Flat in Bolivia', Antipode, 51(4), DOI: 10.1111/anti.12539.

Sanderson, H. (2022) *Volt Rush: the Winners and Losers in the Race to Go Green* (London: Oneworld Publications).

Secretariat of the Convention on Biological Diversity (2011) *The Tkarihwaié: RI Code of Ethical Conduct to Ensure Respect for the Cultural and Intellectual Heritage of*

Indigenous and Local Communities (Montreal: Secretariat of the Convention on Biological Diversity).

Secretariat of the Convention on Biological Diversity (2004) *Akwé: Kon Voluntary Guidelines for the Conduct of Cultural, Environmental and Social Impact Assessment* (Montreal: Secretariat of the Convention on Biological Diversity).

Sepúlveda Rivera, I., R. Molina Otárola, M. del M. Delgado-Serrano and J.E. Guerrero Ginel (2015) 'Aguas, Riego y Cultivos: Cambios y Permanencias en los Ayllus de San Pedro de Atacama', *Estudios Atacameños*, 51, pp. 185–206, DOI: 10.4067/S0718-10432015000200012.

Sherwood, D. (2021) 'Inside Lithium Giant SQM's Struggle to Win over Indigenous Communities in Chile's Atacama', *Reuters*, 15 January, https://www.reuters.com/article/us-chile-lithium-sqm-focus-idUSKBN29K1DB (accessed on 18 January 2021).

Sherwood, D. (2020a) 'Chilean Regulators Scrap Lithium Miner SQM's Environmental Plan', *Reuters*, 1 August, https://uk.reuters.com/article/us-chile-lithium-sqm-idUKKBN24X3Q6 (accessed on 8 September 2020).

Sherwood, D. (2020b) 'Indigenous Groups in Chile's Atacama Push to Shut down Top Lithium Miner SQM', *Reuters*, 14 August, https://www.reuters.com/article/us-chile-lithium-sqm-idUSKCN25A2PB (accessed on 19 August 2020).

Standridge, C.R. and L. Corneal (2014) *Remanufacturing, Repurposing, and Recycling of Post-Vehicle-Application Lithium-Ion Batteries*, No. 12–20 (San José: Mineta National Transit Research Consortium), https://transweb.sjsu.edu/sites/default/files/1137-post-vehicle-Li-Ion-recycling.pdf (accessed on 7 November 2022).

Sultana, F. (2021) 'Progress Report in Political Ecology II: Conjunctures, Crises, and Critical Publics', *Progress in Human Geography*, p. 03091325211028665, DOI: 10.1177/03091325211028665.

Sultana, F. (2020) 'Political Ecology 1: From Margins to Center', *Progress in Human Geography*, p. 0309132520936751, DOI: 10.1177/0309132520936751.

Svampa, M. (2013) 'Consenso de Los Commodities y Lenguajes de Valorización En América Latina', *Nueva Sociedad*, 244.

Swyngedouw, E. (2004) *Social Power and the Urbanization of Water* (Oxford: Oxford University Press).

SQM (Sociedad Química y Minera de Chile) (2021) *Reporte de Sostenibilidad* (Santiago: SQM) https://www.sqm.com/wp-content/uploads/2022/05/reporte-de-sostenibilidad-2021-v15_compressed.pdf (accessed on 7 November 2022).

Tironi, M. and J. Barandiarán (2014) 'Neoliberalism as Political Technology: Expertise, Energy, and Democracy in Chile', in E. Medina, I. da C. Marques and C. Holmes (eds.) *Beyond Imported Magic: Essays on Science, Technology, and Society in Latin America* (MIT Press), pp. 305–330.

Toscano, A. (2018) 'Antiphysis/Antipraxis: Universal Exhaustion and the Tragedy of Materiality', *Mediations*, 31(2), pp. 125–144, http://mediationsjournal.org/articles/antiphysis-antipraxis (accessed on 7 November 2022).

Turner, J.M. (2015) 'Following the Pb: an Envirotechnical Approach to Lead-Acid Batteries in the United States', *Environmental History*, 20(1), pp. 29–56, DOI: 10.1093/envhis/emu128.

UNESCO (2005) *The Precautionary Principle* (Paris: UNESCO, World Commission on the Ethics of Scientific Knowledge and Technology), https://unesdoc.unesco.org/ark:/48223/pf0000139578 (accessed on 7 November 2022).

UNESCO (1998) *San Pedro de Atacama*, (Paris: UNESCO, World Heritage Centre) https://whc.unesco.org/en/tentativelists/1191/ (accessed on 25 October 2021).

USGS (U.S. Geological Survey) (2021) 'Lithium', *Mineral Commodity Summaries*, https://pubs.usgs.gov/periodicals/mcs2021/mcs2021-lithium.pdf,(WashingtonD.C.:USGS) (accessed on 7 November 2022).

Voskoboynik, D.M. and D. Andreucci (2021) 'Greening Extractivism: Environmental Discourses and Resource Governance in the 'Lithium Triangle'', *Environment and Planning E: Nature and Space*, DOI: 10.1177/25148486211006345.

Voyles, T.B. (2015) *Wastelanding: Legacies of Uranium Mining in Navajo Country* (Minneapolis: University of Minnesota Press).

Wang, G., S. Mang, H. Cai, S. Liu, Z.-Q. Zhang, L. Wang and J. Innes (2016) 'Integrated Watershed Management: Evolution, Development and Emerging Trends', *Journal of Forestry Research*, 27, DOI: 10.1007/s11676-016-0293-3.

Whyte, K.P. (2013) 'On the Role of Traditional Ecological Knowledge as a Collaborative Concept: a Philosophical Study', *Ecological Processes*, 2(7), DOI: 10.1186/2192-1709-2-7.

Wit, M.M. de (2021) 'What Grows from a Pandemic? Toward an Abolitionist Agroecology', *The Journal of Peasant Studies*, 48(1), pp. 99–136, DOI: 10.1080/03066150.2020.1854741.

Wynter, S. (1971) 'Novel and History, Plot and Plantation', *Savacou*, 5, pp. 95–102.

Xiong, S., J. Ji and X. Ma (2020) 'Environmental and Economic Evaluation of Remanufacturing Lithium-Ion Batteries from Electric Vehicles', *Waste Management*, 102, pp. 579–586, DOI: 10.1016/j.wasman.2019.11.013.

Yáñez, N. and R. Molina (eds.) (2011) *Las Aguas Indígenas En Chile* (Santiago: LOM Ediciones), http://www.digitaliapublishing.com/a/18267/las-aguas-indigenas-en-chile (accessed on 30 September 2019).

CHAPTER 11

Green Masquerade: Neo-liberalism, Extractive Renewable Energy Transitions, and the 'Good' Anthropocene in South Africa

Michelle Pressend

Abstract

This chapter examines the 'green' energy developments apparent in the South African government's energy policy and renewable energy programme. In 2011, the South African government introduced the Renewable Energy Independent Power Producer Procurement Programme as a new policy imperative for electricity generation from renewable energy sources through public–private partnerships. The Programme has been hailed for attracting a huge amount of direct foreign investment in climate mitigation in South Africa. This chapter analyses the material nature of the Programme and the public–private partnership investment conditions, based on a case study of the Tsitsikamma Community Wind Farm in the Eastern Cape in South Africa, an electricity generation project initiated prior to the introduction of the Independent Power Producer renewable energy programme on community reclaimed land. This community was a willing partner in the wind energy investment partnership. Despite their inclusion in this techno-capitalist development project, however, the material well-being of members of this community remains unchanged, as does the degraded state of the commercial agricultural land involved. The chapter argues that the capitalist neo-liberal logic of alternative 'green' energy interventions in investment models such as this renewable energy programme is embedded in the machinations of the extractivist productivist model through 'new' forms of financialisaton for capital accumulation.

> Coal and the steam engine did not determine the story, and besides the dates are all wrong [...] One must surely tell of the networks of sugar, precious metals, [...] indigenous genocides, and slavery, with their labour innovations and relocations and recompositions of critters and things sweeping up both human and nonhuman worker of all kinds. The infectious industrial revolution of England mattered hugely, but it is only one player in planet-transforming, historically

 | DOI:10.1163/9789004686182_012

> situated, new enough, worlding relations. The relocation of peoples, microbes, plants, and animals; the leveling of vast forests; and the violent mining of metals preceded the steam engine.
>
> HARAWAY, 2016, 51–52

∵

1 Introduction[1]

The term Anthropocene[2] suggests that all humans are geological agents insofar as their use of fossil fuels causes climate change, and that they have made indelible impacts on the planet's stratigraphic record. The dominant scientific narratives suggest the onset of this period coincides with the invention of the steam engine in 1784. But as Donna Haraway (2016, 51) implies, 'The relocation of peoples, microbes, plants, and animals; the levelling of vast forests; and the violent mining of metals preceded the steam engine [...]' and were underway long before the extraction of coal began. According to Merchant (1980), in the fifteenth and sixteenth centuries in Europe the understanding of humans' relationship with the Earth changed in nature from one of a holistic, organic cosmos to a mechanistic and exploitative approach driven by ideals motivated by ideas of human 'progress'. Structural violence and an extractive relationship disentangled humans and the non-human worlds. The thinking and power of scientific and Cartesian revolutions separated the domain of human relationships in the web of life into dualisms embedded in concepts such as 'Civilisation and Savage' and 'Society and Nature' (Moore, 2014; 2015b; 2016; 2017; Patel and Moore, 2020). Within this Cartesian dualistic thinking, elements of Western European civilisation assumed the position of 'masters and processers of nature' (Descartes in Moore, 2014, 288). Conquest, productivity, and plunder became common sense and commonplace (Patel and Moore, 2020). Cartesian dualism shaped emergent knowledge regimes and 'the modern logics of power as well as thought' (Patel and Moore, 2020, 63).

1 This chapter is based on my PhD research.

2 The term Anthropocene was popularized by Paul Crutzen and Eugene Stoermer and expresses the capacity of the human species to transform planetary elements and how this has reached an unprecedented scale, to the extent that human beings 'have collectively become the "geological agent" capable of changing the global climate through our emissions' (Jonsson, 2015, 55).

Tracing backwards in time beyond the invention of the steam engine traces older roots of human-mediated geological impacts. Caroline Merchant (1980) and Jason Moore (2002) show how agrarian land use strategies in medieval Europe can be linked to the planetary transformation that led to the 'little ice age', a global climatic cooling. Koch et al. assert that the massive extent of indigenous genocide that took place upon the arrival of Europeans in the Americas led to a decline in atmospheric carbon dioxide levels and estimate that '55 million indigenous people died following the European conquest of the Americas beginning in 1492', leading to 'the abandonment and secondary succession of 56 million hectares of land' (Koch et al., 2019, 24). The genocide of indigenous people had far-reaching ecological consequences for diversity, abundance, and stability and for their way of life (Cronon 1983).

Koch et al. (2019) suggest that land use changes in the sixteenth century significantly increased carbon stored in the land, resulting in cooling phenomena. Their research concludes that the Columbian exchange[3] contributed to earth system change before the industrial revolution did so (Koch et al., 2019, 30).

Moore (2015b) states that the Anthropocene discourse is embedded in the well-worn dualism that has separated human relations from the web of life in binary conceptions such as 'Civilisation and Savage' and 'Society and Nature'. Patel and Moore (2020) capitalise the *S* and the N of society and nature to reflect the abstractions that both describe the world and make it. Moore (2015b, 3) describes how ontologically, a dualist frame organises 'Nature' as something to be 'coded [and] quantified [...] to serve economic growth, social development, or some other higher good'. Patel and Moore (2020) refer to these abstractions or generalisations as statements of ontology and epistemology. They are invisible, and their violence is hidden in the dualisms embedded in an ontology of separation, extraction, and domination (Mignolo, 2019; Haraway, 2016; French et al., 2020).

Moving beyond the sources of the pollutants of the Anthropocene, Moore (2015a, 2) states, '[f]rom this perspective, the problem is not the "Age of Humans" but the "Age of Capital". Not Anthropocene, but *Capitalocene*'. Further declaring that Anthropocene describes 'what' is the cause of global warming but does not describe 'how' it came about: capitalism as world-ecology

3 Koch et al. (2019) state that 'The Great Dying of the Indigenous Peoples of the Americas resulted in a human-driven global impact on the Earth System in the two centuries prior to the industrial revolution' (p. 13), and that ecocide, genocide and diseases 'led to the abandonment of enough cleared land in the Americas that the resulting terrestrial carbon uptake had a detectable impact on both atmospheric CO_2 and global surface air temperatures in the two centuries prior to the Industrial Revolution' (p. 30).

entwined with power, profit and life as a way of 'putting the whole of nature to work for capital' (Moore, 2015a, 3), and this applies to both human and non-human nature. This required the mastery of both nature and human nature, whereby women and indigenous and 'black' people and 'people of colour' were excluded from humanity and society, 'designated *only partly* Human' (Moore, 2016, 91). Thus, appropriating the unpaid work of uncommodified human and non-human natures territorially and in symbolic forms into labour productivity and commodity production is underpinned by 'cheapness' and profit accumulation (Moore 2014; 2015a; 2015b; 2016; Patel and Moore, 2020).

In the Anthropocene discourse, 'man' as the 'good Anthropocene'[4] may be—based on post-nature, utilitarian, and eco-modernist ideas of high-technology advancements—considered to have 'good' intentions in terms of the human mastery necessary to address the climate crisis. Some of the chief ideas of the 'good' Anthropocene discourse relevant to the present chapter are 1) economic growth and the expansion of consumer culture are important so that everyone can be affluent, 2) major scientific and technological fixes and inventions, including engineering climate and life, will be needed, and 3) the need to embrace a scientific planetary managerial mindset with regard to the climate crisis through mitigation and adaptation approaches (Crist, 2016, 15). As Crist puts it (2016, 16), 'And while history might just see the human enterprise prevail after overcoming or containing its self-imperiling effects, the course toward world domination should not (or cannot) be stopped: history will keep moving in that direction, with the human enterprise eventually journeying into outer space, mining other planets [...]'. Furthermore, she stresses, 'Anthropocene supporters expect (or hope) that this forward movement will keep materialising variants of progress such as green energy [and] economic development for all [...]' (Crist, 2016, 17). All other relationships and values, including ecological, spiritual, cultural, or aesthetic, are disregarded (Crist, 2016; Szeman and Wentzel, 2021). This notion of the Anthropocene discourse, as Crist (2016, 25) notes, offers 'a techno-scientific pitch for its rationalization [...]'. It fails to make space for alternative framings of humanity and the place of humans and their actions in the web of life (Crist, 2016). This discourse overlooks modernity's social relations and 'how new connections between

4 Stengers (2015) problematises the Anthropocene discourse that makes humans the responsible agent and geological force the cause of climate disorder. She questions current responses to climate change, particularly those in which humanity considers how it might use its powers to master a 'good' Anthropocene. Bonneuil and Fressoz (2016, 87) raise similar concerns that human mastery might be articulated as the 'good' Anthropocene to address climate change.

human nature, global power and production, and the web of life' work (Moore, 2015b, 25).

In South Africa, the domestic manifestation of the 'good' Anthropocene discourse in 'green' energy developments is apparent in the South African government's energy policy and renewable energy programme. In 2011, the government released the country's electricity plan, the Integrated Resource Plan for Electricity (IRP) 2010–30 (Department of Energy, 2011), which announced the introduction of renewable energy into the country's energy mix with the goal of increasing renewable energy capacity to 17,800 gigawatts by 2030. The policy also announced the Renewable Energy Independent Power Producer Procurement Programme (REI4P), a new policy imperative for electricity generation from renewable energy sources. This was a significant undertaking and political decision given that the country's reliance on cheap and abundant supplies of coal-derived electric power is at the heart of South Africa's political, social and economic history (McDonald, 2009). Implementing the REI4P was also a demonstration of the country's commitment to climate change mitigation. According to the government the REI4P is intended to contribute to job creation, social upliftment and a broadening of economic ownership (Department of Energy et al., 2016). The introduction of independent power producers (IPPs) would expand electricity markets through the introduction of a competitive bidding process whereby such producers would obtain 20-year contracts to sell electricity to Eskom (South Africa's electricity utility) as the single buyer. The high-technology, large-scale wind and solar infrastructure of the REI4P is organised as a public–private partnership (PPP).

This chapter analyses the material nature of the REI4P and the public–private partnership investment conditions based on a case study of the Tsitsikamma Community Wind Farm (TCWF) in the Eastern Cape. It argues that the capitalist neo-liberal[5] logic of alternative 'green' energy interventions in investment models such as the REI4P is embedded in the machinations of the extractivist productivist model through 'new' forms financialisaton for capital accumulation. The first section provides a literature review and theoretical underpinnings critical of the Anthropocene discourse. The purpose of this literature review is to show scholarly work on the emerging tensions of the capitalist neo-liberal logic in renewable energy projects, particularly wind energy developments in Mexico, where several large-scale wind farms have been implemented. The second section provides the background and context

5 Capital accumulation in late-stage capitalism predominately occurs through neo-liberal strategies of capitalisation, financialisaton and trade liberalisation, facilitated by the mechanism of international investment rules (Harvey, 2004; Moore, 2015b).

of the TCWF. It situates the location of the TCWF and focuses on the financing of this capital-intensive project. The third section discusses controversies regarding the strategy of favouring investment and the de-risking of the REI4P model. The chapter demonstrates several contradictions and paradoxes with regard to those institutional and financial energy-sector actors that claim to be fostering economic growth and development and propose technoscientific fixes to address the climate crisis and improve community well-being.

2 Conceptual Inspirations and Literature Review

Over the last decade, the concept of the Anthropocene has become ubiquitous across academic disciplines, civil society organisations, multilateral institutions, and policymaking, with wide-ranging global acceptance that 'we' are living in the 'Age of Man' (Moore, 2015a). Crist (2016, 15) suggests that the 'advocacy and elaboration of rationales favoring the term in scientific, environmental, popular writings, and other media [...] communicate a cohesive though not entirely homogeneous set of ideas'. Baskin (2015, 20) argues these ideas and way of thinking about global warming are heavily reliant on 'planetary management and technophilia' and the favouring of geoengineering and other forms of 'green' technology. The Anthropocene discourse places fossil fuel energy at the heart of global warming (Steffen et al., 2007; Chakrabarty, 2009; Morton, 2013; Bonneuil and Fressoz, 2016). But as Patel and Moore (2020, 46) put it,

> We are living with the consequences of a civilization built on cheap energy, a reality verified by climate change. The global political economy of cheap fuel has not only wrought immense human suffering in its extraction but also, of course, remade planetary ecology.

Patel and Moore (2020, 22) refer to 'cheapness' as a strategy that is not only about price, but is also 'a practice, a violence that exploits human and animal, botanical and geological work with little or no compensation'.

The present chapter is inspired by Moore's conceptual framing of world-ecology. World-ecology pays attention to 'how relations of power, production, and reproduction work through the web of life' (Patel and Moore, 2020, 38). This framing is not a theory but rather a perspective and method. As Moore explains:

> World-ecology is a method of bounding and bundling the human/extra-human/web of life relations—a manifold and multi-layered relation that encompasses everything from the micro-biome to the biosphere. And it is a framework for theorizing manifold forms of the human experience past, present, and future.
>
> MOORE, 2015b, 28

The basis of capital accumulation by appropriation is unpaid work that arises out of the rate of exploitation, but it 'depends upon the fruits of appropriation derived from Cheap Natures, understood primarily as the "Four Cheaps" of labour-power, food, energy, and raw materials' (Moore, 2015a, 10). Moore's use of appropriation offers a useful context for the study that differs slightly from that of Marx (1818–83) that deployed appropriation with the exploitation of wage-labour. Moore (2015a, 10) explains that appropriation and accumulation is based on 'those extra-economic processes that identify, secure, and channel unpaid work outside the commodity system into the circuit of capital'. Patel and Moore (2017) expand this to 'seven cheap things': nature, money, work, care, food, energy, and lives. Capitalism as world-ecology entwined with power, profit, and life relates to values of domination and appropriation both of humans—including women, slaves, and indigenous and black/brown peoples—and of extra-human nature such as forests, soils or rivers for capital accumulation (Moore, 2014; 2015a; 2015b; 2016). Thus, appropriating the unpaid work of uncommodified human and non-human natures territorially and in symbolic forms into labour productivity and commodity production is underpinned by 'cheapness' and profit accumulation (Moore, 2014; 2015a; 2015b; 2016; Patel and Moore, 2020).

Globally, the fixation on 'green' economic growth and notions of the 'good' Anthropocene regard renewable energy technologies as a lucrative investment opportunity that will stimulate job creation and improve the well-being of people and the planet, particularly in 'developing' countries (International Energy Agency, 2017; UNEP, 2017; UNDP, 2016). I couch the term 'good' Anthropocene as synonymous with green growth (a.k.a. green capitalism) and draw attention to the burgeoning 'green' neo-liberal agenda in renewable energy transitions through a world-ecology approach. A closer interrogation of the renewable energy policies and processes that insert a neo-liberal agenda under the mantle of climate mitigation is critical to illuminating novel forms of capital accumulation in the present-day world order (Vargas,2020; Dunlap, 2017; 2021; Howe, 2011; 2015; 2019; Gabor, 2021).

A considerable literature exists on the neo-colonialism and neo-liberal consequences of renewable energy transitions in Mexico, where the isthmus of Tehuantepec in Oaxaca has become valued for its wind (Howe, 2011; 2015; Howe and Boyer, 2016; Vargas, 2020; Dunlap, 2017; 2021; Ramirez and Böhm, 2021). Howe's (2011) study of renewable energy transitions shows that local communities have been alienated in a process that echoes economic coloniality, particularly because of investments by Spanish corporations reminiscent of the actions of earlier Spanish colonisers.

Howe's (2015, 232) analysis of Latin American energy transitions and climate change mitigation raises a fundamental and critical question: 'If energy production continues to prioritize destructive and displacing megaprojects, can governments, energy developers, and communities balance the needs of local populations against the development desires of *neo-liberalismo verde*?' Similar approaches are seen in other parts of the world. For example, wind energy development in Norway affects the indigenous Saami community (Normann, 2020). While ancestral reindeer herding is protected by international law, large-scale wind turbines are dispossessing herders of their pastural lands, a practice the Saami peoples have termed 'green colonialism' (Normann, 2020). Howe (2015, 234) emphasises critical concerns about 'international economic investments that purport to enhance 'sustainable livelihoods' *may be beneficial*, both locally and globally but they must also be understood against a backdrop of enduring economic and political interventions. She stresses that these renewable energy initiatives could have the same impact as colonial and corporate extractivism, which have benefitted 'affluent patrons and regions' under the guise of 'clean development' (Howe 2015, 234).

Existing and planned wind farms in South Africa are not on the scale of wind farms on the isthmus of Tehuantepec in Oaxaca, where one wind park alone contains hundreds of turbines. However, these wind farms have in common that 'their value has been carefully metered in terms of both their profits and their greater ethical possibilities in the global reduction of greenhouse gases' (Howe, 2014, 382). Increasingly, alongside growing interest in renewable wind energy, the use-value of wind and its powers has become a desire for technological management (Howe, 2019). As put by (Howe, 2019, 25) 'while the wind may have always mattered, it has now come to matter in different ways'.

Land and spatial concerns are emerging as one of the key political ambiguities of renewable energy (Burke and Stephens, 2018). Large tracts of land are required to host renewable energy infrastructure and harvest wind and solar energy. But the implications of how renewable energy transitions will affect spatial reconfigurations of social, political and economic processes that co-produce patterns of relations to power and production within nature remain under-considered. Huber and McCarthy (2017) highlight that the spatial and material conditions for the maintenance of fossil capitalism are immense. The shift to renewables 'would involve massive production of space around the globe, at almost every conceivable scale—that is, not just using given static areas of land (and sea) in new ways, but fundamentally remaking economic, geopolitical, and material relationships and configurations in myriad ways' (Huber and McCarthy, 2017, 663). These authors stress that the spatially intensive nature of solar and wind technology 'beyond the subterranean energy regime toward renewables might *elevate* land as the centre of energy struggles' (Huber and McCarthy, 2017, 666).

Most REI4P projects are situated in rural areas of South Africa where there is high solar and/or wind intensity, on farmland appropriated under colonialism and apartheid. McEwan (2017, 3) notes that the REI4P has largely overlooked historical land occupation and land appropriation, writing that 'the discursive erasure of land within public debate about renewable energy is particularly notable given that the South African land question is of great political sensitivity [...]'. The most capital-intensive commercial agricultural land is optimally located for both wind and solar energy generation, making it financially viable for commercial farmers to lease their land out for renewable energy infrastructure. Parenti (2016, 170) reminds us that 'the modern state makes and delivers "nature" through place-based property regimes, its production of infrastructure, and its geographical forms of biopower'. The subset of biopower that Parenti (2016, 171) calls 'geopower' is the 'statecraft and technologies of power that make territory and the biosphere accessible, legible, knowable, and utilizable'.

McEwan (2017, 5) explains that 'IPPs thus need to secure agreements with landowners on transfer of ownership or lease rights for REI4P projects; as a consequence of prevailing land ownership patterns, these agreements serve the interests of commercial (mainly white) landowners'. These renewable energy PPPs create new income generating opportunities on commercial agricultural land.

Baker (2015a, 256) raises concerns that while these PPPs contribute to the diversification of the energy mix, 'their introduction still contributes to an electricity-intensive model [predicted in increased demand], with issues of affordability for low-income households unresolved'. Under the REI4P, all renewable energy is transmitted directly to the central grid and thus does not reach the 30 per cent of people not connected to the grid (Baker, 2015a, 257). Access to and affordability of electricity for marginalised communities are not addressed. This is true in both South Africa and Mexico, renewable energy transition projects generally bypassing access to power for communities situated where these very same renewable energy infrastructures are located. In the case of Mexico, mining companies and other commercial operations are the real beneficiaries of the expansion of energy production, not the people living in those territories where the energy is produced (Howe and Boyer, 2016; Dunlap, 2021). In relation to such renewable energy projects, Boyer (2011, 5) warns that in addition to the carbon statecraft crisis, attention should be paid to the role that states, corporations and communities play in so-called 'sustainable' solutions.

3 Background and Context of the TCWF

3.1 *Situating the Case Study*

The TCWF is situated in a small area called Witkleibos[6] in South Africa's Eastern Cape (Figures 11.1 and 11.2). The Tsitsikamma Mfengu's land claim, which was settled in 1994, is often referred to as a successful land restitution and RE4IP project because it involves reclaimed land (Jannecke, 2006; 2008; McEwan, 2017, 5). Six thousand hectares were reclaimed altogether, including Witkleibos, and three more Tsitsikamma Mfengu community areas, called Snyklip, Doriskraal and Nuweplaas. Some Mfengu community members also live in a settlement called Clarkson, which was historically a Moravian mission station. People that previously lived in Doriskraal presently live in a location called Ekuphumleni (popularly called Guava Juice).

The TCWF is particularly interesting and differs from other renewable energy projects in South Africa in noteworthy ways. The initiator of the wind farm, the late Michael Mcebisi 'Mike' Msizi was born in Witkleibos and lived in exile in Denmark during apartheid. There he became inspired by wind turbines and captivated by the idea that wind power could bring affordable electricity to the Tsitsikamma community and enable it to sell surplus electricity to the central grid. When he returned to South Africa in the mid-1990s, he shared his vision with the Tsitsikamma Mfengu[7] community who had resettled on the land. The first distinction of this wind farm is that the idea for it occurred before the South African government had a formal renewable energy policy in

6 Many community members refer to 'Wittekleibosch', so I use 'Witkleibos' to refer to the area but repeat the 'Wittekleibosch' used by interviewees.

7 I am learning basic Xhosa but have no command of the Xhosa language. Peires (2011) explains that the 'word "Mfengu" derives from a verb, ukumfenguza, which means "wandering around homelessly looking for work"'. Peires uses '*amaMfengu*' to describe the people and '*Mfengu*', without the prefix, as an adjective. Peires points out that 'revisionists tend to prefer "Fingo" to demonstrate their conviction that the term was coined by the British colonist'. In this study, I use the English construction of the terms 'Mfengu' and 'Xhosa'. I use 'Tsitsikamma Mfengu' to refer to the community.

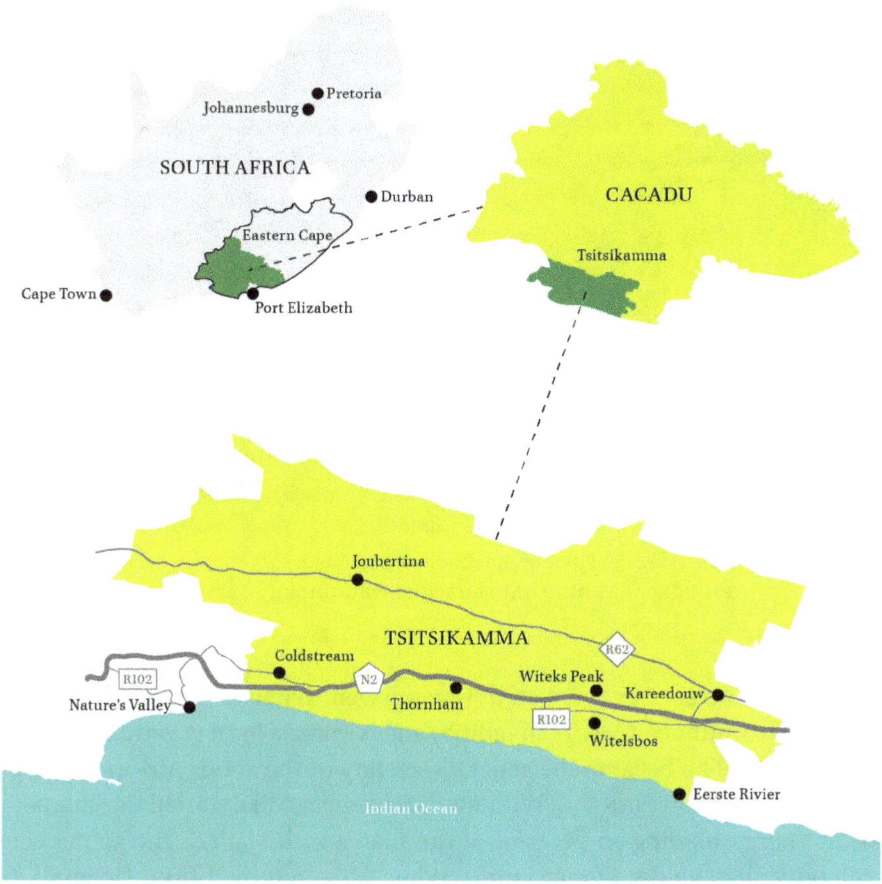

FIGURE 11.1 Map locating the Tsitsikamma geographical area in South Africa
SOURCE: AUTHOR, ADAPTED FROM TSITSIKAMMA TRAVEL

place and was initiated in anticipation that in future it would be possible to sell electricity generated there back to the grid. Secondly, under the Tsitsikamma Development Trust (TDT), the TCWF involved an organised community partnership from the outset, unlike similar projects where arbitrary communities within a 50 km radius might have to forge such a relationship in order to 'benefit' from renewable energy investment projects. Thirdly, the land on which the wind farm was built and operates is communally owned reclaimed land whereas most other projects are built on private commercial farms, which are predominantly white-owned in South Africa.

Mike Msizi was very influential in the community; he was a political exile and worked for the South African Congress of Trade Unions (SATCU) and African

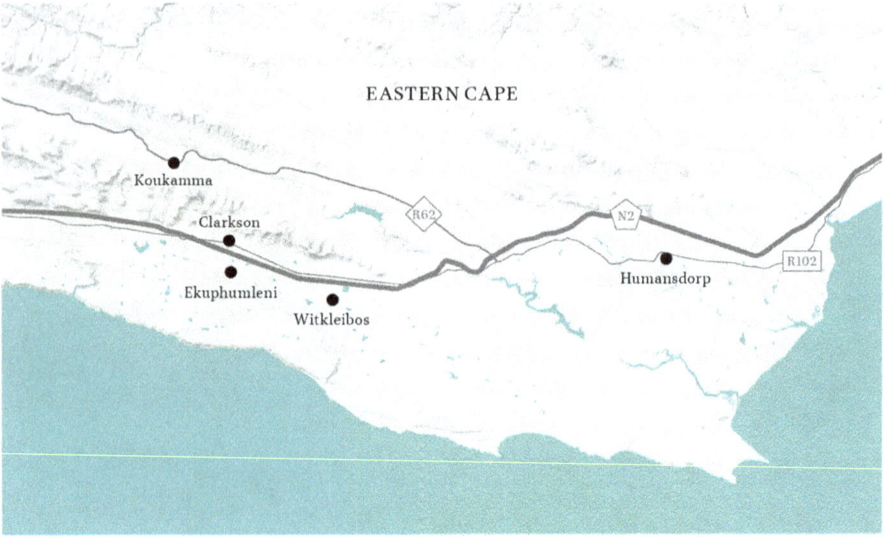

FIGURE 11.2 Physical map of part of the south-eastern Cape
SOURCE: AUTHOR, ADAPTED FROM WEGO.HERE

National Congress (ANC) office in Copenhagen. When he returned to South Africa, he continued to work in politics and became a local government councillor. In 2008 he became the general secretary of the South African National Civic Organisation (SANCO). With Mark Scheepers, Mike started the company Watt Energy, holding 70 per cent of the shares with Mark as the 30 per cent minority shareholder (Young, 2016). When Mike returned from Denmark in the mid-1990s, he pursued the idea and shared his vision of a wind farm with the Tsitsikamma Mfengu, and the community agreed to offer some reclaimed land to host the farm.

Most importantly, Msizi needed to finance the wind farm. Initially it was hoped that the financing could be obtained from Denmark. The Danish Embassy's Development Counsellor paid for a feasibility study (Young, 2016). Young, pointed, out 'in Denmark many wind farms are wholly owned by farmers or co-operatives' (2016, 171). As the Embassy was interested in 'community upliftment' and the land on which the TCWF would be built was community owned, the Danish Embassy's Development Counsellor in 2009 considered funding the project (Young 2016). While the Danes were supportive, uncertainty reigned over the future of renewable energy in South Africa, and there were no guarantees that Eskom would deploy an optimal buy-back policy for the electricity that could be generated by the wind farm. Exxaro, South Africa's second largest coal company, through their 'clean energy' initiative obtained carbon credits. These credits were sold to the Danish oil and gas parastatal Danish Oil and Natural Gas (DONG). Through this transaction with DONG and Exxaro, the Danish Embassy introduced to Mike Msizi the Exxaro representative (Young 2016). Exxaro had an interest in pursuing renewable energy in the future, and the partnership with Mike Msizi and the Tsitsikamma Mfengu community provided it with an opportunity to invest in the wind farm project through its 'clean energy' offshoot Cennergi (discussed in detail below). In addition, Exarro saw the project as a way of assisting the struggling community, including by setting up a school bus service, building a creche and cattle kraal, and employing a range of other initiatives, all as part of its corporate philanthropy measures. Moreover, the REI4P provided the institutional framework and investment parameters necessary to implement renewable energy projects in South Africa. Sadly, 'Mike' Msizi passed away following a car accident in 2012. His 70 per cent share in Watt Energy passed to his wife and son.

My fieldwork in 2016 and 2017 immersed me in the materiality (configuration of the material matter) of relations in the making of the TCWF. I focused on the patterns of material nature of the land (the soil, typography, vegetation among other material elements and relationships to the land) on the wind farm, the stories and narratives gathered in conversations with community members and interviews with the key energy actors involved, including the government and the corporation, and on the material nature of the REI4P as an energy policy. Particular attention is paid in this study to 'silent' actors and voices—those rendered invisible and/or non-credible and subjects of capitalist machinations (de Sousa Santos, 2006); that is, community members and the land. I employed mixed methodologies, using archival research, oral narratives, interviews, photo stories, embedded ethnography (immersive fieldwork and participant observation) and workshops. Consent forms were signed by all interviewees. Government officials preferred to remain anonymous.

When the Tsitskamma Mfengu reclaimed the land in 1994, many people moved back in anticipation of returning to their small holdings, four-and-a-half-morgen (3.87 hectare) plots.

One of the community members, who was born and raised in Witkleibos, explained:

> Wittekleibosch Tsitsikamma didn't look like it is now. Then we used to plough our fields, we depended on working the land, cutting crops and all that stuff; people didn't have to work that time, we worked for ourselves. The land was beautiful and rich at that time, so whatever you planted grew up nicely. So we were, each and every one, all had their

> four-and-a-half-*morgen* piece of land. We had livestock, cattle, goats and, you know, chickens, pigs ... whatever.
>
> Witkleibos, 8 June 2016

Another community member, born in Snyklip in 1932, recalled:

> We had cattle, we had everything ... we had a four-and-a-half-*morgen* piece of land. The water was different then, it was clean straight from the ground. Now the water we get in Wittekleibosch is not clean. The ground was fertile and we used cow manure, and the land was very rich, so it was easy to grow vegetables.
>
> Witkleibos, 15 June 2016

But because the land of the amaMfengu claim incorporated 15 forestry farms and 19 privately owned dairy farms (Jordan, 2014), the beneficiaries of the land had rights but no decision-making power over the land (Jannecke, 2008). The only option for this community was to enter into a capitalist productivist relationship through a joint venture with the commercial farmers who had purchased the land from the apartheid-era government and had chosen to remain. This partnership was initially meant to last ten years but has been renewed on a continual basis.

The people that chose to return were allocated space in the vacant lands of the dairy farms. They received a government housing grant to build RDP (Reconstruction and Development Programme) houses. These tiny, poorly constructed brick houses were initially intended to be built on 50-meter square plots of land. The community members were unhappy with this proposal and the TDT negotiated with the government to extend the portion of land available for individual houses. The idea of creating an agricultural village was put forward, but this was rejected by the government. The compromise was that beneficiaries were offered RDP houses on slightly larger plots of land (Figure 11.3). But these were still only a fraction of the size of the plots—of almost four hectares per family—that people had lived on before they were displaced.

The beneficiaries were promised an income from the dairy farms' land rentals and a portion of the 50 per cent dividend from the farms' profits. But those who returned live in grim conditions. The houses consist of a lounge and kitchenette and two other rooms, many had no electricity, and some have asbestos roofs without a ceiling lining. By the time the claim was settled, the land was largely deforested and had become monoculture pine forest and pasture for the dairy farms. The soil is degraded, making it challenging for people

FIGURE 11.3 RDP houses in Witkleibos
SOURCE: AUTHOR, 2016

to cultivate their own food crops. They are far from schools, children walked a long distance, and no public transport is available. Many people hitch a ride to town and the hospital, and private transport is arranged when the elderly need to go into town at month end. In the narrative conversations with community members, people explained that they did not expect that the land they once lived on would turn out to be a location/settlement. Access to these locations is challenging, with poor quality gravel roads littered with huge potholes (see Figure 11.4).

The houses that do have electricity were only connected in 2008, 14 years after South Africa became a democratic state. This community's connection to the grid was brought about mostly through intense lobbying of Eskom by the late Mike Msizi. Because the community was categorised as low-consumption it is charged a flat rate with no service charge and in addition receives its first 50 kWh/month free of charge. Although low-income households receive this free initial electricity and pay no service charge, tariffs are higher than those paid by wealthy suburbanites (see McDonald, 2009, 24). Low-income households are forced to use proportionally more of their income for electricity,

FIGURE 11.4 Entrance to Witkleibos following rainfall
SOURCE: AUTHOR, 2016

which means they often have to under consume or are unable to pay their electricity bills.

Energy policy in South Africa followed neo-liberal prescriptions, and energy liberalisation and various forms of electricity privatisation strategies were adopted (McDonald, 2009). The neo-liberal policy shift in the 1990s—when 'user pays' cost recovery and cost-reflective tariff policies were introduced—had huge implications with regard to access and affordability for many low-income households (McDonald, 2002; 2009; Greenberg, 2009). Furthermore, as McDonald (2009, 16) highlights, because millions of people in low-income households simply did not have a regular income with which to 'buy (enough of) the electricity' even when they did have access, people were forced into making 'tragic choices between buying electricity, water, food or clothing'.

Prepaid electricity meters were introduced in 2007. These became very popular with utility managers because they can be used to preclude non-payment problems altogether by forcing households to pay for their electricity in advance. As McDonald (2009, 26) argues, 'This system avoids the costly (political and financial) procedures of cut-offs while effectively downloading the act of cut-offs to households themselves, with people discontinuing their electricity consumption at the point that they no longer have the money to consume'. The installation of electricity meters, McDonald (2009) claims, instituted a self-imposed 'cut-off' for households unable to pay for electricity. The houses on the Tsitsikamma Mfengu's reclaimed land have an electricity meter in the front room, with a plug and many leads and wires webbed around the meter (see Figure 11.5).

A Snyklip resident said she finds it difficult to access electricity because it is too expensive. Though electricity has been provided by the government, the resident said:

> You can switch it on even if it is with R10 [10 rand], and it finishes, there is not much to it, because the stove and things like that use a lot of electricity. You see, we have these small boxes, and you cannot use the four-plate stove, it uses a lot of electricity, and it also makes the electricity trip, so we use the small ones—well I do, I have the small one and most of the time I can use the gas.

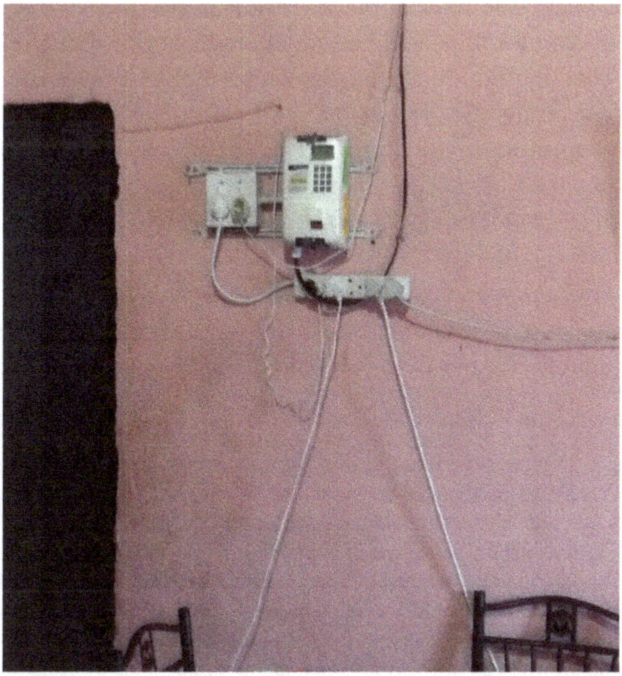

FIGURE 11.5 An electricity meter in a house in Snyklip
SOURCE: AUTHOR, 2016

A community member from Witkleibos added, 'Electricity is from the wind farms, but no light in our houses, still in darkness'.

3.2 *Establishing the Wind Farm under the REI4P*

In 2009, Msizi's dream of a community wind farm almost came true, as representatives of the Danish government met with several other partners at a project launch ceremony in Witkleibos. The signatories were Exxaro, Watt Energy, DONG, European Energy, Vestas, the Danish Embassy, and two financial institutions—Export Credit Agency, which is Danish, and the Investment Fund for Developing Countries (Young, 2016, 175). Exarro agreed to finance the entire project in anticipation that the government would implement a viable renewables policy. With the publication of the Department of Energy's Integrated Resources Plan (Department of Energy, 2011) on 22 October 2010, the key element of which was that South Africa's energy future would include renewable energy, the TCWF had a guaranteed buyer for its electricity.

Two of the major developmental components of the REI4P are 'community upliftment' and black economic empowerment (BEE).[8] The bidding process criteria for REI4P institute measures to improve the lives of communities situated within a 50 km radius of a project, including job creation, enterprise development and socio-economic development. They outline that 'Bidders must assess the needs of communities within a 50 km radius of project sites and prepare strategies covering how these needs will be met with contributions from the project's revenues. Socio-economic development plans must be prepared by bidders and submitted with proposals' (Eberhard, Kolker and Leigland, 2014, 30). The economic development criteria in particular contain several components that the bidder must deliver, each category having a certain weighting (see Table 11.1).

The REI4P has mandatory provisions for communities to hold equity of or exercise a degree of ownership over wind and solar farms, the required figure being between 2.5 per cent and 5 per cent (McDaid, 2014). The government

8 South African state policies promote redistribution through the economic inclusion of the historically marginalised under the auspices of 'inclusive growth' to ensure greater market ownership by the black population. In the postcolonial and post-apartheid era, government-facilitated capital accumulation encompasses ways of incorporating the previously marginalised through market shareholding and ownership, procuring services from black-owned businesses and practicing other forms of black economic empowerment (BEE) as forms of active participation in the economic matrix and redistribution. The South African government favours economic growth and 'inclusive economic development' as a means of redistributing the 'wealth' of the country, considered to be largely in the hands of the white minority (National Development Plan, 2012).

TABLE 11.1 Economic development scorecard weightings

Economic development category	Weighting
Job creation	25%
Local content	25%
Ownership	15%
Management control	5%
Preferential control	10%
Enterprise development	5%
Socio-economic development	15%

SOURCE: AUTHOR, ADAPTED FROM WWF–SA (2015)

and multinational energy corporations facilitate the loan process working with banks and other financial institutions to ensure this degree of community ownership. This credit arrangement is also necessary if corporate investors are to fulfil their BEE obligations. A South African Treasury official stated that 'The big thing is compliance with BEE regulation […] So IPPs must comply with laws and regulations passed by departments that are applicable. It has to show black economic empowerment'.[9] The REI4P requires that projects involve at least 40 per cent participation from South African entities and a minimum of 12 per cent black ownership (with a target of 20 per cent), and that at least 2.5 per cent of the project be owned by communities living within the 50 km radius (Baker, 2015b, 150).

Through its economic inclusion policy, the government has encouraged communities that were designated subaltern to enter into a system of capital accumulation on the premise of economic wealth creation for black people. In the case of the TWCF, the TDT holds a 9 per cent share on behalf of the community. These shares were purchased using a USD 3.87 million (ZAR 45 million) bank loan taken out by Cennergi/Exxaro. A larger shareholding would mean a larger dividend would be paid out to the TDT and thus, theoretically, to the beneficiaries of the land. The investor emphasised that the best part of the TCWF story is that

9 Interview with a Treasury official, 9 November 2016.

> The Tsitsikamma Development Trust or the landowner has a 9 per cent shareholding [...] 2.5 per cent of that 9 per cent is interest free, and the rest is repayable carried interest. So, we gave all the money, and we acted like a bank, and they must give it back to us over time.

He also indicated that the project would offer much more in the long run, especially in terms of the financial arrangement and returns to the community:

> In our bid, we promised to spend 2.1 per cent of the money on socio-economic development [SED] and enterprise development. So, 1.5 per cent is SED and 0.6 per cent is enterprise development. So, to give you an idea of that, it's 20 000 rand [approximately USD 1,700] per day for 20 years.

The assumption behind the REI4P is that by including criteria for local economic development and social economic development, enterprise development, and local ownership, which should be met from contributions from the project's revenues, local well-being will be improved as will climate mitigation. However, reviews carried out by Bode (2014) and McDaid (2014) of current REI4P projects highlight several concerns in the socio-economic development dimension.

At the beginning of the investment, Exarro's clean energy subsidiary Cennergi was in an equal partnership with Tata, an Indian corporation that has significant experience in wind energy, and the two constituted the major investors in TCWF, owning 75 per cent of shares. The TDT as the community trust held 9 per cent, and the remaining partner was Watt Energy, which owned 16 per cent (see Figures 11.6 and 11.7). Watt Energy was acrimoniously liquidated following Mike Msizi's death in 2012 (Carlisle, 2015), and at the time of my fieldwork the purchase of this 16 per cent of shares was unresolved.

This shareholding arrangement has gone through several changes since its inception, and these are discussed further in section 4 of this chapter.

During conversations with community members, most expressed that the wind farm was a positive initiative. The community was especially enthusiastic when Mike Msizi was still alive. Community members felt that they were part of the discussions on establishing the wind farm and that they were always kept informed. Some individuals even went on site visits to the Darling wind farm in the Western Cape to get a sense of how these turbines work. The community members I spoke with expressed that lots of promises were made with regard to community upliftment. Mike conveyed, 'we will bring solar geysers, build libraries, play fields for children' (personal communication, 2016). For

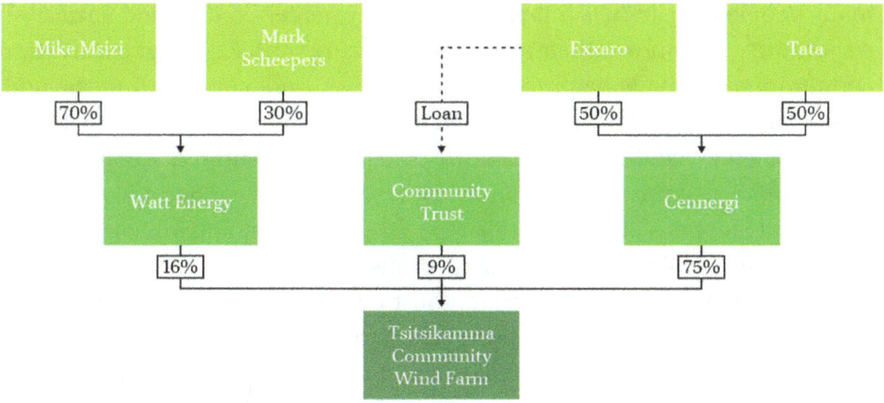

FIGURE 11.6 Initial structure of the Tsitsikamma Community Wind Farm
SOURCE: AUTHOR

FIGURE 11.7 Tsitsikamma Community Wind Farm signage
SOURCE: AUTHOR, 2016

many people education is important, and they perceived the wind farm as an opportunity to improve their skills and to secure jobs. Cennergi contributed certain improvements before the wind turbines were connected to the grid. These included building a crèche, arranging transport to schools, upgrading the Trust office, and building a cattle kraal. On the surface, Exxaro's clean energy offshoot appears to be an exemplary investor working towards what Burke and Stephens (2018) describe as inclusivity, equity and influence among communities involved with renewable projects.

What is, however, overlooked amid just energy transitions, energy democracy, and 'green' energy growth prospects is the trajectory of techno-capitalist development that instead works to facilitate the inclusion of people in capitalist developments (Dunlap, 2021). These local economic development projects do not allow for 'perspectives outside the dominant culture of modernity, industrial development and universal ideas of human rights' (Dunlap, 2021). The politics of 'inclusion' largely ignores a politics that recognises the agency of the 'the other'—invisibilised, marginalised, depoliticised—and engagement with the more-than-human world[10] (de Sousa Santos, 2006; Gibson-Graham, 2007; Gibson-Graham, Hill and Law, 2016). Modernity's dualisms, as stressed by Patel and Moore (2020, 202), not only 'describe and categorize the world but [have] served practically to dominate and cheapen the lives of nearly all humans and the rest of nature'. Understanding capitalism as a world-ecology of power, capital, and nature helps us see how deeply each half of the society and nature dualism is embedded in the other, and how mightily the powerful have worked to police and sharpen the boundaries between them (Patel and Moore, 2020, 202).

As stressed by Patel and Moore (2020, 202), what remains intact is 'cheapness' as a 'set of strategies to manage relations between capitalism and the web of life by temporarily fixing capitalism's crises'. 'Cheapness'—from a geo-cultural perspective related to the ethical-political devaluation of cheap lives and the labour of woman, nature and colonies—is central to thriving capital accumulation (Moore 2021). Moore (2021) also stresses that sexism and racism are used as geo-cultural strategies of devaluation in the interests of driving down labour costs. What becomes visible is the race and class divide historically constructed in nature and society abstractions, where the work of the black peoples is laborious and exploitative. Salleh (1996, 156), a Marxian

---

10 It is a term used to counter and surpass the dominance of the colonial modernist human-centric worldview underpinned Society and Nature dualisms, which separate humans from nature. David Abram coined the phrase "more-than-human world" as way of referring to earthly nature.

eco-feminist, notes that the worker is not fully reimbursed for his or her time and energy because the energy of labour is undervalued in relation to surplus and use values based on exchange value or labour costs. The low-skilled worker is usually underpaid in the labour–wage exchange. In the neo-liberal regime, cheap labour was made possible through a new regime of 'forced underconsumption' (Araghi in Moore 2014, 300). People's dispossession via 'global enclosures' "were realised through structural adjustment programmes and market liberalization, restructured agrarian class relations worldwide, dispossessing hundreds of millions of peasants worldwide" (Araghi in Moore 2014, 300). This neoliberal strategy not only expanded the proletariat but people simply did have enough money live dignified lives Another register of 'cheap nature' is as a political project for the creation of markets under capitalism, one that is secured by the political forces of the political mechanisms of imperialism, during which cheapness is secured and periodically restructured into 'new' forms of capital accumulation (Moore, 2021).

4 Illuminating the Neo-liberal Nature of the REI4P

4.1 *Creating Favourable Conditions for Investors: Strategies for Addressing Surplus Capital Accumulation in 'Development' Financing?*

During the 2008 Copenhagen climate change negotiations, South Africa pledged a 34 per cent reduction in its carbon emissions by 2020 and a 42 per cent reduction by 2025 (Baker, 2015a). Since 2007 South Africa has experienced a worsening power crisis resulting in extensive power cuts. This is the result of ageing coal power stations and delays in completing the two key large-scale coal power stations of Medupi and Kusile, and of a crisis at Eskom. In this context, the government requires immense financing levels for South Africa's energy transition and infrastructure.

The introduction of IPPs into the renewable energy systems is widely celebrated in terms of climate change mitigation, the generation of additional electricity, and attracting private sector involvement to address energy market 'inefficiencies' (Rennkamp et al., 2017, 216; WWF-SA, 2015, 12). The government, investors, some non-governmental organisations and some academics consider the REI4P a watertight vehicle for capital investment in renewable energy technologies that guarantees return on investment and eliminates the risks of corruption (Eberhard in McEwan, 2017). The REI4P has been hailed for attracting a huge amount of direct foreign investment and is considered a success by the government, with 5,243 megawatts of renewable energy provided by USD 16 billion of private investment, which the South African government regards as a 'significant investment in mitigations' (Rennkamp et al., 2017).

But as stressed by Jessop (2013), Parenti (2016) and Le Billon and Sommerville (2016), the state must create favourable conditions to attract increased investment in renewable energy projects. Treasury officials interviewed also emphasised that South Africa must provide quite attractive terms for investors and put a price cap in place in the electricity purchase agreement.

> The price has come down dramatically from bid window 1 to bid window 4; [t]he price is now 69 c[ents] per kWh [kilowatt-hour], [which is a] 67% [fall]. It was R2 [2 rand] something and coal is ranged at 82 c[ents] per kWh so it is cheaper than coal. And we would not have had this if we didn't take the risk and offer those terms to attract the investor. The thing is, because of the policy uncertainty in the country we are not really a prime destination for foreign investment.
>
> Personal communication, 2016

South Africa has become a prime investment opportunity for renewable energy operators (Baker, 2015b). Energy Minister Jeff Radebe has signed contracts with 27 new renewable energy IPPs. He considered these new contracts to be the biggest IPP procurement by the department between 2016 and 2018, representing a total of almost USD 4.5 billion (ZAR 56 billion) in investment (Khumalo, 2018). Favourable conditions created to attract investment range from access to land to guaranteed payments to fiscal measures to reduce investment costs, amongst others. Thus, as pointed out by Le Billon and Sommerville (2016), governments would have to marshal narratives about both attractive returns for financiers and supposed social benefits. These authors also point out that one of the key contradictions is that the government often misrepresents investments as public revenues and compensation for disruption in local communities (Le Billon and Sommerville, 2016). Making investable projects attractive also requires reforms at the institutional level in the form of changes to regulatory regimes and corporate governance that contribute to securing investor access (Le Billon and Sommerville, 2016, 220). As pointed out by Gabor (2021), the development of 'investable' projects requires a two-pronged strategy: first, the reorienting of the fiscal and monetary arm of the state in order to de-risk development asset classes so that there are steady cash flows for investors, and second, the re-engineering of local financial systems in the image of US market-based finance to allow portfolio investors easy entry into, and exit from, new asset classes (2021, 431). In an era in which 'cheap natures' are being depleted and becoming more expensive, capitalism finds new financial

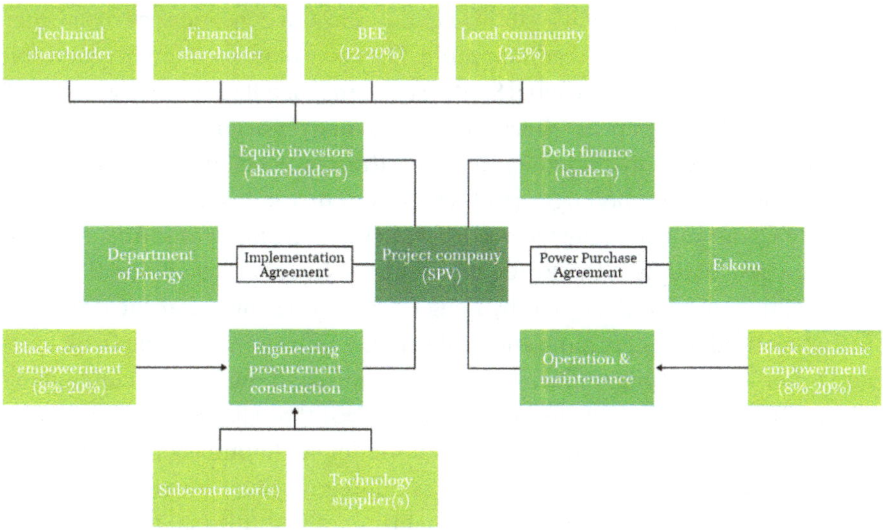

FIGURE 11.8 The structure of project finance under the REI4P
SOURCE: AUTHOR, ADAPTED FROM BAKER (2015B)

engineering capital accumulation strategies. As Patel and Moore (2020, 88) put it, 'The ever-increasing sophistication of financial engineering emerges not as "the rise of the quants"[11] but as the outcome of centuries of accumulation[s], each with its distinctive ways of organizing capital, power, and nature'.

Baker (2015b) raised concerns that South Africa's renewable energy sector is likely to 'rest increasingly with financial investors as shareholdings become tradable financial assets' (2015b, 148) because of the structure and finance mechanisms of the REI4P. She also notes the complex ownership structures 'involving international, national, private and public players, black and local community shareholders' (Baker, 2015b, 150) (see Figure 11.8).

Baker (2015b, 147) is particularly concerned about the implications of 'on-selling' shares given the trend of financialisaton in the South African economy. She questions whether on-selling—including to pension funds, insurers and other institutional investors—will potentially contribute to a trend of capital flight through financial institutions listed in South Africa but with their headquarters situated abroad (Baker, 2015b, 155). She also clearly suspects the crisis of accumulation will lead to the circulation of excess money in the system and

11 'Quant' is shorthand for quantitative analyst, so, someone expert in the analysis and management of quantitative data, particularly that of a financial nature (See Read, 2012).

result in on-selling that will result in a and in the as a consequence of speculation and the expansion of credit for profit. The wave of investment in renewable energy, particularly in the Global South, is making installations energy technology less and less expensive (because there is an over-accumulation of capital that wants to invest in climate mitigation); thus, projects that are funded with private money must be larger (to lower costs) or the investment conditions need be favourable in higher risks context to generate higher returns. A review of renewable energy in the BRICS (the emerging economies of Brazil, Russia, India, China and South Africa) by Zeng et al. (2017) shows that the dominant financing models for current renewable energy transitions include bank loans and other institutional financing, industry funds, and international financing. The authors of the review also point out (p. 870) that all five BRICS countries have adopted 'the international financial model, with funds coming from foreign governments, international banks and foreign private investors'.

Gabor stresses (2021, 434) that 'the inclusion of institutional investors, from hedge and pension funds to insurance companies and sovereign wealth funds, and asset managers as critical stakeholders, upgraded the de-risking renewables strategy into a full-blown, ambitious 'development as de-risking' paradigm'. In this way, risk is transferred to the balance sheet of the state (Gabor, 2021). According to Gabor (2021) the development as de-risking paradigm puts states 'under pressure to institutionally codify risk-proofing arrangements, guaranteeing private financial profits in the name of aligning sustainable projects with the preferred risk/return profile of institutional investors' (Gabor, 2021, 453).

A Treasury official, during an interview regarding the introduction of independent power producers, told me, '[…] Bringing in private providers, it has shown that everything is better—the rate of return and all the risk has been passed on to the private partner, and they are still doing it cheaper than Eskom'. The same official went on to explain how 'an advantage of the shift to the IPPs is that you are purchasing the product, which is electricity. While Eskom owns that asset, it is not about ownership of the asset anymore'. This shift from state capitalism to neo-liberal capitalism ostensibly reduces the state's financial responsibility for infrastructure development, which is now borne by the private sector via PPPs. The official also pointed out that 'delays in Eskom generation are huge compared to the IPPs—they [the IPPs] deliver [and] reduce cost'. So, for the Treasury, 'It is about passing the risk; with Eskom, the risk unfortunately is on us as the fiscus and the taxpayer at the end of the day. If you contract a private provider, the risk is on them'.

The REI4P, constructed as a PPP, was introduced in South Africa in 1998. Gabor (2021, 430) explains that in PPPs 'the private sector commits to finance, construct and manage public services as long as the state, with multilateral development bank (MDB) support via blended finance, shares the risk by guaranteeing payment flows to PPP operators and investors'. In PPPs, this financial strategy of a 'de-risking state can be understood as a project that seeks to extend the infrastructural dependence of the state on private finance [...]' and transforms a range of infrastructure sectors into asset classes, including water, housing, energy, health, education, transport, and even nature, 'which is code for creating de-risking partnerships' (Gabor, 2021, 436). Gabor (2021, 431) also points out that this is not simply an agenda to privatise (social) infrastructure. It is much more. The development of 'investable' projects requires changes in financial regulation and corporate governance that secure the investment. The 'Wall Street Consensus [WSC] re-imagines international development interventions as opportunities' and is a state-building project that puts in place the institutional basis for a new regime of de-risking as accumulation (Gabor, 2021, 453). In contemporary forms of capital accumulation, Gabor (2021, 432) explains, the de-risking development paradigm of the WSC protects bondholders from having to participate in the debt renegotiations that may be required by poor and emerging countries. This investment arrangement also further threatens the developmental policy space by narrowing the state's scope for achieving just energy transitions and for putting in place mechanisms whereby 'the burden of structural change does not disproportionately fall on the poor' (Gabor, 2021, 432).

4.2 *Questions Concerning the On-selling of Shares in the TWCF*

Baker (2015b) has raised concerns over the on-selling of debt purchased through loans. Investors consider on-selling as a mechanism by which returns can be redistributed, creating a secondary market in debt and equity that in turn generates further investment in renewable energy in order to reduce capital costs (Baker, 2015b). With this in mind, we now return to the unresolved matter of Watt Energy's 16 per cent share in the TCWF. These shares were bought in October 2020 by Kruger International, an asset management company in partnership with GAIA Fund Managers (GFM), an investment manager specialising in agriculture and infrastructure[12] (Cairns, 2020). These shares were incorporated into the investment holding company GAIA Fund 1 (GF1), a

12 I consulted a finance specialist to help me understand and explain changes in the shareholding arrangement of the TWCF. Kruger International is a unit trust fund and bought the shares in October 2020. While Kruger International bought the issued preference shares in GAIA Fund 1, those shares (along with GAIA ordinary shares) trade on the stock exchange, and so may have changed hands.

parent entity that conducts no business operations. The purpose of this holding company is to hold stock or membership interest in other companies. On 12 October 2020, Kruger International, a unit trust company, stated in a press release that preference shares would be bought from its various funds and that proceeds of the listing would be 'used by the Fund to buy a 16% indirect shareholding in the Tsitsikamma Community Wind Farm' (Kruger International, 2020). The funding structures of GFM and Kruger International allow for direct investment in the renewables project within a collective investment scheme structure. Kruger International bought the preference shares issued by GAIA Fund (GF1).

A 2020 Citywire article praises unit trust access to infrastructure projects, saying that one of South Africa's economic imperatives is to encourage more private investment into infrastructure projects. As the government has run out of money to finance this kind of development, capital has to be sourced from elsewhere (Cairns, 2020). Keen to understand this purchase of shares in the TCWF, I consulted a finance expert, who was able to explain the complex financial engineering involved in the new structure of the TWCF (see Figure 11.9). While it would be possible to further elaborate on this matter, for example by examining more closely the vehicles used for selling and buying the shares on the stock exchange, such elaboration is beyond the scope of this chapter.

In summary, RE Times, which is essentially a shell company, acquired 16 per cent of the TCWF. Msizi's widow and son own 70 per cent of RE Times and the other 30 per cent, which was previously owned by the minority shareholder, Watt Energy, has been put into the TCWF Investment Special Purpose Vehicle (SPV). So, there is 11.2 per cent BEE ownership and community ownership is 9 per cent, meeting the BEE ownership criteria. It was also critical for Cennergi, as the main investor in the TCWF, to fulfil the BEE criteria of the REI4P following Mike's death to meet legal requirements. Despite all these arrangements, meanwhile, for the Mfengu communities living in poverty-stricken conditions improved well-being and the benefits of the monetisation of their reclaimed land are both yet to be realised. This situation raises concerns about the illusion of BEE, and Baker (2015b, 254) notes that the 'BEE has primarily resulted in the enrichment of an unproductive black elite with limited trickle-down potential, rather than a tool for genuine socio-economic transformation'.

The REI4P is considered a success in that it attracts investment for renewable energy transitions. But it is essentially an investment frontier for surplus private finance (cheap money) underpinned by productivity and practice that put nature (both human and non-human) to work as cheaply as possible. Since accumulation through 'cheap natures' is diminishing and becoming expensive, surplus capital requires new vehicles, and new places for new investments to

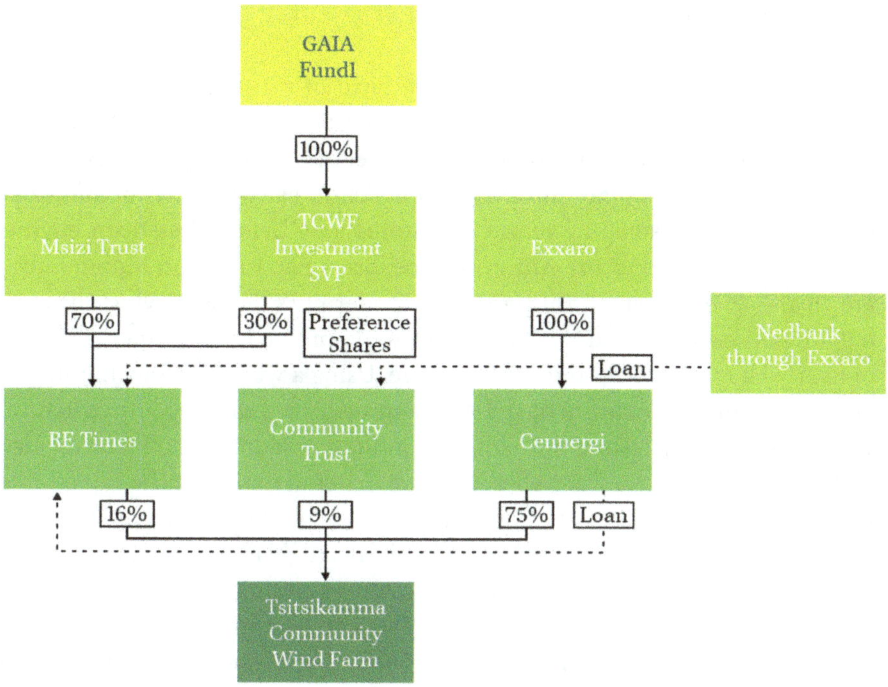

FIGURE 11.9 The current structure of the TCWF
SOURCE: AUTHOR, BASED ON THE CONSULTATION OF A FINANCE EXPERT

land. 'Green' energy solutions and PPP investment models such as the REI4P are embedded in the machinations of the productivist model through 'new' forms of financialization. Gabor (2021) has pointed out that this investment strategy is a state-building project that puts in place the institutional basis for a new regime of de-risking as accumulation. By opening new frontiers for accumulation, capitalism thus expands, and this is how it 'controls a wider set of life-making relations' that 'do not appear on a balance sheet or profit and loss statement' (Patel and Moore, 2020, 19).

By expanding across new frontiers, capitalism controls a wider set of life-making relations. These frontiers are sites where power is exercised, and not just economic power. But capitalism's strategies of cheapness and profit constitute 'a practice, a violence that mobilises all kinds of work – human and animal, botanical and geological – with as little compensation as possible' (Patel and Moore, 2020, 22). The vision of providing electricity for the Mfengu communities and selling the excess to the grid was deferred because the wind farm could only be implemented within the framework and the investment conditions of the REI4P.

5 Conclusion

The Anthropocene discourse situates the birth of this new planetary epoch during the Industrial Revolution and is primarily interested in replacing fossil fuel energy generation 'resources' with renewable energy. But as Moore (2014, 596) observes, 'the erasure of capitalism's early-modern origins, and its extraordinary reshaping of global natures long before the steam engine' is largely overlooked in the Anthropocene discourse. Patel and Moore (2017) are clear—at the heart of this crisis lies modernity's dualism, which has not only organised the world but has served to dominate and cheapen the lives of nearly all humans and the rest of nature. Using a world-ecology framing to analyse the material nature of the REI4P has exposed the ongoing structural violence of capital, despite the 'noble' intentions of addressing climate change and improving community well-being. The material nature of the Renewable Energy Independent Power Producer Procurement Programme reveals the invasiveness of modernity's alienating of social relations, an invasiveness apparent in patterns of accumulation, ways of the thinking, and the strategies that foster 'cheapness' and profit. The Tsitsikamma Community Wind Farm—although conceived of prior to the launch of the REI4P, and raising the prospect of donor funding from Denmark and eventually being funded by Exxaro—became enmeshed in the de-risking parameters of the REI4P. As this chapter has shown, the REI4P, organised in the form of a paradigm of de-risking, can be characterised as a frontier, but not only in the sense of a settler–colonial frontier with regard to land appropriation. As Patel and Moore (2017, 30) explain, it also constitutes a 'place [that] encounters all kind[s] of nature—humans included' and is about reducing the cost of doing business. These same authors also stress that 'a frontier is a site where crisis encourages new strategies for profit' (Patel and Moore, 2020, 18–19). Frontiers are important in these processes because they offer new sites where 'cheap things can be seized—and the cheap work of humans and other natures can be coerced' (Patel and Moore, 2020, 22). In essence, renewable energy technology 'fixes', with their planetary management aspirations, become a 'fix' for ensuring 'cheap' money a place to land. The sophisticated strategies of financial engineering revealed in this chapter point, in the words of Patel and Moore (2020, 88), to an 'outcome of centuries of accumulation[s], each with its distinctive ways of organizing capital, power, and nature'.

References

Araghi, F. (2000) 'The Great Global Enclosure of Our Times', in F. Magdoff, J. Bellamy Foster, and F. Buttel (eds.) *Hungry for Profit* (New York: Monthly Review Press).

Baker, L. (2015a) 'Renewable energy in South Africa's minerals-energy complex: a "low carbon" transition?', *Review of African Political Economy*, 42(144), pp. 245–61, DOI: 10.1080/03056244.2014.953471.

Baker, L. (2015b) 'The evolving role of finance in South Africa's renewable energy sector', *Geoforum*, 64, pp. 146–56, DOI: 10.1016/j.geoforum.2015.06.017.

Baskin, J. (2015) 'Paradigm Dressed as Epoch: the Ideology of the Anthropocene', *Environmental Values*, 24(1), pp. 9–29, DOI: 10.3197/096327115X14183182353746.

Bode, C. (2014) *An Analysis of Collective Ownership Models to Promote Renewable Energy Development and Climate Justice in South Africa*, Master's Thesis (Potchefstroom: North-West University), https://repository.nwu.ac.za/bitstream/handle/10394/10004/Bode_CC.pdf?sequence=1 (accessed on 9 December 2022).

Bonneuil, C. and J. Fressoz (2016) *Shock of the Anthropocene: the Earth, History and Us* (London: Verso).

Boyer, D. (2011) 'Energopolitics and the Anthropology of Energy', *Anthropology News*, DOI: 10.1111/j.1556-3502.2011.52505.x.

Burke, M. J. and J. C. Stephens (2018) 'Political power and renewable energy futures: a critical review', *Energy Research and Social Science*, 35, pp. 78–93, DOI: 10.1016/J.ERSS.2017.10.018.

Cairns, P. (2020) 'Is this how SA unit trusts will get exposure to infrastructure?', *Citywire South Africa*, 28 October, https://citywire.com/za/news/is-this-how-sa-unit-trusts-will-get-exposure-to-infrastructure/a1418138 (accessed on 15 February 2021).

Carlisle, A. (2015) 'Major players in Tsitsikamma wind farm wound up', *Herald*, 24 Sep, http://www.pressreader.com/south-africa/the-herald-south-africa/20150924/281621009137052/TextView (accessed on 3 April 2023).

Chakrabarty, D. (2009) 'The Climate of History: Four Theses', *Critical inquiry*, 35 (2), 197–222.

Crist, E. (2016) 'On the Poverty of Our Nomenclature', in J. W. Moore (ed.) *Anthropocene or Capitalocene? Nature, History and the Crisis of Capitalism* (Oakland: PM).

Cronon, W. (1983) *Changes in the land: Indians, colonists, and the ecology of New England* (New York: Hill and Wang.Press), pp. 14–33.

Department of Energy (2011) *Integrated Resource Plan for Electricity 2010–2030* (Pretoria: Republic of South Africa), https://www.energy.gov.za/irp/irp%20files/irp2010_2030_final_report_20110325.pdf (accessed on 3 April 2023).

Department of Energy, National Treasury, Development Bank Southern Africa (2016) *Independent Power Producers Procurement Programme (IPPP): an Overview* (Pretoria: Republic of South Africa).

De Sousa Santos, B. (2006) 'The World Social Forum as epistemology of the South', in *The Rise of the Global Left: the World Social Forum and Beyond* (London and New York: Zed Books), pp. 13–34.

Dunlap, A. (2021) 'More wind energy colonialism(s) in Oaxaca? Reasonable findings, unacceptable development', *Energy Research and Social Science*, 82, DOI: 10.1016/j.erss.2021.102304.

Dunlap, A. (2017) 'The town is surrounded: from climate concerns to life under wind turbines in La Ventosa, Mexico', *Human Geography*, 10(2), pp. 16–36.

Eberhard, A., J. Kolker and J. Leigland (2014) *South Africa's Renewable Energy IPP Procurement Programme: Success Factors and Lessons* (Washington, DC: World Bank Group and PPIAF), https://openknowledge.worldbank.org/bitstream/handle/10986/20039/ACS88260WP0P1482120Box385262B00PUBLIC0.pdf?sequence=1&isAllowed=y (accessed on 9 December 2022).

Gabor, D. (2021) 'The Wall Street Consensus', *Development and Change*, 52(3), pp. 429–459, DOI: 10.1111/dech.12645.

Gibson-Graham, J. K. (2007) 'Surplus Possibilities: Post-development and Community Economies', in A. Ziai (ed.) *Exploring Post-development: Theory and Practice, Problems and Perspectives* (London: Routledge), pp. 145–162.

Gibson-Graham, J. K., A. Hill and L. Law (2016) 'Re-embedding economies in ecologies: resilience building in more than human communities', *Building Research and Information*, 44(7), pp. 703–716, DOI: 10.1080/09613218.2016.1213059.

Greenberg, S. (2009) 'The repositioning of Eskom in post-apartheid South Africa', in D. McDonald (ed.). *Electric capitalism: Recolonising Africa on the power grid* (London: Earthscan Publication), pp 73–108.

Haraway, D. J. (2016) 'Staying with the Trouble: Anthropocene, Capitalocene, Chthulucene', in J.W. Moore. (ed.) *Anthropocene or Capitalocene? Nature, History and the Crisis of Capitalism* (Oakland: PM Press), pp. 34–77.

Harvey, D. (2004) 'The "New" Imperialism: Accumulation by Dispossession', *Socialist Register*, 40, pp. 63–87, DOI: 10.4324/9781315251196-10.

Howe, C. (2019) *Ecologics* (Durham, NC: Duke University Press).

Howe, C. (2015) 'Latin America in the Anthropocene: Energy Transitions and Climate Change Mitigations', *The Journal of Latin American and Caribbean Anthropology*, 20(2), pp. 231–241, DOI: 10.1111/jlca.12146.

Howe, C. (2014) 'Anthropocenic Ecoauthority: The Winds of Oaxaca', *Anthropological Quarterly*, 87(2), pp. 381–404, https://www.jstor.org/stable/43652703.

Howe, C. (2011) 'Logics of Wind: Development Desires over Oaxaca', *Anthropology News*, 52(5), p. 8, DOI: 10.1111/j.1556-3502.2011.52508.x.

Howe, C. and D. Boyer (2016) 'Aeolian Extractivism and Community Wind in Southern Mexico', *Public Culture*, 28 (2), pp. 215–235, DOI: 10.1215/08992363-3427427.

Huber, M. T. and J. McCarthy (2017) 'Beyond the subterranean energy regime? Fuel, land use and the production of space', *Transactions of the Institute of British Geographers*, 42(4), pp. 655–668, DOI: 10.1111/tran.12182.

IEA (International Energy Agency) (2017) *Energy Access Outlook Report 2017. World Outlook Special Report*, (Paris: IEA), https://www.iea.org/reports/energy-access-outlook-2017 (accessed on 3 April 2023).

Jannecke, C. (2006) 'Constituting Community: the Contested Rural Land Claim of the Tsitsikamma'Fingo/Mfengu'and Clarkson Moravian Mission in South Africa', *Kronos: Journal of Cape History*, 32, pp. 192–215.

Jannecke, C. (2008) 'Strategies of Representation in Tsitsikamma Fingo/Mfengu Land Restitution Claims', *South African Historical Journal*, 60(3), pp. 452–476, DOI: 10.1080/02582470802417508.

Jessop, B. (2013) 'Revisiting the regulation approach: Critical reflections on the contradictions, dilemmas, fixes and crisis dynamics of growth regimes', *Capital and Class*, 37(1), pp. 5–24, DOI: 10.1177/0309816812472968.

Jonsson, F. (2015) 'Anthropocene Blues: Abundance, Energy, Limits', in F. Felcht and K. Ritson (eds), *The Imagination of Limits: Exploring Scarcity and Abundance*, RCC Perspectives, 2, pp. 55–63.

Jordan, B. (2014) 'Pensioner's hopes for his promised land turn to dust: Ancestral home feels like another dumping ground', *Sunday Times*, 3 August, https://www.timeslive.co.za/sunday-times/lifestyle/2014-08-03-pensioners-hopes-for-his-promised-land-turn-to-dust/ (accessed on 3 April 2023).

Khumalo, S. (2018) 'Jeff Radebe signs renewable energy contracts after more than two years of delays', *Mail & Guardian*, 4 April, https://mg.co.za/article/2018-04-04-signing-of-renewable-energy-contracts-delayed-but-only-for-a-few-hours/ (accessed on 16 July 2019).

Koch, A., C. Brierley, M. M. Maslin and S. L. Lewis (2019) 'Earth system impacts of the European arrival and Great Dying in the Americas after 1492', *Quaternary Science Reviews*, 207, pp. 13–36, DOI: 10.1016/j.quascirev.2018.12.004.

Kruger International (2020) *Kruger International's fund becomes the first unit trust in SA to invest directly in infrastructure for renewable energy*, press release, 14 October, https://www.krugerinternasionaal.co.za/2020/10/14/tsitsikamma-community-wind-farm-investment/ (accessed on 9 September 2022).

Le Billon, P. and M. Sommerville (2016) 'Landing capital and assembling 'investable land' in the extractive and agricultural sectors', *Geoforum*, 82, pp. 212–224, DOI: 10.1016/j.geoforum.2016.08.011.

McDaid, L. (2014) *Renewable Energy Independent Power Producer Procurement Programme Review* (South Africa: Electricity Governance Initiative and World Resources Institute), https://thegreenconnection.org.za/wp-content/uploads/2021/10/EGI-Renewable-Energy-Independent-Power-Producer-Procurement-Programme-Reveiw-Aug2014.pdf (accessed on 12 December 2022).

McDonald, D. (2009) *Electric Capitalism: Recolonising Africa on the Power Grid* (London: Earthscan Publication).

Mcdonald, D. (2002) 'No money, no service: South Africa's attempts to recover service costs for water and power are harming its poorest citizens', *Alternative Journal*, 28(2), pp.16–20, https://go.gale.com/ps/i.do?id=GALE%7CA84667579&sid=googleScholar&v=2.1&it=r&linkaccess=abs&issn=12057398&p=AONE&sw=w&userGroupName=anon%7Eb5ccad89 (accessed on 3 April 2023).

McEwan, C. (2017) 'Spatial processes and politics of renewable energy transition: Land, zones and frictions in South Africa', *Political Geography*, 56, pp. 1–12, DOI: 10.1016/j.polgeo.2016.10.001.

Merchant, C. (1980) *The Death of Nature: Women, Ecology, and the Scientific Revolution* (New York: Harper and Row).

Mignolo, W. (2019) 'Sustainable development or sustainable economies? Ideas towards living in harmony and plenitude', *Socioscapes : international journal of societies, politics and cultures*, 1(1), http://digital.casalini.it/10.48250/1004.

Moore, J.W. (2021) *Climate, Class and the Great Frontier: from Primitive Accumulation to the Great Implosion*, unpublished paper (USA: Binghamton University, World-Ecology Research Group), https://jasonwmoore.com/wp-content/uploads/2021/09/Moore-Class-Climate-and-the-Great-Frontier-circulating-September-2021.pdf (accessed on 10 July 2022).

Moore, J.W. (2017) 'The Capitalocene, Part I: on the nature and origins of our ecological crisis', *The Journal of Peasant Studies*. 44(3), DOI: 10.1080/03066150.2016.1235036.

Moore, J.W. (2016) 'The Rise of Cheap Nature', in *Anthropocene or Capitalocene? Nature, History, and the Crisis of Capitalism* (Oakland: PM Press), pp. 78–116.

Moore, J. W. (2015a) 'Putting Nature to Work', in C. Wee, J. Schönenbach and O. Arndt (eds.) *Supramarkt: a Micro-toolkit for Disobedient consumers, or How to Frack the Fatal Forces of the Capitalocene* (Gothenburg: Irene Books), pp. 69–117.

Moore, J. W. (2015b) *Capitalism in the Web of Life: Ecology and the Accumulation of Capital* (London: Verso Books).

Moore, J. W. (2014) 'The End of Cheap Nature or: How I Learned to Stop Worrying about "the" Environment and Love the Crisis of Capitalism', in C. Suter and C. Chase-Dunn (eds.) *Structures of the World Political Economy and the Future of Global Conflict and Cooperation* (Zurich: LIT Verlag).

Moore, J. W. (2002) 'The Crisis of Feudalism: an Environmental History', *Organization and Environment*, 15(3), pp. 301–322, DOI: 10.1177/1086026602153008.

Morton, T. (2013) *Hyperobjects : Philosophy and Ecology after the End of the World* (Minneapolis: University of Minnesota Press).

National Development Planning Commission (2012) *National Development Plan 2030—Our future make it work* (Pretoria: Government of South Africa), https://www.gov.za/sites/default/files/gcis_document/201409/ndp-2030-our-future-make-it-workr.pdf (accessed on 28 February 2018).

Normann, S. (2020) 'Green colonialism in the Nordic context: Exploring Southern Saami representations of wind energy development', *Journal of community psychology*, 49 (1), pp. 77–94.

Parenti, E. (2016) 'Environmental-Making in the Capitalocene: Political Ecology of the State', in J.W. Moore (ed.) *Anthropocene or Capitalocene? Nature, History and the Crisis of Capitalism* (Oakland, CA: PM Press). pp 166–184.

Patel, R and J.W. Moore (2020) *A History of the World in Seven Cheap Things: a Guide to Capitalism, Nature and the Future of the Planet* (London: Verso).

Ramirez, J. and S. Böhm (2021) 'Transactional colonialism in wind energy investments: Energy injustices against vulnerable people in the Isthmus of Tehuantepec', *Energy Research and Social Science*, 78, DOI: 10.1016/j.erss.2021.102135.

Read, C. (2012) *The Rise of the Quants: Marschak, Sharpe, Black, Scholes, and Merton* (London: Palgrave Macmillan).

Rennkamp, B., S. Haunss, K. Wongsa, A. Ortega and E. Casamadrid (2017) 'Competing coalitions: the politics of renewable energy and fossil fuels in Mexico, South Africa and Thailand', *Energy Research and Social Science*, 34, pp. 214–223, DOI: 10.1016/j.erss.2017.07.012.

Salleh, A. (1996) *Ecofeminism as Politics : Nature, Marx and the Postmodern* (London: Zed Books).

Steffen, W., P. Cruzen and J. McNeill (2007) 'The Anthropocene: Are Humans Now Overwhelming the Great Forces of Nature?', *Ambio*, 36(8), pp. 614–621.

Stengers, I. (2015) 'Accepting the reality of Gaia—a fundamental shift?' in C. Hamilton, F. Gemenne and C. Bonneuil (eds.) *The Anthropocene and the Global Environmental Crisis: Re-thinking Modernity in a New Epoch* (London: Routledge).

Szeman, I. and J. Wenzel (2021) 'What do we talk about when we talk about extractivism?', *Textual Practice*, 35(3), pp. 505–523, DOI: 10.1080/0950236X.2021.1889829.

UNDP (United Nations Development Programme) (2016) *Human Development Report 2016: Human Development for Everyone,* (New York: UNDP), https://sustainabledevelopment.un.org/content/documents/25212016_human_development_report.pdf (accessed on 3 April 2023).

UNEP (United Nations Environment Programme) (2017) *Renewable Energy and Energy Efficiency in Developing Countries: Contributions to Reducing Global Emissions*, Third Report 2017 (Nairobi: UNEP), https://www.unep.org/resources/report/renewable-energy-and-energy-efficiency-developing-countries-contributions-0 (accessed on 3 April 2023).

Vargas, N. (2020) 'The Effects of the Wind Farms on the Indigenous Zapotec Community of the Isthmus of Tehuantepec, Mexico', *Occam's Razor*, 10, https://cedar.wwu.edu/orwwu/vol10/iss1/3 (accessed on 28 January 2022).

WWF-SA (World Wide Fund for Nature South Africa) (2015) *A Review of the Local Community Development Requirements in South Africa's Renewable Procurement*

Programme (Pretoria: WWF-SA) http://awsassets.wwf.org.za/downloads/local_community_development_report_20150618.pdf (accessed 30 June 2015).

Young, J. (2016) *Just Imagine: the story of Mike Msizi, the Tsitsikamma Mfengu and the Tsitsikamma Community Wind Farm* (Cape Town: CTP Printers).

Zeng, S., Y. Liu, C. Liu and X. Nan (2017) 'A review of renewable energy investment in the BRICS countries: History, models, problems and solutions', *Renewable and Sustainable Energy Reviews*, 74, pp. 860–872, DOI: 10.1016/j.rser.2017.03.016.

CHAPTER 12

Electric Vehicle Paradise? Exploring the Value Chains of Green Extractivism

Devyn Remme, Siddharth Sareen, Håvard Haarstad and Kjetil Rommetveit

Abstract

Norway has the world-class ambition to make transport more sustainable and climate friendly. Its electric vehicle (EV) rollout is celebrated by and aspirational for other countries, manifesting the imaginary of technological solutions for sustainable mobility. This chapter undertakes a critically constructive analysis of the value chains of this rollout, tracing the production, usage and discard of EVs. Our point of departure in Norway's EV rollout serves to map broader implications of a rapid, massive shift towards electric transport. We map relevant externalities associated with, for example, the mining of raw materials and with modes of digitalisation that run counter to circular economy principles. The requisite resources for the transition to renewably powered, electrified transportation—notably batteries—are sourced in the global South, whereas their consumption and industries that reuse and recycle valuable minerals are emerging in the global North. The uneven distribution of benefits and burdens is increasingly being criticised as green extractivism for an imperial mode of living. By paying attention to site-specific struggles over resources, our mapping demonstrates that practices of legitimation have yet to be welded with holistic accountability. By piecing together some major links along the value chains of Norway's EV rollout, we argue for a global perspective on this transition.

1 Introduction

Norway's electric vehicle (EV) rollout has made global headlines for multiple reasons: its all-inclusive incentive packages for electric cars (de Rubens et al., 2020), world-leading battery EV market share per capita (Figenbaum, 2020), and impressive EV charging infrastructure coverage (Funke et al., 2019). Thus far, the rollout remains a largely middle-and upper-class phenomenon (Fevang et al., 2021; Fjørtoft and Pilskog, 2020), relatively limited to electric cars compared to the global leader China with its massive electrified bus

 | DOI:10.1163/9789004686182_013

fleets (Li et al., 2020). Notably, this is beginning to change, with the procurement of electric buses (Thorne et al., 2021), expansion of light rail systems (Engebretsen, Christiansen and Strand, 2017) and advent of electric ferries along Norway's western coast (Njøs et al., 2020). The expansion of EVs has been criticised for perpetuating over consumption and overshadowing efforts to shift away from automobility and towards walking, cycling and public transportation (Henderson, 2020; Remme, Sareen and Haarstad, 2022). We concur that Norway's EV revolution merits critical attention but will show that critical attention should not be only paid to the effects within the country's cities—the EV revolution has global implications.

The Norwegian case has captured the imagination of innovation and diffusion scholars, notably in economic geography, transition studies and transport policy. Accounting for the diverse spatial–temporal implications of the rollout, however, requires holistic analysis of its value chain. This work is underway (see Henderson, 2020; Sovacool, 2019; Chester and Horvath, 2009), and includes a focus on lithium extraction as the colonial shadow of electromobility (Blair et al., chapter 10 in this volume; Jerez, Garcés and Torres, 2021; Schlosser, 2020) and the greenwashing of an imperial mode of living (Post, chapter 2 in this volume; Anlauf, 2017).

However, translocal aspects of EV rollout remain obfuscated in low-carbon transition narratives (Sareen and Grandin, 2020). EVs come from somewhere (which entails extraction and heavy material transport), exist somewhere (which means occupying limited public space and shaping spatial planning), and go somewhere (which implies end-of-life arrangements and limited material salvage). This necessitates a broader analysis of the implications of Norway's EV revolution. This chapter is based on a preliminary mapping and critically constructive analysis of the EV value chain, from mineral extraction to battery recycling, juxtaposed with popular imaginaries of Norway's EV revolution.

A major focus is lithium-ion (Li-ion) batteries, for which technological and market options are dynamic, but also characterised by persistent constraints: spatial concentrations of reserves, battery production hubs, limited demand centres, and resource-specific bottlenecks (Mayyas, Steward and Mann, 2019), notably involving cobalt (Olivetti et al., 2017). Limited knowledge on socio-environmental impacts is a cause for concern (Agusdinata et al., 2018; Klinger, 2017). Understanding of the recycling and reuse of Li-ion batteries is also only nascent (Rykalova, 2019; Gaines, 2019). Scholars identify value chain integration, involving diverse actors, as a key challenge (Mossali et al., 2020); this recognition has led to calls for circular economy business models and governmental priority-setting (Wrålsen et al., 2021).

We offer an overarching account, admittedly brief, of how the Norwegian EV imaginary mobilises a value chain and metabolises a rollout. Our analysis considers extraction, circular economy principles, translocal equity agendas (Sareen and Grandin, 2020), and disposal (Green, 2017). Situating the rollout in a global perspective, we analyse its implications for sites of extraction, discard and salvage, aspects that remain neglected relative to usage.

The next section reviews the literature on extraction, consumption and the afterlives of EVs, and their discursive construction as a sociotechnical imaginary. It combines longitudinal (life cycle and circular economy) and translocal (value chain) approaches to provide a robust spatial–temporal conceptual basis. Next we present an analytical framework, and employ it to structure the empirical analysis in the fourth section. The final section discusses key takeaways that stem from the empirical analysis and argues for a fuller knowledge base that privileges holistic spatiality over geographical immediacy, to question systemic logics that glorify 'greener' consumption, and to work towards systemic scaling and institutionalisation.

2 Material–Semiotic Mapping: Seeing Upstream, Seeing Downstream

EVs come with unintended socio-environmental consequences that remain understudied and uncertain (Lis et al., 2018; Di Felice, Renner and Giampietro, 2021; Xu et al., 2020). Looking at EVs from a wide perspective, going beyond the narratives of national policy success, reveals a host of unaddressed challenges. These include virtual water export due to lithium extraction in groundwater-reliant communities (Blair et al., chapter 10 in this volume; Ma, Opp and Dang, 2020; Liu and Agusdinata, 2020), labour exploitation and worsening inequality due to extraction at remote sites (Sovacool, 2019; Dunlap, Chapter 3 in this volume), the greenwashing of unsustainable environmental consumption (Swilling et al., 2013; Nguyen and Davidson, 2017), a lack of incentives and reliable monitoring of compliance with circular economy principles related to disposal and planned obsolescence (Velázquez-Martínez et al., 2019) and fragmented examples of sporadic improvisation without a systemic and scalable logic (Wrålsen et al., 2021).

In a more general sense, the drawbacks of extractive industries and the challenges of recycling merit greater attention as well (Olivetti et al., 2017; Bonelli and Dorador, 2021; Schlosser, 2020). Estimates of raw material availability and bottlenecks depend on many factors: how existing reserves are measured (Vikström, Davidsson and M. Höök, 2013), and what assumptions are made when predicting demand acceleration. Life cycle emission assessments vary greatly based on assumptions about electricity mixes (Girardi, Gargiulo and Brambilla, 2015), extraction and manufacture processes (Hawkins et al., 2013), user behaviour (Yuksel et al., 2016), vehicle weight (Nealer and Hendrickson, 2015), battery durability (Ellingsen et al., 2016), reuse potential, recycling (Gaines, 2014) and disposal (Hendrickson et al., 2015).

Furthermore, a transition focused on electric cars requires the massive decarbonisation of electric grids; this relies on extractive industries similar to those that enable electric cars (Kramarz, Park and Johnson, 2021). The argument for EV rollouts thus routinely goes hand in hand with the larger argument that a transition to 100 per cent renewable energy by 2050, without reducing energy use, is 'technically and economically feasible with little downside' (Jacobsen et al., 2015, 1). This overlooks the wider political ecologies involved in EV production. As BloombergNEF,[1] a key market analyst puts it:

> And what about all the lithium and other finite materials used in the batteries? BNEF analysed those markets as well and found they're just not an issue. Through 2030, battery packs will require less than 1% of the known reserves of lithium, nickel, manganese, and copper. They'll require 4% of the world's cobalt.

This quote illustrates the tendency to reduce these resources to global commodities, removed from the sociocultural and political economic contexts of extraction.

Yet markets are never independent of these wider relations (Callon, 1998). Linking a product and its consumer entails a great deal of work (Tsing, 2005); notably the discursive construction of sociotechnical imaginaries of some products as more just and sustainable, and therefore more desirable, than others. Mainstream economics abstracts the functioning of markets away from such relations and imaginaries of salvation through technological innovation work to construct EVs as 'zero emissions'. This semiotic manoeuvre makes negative externalities disappear, ignoring environmental pollution and social displacement at remote sites of extraction and failing to account for the high carbon and water intensity present in the extraction, manufacture, and discard of Li-ion batteries. Correspondingly, reductive visions of EVs as sustainable obscure the spatially uneven distribution of benefits and burdens.

While some of these uncertainties and gaps in knowledge can be reduced with greater information and quantitative analysis, others are more intractable.

1 https://about.bnef.com/ (accessed on 30 August 2023).

Di Felice, Renner and Giampietro (2021, 2) argue that 'the existence of irreducible uncertainties in the EV knowledge base points to a broader question of how science and policy interact in the co-creation of sustainability transition pathways' in ways that legitimise some agendas and foreclose others. Reports that project the demand for EVs and the availability of critical materials, including the initial labelling of some materials as 'critical', co-shape imaginaries that inform societal policies, attitudes, and efforts (Strand et al., 2018). The recursive relationship between imaginaries and policies can be aptly framed using the sociotechnical imaginaries approach (Di Felice, Renner and Giampietro, 2021; Bergman, Schwanen and Sovacool, 2017).

Focusing on national policy plans, Jasanoff and Kim (2009, 120) define imaginaries as 'collectively imagined forms of social life and social order reflected in the design and fulfilment of nation-specific scientific and/or technological projects'. Scholarship on sociotechnical imaginaries of EVs has mostly focused on imaginaries of and about users, and propagated by policymakers (Skjølsvold and Ryghaug, 2020; Di Felice, Renner and Giampietro, 2021; Bergman, Schwanen and Sovacool, 2017; Anfinsen, Lagesen and Ryghaug, 2019). These accounts characterise EV imaginaries as linked with ideas of ecomodernism, progress, techno-optimism, prosperity, low-carbon futures, environmental responsibility, green growth, and automobility as individual freedom. Less attention has been devoted to the vested interests that shape such imaginaries, which itself underscores how influential the (significantly Nordic)[2] imaginary of EVs as unequivocally positive has become.

The positive feedback loop between this imaginary and EV rollout policies has reinforced the positing of EVs as a solution and supported knowledge production on acceleration rather than on critical assessment of the justifications for the solution itself (e.g., Kotilainen et al., 2019). Justifications that promote EVs have been challenged by critical mobility scholars and extractivism scholars who have demonstrated the negative socio-environmental effects of car dependence and advocated for collective and active transport solutions and infrastructures (Henderson, 2020; Urry, 2004; Holden et al., 2020; Mattoili et al., 2020). While of interest to municipal planners, such studies seem to have had less impact on EV imaginaries among national policymakers.

This perspective also draws us towards a properly global frame of reference and postcolonial perspectives. Scholars of extractivism offer a direct critique of hegemonic EV imaginaries in relation to lithium operations in Latin America,

2 A 2021 Super Bowl commercial by General Motors featuring Will Ferrell called on the United States to catch up with Norway's electric vehicle transition, recognising it as a global leader: https://www.youtube.com/watch?v=mdsPvbSpB2Y (accessed on 18 July 2022).

'whereby extraction and valorisation of mineral resources is rendered not only compatible with "sustainable development," but necessary to it' (Voskoboynik and Andreucci, 2021, 16). Jerez, Garcés and Torres (2021, 1) argue that the 'green economy in the global north relies on green extractivism in the global south', as do Dunlap and Jacobsen (2020) and Riofrancos (2019). Anlauf (2017) and Schlosser (2020) combine green extractivism and the 'imperial mode of living' to frame the drivers and consequences of EVs. The 'imperial mode of living' signals how 'people's everyday practices, including individual and societal orientations, as well as identities, rely heavily on: (i) the unlimited appropriation of resources; (ii) a disproportionate claim to global and local ecosystems and sinks; and (iii) cheap labour from elsewhere' (Brand and Wissen, 2013, 152). Yet the dominant enthusiasm for electric automobility largely ignores these critiques, which occupy more radical discursive spaces.

The preceding literature review reveals a need for more holistic analysis of the political ecologies that underpin EV rollouts. There are multiple studies that point to aspects of the upstream and downstream effects of EVs. But there is a need for a framing on these analyses that connects the dots of these seemingly separate effects and developments. Therefore, in the next section we will outline an analytical approach that draws on the concept of commodity chains.

3 Towards a Value Chain Perspective on Electric Vehicles

In this chapter we argue for an analysis of the value chains of EVs and the imaginaries that mobilise them, focusing on how value is constructed, extracted, and concentrated along the EV commodity chain. Hopkins and Wallerstein (1977) coined the term 'commodity chains' in order to 'ground abstract-prone analysis of economic globalization in the everyday practices of firms, workers, households, states, and consumers' (Bair and Werner, 2011, 1). A commodity is the outcome of relational processes that connect actors and activities across space; studying processes linked to a particular commodity can thus unpack complex characteristics of the global economy.

Analysing the structure of the hydrocarbons value chain, Bridge (2010) identified key actors and imperatives that perpetuate the oil industry despite widespread recognition that climate change can and should be mitigated through emissions reductions. Scholars of science and technology studies highlight concrete mechanisms such as standards and certification schemes within value chains (Callon, 1998). These efforts clarify how value chains are constituted through material and semiotic transformations that produce commodities, products and pollution. For instance, Hartwick (1998) demonstrates the material–semiotic links between advertisements for gold, jewellery factories in Italy, male gold mine migrants in apartheid South Africa and their 'gold widows' in Lesotho.

Our mapping of the EV value chain is more preliminary than comprehensive, approached as a distributed web of nodes in dynamic relations co-constituted with market and political conditions. A comprehensive accounting of the impacts of EVs would feature detailed insight into different life cycle stages and connections across sectors; here we aim to provide an accessible overview, not an exhaustive one. A key point is that commodities travel in value chains whereas contextual information about labour conditions, environmental costs and other power relations does not. We aim to elucidate the impact of EVs in a manner that lays bare sociotechnical imaginaries reliant on green extractivism that perpetuate an imperial mode of living, curtailing opportunities for more globally just futures.

Our three-part analysis pulls together a wide range of existing work to better understand aspects of EV value chains from extraction, through consumption, to afterlives. To ensure meaningful depth on key selected aspects, we omit the stage between extraction and consumption, which includes multiple steps of transport, processing and manufacture. For instance, refinement requires energy intensive high temperatures and large volumes of water, and produces toxic by-products such as fluoride and sulfuric acid. In addition, the manufacture of semiconductors and battery cells and packs, and vehicle assembly, entail their own shifting geographies and socio-environmental impacts. This limit to scope is commensurate with our current effort and aimed at motivating future research with greater coverage and depth. To balance scale and resolution, we include global and regional trends alongside situated contextual details directed by relevance and representativeness.

Analysts have noted that *extraction* takes place far from the public eye. We hold that this invisibility of conditions of production for end users is essential to maintaining a glossy EV imaginary. The stage of *consumption* includes marketing, sale and usage, and is reliant on the prominence of spectacle and the performativity of the EV imaginary to shape public opinion and to lobby policymakers, in order to make EVs available and desirable to a wide set of publics. Finally, *afterlives* include the used car and spares market, salvage, and discard, categories that are emergent in the least formalised and regulated part of EV rollouts, where actors improvise to fill gaps and gain positional advantages on matters such as refurbishing, recycling and disposal.

To examine these three stages of the value chain for EVs deployed in Norway, we draw on peer-reviewed and grey literature, media reports, and primary observations from industry events, including the Nordic EV summit and Nordic Battery Thursdays during late 2021. The Nordic EV summit is co-organised by the Norwegian EV association (which promotes the interests of EV users and has over 75,000 members) and Norway Trade Fairs (Norway's largest exhibition centre). Nordic Battery Thursdays is co-organised by trade and industry lobby groups Business Finland and Business Sweden, the government funding organisation Innovation Norway, and EBA 2050, an industrial development programme of the European Battery Alliance (EBA). The last of these is driven by EIT InnoEnergy, an independent European Union (EU) body aiming to strengthen European competitiveness in sustainable energy. Both events are geared towards bringing industry actors and policymakers together to develop best practices for the sector and exhibit new technologies and companies.

Our overall mapping exercise is informed by the observation that industry actors continue to routinely refer to 'sustainable', 'ethical', and 'clean' mining, as critiqued by, for example, Whitmore (2006) and later by Han Onn and Woodley (2014). Such desirable forms of mining are to be delivered through 'traceable' and 'transparent' supply chains. The relationship between sustainable/ethical relations and traceability/transparency seems to be taken for granted, indicating that any current lack of accountability is assumed to be the result of incomplete information. The assumption that more data is the key to sustainability is an important element in how private industry actors and policymakers are interacting to co-create sustainability transition pathways.

4 Mapping and Analysis

We now present our analysis of three stages in the value chain of the EV roll-out in Norway. Global electric car sales have grown exponentially since 2010 (IEA, 2020). Despite overall car sales slumping by a fifth during the pandemic in 2020, electric car sales continued to accelerate (IEA, 2020). In Norway, electric cars surpassed a 20 per cent share of the total car fleet in 2020. Solidifying Norway's position as the global EV capital, 2021 saw electric cars comprise over 60 per cent of new car sales.

There are more than 140 components in an average car, regardless of fuel type. Electric vehicles contain many of the same materials as internal combustion engine vehicles, including steel, lead, plastics, aluminium, and a variety of chemicals that cause emissions (Hawkins et al., 2013; Henderson, 2020). Here we focus on the elements that are particular to the Li-ion batteries in EVs, rather than the materials they have in common with fossil fuel–powered cars.

4.1 *Extraction*

> Meeting climate goals will turbo charge the demand for raw materials.
>
> European Battery Alliance Programme Director at the Nordic EV Summit, 2021

Meeting the projected demand for the raw materials used in EVs is a major topic at industry events and in policy documents such as the EU action plan on the circular economy and the Norwegian national strategy for a green and circular economy. One of the top priorities of the European Battery Alliance (EBA, 2021), a partner in the EU Circular Economy Action Plan, is to 'secure access to sustainably produced battery raw materials at reasonable cost'. At the Nordic EV summit, participants repeatedly used the terms 'ethical', 'clean' and 'sustainable' mining. The moderator declared, 'We can do it if we set our minds to it'. The EBA director claimed, 'development of sustainable, traceable and transparent supply chains [is] a prerequisite to sustain[ing] [...] continued market growth'. Exactly how traceability and transparency contribute to environmental sustainability is left unspecified.

We focus in on cobalt sourcing to explore this imaginary further. Cobalt is currently listed as a 'critical resource' in the EU and is required for the Li-ion batteries found in Norwegian EVs. The Democratic Republic of Congo (DRC) supplies 60 per cent of the world's cobalt and conditions for miners are frequently abhorrent (Niarchos, 2021). As a panel moderator at Nordic Battery Thursdays stated, 'all of us know that there are problems with mining cobalt so removing it will give sustainability benefits'. However, the potential negative consequences of developing battery technologies without cobalt include abandoning commitments to improve conditions at extraction sites and to provide opportunities for economic development (Sovacool, 2019), reducing electric vehicles' range, displacing the demand to other minerals and undermining the economic viability of recycling industries.

While Chinese companies dominate cobalt extraction and refining, they are not the only player. Glencore, incorporated in Switzerland, is the world's largest publicly traded commodity supplier and operates two of the largest mines in the DRC. In June 2020, Tesla signed a long-term contract to source cobalt from Glencore for its factories in Berlin and Shanghai (Stringer and Biesheuvel, 2020). Concomitant with the wider discourse, Glencore consistently links 'responsible' and 'ethical' sourcing with 'transparency' and 'traceability' in their supply chain. Traceability and transparency are further reduced to tracking and certification schemes. Until recently these were supposed to ensure that the cobalt was extracted from officially sanctioned industrial mines rather than by artisanal or small-scale miners. After signing the deal with Tesla, Glencore announced the launch of the Fair Cobalt Alliance, which it claims will work to improve conditions in the informal sector and encourage battery manufacturers not to engineer out Congolese cobalt.

Exposure to cobalt is associated with a number of health risks including DNA damage (Banza Lubaba Nkulu et al., 2009; 2018), higher risk of congenital birth defects (Kayembe Kitenge et al., 2020a) and potentially fatal lung disease (Kayembe Kitenge et al., 2020b). Studies have found very high concentrations of the element and other metals in the urine of children around mining sites (Kayembe Kitenge et al., 2020b). Cobalt mining in the DRC is notoriously implicated in child labour (Niarchos, 2021; Faber, Krause and Sánchez de la Sierra, 2017; Chohan, 2018). In 2019 a lawsuit was filed in the US against Tesla and other significant buyers of cobalt on behalf of children who were maimed or killed in tunnel or wall collapses while mining cobalt in the DRC. The plaintiffs asserted claims of forced child labour in violation of the Trafficking Victims Protection Reauthorization Act. The companies claimed 'they did not have "requisite knowledge" of the abuses at the specific mining sites mentioned, and that "knowledge of a general problem in an industry [...] is insufficient" to prove they knew about the violations that had injured the plaintiffs' (BHRRC, 2021). In 2021 the case was dismissed, partly because the Judge asserted 'the harm they [the plaintiffs] allege is not traceable to any defendant' (BHRRC, 2021).

Local organisations representing miners claim the big mining companies use subcontractors to avoid accountability (Pettison, 2021). Subcontractors can end contracts with miners at any time, contributing to a climate of fear and attrition that discourages workers from organising for better pay or holding their employers accountable for safety or environmental hazards. Additionally, Glencore has employed other tactics, such as shell companies and jurisdictional arbitrage, to avoid financial accountability (Public Eye, 2017). In 2017 a human rights watch group filed a lawsuit leading to the Swiss Federal Prosecutor's office opening a criminal investigation into Glencore for its failure to prevent alleged corruption in the DRC. In 2019 Glencore lost a landmark case in Australia regarding the legality of using leaked documents as evidence in investigations of financial crimes. Glencore Chief, Ivan Glasenberg, said in a speech following the decision, 'At least in the Congo they need you, they want you there and if they start changing the rules, you may not continue investing' (Chenoweth, 2019).

At COP26, the Congolese Deputy Prime Minister and Minister for the Environment, Eve Bazaiba, announced to the ambassador of Switzerland and the public that the DRC plans to block Glencore from exporting raw materials from the country: 'We can no longer accept these exports. We too must move towards ecological transition. Cobalt cannot be exported, transformed and manufactured into batteries outside the country, while we are reduced to selling our teeth to afford a green vehicle' (Landgrand, 2021). Glencore has not responded to the announcement and its website hosts plans to expand mining operations in the DRC, although in May 2022 the corporation pled guilty to violating the Foreign Corrupt Practices Act and to a commodity price manipulation scheme (USDOJ, 2022). Glencore's actions included more than USD 100 million worth of bribes to officials in Brazil, Cameroon, Ivory Coast, Equatorial Guinea, Nigeria, Congo (DRC), South Sudan and Venezuela between 2007 and 2018. As a result, the African Energy Chamber has requested that Glencore lose its membership of the Extractive Industry's Transparency Initiative (EITI), although the EITI has issued a statement saying that it welcomes recent actions taken by Glencore to remedy the situation and encourages the corporation's active participation in the EITI to ensure that 'we can learn from this unfortunate experience and identify measures that will prevent it from happening again' (EITI, 2022). In April 2022, the governments of the DRC and Zambia signed a cooperation agreement to establish a Battery Council and integrate the EV value chain within their territories, including plans to build processing plants and an EV battery factory (Wansi, 2022).

4.2 *Consumption*

The dominant narrative about Norwegian EV adoption holds that it is the result of demand-oriented climate change policies. For example, an article in *The Guardian* claims that 'Norway's lead on electric cars has been driven by the government backing them with a wide range of generous incentives and perks, as a way of meeting its climate change ambitions' (Vaughan, 2017). However, EV policies in Norway have evolved over time from their original intent to stimulate industrial development (Skjølsvold and Ryghaug, 2020). Since the turn towards demand-oriented policies, imaginaries of EVs as environmentally friendly and of those who drive them as 'good', 'green citizens' (Green, Steinbach and Datta, 2012) have been crucial aspects of EV promotion (Ingeborgrud and Ryghaug, 2019). User surveys have found that EV owners in Norway are often motivated by concern for the environment in addition to economic incentives (Thronsen, 2019; Tvinnereim and Ferguson-Cradler, 2020; Anfinsen, 2021).

A representative for Northvolt, a battery manufacturing company in Norway, stated at an industry event that 'When we started out "sustainability" was a nice, cute extra bonus but not important for the customers. Now it is central'. Research on consumer motivations reveals that Norwegian EV owners claim to be environmentally motivated (Anfinsen, Lagesen and Ryghaug, 2019); it is, however, difficult to say how 'real' these self-reported motivations are. There are a plethora of consumer outreach and awareness campaigns working to promote EV adoption in Norway and the rest of Europe (Jin and Slowvik, 2017). One of the priority areas for the EBA, which is present at most Nordic EV industry events, is to 'Involve the EU citizens in the journey: inform, educate and motivate' because, 'public-sector efforts (education in schools, role modelling and so on) should be invested in the general population's awareness and understanding of the entire value chain so that there is relevant societal appropriation from the start' (EBA, 2021). Given the materials present on the Alliance's website, we take this statement to refer to highlighting EV industry–related economic opportunities in European regions, including with regard to manufacturing and recycling, rather than to informing consumers about the potential negative impacts of EV value chains outside Europe.

While the success of EV promotion campaigns is often measured in Norway by the percentage of the car fleet that is electric, far less attention is paid to how many kilometres are driven in electric vehicles and whether they are purchased in addition to fossil fuel vehicles or replace them. In 2019, less than 10 per cent of the kilometres driven in personal vehicles were driven with electric cars (Moberg, 2020). Reports show that EVs in Norway are usually second or third cars in a household (Fjørtoft and Pilskog, 2020). Drivers use their conventional vehicles for longer drives, for example to vacation homes, which are popular in Norway (RVU, 2019).

There are also concerns about elite capture of the benefits of EV subsidies (Fevang et al., 2021; Wågsæther et al., 2022). As of 2019, 37 per cent of Norway's electric vehicles were owned by households in the top ten percentile of income earners and 58 per cent were owned by those in the top 20 percentile (Fjørtoft and Pilskog, 2020). In 2018, EV subsidies amounted to approximately USD 883 million (7.2 billion Norwegian kroners, or approximately 739 million euros), and the figure was USD 1.28 billion (11 billion Norwegian kroners, or approximately 1.1 billion euros) in 2019[3] (Fjørtoft and Pilskog, 2020). These subsidies are in addition to exemption from or vastly discounted road tolls, which has raised the cost of tolls for fossil fuel–vehicle drivers (Krehic, 2019). The recent political backlash against road tolls has centred on claims of social injustice and pushing back on depoliticised and moralising sustainable mobility agendas (Wanvik and Haarstad 2021; Wågsæther et al., 2022).

The director of Norway's Institute of Transport Economics (TØI) recently held that the Norwegian government must end the economic subsidies for electric vehicles because they are outcompeting efforts to promote public

3 The conversions in this chapter use the appropriate historical exchange rates.

transportation (Bentszrød, 2021). In 2019, a 'technology expert panel' recommended the government replace the 'zero growth in personal traffic target' currently governing transportation policy and funding in every Norwegian city with a 'zero emissions' target, because of EV adoption. This proposal was written into the last National Transport Plan for review (Regjeringen, 2019). The change would have major implications for the urban planning paradigm that has been guiding development for several decades including compact city building and prioritising walking, cycling and public transport. The national government recently approved several new intercity superhighways, replacing two lanes with four and building mega infrastructure such as bridges and undersea tunnels, signalling that automobility will remain a central element of transportation planning in Norway.

The Norwegian EV imaginary is further shaped by strategic efforts to convince and mobilise consumers through evangelising the desirability and sustainability of EVs. When lobby groups such as the union for electric car owners declare, 'we can do it if we set our minds to it' (referring to sustainable and ethical mining), they are part of constructing the 'ecomodern' discourse that relies on salvation through technological innovation and sustained economic growth. Without more concrete mechanisms that explicate the relationship between 'sustainable' or 'ethical' mining and 'traceable, transparent' supply chains, we interpret these discursive constructions as legitimation practices that remain to be fully operationalised for accountability.

4.3 *Afterlives*

Circular economy models are increasingly presented as the solution to potential supply shortages and environmental damage related to the electric vehicle transition (Wrålsen et al., 2021; Rallo et al., 2020). The EU is keen for circular economy models to deliver ecological modernisation—reconciling continuous economic growth measured by GDP with reducing emissions and environmental degradation (EC, 2020). New 'regulations for sustainable batteries' under the EU's circular economy action plan began taking effect in January 2022. The aspiration of circular economics is to avoid or reduce the exploitation of raw materials by closing material and energy loops in biological and technical cycles and lengthening the life cycle of goods (Prieto-Sandoval, Jaca and Ormazabal, 2018). Examples include reuse for stationary energy storage (Kamath et al., 2020) and recovering valuable materials through recycling (Baars et al., 2021; Jiao and Evens, 2016). However, analysts are sceptical this will have any impact on expanding primary extraction in the next few decades (Gaines, 2014; Xu et al., 2020).

In 2019, 1,400 electric and hybrid cars were scrapped in Norway and most of these were less than five years old (Myklebust, 2021). This is partially due to insurance industry standards, which dictate if the cost of repairs exceeds 60 per cent of the cost of a new car, the vehicle should be scrapped. However, installing used parts renders new car guarantees void, leading to substantially inflated prices for repairs (Myklebust, 2021; Stumpf, 2021). In Norway, only 2 per cent of the total amount of vehicle repairs are carried out with used parts (Myklebust, 2021; Stumpf, 2021). Right to repair (RtR) legislation may increase the lifespan of electric vehicles by allowing independent repair shops access to the same diagnostic data as automobile manufacturers (Myklebust, 2021; Stumpf, 2021). Car manufacturers have lobbied against RtR proposals, using a variety of arguments including safety concerns related to batteries, cybersecurity, and possible violation of emissions regulations.[4] Tesla, a major EV supplier to the Norwegian market, has punished customers who obtain unauthorised repairs, including by permanently disabling access to its Supercharging network and fast charging using third-party chargers for any 'unsupported' repairs (Stumpf, 2021).

Once batteries are too degraded for use in EVs they retain more than two-thirds of their usable energy storage capacity and may provide five to eight years more service in a secondary application (Ambrose et al., 2020). A second use battery is functional until it reaches 60 per cent of its initial capacity, at which point it is sent for recycling or disposal (Cicconi et al., 2012). Reuse for stationary energy storage is still uncommon but expected to grow (Cicconi et al., 2012; Wrålsen et al., 2021). However, extending the life of batteries through reuse applications delays their entry into recycling, thereby contributing to further primary extraction in the meantime (Gaines, 2019).

The projected massive demand for battery recycling and disposal is increasingly connected to national discourses around 'new green industries and jobs' and 'green growth' (Grobæk, 2021). State-backed industries for recycling are being established, including Europe's largest recycling plant, in Poland (Reiserer, 2021), and another in Norway. However, the projected demand far outstrips the projected capacity (Wrålsen et al., 2021; Olivetti et al., 2017; Gaines, 2019). Battery pack designs are not standardised or optimised for easy disassembly and recovery of valuable materials (Ambrose et al., 2020; Kamath

4 In 2020, the Alliance for Automotive Innovation, a trade group that includes almost every large auto manufacturer and original equipment manufacturer relevant to the EV space, filed a suit against RtR legislation in the United States. In addition to court proceedings, the group also ran advertisements suggesting that RtR legislation would put women at risk and benefit 'sexual predators' (Gault, 2020).

et al., 2020). EV batteries were exported from Norway to China until 2018 when China stopped accepting them. Since then, batteries are stored and dismantled in Norway before some of them are sent onwards to recycling plants in Belgium, Germany or Canada (Brandslet, 2019). Almost no lithium or graphite is recovered because it is not cost-effective compared with primary supplies. Recycling is geared towards recovering cobalt, nickel and copper (EC, 2020). The volume of recovered metals used in battery manufacturing is currently low but new EU battery regulations state that EV batteries will have to declare the content of recycled cobalt, lead, lithium and nickel from 1 January 2027, and by 2030 batteries will need to contain minimum levels of recycled materials (EC, 2020). Alternative battery chemistries, such as LFP (Lithium iron phosphate),[5] that do not require cobalt are attractive to manufacturers but risk undermining nascent industries for recycling because cobalt is what makes recycling economically viable at this stage (Gaines, 2019).

5 Conclusion

The negative consequences of mass EV adoption have largely been neglected within the dominant Norwegian EV imaginary. While the Norwegian EV phenomenon is ostensibly driven by climate and sustainability concerns, it can be characterised as an ecomodernist discourse that wilfully ignores its own limitations. Problems highlighted in our analysis show cracks growing between the sociotechnical imaginary of electric vehicles and the sobering reality. There is a need for a more holistic analysis of the negative externalities of EV rollout. In this chapter we have argued for a commodity chain perspective in order to capture the wide range of effects of EVs and their extensive rollout. We have sought to extend the form of reductionist accounting that dominates both policy and scholarship on EVs to capture more of what is at stake for communities and ecologies during the transition to EVs. This approach reveals the implicit normative claims that make it possible to discursively separate matter from its entanglements and mobilise imaginaries about green electromobility.

It is not that aggregate, quantitative knowledge related to energy and resources is not useful, but that cost–benefit analyses that assume fungible people and places obscure situated injustices and privilege geographic immediacy over holistic spatiality. The materials required for electric vehicles are

5 In 2021 Tesla announced it will be using LFP batteries for some of its vehicles and stationary storage, *CNBC*, https://www.cnbc.com/2021/10/20/tesla-switching-to-lfp-batteries-in-all-standard-range-cars.html (accessed on 9 March 2023).

embedded in global supply chains that outsource emissions and environmental degradation from the Norwegian territory, where these cars are driven. This enables the construction of EVs as 'zero emission', and as singularly positive for the climate. Creative accounting that outsources emissions and other environmental degradations to the global South, while promoting a narrative of leading the way in climate change mitigation, perpetuates the colonial exploitation that undergirds modernity's strategic relations of power and production. This form of accounting is not only unjust, it also ensures that we will surpass the bio-geo-chemical tipping points we are rapidly approaching or, in some cases, have already passed.

This chapter analysed the global social and environmental consequences of the Norwegian EV imaginary and offers three key areas in need of attention from future research and policy design:

1. Industry actors link the terms 'responsible', 'ethical' and 'sustainable' mining with traceability and transparency in their supply chains. These terms are used to legitimise extraction for electric vehicles; however, policies should be informed more by research on how legitimation practices are linked (or not) with long-term accountability towards impacted places and people.
2. Circular economy regulations should prioritise deepening the mitigation potential of EVs and benefiting people and ecologies all along value chains, especially extraction sites, not just benefit the actors who are well positioned to leverage economic opportunities in the global North, perpetuating the imperial mode of living through green extractivism.
3. It is vital to maintain and promote imaginaries of urban sustainable mobility in policy circles beyond EVs. The passionate and dedicated innovators and advocates of electric vehicles as a mitigation effort must be supported by simultaneous and radical reductions in energy and resource use. It is not about technological *or* social innovations, cars *or* no cars; it's about holistic approaches for deep decarbonisation and global justice.

Although circular economy models aim to lengthen the life of electric vehicles and thereby reduce the demand for extraction, there is a danger that the value added in practice will largely be captured in the global North through new market opportunities in the reuse and recycling industries while extraction in the global South will continue to expand. According to dominant imaginaries, the demand for EVs and other uses for Li-ion batteries is expected to soar far beyond the capacity of emergent reuse and recycling industries to provide the materials for battery production, let alone at competitive prices. If the circular economy is primarily focused on integrating waste streams into economic growth practices in the global North, it perpetuates the imperial mode of living based on green extractivism. Our findings resonate with Anlauf's (2017, 191) argument that green economy strategies, such as the EU Circular Economy Action Plan, rely on 'asymmetries of power, and spatially and temporarily externalise ecological and social costs' and that '[t]herefore, they fail to promote socio-ecological justice, but are rather "greening" the imperial mode of living'.

Despite the socio-ecological costs of extraction, there is an argument that reducing emissions from transportation in wealthy countries benefits everyone because the effects of mitigation are global. From that perspective, the most vulnerable countries benefit even more from the transition to EVs than the countries in which they are primarily driven. However, there are other pathways to mitigating emissions from transportation that require far less resources per person than automobility. Seeing systemic embeddedness is central to our ability to reason about the future. Our analysis demonstrates why rapid technological innovation and deployment that reduce emissions and energy and resource use must be coupled with radical reductions in energy and resource use delivered through political and social change. Limited natural resources, energy and urban space will prevent most of the world's population from ever owning a private vehicle. Those most negatively impacted by the production of EVs are often the least likely to drive one, exemplifying the imperial mode of living linked with green extractivism.

Acknowledgements

The authors acknowledge the support of the University of Bergen through its Global Challenges strategic area, and the Research Council of Norway (grant 321421) and JPI Climate funded project Responsive Organising for Low Emission Societies (ROLES).

References

Agusdinata, D.B., W. Liu, H. Eakin and H. Romero (2018) 'Socio-environmental impacts of lithium mineral extraction: towards a research agenda', *Environmental Research Letters*, 13(12), 123001, DOI: 10.1088/1748-9326/aae9b1.

Ambrose, H., A. Kendall, M. Slattery and T. Steckel (2020) *Battery Second-life: Unpacking opportunities and barriers for the reuse of electric vehicle batteries*, Prepared for CalRecycle and the AB2832 Working Group.

Anfinsen, M. (2021) 'Between stability and change: Tensions in the Norwegian electric mobility transition', *Social Studies of Science*, 51(6), pp. 895–913, DOI: 10.1177/03063127211022842.

Anfinsen, M., V.A. Lagesen and M. Ryghaug (2019) 'Green and gendered? Cultural perspectives on the road towards electric vehicles in Norway', *Transportation research. Part D, Transport and environment*, 71, pp. 37–46.

Anlauf, A. (2017) 'Greening the imperial mode of living? Socio.ecological (in)justice, electromobility and the lithium mining of Argentina', in M. Pichler, C. Staritz, K. Küblböck, C. Plank, W. Raza and F. Ruiz Peyr (eds.) *Fairness and Justice in Natural Resource Politics* (London: Routledge), pp. 176–192, DOI: 10.4324/9781315638058.

Baars, J., T. Domenech, R. Bleischwitz et al. (2021) 'Circular economy strategies for electric vehicle batteries reduce reliance on raw materials', *Nat Sustain*, 4, pp. 71–79.

Bair, J. and M. Werner (2011) 'Commodity Chains and the Uneven Geographies of Global Capitalism: a Disarticulations Perspective', *Environment and Planning A: Economy and Space*, 43(5), pp. 988–997, DOI: 10.1068/a43505.

Bentszrød, S.B. (2021) 'TØI-sjefen: – Elbiler kommer til å utkonkurrere kollektivtrafikken', *Aftenposten*, August 21, https://www.aftenposten.no/norge/i/G3P946/toei-sjefen-elbiler-kommer-til-aa-utkonkurrere-kollektivtrafikken (accessed on 23 September 2021).

Banza Lubaba Nkulu, C., L. Casas and V. Haufroid et al. (2018) 'Sustainability of artisanal mining of cobalt in DR Congo', *Nature Sustainability*, 1, pp. 495–504, DOI: 10.1038/s41893-018-0139-4.

Banza Lubaba Nkulu, C., et al. (2009) 'High human exposure to cobalt and other metals in Katanga, a mining area of the Democratic Republic of Congo', *Environmental Research*, 109(6), pp. 745–752, DOI: 10.1016/j.envres.2009.04.012.

Bergman, N., T. Schwanen, B.K. Sovacool (2017) 'Imagined people, behaviour and future mobility: Insights from visions of electric vehicles and car clubs in the United Kingdom', *Transport Policy*, 59, DOI: 10.1016/j.tranpol.2017.07.016.

BHRRC (Business and Human Rights Resource Centre) (2021) 'Lawsuit against Apple, Google, Tesla, and others (re child labour, DRC)' (London, New York: BHRRC), https://www.business-humanrights.org/en/latest-news/lawsuit-against-apple-google-tesla-and-others-re-child-labour-drc/ (accessed on 15 February 2022).

Bonelli, B. and C. Dorador (2021) 'Endangered Salares: micro-disasters in Northern Chile', *Tapuya: Latin American Science, Technology and Society*, 4(1), DOI: 10.1080/25729861.2021.1968634.

Brand, U. and M. Wissen (2013) 'Crisis and continuity of capitalist society-nature relationships: the imperial mode of living and the limits to environmental governance', *Review of international political economy: RIPE*, 20(4), pp. 687–71, DOI: 10.1080/09692290.2012.691077.

Brandslet, S. (2019) 'Lithium can now be recycled', *Norwegian SciTech News*, 10 December, https://norwegianscitechnews.com/2019/12/lithium-can-now-be-recycled/ (accessed on 15 August 2022).

Bridge, G. (2010) 'Resource geographies I: Making carbon economies, old and new', *Progress in Human Geography*, 35(6), pp. 820–834, DOI: 10.1177/0309132510385524.

Callon, M. (1998) *The Laws of the Markets* (Hoboken: Wiley-Blackwell).

Chenoweth, N. (2019) 'Glencore's real Paradise Papers problem', *Australian Financial Review*, August 23, https://www.afr.com/rear-window/glencore-s-real-paradise-papers-problem-20190822-p52jq7 (accessed on 23 February 2022).

Chester, M. and A. Horvath (2009) 'Environmental assessment of passenger transportation should include infrastructure and supply chains', *Environmental Research Letters*, 4(2), 024008, DOI: 10.1088/1748-9326/4/2/024008.

Cicconi, P., D. Landi, A. Morbidoni and M. Germani (2012) *Feasibility analysis of second life applications for Li-Ion cells used in electric powertrain using environmental indicators*, IEEE International Energy Conference and Exhibition (ENERGYCON), pp. 985–990.

Chohan, U. (2018) 'Blockchain and the extractive industries: cobalt case study', *SSRN Electron. J.*, DOI: 10.2139/ssrn.3138271.

De Rubens, G.Z., L. Noel, J. Kester and B.K. Sovacool (2020) 'The market case for electric mobility: Investigating electric vehicle business models for mass adoption', *Energy*, 194, 116841, DOI: 10.1016/j.energy.2019.116841.

Di Felice, L.J., A. Renner and M. Giampietro (2021) 'Why should the EU implement electric vehicles? Viewing the relationship between evidence and dominant policy solutions through the lens of complexity', *Environmental Science & Policy*, 123, pp. 1–10, DOI: 10.1016/j.envsci.2021.05.002.

Dunlap, A. and J. Jakobsen (2020) *The Violent Technologies of Extraction: Political Ecology, Critical Agrarian Studies and the Capitalist Worldeater* (London: Palgrave).

EBA (European Battery Alliance) (2021) *Priority Actions* (Eindhoven: EBA), https://www.eba250.com/actions-projects/priority-actions/ (accessed on 23 February 2022).

EC (European Commission) (2020) *Circular economy action plan: for a cleaner and more competitive Europe*, Off. J. Eur. Union (Brussels: European Commission).

EITI (Extractive Industry Transparency Initiative) (2022) *Statement from the EITI board chair on the Glencore bribery case*, Statement from Rt Hon. Helen Clark, 26 May, https://eiti.org/articles/statement-eiti-board-chair-glencore-bribery-case (accessed on 27 June 2022).

Ellingsen, L.A. W., B. Singh and A.H. Strømman (2016). 'The size and range effect: lifecycle greenhouse gas emissions of electric vehicles', *Environmental Research Letters*, 11(5), DOI: 10.1088/1748-9326/11/5/054010.

Engebretsen, Ø., P. Christiansen and A. Strand (2017) 'Bergen light rail–Effects on travel behaviour', *Journal of Transport Geography*, 62, pp. 111–121, DOI: 10.1016/j.jtrangeo.2017.05.013.

Faber, B., B. Krause and R. Sánchez de la Sierra (2017) *Artisanal mining, livelihoods, and child labor in the cobalt supply chain of the Democratic Republic of Congo* (UC Berkeley: Center for Effective Global Action), https://escholarship.org/uc/item/17m9g4wm (accessed on 23 February 2022).

Fevang, E., E. Figenbaum, L. Fridstrøm, A.H. Halse, K.E. Hauge, B.G. Johansen and O. Raaum (2021) 'Who goes electric? The anatomy of electric car ownership in Norway', *Transportation Research Part D: Transport and Environment*, 92, 102727, DOI: 10.1016/j.trd.2021.102727.

Figenbaum, E. (2020) 'Norway: the world leader in BEV adoption', in *Who's driving electric cars* (Wiesbaden: Springer, Cham), pp. 89–120.

Fjørtoft, T. and G. Pilskog (2020) 'Dei rikaste kjøpte 4 av 10 elbilar', *Statistics Norway*, 14, https://www.ssb.no/transport-og-reiseliv/artikler-og-publikasjoner/dei-rikaste-kjopte-4-av-10-elbilar (accessed on 21 September 2021).

Funke, S.Á., F. Sprei, T. Gnann and P. Plötz (2019) 'How much charging infrastructure do electric vehicles need? A review of the evidence and international comparison', *Transportation Research Part D: Transport and Environment*, 77, pp. 224–242, DOI: 10.1016/j.trd.2019.10.024.

Gaines, L. (2019) 'Profitable Recycling of Low-Cobalt Lithium-Ion Batteries Will Depend on New Process Developments', *One Earth*, 1(4), pp. 413–415, DOI: 10.1016/j.oneear.2019.12.001.

Gaines, L. (2014) 'The future of automotive lithium-ion battery recycling: charting a sustainable course', *Sustainable Materials and Technologies*, 1–2, pp. 2–7, DOI: 10.1016/j.susmat.2014.10.001.

Gault, M. (2020) 'Auto Industry TV Ads Claim Right to Repair Benefits 'Sexual Predators'', *Vice*, September 1, https://www.vice.com/en/article/qj4ayw/auto-industry-tv-ads-claim-right-to-repair-benefits-sexual-predators (accessed on 9 August 2022).

Girardi, P., A. Gargiulo and P.C. Brambilla (2015) 'A comparative LCA of an electric vehicle and an internal combustion engine vehicle using the appropriate power mix: the Italian case study', The *International Journal of Life Cycle Assessment*, 20, pp. 1127–1142, DOI: 10.1007/s11367-015-0903-x.

Green, M. (2017) 'Aspects of battery legislation in recycling and Re-use', *Johnson Matthey Technology Review*, 61, pp. 87–92, DOI: 10.1595/205651317X694894.

Green, J., R. Steinbach and J. Datta (2012) 'The Travelling Citizen: Emergent Discourses of Moral Mobility in a Study of Cycling in London', *Sociology* (Oxford), 46(2), pp. 272–289, DOI: 10.1177/0038038511419193.

Grobæk (2021) 'Building a circular battery economy in Norway', *The Explorer*, February 22, https://www.theexplorer.no/stories/energy/building-a-circular-battery-economy-in-norway/ (accessed on 21 October 2021).

Han Onn, A. and A. Woodley (2014) 'A discourse analysis on how the sustainability agenda is defined within the mining industry', *Journal of cleaner production*, 84, pp. 116–127.

Hartwick, E. (1998) 'Geographies of Consumption: a Commodity-Chain Approach', *Environment and Planning D: Society and Space*, 16(4), pp. 423–437, DOI: 10.1068/a3256.

Hawkins, T., B. Singh, G. Majeau-Bettez and A. Hammer Strømman (2013) 'Comparative environmental life cycle assessment of conventional and electric vehicles', *Journal of Industrial Ecology*, 17(1), pp. 53–64, DOI: 10.1111/j.1530-9290.2012.00532.x.

Henderson, J. (2020) 'EVs are not the answer: a mobility justice critique of electric vehicle transitions', *Annals of the American Association of Geographers*, 110(6), pp. 1993–2010, DOI: 10.1080/24694452.2020.1744422.

Hendrickson, T.P., O. Kavvada, N. Shah, R. Sathre and C.D. Scown (2015) 'Life-cycle implications and supply chain logistics of electric vehicle battery recycling in California', *Environmental Research Letters*, 10(1), DOI: 10.1088/1748-9326/10/1/014011.

Holden, E., D. Banister, S. Gössling, G. Gilpin and K. Linnerud (2020) 'Grand Narratives for sustainable mobility: A conceptual review', *Energy Research & Social Science*, 65, 101454.

Hopkins, T, and I. Wallerstein (1977) 'Patterns of Development of the Modern World-System', *Review – Fernand Braudel Center for the Study of Economies, Historical Systems, and Civilizations*, 1(2), pp. 111–145.

IEA (The International Energy Agency) (2020) *Key World Energy Statistics 2020* (Paris: IEA), https://www.iea.org/reports/key-world-energy-statistics-2020 (accessed on 23 February 2021).

Ingeborgrud, L., and M. Ryghaug (2019) 'The role of practical, cognitive and symbolic factors in the successful implementation of battery electric vehicles in Norway', *Transportation Research Part A: Policy and Practice*, 130, pp. 507–516.

Jacobson, M.Z., M.A. Delucchi, G. Bazouin, Z.A. Bauer, C. Heavey, E. Fisher, E., and T.W. Yeskoo (2015) '100% clean and renewable wind, water, and sunlight (WWS) all-sector energy roadmaps for the 50 United States', *Energy & Environmental Science*, 8(7), 2093–2117

Jasanoff, S. and S.H. Kim (2009) 'Containing the atom: sociotechnical imaginaries and nuclear power in the United States and South Korea', *Minerva*, 47, pp. 119–146, DOI: 10.1007/s11024-009-9124-4.

Jiao, N. and S. Evans (2016) 'Secondary use of electric vehicle batteries and potential impacts on business models', *Journal of Industrial and Production Eng*ineering, 33(5), pp. 348–354, DOI: 10.1080/21681015.2016.1172125.

Jin, L. and P. Slowvik (2017) *Literature review of electric vehicle consumer awareness and outreach activities*, ICCT Working paper, March 21 (Washington, D.C.: International Council on Clean Transportation (ICCT)), https://theicct.org/publication/literature-review-of-electric-vehicle-consumer-awareness-and-outreach/ (accessed on 18 July 2022).

Jerez, B., I. Garcés and R. Torres (2021) 'Lithium extractivism and water injustices in the Salar de Atacama, Chile: the colonial shadow of green electromobility', *Political Geography*, 87, 102382, DOI: 10.1016/j.polgeo.2021.102382.

Kamath, D., R. Arsenault, H.C. Kim and A. Anctil (2020) 'Economic and environmental feasibility of second-life lithium-ion batteries as fast-charging energy storage', *Environmental Science and Technology*, 54, pp. 6878–6887, DOI: 10.1021/acs.est.9b05883.

Kayembe Kitenge, T. et al. (2020a) 'Agnathia otocephaly: a case from the Katanga Copperbelt', *Birth defects research*, 112(16), pp. 1287–1291, DOI: 10.1002/bdr2.1758.

Kayembe Kitenge, T. et al. (2020b) 'Respiratory Health and Urinary Trace Metals among Artisanal Stone-Crushers: a Cross-Sectional Study in Lubumbashi, DR Congo', *International journal of environmental research and public health*, 17(24), 9384, DOI: 10.3390/ijerph17249384.

Klinger, J.M. (2017) *Rare Earth Frontiers: from Terrestrial Subsoils to Lunar Landscapes*, (Ithaca: Cornell University Press).

Kotilainen, K., P. Aalto, J. Valta, A. Rautiainen, M. Kojo and B.K. Sovacool (2019) 'From path dependence to policy mixes for Nordic electric mobility: Lessons for accelerating future transport transitions', *Policy sciences*, 52(4), pp. 573–600, DOI: 10.1007/s11077-019-09361-3.

Kramarz, T., S. Park and C. Johnson (2021) 'Governing the dark side of renewable energy: A typology of global displacements', *Energy Research & Social Science*, 74, 101902, DOI: 10.1016/j.erss.2020.101902.

Krehic, L. (2019) *A free rider problem? The effect of electric vehicles on urban toll prices in Norway*, Working Paper No. 17819, (Trondheim: Norwegian University of Science and Technology), http://www.svt.ntnu.no/iso/WP/2019/2_19.pdf (accessed on 30 August 2023).

Landgrand, M. (2021) 'Switzerland and Glencore reined in by DRC: "The resources belong to us"', *Geneva Solutions news*, November 6, https://genevasolutions.news/climate/drc-puts-foot-down-on-glencore-the-resources-belong-to-us (accessed on 23 February 2022).

Li, M., H. Ye, X. Liao, J. Ji and X. Ma (2020) 'How Shenzhen, China pioneered the widespread adoption of electric vehicles in a major city: Implications for global implementation', *Wiley Interdisciplinary Reviews: Energy and Environment*, 9(4), e373, DOI: 10.1002/wene.373.

Lis, A., A. Wagner, F. Ruzzenenti and H.J. Walnum (2018) 'Envisaging the unintended socio-technical consequences of a transition from fossil fuel-based to electric mobility', *Shape energy research design challenge* (Cambridge: Shape Energy), https://ruj.uj.edu.pl/xmlui/bitstream/handle/item/61406/lis_wagner_ruzzenenti_walnum_envisaging_the_unintended_socio-technical_2018.pdf?sequence=1&isAllowed=y (accessed on 18 July 2022).

Liu, W. and D.B. Agusdinata (2020) 'Interdependencies of lithium mining and communities sustainability in Salar de Atacama, Chile', *Journal of Cleaner Production*, 260, 120838, DOI: 10.1016/j.jclepro.2020.120838.

Ma, W., C. Opp and D. Yang (2020) 'Past, present, and future of virtual water and water footprint', *Water*, 12(11), 3068, DOI: 10.3390/w12113068.

Mattioli, G., G. Roberts, J.K. Steinberger and A. Brown (2020) 'The political economy of car dependence: A systems of provision approach.', *Energy Research & Social Science*, 66, 101486.

Mayyas, A., D. Steward and M. Mann (2019) 'The case for recycling: Overview and challenges in the material supply chain for automotive li-ion batteries', *Sustainable Materials and Technologies*, 19, e00087, DOI: 10.1016/j.susmat.2018.e00087.

Moberg, K. (2020) 'Ferskt tallmateriale fra SSB viser: Bensin-og dieselbilene vil dominere i mange år', *Motor*, 26 March (Oslo: *Motor*).

Mossali, E., N. Picone, L. Gentilini, O. Rodrìguez, J.M. Pérez and M. Colledani (2020) 'Lithium-ion batteries towards circular economy: A literature review of opportunities and issues of recycling treatments', *Journal of environmental management*, 264, 110500, DOI: 10.1016/j.jenvman.2020.110500.

Myklebust, M. (2021) 'Hvorfor lønner det seg å kaste bilen?', *NRK*, January 6, https://www.nrk.no/dokumentar/xl/hvorfor-lonner-det-seg-a-kaste-bilen_-1.15232892 (accessed on 23 September 2021).

Nealer, R. and T.P. Hendrickson (2015) 'Review of recent lifecycle assessments of energy and greenhouse gas emissions for electric vehicles', *Current Sustainable/Renewable Energy Reports*, 2, pp. 66–73, DOI: 10.1007/s40518-015-0033-x.

Nguyen, T.M.P. and K. Davidson (2017) 'Contesting green technology in the city: techno-apartheid or equitable modernisation?', *International Planning Studies*, 22(4), pp. 400–414, DOI: 10.1080/13563475.2017.1307719.

Niarchos, N. (2021) 'The Dark Side of Congo's Cobalt Rush', *The New Yorker*, May 24.

Njøs, R., S.G. Sjøtun, S.E. Jakobsen and A. Fløysand (2020) 'Expanding analyses of path creation: Interconnections between territory and technology', *Economic Geography*, 96(3), pp. 266–288, DOI: 10.1080/00130095.2020.1756768.

Olivetti, E.A., G. Ceder, G.G. Gaustad and X. Fu (2017) 'Lithium-ion battery supply chain considerations: analysis of potential bottlenecks in critical metals', *Joule*, 1(2), pp. 229–243, DOI: 10.1016/j.joule.2017.08.019.

Pettison, P. (2021) '"Like slave and master": DRC miners toil for 30p an hour to fuel electric cars', *The Guardian*, https://www.theguardian.com/global-development/2021/nov/08/cobalt-drc-miners-toil-for-30p-an-hour-to-fuel-electric-cars (accessed on 15 February 2021).

Prieto-Sandoval, V., C. Jaca and M. Ormazabal (2018) 'Towards a consensus on the circular economy', *Journal of Cleaner Production*, 179, pp. 605–615, DOI: 10.1016/j.jclepro.2017.12.224.

Public Eye (2017) 'Glencore's Murky Deals in the DRC', https://www.publiceye.ch/en/topics/commodities-trading/glencore-in-drc (accessed on 23 February 2022).

Rallo, H., L. Canals Casals, D. De La Torre, R. Reinhardt, C. Marchante and B. Amante (2020) 'Lithium-ion battery 2nd life used as a stationary energy storage system: ageing and economic analysis in two real cases', *Journal of Cleaner Production*, 272, 122584, DOI: 10.1016/j.jclepro.2020.122584.

Regjeringen (2019) *Nasjonal transportplan 2022–2033*, Oppdrag 5: byområdene. 01.10, https://www.regjeringen.no/contentassets/12d4b3bcdad74d368f58f2d5abbd8ced/virksomhetenes-fellessvar-oppdrag-5.pdf (accessed on 19 July 2022).

Reiserer, A. (2021) *With EBRD financing, Poland builds first recycling plant for car batteries* (London: European Bank for Reconstruction and Development), https://www.ebrd.com/news/2021/with-ebrd-financing-poland-builds-first-recycling-plant-for-car-batteries-.html (accessed on 30 August 2023).

Remme, D., S. Sareen and H. Haarstad (2022) 'Who benefits from sustainable mobility transitions? Social inclusion, populist resistance and elite capture in Bergen, Norway', *Journal of Transport Geography*, 105, 103475, DOI: 10.1016/j.jtrangeo.2022.103475.

Riofrancos, T. (2019) 'What Green Costs', *Logic*, 9, 7 December, https://logicmag.io/nature/what-green-costs/ (accessed on 20 January 2021).

Rykalova, O. (2019) *Understanding drivers and barriers for industry formation around re-use and recycling of electric vehicle lithium-ion batteries in Norway*, MA thesis (Oslo: University of Oslo).

RVU (Reisevaner undersøkelse) (2019) *The national travel habits survey*, https://www.vegvesen.no/fag/fokusomrader/nasjonal-transportplan/den-nasjonale-reisevaneundersokelsen/reisevaner-2019/ (accessed on 23 February 2022).

Sareen, S. and J. Grandin (2020) 'European green capitals: branding, spatial dislocation or catalysts for change?', *Geografiska Annaler: Series B, Human Geography*, 102(1), pp. 101–117, DOI: 10.1080/04353684.2019.1667258.

Schlosser, N. (2020) *Externalized costs of electric automobility: Social-ecological conflicts of lithium extraction in Chile*, Working Paper No. 144/2020 (Berlin: Institute for International Political Economy (IPE)), https://www.ipe-berlin.org/fileadmin/institut-ipe/Dokumente/Working_Papers/ipe_working_paper_144.pdf (accessed on 19 July 2022).

Skjølsvold, T.M. and M. Ryghaug (2020) 'Temporal echoes and cross-geography policy effects: Multiple levels of transition governance and the electric vehicle breakthrough', *Environmental Innovation and Societal Transitions*, 35, pp. 232–240, DOI: 10.1016/j.eist.2019.06.004.

Sovacool, B. (2019) 'The precarious political economy of cobalt: Balancing prosperity, poverty, and brutality in artisanal and industrial mining in the Democratic Republic of the Congo', *The extractive industries and society*, 6(3), pp. 915–939, DOI: 10.1016/j.exis.2019.05.018.

Strand, R., A. Saltelli, M. Giampietro, K. Rommetveit and S. Funtowicz (2018) 'New narratives for innovation', *Journal of Cleaner Prod*uction, 197(2), pp. 1849–1853, DOI: 10.1016/j.jclepro.2016.10.194.

Stringer, D. and T. Biesheuvel (2020) 'Tesla strikes deal to buy cobalt from Glencore ahead of future supply squeeze', *Bloomberg News*, June 16, https://financialpost.com/commodities/mining/tesla-buys-glencore-cobalt (accessed on 13 February 2022).

Stumpf, R. (2021) 'Tesla's $16,000 Quote for a $700 Fix Is Why Right to Repair Matters', *The Drive*, July 12, https://www.thedrive.com/news/41493/teslas-16000-quote-for-a-700-fix-is-why-right-to-repair-matters (accessed on 24 September 2021).

Swilling, M., B. Robinson, S. Marvin, M. Hodson and M. Hajer (2013) *City-Level Decoupling: Urban resource flows and the governance of infrastructure transitions*, a report of the working group on cities of the international resource panel (Oslo: Arendal UNEP), https://www.grida.no/publications/237 (accessed on 19 July 2022).

Thorne, R.J., I. Beate Hovi, E. Figenbaum, D.R. Pinchasik, A.H. Amundsen and R. Hagman (2021) 'Facilitating adoption of electric buses through policy: Learnings from a trial in Norway', *Energy Policy*, 155, DOI: 10.1016/j.enpol.2021.112310.

Thronsen, M. (2019) 'Norske elbilister stadig mer opptatt av klima', *Norsk Elbilforening*, July 4, https://elbil.no/norske-elbilister-stadig-mer-opptatt-av-klima/ (accessed on 23 February 2022).

Tsing, A.L. (2005) *Friction: an ethnography of global connection* (Princeton, New Jersey: Princeton University Press).

Tvinnereim, E. and G. Ferguson-Cradler (2020) 'Electric vehicles from novelty to controversy: Analyzing environmental and fairness claims in open-ended survey questions', *APSA Preprints*, DOI: 10.33774/apsa-2020-6s44w.

Urry, J. (2004) 'The 'system'of automobility', *Theory, culture & society*, 21(4-5), pp. 25–39.

USDOJ (US Department of Justice) (2022) *Glencore entered guilty pleas to foreign bribery and market manipulation schemes*, Press release Nr. 22–554, May 24 (Washington D.C.: DOJ Office of public affairs), https://www.justice.gov/opa/pr/glencore-entered-guilty-pleas-foreign-bribery-and-market-manipulation-schemes (accessed on 27 June 2022).

Vaughan, A. (2017) 'Norway Leads Way on Electric Cars: 'It's Part of a Green Taxation Shift'', *The Guardian*, https://www.theguardian.com/environment/2017/dec/25/norway-leads-way-electric-cars-green-taxation-shift (accessed on 25 February 2022).

Velázquez-Martínez, O., J. Valio, A. Santasalo-Aarnio, M. Reuter and R. Serna-Guerrero (2019) 'A critical review of lithium-ion battery recycling processes from a circular economy perspective', *Batteries*, 5(4), 68, DOI: 10.3390/batteries5040068.

Vikström, H., S. Davidsson and M. Höök (2013) 'Lithium availability and future production outlooks', *Applied Energy*, 110 (2013), pp. 252–266, DOI: 10.1016/j.apenergy.2013.04.005.

Voskoboynik, D.M. and D. Andreucci (2022) 'Greening extractivism: Environmental discourses and resource governance in the 'Lithium Triangle'', *Environment and planning E: Nature and space*, 5(2), pp. 787-809, DOI: 10.1177/25148486211006345.

Wansi, B. (2022) 'DRC/Zambia: an agreement to manufacture batteries for electric vehicles', *Afrik21*, May 9, https://www.afrik21.africa/en/drc-zambia-an-agreement-to-manufacture-batteries-for-electric-vehicles/ (accessed on 24 June 2022).

Whitmore, A. (2006) 'The Emperor's New Clothes: Sustainable Mining?', *Journal of Cleaner Production*, 14(3), pp. 309–314.

Wrålsen, B., V. Prieto-Sandoval, A. Mejia-Villa, R. O'Born, M. Hellström and B. Faessler (2021) 'Circular business models for lithium-ion batteries-Stakeholders, barriers, and drivers', *Journal of Cleaner Production*, 317, 128393, DOI: 10.1016/j.jclepro.2021.128393.

Wågsæther, K., D. Remme, S. Sareen and H. Haarstad (2022) 'The justice pitfalls of a sustainable transport transition', *Environment and Planning F*, DOI: 10.1177/26349825221082169.

Xu, C., Q. Dai, L. Gaines et al. (2020) 'Future material demand for automotive lithium-based batteries', *Communications Materials*, 1, DOI: 10.1038/s43246-020-00095-x.

Yuksel, T., M.A.M. Tamayao, C. Hendrickson, I.M.L. Azevedo and J.J. Michalek (2016) 'Effect of regional grid mix, driving patterns and climate on the comparative carbon footprint of gasoline and plug-in electric vehicles in the United States', *Environmental Research Letters*, 11(4), pp. 1–13, DOI: 10.1088/1748-9326/11/4/044007.

Index

www.ingramcontent.com/pod-product-compliance
Lightning Source LLC
LaVergne TN
LVHW021117300926
849160LV00010B/760
9789004538856